Devon & Cornwal

Special Iss

Frontispiece.   Mrs Margery Rowe.

Devon & Cornwall Notes & Queries

DEVON DOCUMENTS

in honour of Mrs Margery Rowe

Edited by
Todd Gray
BA, PhD, FRHistS

1996

First published in 1996
by Devon & Cornwall Notes & Queries
3 Johnstone Drive,
Tiverton EX16 5BU
UK

Second impression July 1996

© Devon & Cornwall Notes & Queries and Todd Gray
1996

No part of this publication
may be reproduced, stored in a retrieval system,
or transmitted in any form, or by any means, electronic,
mechanical, photocopying, recording or otherwise,
without the prior permission
of the copyright holders.

ISBN 0 95283 620 3

Typeset for the Society by
Colin Bakké Typesetting, Exeter

Printed and bound for the Society by
Short Run Press, Exeter

CONTENTS

Frontispiece: *Mrs Margery Rowe*
List of Contributors ix
Preface
  Todd Gray xi
List of Abbreviations xiii
Margery Rowe
  John Draisey, Audrey Erskine & Joyce Youings xv
Sir William Courten and Mark Pierce's Map of Cullompton of 1633
  Mary Ravenhill xix
  Plates . . . . between pages xx & xxi
  1. Map by Mark Pierce, 1633
  2. Detail of Cartouche
  3. Detail of Cullompton
  4. Detail of Ponsford

1. *Norman Annett*
   A Breach of Promise, c.1579 1
2. *Frank Barlow*
   A Few Twelfth- and Thirteenth-Century Plympton Pieces . . 2
3. *Jonathan Barry*
   Exeter in 1688: The Trial of the Seven Bishops 7
4. *Sue Berry*
   The Travel Journals of Elizabeth Ernst; North Devon in the 1840s 14
5. *Susan Bradshaw*
   The Teaching of Honiton Lacemaking in the Early Twentieth Century 17
6. *Mark Brayshay*
   Defence Preparations in Devon Against the Arrival of the Spanish Armada: 'So doth the state of this countrye reste quiet in orderlye readynes' 20

7. *Paul Brough*
   A Seventeenth-Century Survey of Hardwick Farm 26
8. *John Brunton*
   A Brawl at a Shobrooke Parish Meeting, c.1758 27
9. *Margaret Burgess*
   A Holiday in Sidmouth, June 1933 31
10. *Richard Burley*
    One Last Chance: A Passage to New York, 1751 34
11. *Brian Carpenter*
    'Remarkable Occurrences' Viewed from Exeter, 1754–1809 . . 37
12. *Veronica Chesher*
    The Glebe Terrier of Cheriton Bishop, 1680 41
13. *Michael Dickinson*
    An Early Crew List from the Newfoundland Trade;
    The *Prosperous* of Appledore in 1739 49
14. *Angela Doughty*
    'Designed and executed by John Kendall AD 1818':
    Exeter Cathedral's New Reredos 52
15. *John Draisey*
    Discordant Notes or A Broken Consort;
    Exeter's Waits in 1631 62
16. *Michael Duffy*
    The Channel Fleet in Torbay in 1800 66
17. *Colin Edwards*
    'having altogeather forgotten his hande wrytinge';
    Two Early-Seventeenth-Century Letters and Clatworthy . . . 68
18. *Audrey Erskine*
    The Closing and Reopening of a Chapter, 1646 and 1660 . . 72
19. *H.S.A. Fox*
    Fishing in Cockington Documents 76
20. *Ian Gowers*
    The Sermon of Richard Saunders of Kentisbeare, 1651 . . . 82
21. *Alison Grant*
    Stopping up the Market Place: Crock Street and
    Barnstaple's Potters in the Seventeenth Century 86
22. *Todd Gray*
    William Lucombe and the Iron Oaks of Hillersden in 1796 . 88

CONTENTS

23. *Tom Greeves*
    The Bounds of Meavy Parish, 1613 90

24. *Josephine Halloran*
    A Gentleman's Travel Journal on Dartmoor in 1856 93

25. *Michael Havinden*
    Improvements to the Park of Castle Hill, Filleigh, and the Conversion of an Old Lime Kiln into a Mock Fort, 1769–70 97

26. *S.D. Hobbs*
    'To cure the mind's wrong biass, Spleen, some recommend the bowling-green' 100

27. *Christopher Holdsworth*
    A Confession of his Drunkeness by George Boone of Bradninch, 1717 102

28. *Roger J.P. Kain*
    Landscape and Farming in the Mid-Nineteenth Century: Extracts from the Tithe Files of Two Moorland Edge Parishes—Holne (Dartmoor) and High Bray (Exmoor) . . . 108

29. *Maryanne Kowaleski*
    An Exeter Man Renounces the Freedom of the City, May 1312 110

30. *Susan Laithwaite*
    A Dutch Officer in Moretonhampstead, c.1807 116

31. *Ian Maxted*
    A Common Culture?: The Inventory of Michael Harte, Bookseller of Exeter, 1615 119

32. *Nigel Morgan*
    The Social Tone of Torquay in the 1920s 129

33. *Christine North*
    'It was only a copy of the Doomsday book . . .'; William Wynne's Travels through Devon in 1755 131

34. *Nicholas Orme*
    Three Early Devon Wills 136

35. *Deborah Phillips*
    An Angel at Castle Street: Extracts from the Autograph Book of Nurse Georgina Blatwayt when Nursing at No. 5 Temporary Hospital, Castle Street, Exeter 141

36. *M.C. Phillips*
 Revd John Jago and his Survey of Tavistock of 1784;
 Demographic Changes, 1741–1871 and their Association
 with Mining Developments 145
37. *Steven Pugsley*
 Mother Hubbard and Housekeeping at Kitley in 1869 154
38. *Stephen K. Roberts*
 Devon Justices of the Peace, 1643–60 157
39. *Michael Smith*
 A Family at Risk: The Thornes of Cruwys Morchard
 in 1793 166
40. *W.B. Stephens*
 Theresa Parker of Saltram, 1745–75 172
41. *M.J. Stoyle*
 'The Counterfeit King': Popular Reaction to the
 Accession of King James I, 1603 177
42. *Roger F.S. Thorne*
 'Holy Enterprises': Victorian Folk Religion at Chagford . . 183
43. *John F. Travis*
 An Enclosure Dispute at Lynton in 1854 190
44. *Alice Wells*
 Peter Orlando Hutchinson and his Cats in the Late
 Nineteenth Century 197
45. *Margaret Westcott*
 Surveying the Estates of Henry Courtenay, Earl of
 Devon, Marquis of Exeter and Traitor, 1543–4 199
46. *Mary Wolffe*
 A Devon Muster in June 1639 204
47. *Tim Wormleighton*
 An Eighteenth-Century Tour of Plymouth 207
48. *Joyce Youings*
 Devon Monastic Bells 210

A Checklist of the Writings of Margery Rowe
 Ian Maxted 215
Index 219

LIST OF CONTRIBUTORS

Norman Annett is Chairman of the Council of the Devonshire Association and Honorary Secretary of *Devon & Cornwall Notes & Queries*.
Frank Barlow is Emeritus Professor of History, University of Exeter.
Jonathan Barry is Senior Lecturer, Department of History and Archaeology, University of Exeter.
Sue Berry is Senior Archivist, Somerset Archive and Record Service.
Susan Bradshaw is Senior Conservator, Devon Record Office.
Dr Mark Brayshay is Principal Lecturer in Geography, Department of Geographical Sciences, University of Plymouth.
Paul Brough is Senior Archivist, West Devon Record Office.
John Brunton is Archivist, Devon Record Office.
Margaret Burgess is Conservation Assistant, Devon Record Office.
Richard Burley is Senior Archivist, Bristol Record Office.
Brian Carpenter is Archivist, Devon Record Office.
Veronica Chesher is Honorary Research Fellow, Department of Continuing and Adult Education and the Institute of Cornish Studies, University of Exeter.
Michael Dickinson is former Senior Assistant Archivist, Devon Record Office.
Angela Doughty is Archivist of Exeter Cathedral.
John Draisey is Senior Archivist, Devon Record Office, and Editor of *Devon & Cornwall Notes & Queries*.
Dr Michael Duffy is Senior Lecturer, Department of History and Archaeology and Director of the Centre for Maritime Studies, University of Exeter. He is also Editor of *Mariner's Mirror*.
Colin Edwards is Principal Archivist, Cornwall Record Office.
Audrey Erskine is former Lecturer in Palaeography and former Cathedral Archivist, University of Exeter.
H.S.A. Fox is Senior Lecturer in English Topography, Department of English Local History, University of Leicester.
Ian Gowers is former Senior Lecturer in History, Liverpool Polytechnic.
Dr Alison Grant is Chairman, North Devon Maritime Museum.
Dr Todd Gray is Leverhulme Research Fellow, Department of History and Archaeology, University of Exeter.

Dr Tom Greeves is a Cultural Environmentalist and Editor of *Transactions of the Devonshire Association*.
Josephine Halloran is Archives Assistant, Devon Record Office.
Michael Havinden is former Senior Lecturer, Department of Economic and Social History, University of Exeter.
S.D. Hobbs is Wiltshire County Archivist.
Christopher Holdsworth is Professor of Medieval History, University of Exeter.
Roger J.P. Kain is Montefiore Professor of Geography, University of Exeter.
Maryanne Kowaleski is Associate Professor, Department of History, Fordham University.
Susan Laithwaite is Archivist, Devon Record Office.
Ian Maxted is Devon County Local Studies Librarian.
Dr Nigel Morgan is Lecturer, University of Wales Institute, Cardiff.
Christine North is Cornwall County Archivist and Editor of *Journal of the Royal Institution of Cornwall*.
Nicholas Orme is Professor of History, University of Exeter, and Joint Editor at the Devon and Cornwall Record Society.
Deborah Phillips is Archive Conservator, Devon Record Office.
Dr M.C. Phillips is Senior Research Officer, Devon Probation Services.
Steven Pugsley is Chairman, Devon Gardens Trust.
Mary Ravenhill is a graduate of the University of Exeter.
Dr Stephen K. Roberts is Tutor Organizer, Workers' Educational Association, West Mercia District.
Revd Michael Smith is former Rector of Silverton, and Visiting Research Fellow, University of Plymouth.
Dr W.B. Stephens is Honorary Research Fellow, School of Archive, University College, London, and is a former Reader and sometime Dean of the Faculty of Education, University of Leeds.
Dr M.J. Stoyle is Lecturer, Department of History, University of Southampton.
Roger F.S. Thorne is Honorary Methodist District Archivist.
Dr John F. Travis is Tutor, Department of Continuing & Adult Education, University of Exeter.
Alice Wells is Archives Assistant, Devon Record Office.
Margaret Westcott is former Local Studies Librarian, Westcountry Studies Library.
Dr Mary Wolffe is currently completing *Gentry Leaders in Peace and War; the Gentry Governors of Devon in the early seventeenth century*.
Tim Wormleighton is Senior Archivist, North Devon Record Office.
Joyce Youings is Emeritus Professor of History, University of Exeter.

PREFACE

It is particularly appropriate that *Devon & Cornwall Notes & Queries* publishes this volume given that Margery acted as Editor for twenty-four years. This book is comprised of contributions from those in the archives world, many of whom have edited a personal favourite document, and from historians whose pieces reflect a specialized interest; all are concerned with an aspect of Devon's history. As will be read in the Appreciation many of these documents reflect Margery's personal interests in travel, music and cats as well as professional ones in Exeter and Devon. One is even concerned with archive management (albeit 350 years ago). Such is the appreciation for Margery's contribution to Devon studies that it would have been possible to have made this volume double or probably treble in its size but publishing practicalities makes this impossible. I apologize to all those who would have also liked to have contributed.

A volume of this size would have been beyond the financial capabilities of *DCNQ* without the greatly appreciated support from the Centre for South-Western Historical Studies, Centre for Maritime Historical Studies, Department of History & Archaeology (all at the University of Exeter), the Devon & Cornwall Record Society, Devon Archaeological Society, Devon Family History Society, Devon Gardens Trust, Devon History Society, Devonshire Association, HFC Hamilton Bank, North Devon Athenaeum, South West Maritime History Society and Zurich Municipal. I would also like to thank Grant Harrison, Dr Richard Willis of Exeter University Press for his advice, Mrs Jennifer Warren for typing the majority of the contributions, Mr Michael Rouillard for his assistance with the subscription leaflets, Mrs Sue Rouillard for the care with which she has designed the cover, Mr Seán Goddard for the Frontispiece and Mr Colin Bakké for his expertise in the typesetting. The officers of *Notes & Queries*, particularly Mr Norman Annett, Mr Ian Maxted and Mr John Draisey, must also be thanked for their enthusiastic support of this volume.

Modernization of spelling in documents is at the discretion of each contributor but variant spellings of place-names have been retained, in italic, with modern spelling generally given, in the first case, immediately afterwards in square brackets: for example, *Tincombe* [Teigncombe]. Square brackets have been used to denote all editorial insertions. Latin has normally been translated into English and italicized. For permission to publish these documents I would like to thank Lady Margaret Fortescue, Mrs D. Bury, the Dean & Chapter of Exeter Cathedral, Anstey, Sargent and Probert Solicitors, Barnstaple Town Council, the Bodleian Library, Bristol Record Office, British Library, Cambridge University Library, Chagford Methodist Circuit, Cornwall Record Office, Devon County Council, Devon Record Office, Diocese of Exeter, Exeter City Council, West Yorkshire Archives Service (Leeds), North Devon Record Office, the Controller of her Majesty's Stationary Office (in respect of Crown copyright material in the Public Record Office), Religious Society of Friends, Somerset Record Office, Stafford Record Office, Tavistock Parish Council, Torquay Central Library, West Devon Record Office and Wiltshire Record Office. Finally, although Margery is herself no stranger to the production of *festschrifts*, I would nevertheless like to apologize to her for the considerable inaccuracies told to her concerning the use made of many of these documents during the preparation of this volume.

Todd Gray

ABBREVIATIONS

CSPD *Calendar State Papers Domestic*
DAT *Devonshire Association Transactions*
DCNQ *Devon & Cornwall Notes & Queries*
DH *Devon Historian*
DNB *Dictionary National Biography*
HMC *Historical Manuscripts Commission*
JRIC *Journal Royal Institution of Cornwall*

BL British Library
BRO Bristol Record Office
CRO Cornwall Record Office
D&C Dean & Chapter Archives (Exeter)
DCRS Devon & Cornwall Record Society
DRO Devon Record Office
NDRO North Devon Record Office
PRO Public Record Office
SRO Somerset Record Office
WDRO West Devon Record Office
WRO Wiltshire Record Office
WSL Westcountry Studies Library

MARGERY ROWE

IN MARGERY ROWE historians of Devon and Exeter have had a good friend. As keeper of the archives of the county of Devon, the city and diocese of Exeter and, more recently, of the dean and chapter of Exeter Cathedral she has facilitated the researches of literally thousands of researchers a year who come from all over the world to join the local 'regulars', seeking anything from family history to that small local clue which will illuminate the history of some national institution. Postgraduates in particular have learned much from Margery and her colleagues. As she herself would be the first to acknowledge, she inherited an established and well-run record office and by general consent the finest collection of provincial records in Great Britain. Besides her professional expertise as an archivist she is also a practitioner in her own right, having contributed much to the writing of Devon's history, not least in editing its records for publication and using her own extensive experience to guide others embarking on that rigorous task. Finally, and well beyond the call of duty, she has been editor of one of the westcountry's best-loved historical journals. Inevitably, in the course of a long career, she has played an important part in her professional organizations. In all of these multifarious activities she has won many friends.

Born in Northamptonshire two days after Christmas 1933, Margery Mary Sparkes went to Manchester High School for Girls before proceeding to Manchester University in 1952 to read History in a department presided over by that fine medieval scholar Professor Christopher Cheney. She graduated in 1955 and took the diploma course in Palaeography and Archive Administration at University College London before being appointed as archivist in the then Exeter City Record Office on 20 August 1956. She had already spent a short period listing deeds for the Harroby Manuscripts Trust at Burnt Norton. She obtained the Diploma in 1959, her dissertation being a listing, with introduction, of the documents of the Mallock family of Cockington, a collection which has never ceased to interest her. In 1960 she was promoted to Senior Assistant Archivist, and in 1965 to Senior Archivist, a post she filled until the great local government reorganization of 1974 when the Exeter City Record Office became the East Devon Office and

Margery the East Devon Area Archivist. In 1977, following the retirement of Peter Kennedy, she became, first, 'Head of Record Services' and eventually Devon County Archivist.

Meanwhile her marriage, in 1961, to David Rowe, provided her with a private life within which relaxations such as gardening, making preserves and playing with a cat have been combined with periods of heavy family responsibility. David and Margery have been venturesome in their choice of holidays but even a series of calamities in India in 1990 has not quenched their enthusiasm for foreign travel.

The last two decades have been demanding, both in the opportunities for developing and expanding the services of the Devon Record Office and for the pressures consequent both on the local government reorganization of recent years and on the cuts in resources inflicted by an unsympathetic Treasury. But in good times and in bad Margery has set her staff an example of cheerful resignation and determination to make the best of it. This has been all too evident to all who, as searchers, sympathized but could do little to help. The complicated move in 1977 from Concord House to the City Library building (the third in the history of the Devon Record Office though the City records have always been there) was the biggest physical upheaval but the regular arrival of documents and the ever-increasing number of readers have kept the whole office on its toes. Nothing ever stood still. A development which undoubtedly gave Margery great satisfaction was the creation in 1988 of a branch office in north Devon with its own staff, in addition to that already in existence in Plymouth, and the subsequent establishment of service points in various local libraries, first in Torquay and later in Colyton, Tiverton, Okehampton, Totnes, Tavistock and Appledore, with members of the central and branch office staff in occasional attendance. An earlier and much more controversial innovation was the introduction in 1981 of charges (except for readers engaged in educational work) which partly financed a microfilming programme and an increase in the number of microfiches and viewers. Other efforts to help searchers have been a huge indexing programme, the appointment of a record searcher for dealing with postal inquiries, the provision of aids to reading documents, short guides to types of record, good reprographic services and, since 1988, a regular *Newsletter* packed with interest. These, and many other efforts to help searchers, have made the DRO one of the most user-friendly local record offices in the country. Special mention, too, must be made of Margery's exhibitions, continuing precedents set by her predecessors, year after year producing a wide diversity of splendidly-presented exhibitions, both in the vestibules of the office and circulating around the county, apparently effortlessly springing to life for special occasions, either for a local event or, when called for, to respond on a grander scale to a civic or national commemoration. Needless to say all such activities have not only made the DRO better known throughout the county but have in turn created more and more demands from a public increasingly curious about the past.

In addition to her full-time work in the office Margery also found the time to edit and prepare for publication no less than three volumes for the Devon and Cornwall Record Society, *Exeter Freemen 1266–1967*, with Andrew Jackson, in 1973, *Tudor Exeter: Tax Assessments 1489–1595* in 1977 and, with John Draisey, *The Receivers' Accounts of the city of Exeter 1304–1353* in 1989. In 1992 she succeeded Joyce Youings as the Society's General Editor for post-medieval publications. She had already, in 1970, succeeded her former colleague, Margaret Cash, as editor of *Devon and Cornwall Notes and Queries*, faithfully producing two numbers a year until relinquishing this very time-consuming responsibility in 1994. At various times she has been a member of the governing bodies of the Devon History Society, the Centre for South Western Historical Studies, the Centre for Maritime Historical Studies and, more recently, has chaired the Archives and Research Committee of the Devon Gardens Trust. She has also served as financial secretary of the Association of County Archivists, as well as playing other active roles in the affairs of that body including Principal Advisor to the Leverhulme Local Maritime Archives Project.

Margery retires as Devon County Archivist in June 1996 after forty years service. These have been forty years of tremendous change and development in the whole concept of local archives administration, and of the use as well as the conservation of records, and she has throughout kept in the lead of these developments. She is an 'old-fashioned' county archivist only in the sense that she is a true archivist, whose basic need is a hands-on contact with her documents, not a management figure organizing from behind a closed office door her dealings with her committees and the activities of her staff. She has always been out front, asking nothing of anyone that she would not do herself. And she is physically tough—how else could she put in such punishingly long hours, and who else would react to a bout of shingles with the remark that she was more comfortable in the office because it was a little boring to be off sick? Always ready to make personal contact, ready to dip into her apparently bottomless well of knowledge about the vast collections in her charge (and of the printed sources and illustrations in the West Country Studies Library, too, for that matter), she has presided with quiet authority imbued with humour and a complete lack of pretentiousness over a record office in which there is usually the feeling of a touch of fun about the place.

What will we do without her? Fortunately we shall not have to. Margery and David will continue to live near Exeter and for a time at least Margery is being retained as a part-time consultant archivist by Devon County Council. Long may she enjoy the company of historical records and the respect and affection of all who consult them.

John Draisey
Audrey Erskine
Joyce Youings

Sir William Courten and Mark Pierces's Map of Cullompton of 1633

The map,[1] of which the cartouche is illustrated on Plates 1 and 2, shows the small town of Cullompton and three areas in the immediate vicinity as they were in 1633. The cartouche informs us that this constituted the 'Barton & Mannor of Padbrooke and *Paunsford* [Ponsford] in the Parishes of Cullompton & Bradninch in the Countye of Devon'. These lands were 'parcell of the possessions of the Right Wor[shipfu]ll Sir William Courten of London Knight who caused this survey to be taken'.[2]

Sir William Courten (1572–1636)[3] was a highly successful merchant who traded not only in Europe but also in the West and East Indies. He was a man of great energy and enterprise who, in his later years, invested some of his wealth in land. He lent money to the Crown, acquired land principally in the Midlands but also elsewhere in the country; in 1625 he purchased the Manor of Laxton in Nottinghamshire. He never visited Laxton but he and his son were interested in developing its potential, principally by converting customary tenures into economic rents reflecting prevailing land values, and in consolidating their land holdings.[4] If not completely successful in all his ventures, Sir William Courten still had a substantial income from his estate purchases, thought to amount to £6,500 a year in 1633 with a capital base of £128,000.[5] It is against this background that the map of Cullompton must be evaluated.

The map, drawn on vellum, measures 45.5 inches (115.5 cm) east to west and 30.375 inches (76.6 cm) north to south. Wide margins coloured black, yellow, blue and yellow border the map. The linear scale, SCALA PERTICARUM, of 150 perches, with the first division marked in single perches, represents a scale of 1:3,960 or one inch to 20 perches. A pair of dividers is placed above the scale. The compass-rose shows the map to be oriented with north at the lower left-hand corner, perhaps to give prominence to the rural areas of Padbrooke, Ponsford and Knowle, and the southern outskirts of Cullompton where Sir William Courten also owned land. It is fortunate that there was space on the map to include the whole of Cullompton (see Plate 3), although this was not part of the estate. The compass-rose shows cardinals and half-cardinals in light and dark blue, and the quarter-cardinals in red and white with three outer circles subdivided into 16,

32, and 64 divisions respectively. The centre is decorated with a globe showing the Atlantic Ocean with the peripheral land masses of Europe, America, and the Southern Continent oriented correctly. North is marked by a fleur-de-lys with south, east, and west also designated individually.

The 'rural' information, when taken with that in the accompanying survey book is considerable. Rivers are shown coloured blue and varying in width but, with the exception of the Culm, only where they pass through or form the boundary of land which is mapped. Fields are coloured according to the various holdings of Sir William Courten's tenants but those which are the property of others are left plain, though the owners are named. Within each field are numbers, letters or symbols for easy reference to the accompanying written survey. Orchards, copses and woods are shown with tree symbols, and the Survey Book makes it clear that these symbols do represent the reality of the landscape. For example, the Survey Book lists 'the Syte of the Barton House [of Padbrooke] with the Barnes and other outhouses, the gardens courtyards forstall & 3 orchards' which can all be seen on the map.[6]

There is little indication of relief except perhaps the deeper green colouring on either bank of the stream rising at Combe Farm which supplied Cullompton with its water. The boundaries of the fields north-west of Ponsford (see Plate 4) follow the slopes marked by the contour lines on the Ordnance Survey six-inch map and the names given in the Survey Book suggest the shape of the ground, for example Hither Cliffe and Hilly Meadow. Land use is not indicated; again, it is the accompanying Survey Book which gives an extra dimension to this map. The accuracy of the field survey is remarkable; when compared with the Ordnance Survey six-inch map, not only the principal field boundaries, but also small changes of direction of hedgerow and stream are faithfully recorded. This is especially true of Padbrooke and Knowle but even in Ponsford, where some detail is more difficult to trace, the basic structure of the land can easily be related to the map. The town of Cullompton, though representing but a small part of Sir William Courten's estate, was surveyed and drawn with the same care and accuracy as the rest of the map. The street pattern is fundamentally the same in 1996 as it was in 1633; the wider area where the market was held, the roads to Tiverton and Ponsford, the small lanes leading to the church and to the mill are all present. Buildings are shown in elevation and it is of interest that only two are shown with blue (conventionally, slate) roofs; one is the church and the other the house now known as Walronds. This was begun in 1603 by Sir John Petre, and completed in

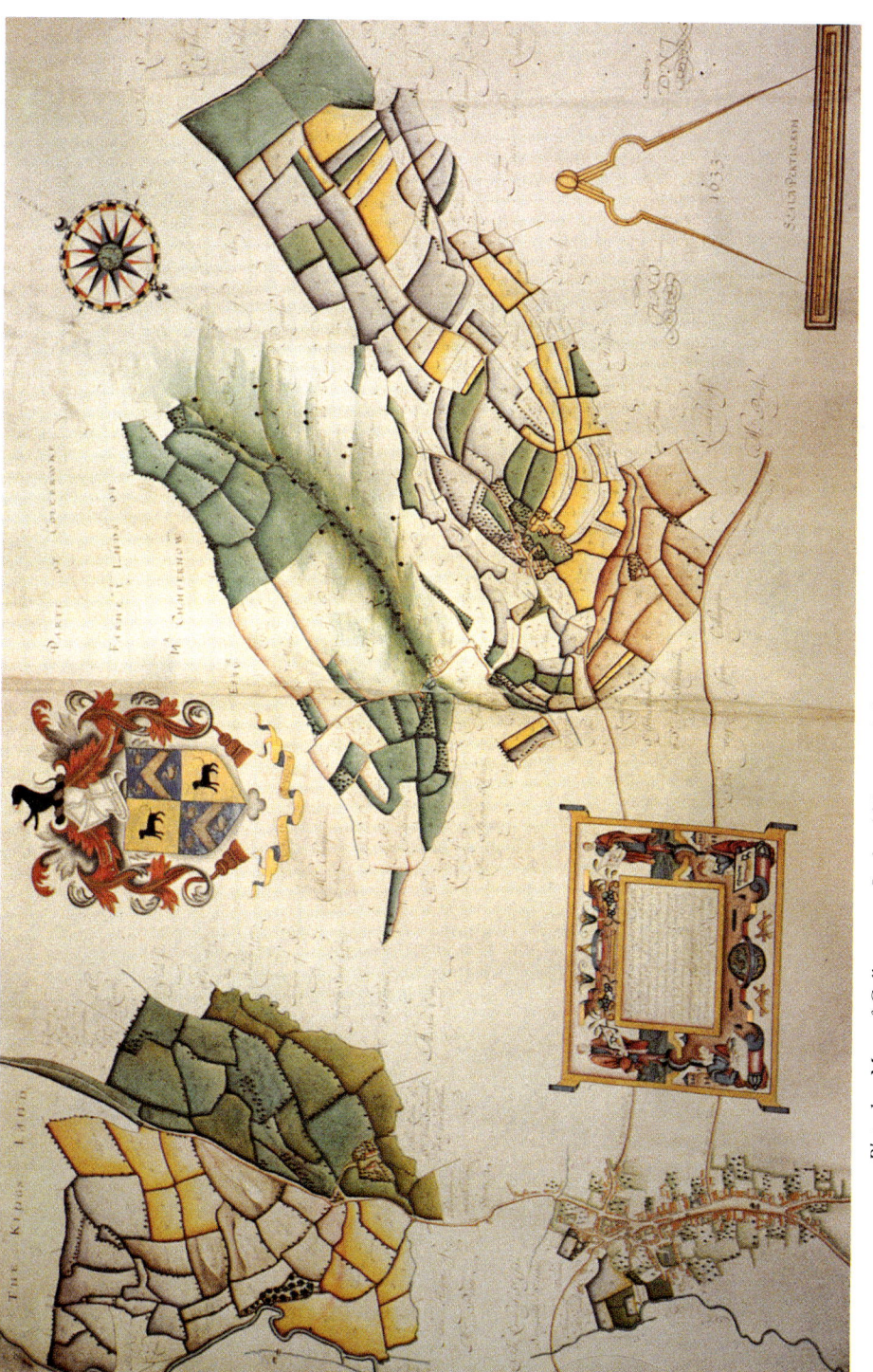

Plate 1. Map of Cullompton. It should be noted that the map is oriented with North at the lower left.

Plate 2. The cartouche surrounding the title and informative detail about the map. The figures illustrate the construction, purpose and use of the map; the background indicates the commercial interests of the owner.

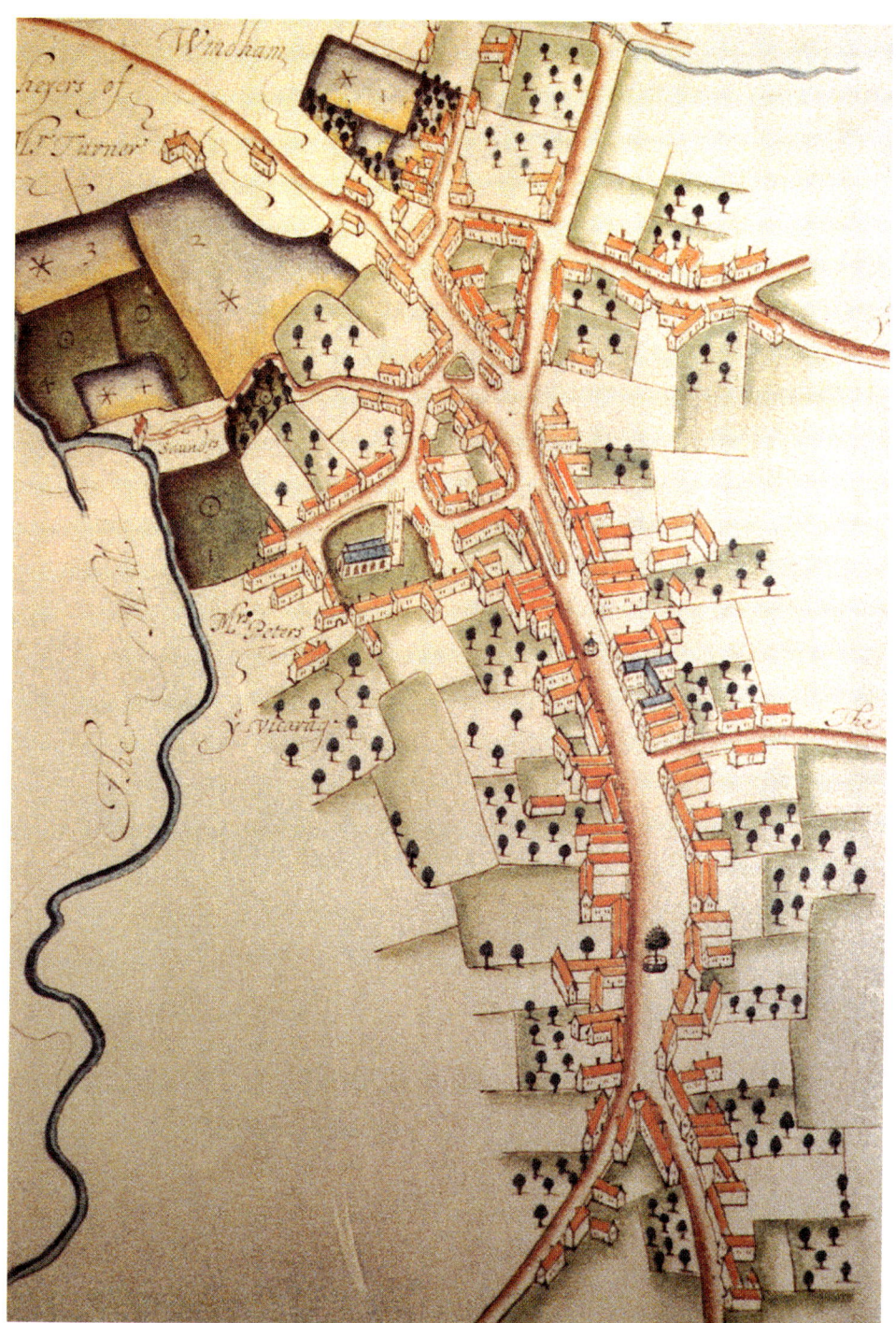

Plate 3. The town of Cullompton.

Plate 4. The barton and manor of Ponsford.

1605;[7] it consisted of one central block and two wings which can be seen quite clearly on the map.

The map is decorated with Sir William Courten's coat of arms and a most attractive and informative cartouche. The map itself is not signed nor does the Survey Book give any indication of authorship. However, details in the cartouche do help attribute this map to a particular, and well-known surveyor. The cartouche is contained within a frame of strapwork, restrained in style with but a small decoration of fruits and leaves. This decoration, together with the drawings of survey instruments, the globes, and the four male figures are reproduced on the later map of Laxton[8] drawn in 1635 for Sir William Courten by Mark Pierce. This would suggest that the Cullompton map was an earlier commission from that magnate. Other details in the background also illustrate Sir William Courten's distant trading activities; land and sea are shown at the feet of the two figures in the upper half of the cartouche whilst the pair at the lower left and right corners are flanked by buildings which are decidedly oriental in character. It is, however, these four figures which are of particular interest to historians of cartography, for they epitomize much of the history of estate mapping at this period. At the lower left there is a clerk obviously entering details in a survey book which has a map on the opposite page, while on the right the cartographer is drawing a map with his ruler and dividers. Between them are the other tools of their trade, inkwells and pen cases with leather thongs for carrying when in the field. Above, one man consults the completed map and the other studies the survey book with its map alongside the text. It is suggested that these four figures are self-portraits of Mark Pierce,[9] an impression reinforced by four similar figures on a map of Aveley in Essex drawn by Pierce in 1619 for Sir Edward Barrett.[10] This is also accompanied by a Survey Book 'compiled by Samuel Pierse', Mark's father.[11] However, on this Essex map the upper two figures are of a mature man, probably Samuel, and the lower two of a younger assistant, probably Mark. By 1633 Mark seems to have taken over from his father if the 'portraits' on the Cullompton and Laxton maps are to be believed. The use of these four figures is suggestive of the kind of survey work, both written and graphic, that the Pierce family were prepared to undertake.

The sixteenth century saw terriers or written surveys gradually supplemented by graphic representations of the landscape they described.[12] At first, the map was merely an aide-memoire or a sketch drawn to assist the clerk. In time, the map replaced the written description entirely, but more frequently, as in the case of the Cullompton map, it became the dominant element in the fusion of the two traditions, written and graphic. Such maps may have served the ambitions of the new landowners who wanted to 'improve' their recently-acquired estates and so maximize their potential but with maps as well drawn and attractively decorated as this one, landowners could also enjoy a visual representation of the estates they possessed.

Surviving estate maps of the sixteenth and early seventeenth centuries are comparatively rare and a map of the quality of this of Cullompton is especially valuable. It must have been of great use to its owner and given satisfaction to its creator; it is a legacy to be treasured by the people of Devon no less than by those interested in the history of cartography.

Transcription of the Text of the Map Cartouche (See Plate 2)

A PLAT & DESCRIPTION OF ALL / the Landes belonging to the Barton & Mannor / of Padbrooke & *Paunfford* in the Parishes of Cul / lumpton & Bradninch in the Countye of Devon, The / lands of Padbrooke being divided into 4 Tenements are / distinguish[d] by these letters A.B.C.D. from th[e] lands of / *Paunfford*, w[ch] are known by diverse Charract[rs]: w[th]: numb[rs]: / correspondent to a booke of Survey of th[e] said Landes, all / which are parcell of th[e] pofsefsions of th[e] Right Wor[ll] / S[r] William Courten of London Knight

Transcription of the Preliminary Description in the Book of Survey which accompanies the Map

A Booke of Surveye of all the Land belonging to the Barton & Mannor of Padbrooke & *Paunsford* in th[e] Parishes of *Cullumpton* and Bradninch in the County of Devon, as they are estated to divers Tenants houlding the same by Coppy of Court roll for terme of Lives. The Lands of the Barton of *Padbrook* being divided into foure Tenem[ts] are distinguished one from another by these severall letters A:B:C:D:(in the Platt and Description thereof,) and all the Lands of the Mannor of *Paunsford* are distinguished by severall charact[s] vis[t] one Tenem[t] is known by this charact[e] ☿ another by this ♁ And with the said letter or charact[ers] in the Description of every parcell of land, is placed a certain number to be referred to it corresponds to numb[ers] in the margent of this book w[ch] sheweth the name, measure and value thereof wth the Totall Sume of acres belonging to every Tenem[t] and the rents and services they yield & pay to the Lord of the Manno[r]

All which lands are parcell of the possessions of the Right wor[ll] Sir William Courten of London Knight who caused this survey to be taken.
in the year 1633

ACKNOWLEDGEMENTS

I would like to thank William Ravenhill's friends and colleagues, especially Roger Kain, for their help in the preparation of this contribution.

NOTES

1. SRO, Wyndham Collection DD/WY Map of Cullompton 1633. I am grateful to Dr Todd Gray for drawing my attention to this map. Also, a photocopy is in DRO, 2650Z/Z1 a–b.
2. SRO, DD/WR SR 57.
3. *DNB*, vol. IV, (Oxford 1921–1), 1258–60; A. Sarah Bendall (ed.), *Dictionary of Land Surveyors and local Map-makers of Great Britain and Ireland 1530–1850* 2nd ed. (British Library, forthcoming).
4. C. S. and C. S. Orwin, *The Open Fields* (Oxford, 1954), 113, 115; J. D. Chambers, *Laxton* (HMSO, 1964), 8; Charles Wilson, *England's Apprenticeship 1603–1763* (1965), 158.
5. *DNB*, IV, 1259.
6. I. H. Adams, *Agrarian Landscape Terms: a glossary for historical geography* (Institute of British Geographers, London 1976), 95; this is a term used in Kent to describe an open space in a village, more commonly a green.
7. Murray T Foster, 'A Short History of Cullompton', *DAT* 42 (1910), 163.
8. Map of Laxton, Bodleian Library, MS. C 17:48(9a). This was accompanied by a 'Booke of Survaye' also by Mark Pierce. The cartouche and title page from the Survey Book are reproduced in Orwin, *Open Fields*, Frontispiece and 174.
9. Roger Mason, notes to Bodleian Library filmstrip 364.2 (1993).
10. F. G. Emmison (ed.), *Catalogue of Maps in the Essex Record Office 1566–1855* (London 1947), 4b. Map of Aveley, Wennington, Upminster and South Ockendon 1619, D/DL.P1.
11. Emmison, *Catalogue*, 42a, D/DL.M14.
12. A. Sarah Bendall, *Maps Land and Society* (Cambridge, 1992), 28–34; William Ravenhill, 'Estate surveying; the land market, land management and improvement' in J B Harley and David Woodward (eds), *The History of Cartography* (Chicago University Press, forthcoming), III.

Mary Ravenhill

1.   A Breach of Promise, *c*.1579

The annual fairs and revels of the small country towns and villages of the county provided plenty of opportunity for the young people of the parishes to enjoy themselves and each other and that held in North Molton at All Saints was no exception. An examination of the parish registers shows that quite often one of the results of this enjoyment manifested itself some nine months later with the baptism of a child quite bluntly labelled as a 'bastard'. From the late sixteenth century comes a case in point. Emme Kerbye and her brother John were the two surviving children of Henry Kerbye of North Molton and had been christened in the present church within a few months of each other in 1553. In 1578 they were the servants of William Dawe and his wife Joan of North Molton when Emme had an affair with one Richard Troute of North Molton who was then thirty or thirty one years of age.

Troute's promises of marriage proved her undoing. At the end of that year she found herself pregnant, but when she tackled Troute on the subject of an early wedding she found her love's ardour had cooled considerably and his plans for their future changed. Accordingly in January 1579, Emme, no doubt with the backing of her master, brought an action for breach of promise. At the Court of the Archdeacon of Barnstaple, William Dawe, his wife and Emme's brother John, all told the same story of how, after being pressed by Emme's master, Troute had, in their presence promised marriage. Thus we read:

NDRO, Archdeaconry of Barnstaple, Acts and Depositions of Witnesses, 1570

William Dawe of Northmolton who is 40 years of age was produced as a witness and said as follows viz that the monday after St Andrewes day last past he this deponent mett with Richard Troute and asked of hym what he ded myne to frequent Emme Kerby compaynie so muche do you entend to marrie & he sayd at the next mettynge you shall knowe and the next Sunday then following the sayd Richard Troute ded come to this deponents house to dynner & at after dynnert this deponent ded ask hym what answer he wold make to Emme Kerbye and then the sayd Richard Troute ded geve to the sayd Emme Kerbye then beynge present his suite & trothe to marrie with her if he ded endeed marrie with anye woman & she ded in lyke manner to hym / and then this deponent ded aske of hym when he wold marrie her & he sayd yt shall not be longe before I wyll do yt & then he toke the cuppe & ded drynke to her uppon that condition & ded cutte an aple & gave her the one halfe & kepte the other hymselfe in ratifyinge of the marriage and the said Troute ded request this deponent to know what her frende wold geve her & this deponent asked hym what yf her frende wyll geve litell or nothynge with her wyll then leave her and he answered no I wyll marrie with her yf I have not a groett with her / present the sayd sondaye at hearynge of all the premyses this deponent & John his wyfe & John Kerbie his servant.

Despite this fulsome and dramatic proclamation of his intentions it would appear that the possible lack of a dowry may have decided Troute, for in a brief reply to all these allegations he stated 'that he ded not believe they contained anye truth whatsoever'. Unfortunately, but not unexpectedly, there are no further records as to the court's decision or action. However, the parish registers do finish the story of poor Emme and the treacherous Troute: for 1579 there is the entry 'Sylvestar sonne of Emme Kerbye a Bastard was christ the vijth of October' and two years later in 1581, it was entered 'John sonne of Rychard Troute & Joane his wyfe was christ the xijth of maye'. A salutary tale from Acts and Depositions of Witnesses, Archdeaconry of Barnstaple 1570.

Norman Annett

2. A Few Twelfth- and Thirteenth-Century Plympton Pieces

1. Plympton priory and the chapel of St Andrew at Sutton

The collegiate church of Plympton was reformed as an Augustinian priory by Bishop William Warelwast of Exeter in 1121. A powerful neighbour was Reginald I de Vautorte (Maine), who in 1086 held the manor of Trematon as a vassal of the count of Mortain and was given the manor of Sutton (now Plymouth) by King Henry I (1100–35). The same king gave the manor of Plympton to Richard I de Reviers, whose son, Baldwin, was created earl of Exeter or Devon. Reginald de Vautorte tried to detach his manorial church, St Andrew's Sutton, from its mother church, Sts Peter and Paul Plympton; but the priory resisted tenaciously. Document 1a is Bishop William's confirmation in 1137 of the subordination of the chapel to the priory.[1] As will be seen from document 1b, an undisclosed component of the settlement seems to have been the admission of Reginald's illegitimate son, Thomas, the product of his liaison with a daughter of Dunprust, the priest of Sutton, to be vicar of the chapel after Dunprust's son, William Bacini, had either resigned it or died.

Document 1b recites the historical evidence produced by the priory in support of its claim after Thomas's death, which occurred after 1169. A descendant of Reginald I, Juhel de Vautorte, acting as guardian for his nephew, Reginald II, was claiming, in both the royal and the papal court, that the church of Sutton was independent of Plympton and that its patronage belonged to them. On 27 June 1175 at Lambeth Richard archbishop of Canterbury and Roger bishop of Worcester, judges delegate of Pope Alexander III, before whom Juhel had failed to appear, gave a final judgment in favour of the canons, who had relied on Bishop William's charter.[2] Nevertheless, the canons seem usually to have had to accept a Vautorte nominee to the vicarage in return for a pension, which at the time of the dissolution of the monasteries was £8 a year.[3]

Bodleian Library, ms. James 23 (early seventeenth-century extracts from a lost fifteenth-century cartulary), 162–4

1a. *William, by the grace of God bishop of Exeter, sends greetings and God's blessing to all God's beloved faithful to whom this document shall come. We give noticed to you, our most beloved brethren, that the long-standing lawsuit between our brothers, the canons of the church of Plympton, and our dearest son, Reginald de Vautorte, regarding the church of St Andrew at Sutton has, in proceedings before us, at last reached its end. For, when both parties answered our summons, they both, as was pleasing to God, put themselves in the hands of the seniors of the province, so that what these would declare on oath on this matter, they all would accept for ever. Whereupon the old men chosen for this, Leofric of Chadelawda* [Cheddlewood] *and Wulfmaer of Colaford* [Coleford], *declared by oath on the Gospels what they had heard from their elders and committed to mind and also what they personally had most clearly seen in the years which they themselves remembered: viz., that before the Normans conquered England the church of Sutton was considered to be a member of the church of Plympton, and that the parsons of Plympton church had held it peacefully, with its chapels and all its pertinencies, as something belonging to them, until Reginald de Vautorte had, by the king's gift, obtained Sutton. And so, with the matter now at rest, since 'an oath for confirmation is to them an end of all strife'* [Hebr. 6:16], *it is decreed that the canons shall possess that chapel for ever in peace. Therefore, if anyone shall rashly presume to overthrow or disturb this peace, let him know that he is subject to divine justice. And if, when canonically admonished, he shall fail to amend his ways, he shall be bound for ever by a sentence of anathema. And so that this peace shall not be forgotten, we have confirmed it with the witness of this charter and our seal and the appointment of the following witnesses: Robert archdeacon of Exeter, Hugh archdeacon of Totnes, William archdeacon of Cornwall and Edmar of Cuic.*

1b. *The canons* [of Plympton] *also say that Reginald de Vautorte I* [1130–61] *had himself begged the lord prior Geoffrey* [1128–60] *to admit his bastard son, the clerk Thomas, to the vicarage of the church of Sutton subject to an annual pension to be paid to Plympton church, and to present him to William, the lord bishop of Exeter* [1107–37]. *And that this was done. Also in this business they rely on what they have learnt from the clerk Robert, a son of Dunprust the priest of Sutton, and from other old men of that time: that, in the days of King Harold of England, Lyfing bishop of Exeter, Godwin earl of Devonshire, Eadric the sheriff and Dodda the treasurer of Plympton, one of the priests of Plympton named Ælfheah had held the chapel and parish of St Andrew of Sutton in his prebend and commons, and that the chapel was still a wooden building. Ælfheah's son was Sladda the priest, who in turn held the church of Plympton. He was followed by the priest Alnod, and Alnod by his son Dunprust. Thus the church of Plympton continuously and peacefully held the church of Sutton as a chapel, for it had not been dedicated before the Norman conquest of England. Also, after Dunprust, his son, William Bacini, held it of Plympton, and, after him, the clerk Thomas, the son of Reginald de Vautorte and Dunprust's daughter. Thomas, after the death of Bishop William and his father Reginald, to whom King Henry I had granted the manor of Sutton as a fief, acknowledged this in the full chapter of Plympton* [priory]; *and on his deathbed he restored the key of that church to Prior John* [1169–76] *and the canons of Plympton in the presence of witnesses.*

2. Plympton priory and estates at Stokeley and Ashridge

The following Plympton memorandum tells the story of how the priory obtained and held on to these estates. The main supporters of Prior Geoffrey (1128–60) were Bishop William de Warelwast of Exeter (1107–37), the founder of the priory, and his two nephews, the one, a namesake, who, acting as his steward, administered the episcopal estates and held the bishop's feudal courts, the other, a clerk, Robert, who served his uncle as archdeacon and succeeded him as bishop (1138–55). Opposed to the priory were Robert Bevin, whose father Ralf had owned Stokeley (in Stokenham), and his wife, Alice, to whom he had given it as dower, and who attempted to take it to her second husband, Richard the Fleming (fitzConan), provost of the city of Exeter in the 1130s.

Bodleian Library, ms.James 23, 166

Robert I bishop of Exeter confirmed by his charter to the church of Plympton the whole estate of Stokelega [Stokeley] *with its pertinencies for a quarter of a knight's service payable in cash. William de Warelwast, his kinsman, had bought this estate from Robert Bevin*[4] *and gave it with himself to the aforesaid church when he was made a canon there. He also gave with himself, it is said by concession of that bishop, the land of Asrigga, also known as Willelande* [?in Harberton], *with its pertinencies. For at one time, so it is said, it had been the land of the keeper of the bishop's swine. The aforesaid Bishop William gave it to William de Warelwast, his nephew and steward, as payment for his services; and the nephew cultivated it for a long time in his demesne together with Stokeley, which, in the time of Bishop William he had bought from the aforesaid Robert [Bevin] and given to his wife, Alice, a daughter of William de Buz, as dowry. But she ran away from her husband with a certain adulterer; and, when Richard the Fleming, provost of Exeter,[5] married her, she laid claim to Stokeley. The aforesaid Prior Geoffrey [of Plympton] gave her and her husband 4 lbs of silver in return for her renunciation of the land in perpetuity in the presence of many witnesses whose names are written on the great roll, together with the witnesses when the aforesaid Robert Bevin quitclaimed all his rights in that same land to Prior Geoffrey, and, by means of the knife of Robert the Hermit, put it on the altar of St Faith in the chapel of the bishop of Exeter and abjured it upon the Four Gospels. And Prior Geoffrey gave him in return 3 marks of silver.*

3. Bishop William Brewer attempts to capture Plympton castle

In 1224 King Henry III goaded into rebellion one of his father's most faithful and useful mercenary military captains, Fawkes de Bréauté, a Norman. King John had in 1216 rewarded him with marriage to Margaret, widow of Baldwin, son and heir of William de Vernon (Reviers), earl of Devon, who himself was to die in 1217: hence Fawkes's possession of Plympton castle and pretensions to act as earl in the right of his wife and her infant son Baldwin (III). The elevation of this low-born foreigner enraged the Devonshire nobility, particularly the interrelated Vernon-Reviers, Courtenay and Brewer families. The bishop's companion-in-arms, the sheriff of Devon, was his cousin, the baron William Brewer II, who had been given the office on 23 January and was superseded by William de Ralegh on 20 October 1225. Fawkes surrendered to the king (with whom were the Devonshire barons) at Bedford on 15 August, and Plympton castle was surrendered to the bishop some time before 6 September when the king ordered him to hand it over to John of Bayeux.[6]

PRO, SC 1/2 no.184

To his most excellent lord, Henry, by the grace of God the illustrious king of the English, lord of Ireland, duke of Normandy and Aquitaine and count of Anjou, William by divine mercy the humble servant of the church of Exeter sends greetings in Him who grants salvation to kings. I wish to inform your exalted royal majesty that on the festival of St-Peter-in-Chains [1 August] I came to Plympton and showed your excellency's letter to the constable and those who are in the castle, and instructed them most strictly that, in accordance with the royal mandate, they should hand over the castle to me. This they in no wise wanted to do; nor did they do so. I, however, with all the knights and serjeants who were present, remained there for eight whole days at my expense in order to ensure that the garrison of the castle could do no damage outside. And meanwhile I had siege engines, that is to say two mangonels, brought up by the sheriff, and ladders and some other things constructed. On the seventh day, when the sheriff and all the knights who remained in the shire were assembled—for all the barons of the shire are in your army—and the royal mandate, that the sheriff and myself should prevent the garrison getting out to make mischief, was recited to them, they replied unanimously that they could not, and were not obliged to, perform such a custody at a time when their lords, to whom they owed their service, were away in your army. And since I did not dare, or desire, that, in so dangerous a situation, your purpose should in any way be thwarted, especially as that castle is strongly munitioned with serjeants, arms and other engines, I provided, with the common consent of your lieges, that the sheriff with 10 knights and 60 serjeants (half mounted and in armour, half on foot)—to which force I myself have contributed 3 knights and 5 serjeants—should remain in place to carry out the blockade. And since the provisions provided for them from my own resources would not last for more than eight days, it was decided by common consent that provisions for their maintenance should be taken as an aid from the men on the lands which are in the hands of Fawkes [de Bréauté] *in Devon—but without detriment to all your rents, crops and stock and everything else on those lands. These arrangements are to last for a fortnight, until your royal majesty shall indicate what should be done in this business. And, so as to preserve your honour, if supplies from my own properties should suffice, I shall in no way seek outside help. To inform you more fully of all other matters I have briefed my clerk, Master Martin, the bearer of this letter. May the Lord preserve your royal highness and honour for ever.*

NOTES

1. Frank Barlow (ed.), *English Episcopal Acta*, 11 (Exeter, 1046–1184) (1996), nos. 19, 23, 120. For the role of oral tradition in lawsuits, cf. Paul Brand, '"Time out of mind": the knowledge and use of the eleventh- and twelfth-century past in thirteenth-century litigation', *Anglo-Norman Studies*, 16 (1994) 37–54.
2. C.R. Cheney and Bridgett E.A. Jones (eds), *English Episcopal Acta*, 2 (Canterbury, 1162–1190), 156–7; M.G. Cheney, *Roger of Worcester, 1164–79* (1981), 143–4, 284, 335, 344–5.
3. Joyce Youings (ed.), *Devon monastic lands; Calendar of particulars for grants 1536–1558*, DCRS, N.S. 1 (1955), 129.
4. According to Bishop Robert I's charter, dateable to 1138 × 42, which records and confirms Robert Bevin's quitclaim for which he was paid 3 marks and awarded confraternity, a settlement made in the bishop's court, William had bought Stokeley from Robert Bevin's father, Ralf. See Barlow, *English Episcopal Acta* , 11, no. 42.
5. For Richard, see Ruth Easterling, 'List of civic officials of Exeter in the 12th and 13th centuries', *DAT*, 70 (1938), 464.
6. Barlow (ed.), *English Episcopal Acta*, 12 (Exeter, 1186–1257) (1996), no. 267. For the historical background see Kate Norgate, *The minority of Henry III* (1912), 182–3, 223–4, 245; F.M. Powicke, *King Henry and the Lord Edward* (1947), 49–66, *The Thirteenth Century 1216–1307* (1953), 24–8; D.A. Carpenter, *The minority of Henry III* (1990), 344–70. See also *Calendar of Patent Rolls* i *(1216–25)* passim.

Frank Barlow

3. Exeter in 1688: The Trial of the Seven Bishops

On Saturday 30 June 1688 a jury in London found the Archbishop of Canterbury and six other bishops (including those of Bath and Wells and Bristol) not guilty of seditious libel. They had been charged for submitting a petition to King James II, seeking to be excused from reading from their pulpits his Declaration of Indulgence, which suspended the laws penalizing both Roman Catholic and Protestant nonconformity. The bishops' petition was the centrepiece of an Anglican show of defiance towards their Roman Catholic monarch who had, since his accession in 1685 with Anglican support, turned his back on his Tory allies and sought the support of dissenters and 'papists', in both central and local government. By centring their petition on the supposed illegality of dispensing with the laws without Parliamentary approval, the bishops had won the support, in London at least, of many prominent Protestant dissenters, and the 'trial of the seven bishops' is often seen as the decisive moment at which James' strategy of seeking to divide and rule the Protestants failed. On the very same day as the acquittal, seven leading politicians issued an invitation to James's son-in-law, the Dutch stadtholder William of Orange, to invade England to force James to call a free parliament. By November William, whose wife Mary was no longer heir to the throne following the birth of James's son (the 'Old Pretender', James III) on 10 June, had invaded England and established himself in Exeter, en route to London and, eventually, the throne.

The public joy at the bishops' acquittal in London and elsewhere, expressed in the lighting of bonfires (associated with the anti-papist celebrations of November the fifth) is well-documented. But there has only been passing mention, if that, of the riotous scenes that developed at Exeter on Monday 2 July, when news of the acquittal reached the cathedral city.[1] Exeter's bishop, Thomas Lamplugh, had timidly refused to sign the petition, though his successor in 1689, Jonathan Trelawney, was one of the seven bishops. But it is clear from the reports of events on 2 July that, despite official efforts to disperse the crowds, bonfires were lit by supporters of the 'Church of England and Bishops'; bells may also have been rung. Although they were branded a mere 'rabble', respectable citizens such as goldsmiths, vintners and druggists participated alongside humbler artisans in these events. One supporter, at least, expected the Dean of Exeter to be sympathetic to the crowd, perhaps because of his robust refusal to have the Declaration of Indulgence read within his jurisdiction. It may be no coincidence that two centres of disturbance were the Cathedral Close ('St Peter's churchyard') and the area outside Eastgate where the Dean and Chapter's other main jurisdiction, St Sidwell's Fee, began.

Those seeking to disperse the crowds by proclamation and then to put out the bonfires (with the corporate fire engine) were denounced as 'popish rogues'. They were, in fact, the members and officials of the city government, led at this date by dissenters and Whigs whom James had brought to power the previous November, replacing the Tory corporation. The violent actions (as well as disrespectful words) aimed at the mayor, dyer Thomas Jefford, and his officials reveal the depth of animosities between the Anglican and dissenting factions in Exeter. Here most, though not all, of the dissenting community had accepted the toleration James offered, welcomed his Declaration and promised to work with the king to reverse the years of Anglican intolerance 'notwithstanding the opposition of the Bishops party'; a few days earlier Jefford had been knighted by the King, probably when presenting an address of congratulation for the birth of the Prince.[2] It must have been sweet revenge to Thomas Crispin, chief target of prosecution over several decades for holding Presbyterian conventicles, to find himself now on the bench as a city JP, while those prosecuted must have found this judicial reversal as outrageous as they found the bearing of the civic sword before the mayor to worship at a nonconformist meeting (probably the James meeting house built in 1687). Many of the witnesses were clearly supporters of the Corporation, as is indicated by their appearance in the list of those enfranchised by it in late August and early September 1688.

There is no sign that this disturbance was ever reported officially to London, perhaps because the Corporation did not wish to reveal the extent of opposition to its policy.[3] But two months later this 'notorious riot' was still producing violent recriminations, and the internal divisions reflected in this incident do much to explain why Exeter, the 'ever-loyal' cathedral city, opened its gates to William in November. Most Tories had found James' actions so repugnant that they lost the will to support him actively: the bishop and dean fled while several leading prebendaries rallied to William. The Whigs were divided, those who had collaborated with James, like Jefford, being discredited, while the Whigs who rallied to William soon found themselves outmanoeuvred in corporate affairs. They did better in parliamentary elections, where the dissenting vote was critical, but even here the power of the 'church party' often proved superior. Ironically one famous Tory victory, in 1698, saw Bishop Trelawney supporting the election as MP of Sir Bartholemew Shower, an Exonian who had been recommended by James' electoral agents in 1688 as a suitable partner for Jefford as a prospective MP for Exeter, and, as recorder of London in 1688, had been one of the prosecuting counsel at the trial of the seven bishops.[4]

DRO, ECA, Book 66

fo.198r. [before Thomas Chrispin Ar[miger]. deputy mayor[5] & Thomas Atherton Ar. JP.[6] 3 July 1688]

Tho Clerke jnr gent undersheriff of the said City and County[7] and George Rogers one of the Serjeants att Mace[8] being yesterday towards the Evening without the Westgate of the said City in pursuance of Mr Mayor's[9] proclamation made that all person should retyre to their habitations were assaulted and wounded by severall persons there mett in a ryotous and tumultuous manner.[10]

Robert Skilton of this city weaver deposeth that Robert Brend feltmaker[11] being yesterday in St Peter's Churchyard,[12] Mr Mayor's proclamation being made that all persons then and there present should cease making of Bonfires and depart to their own habitations, the said Brend cryed 'sound, sound' and gave this deponent ill language.

William Browne of this city cordwyner[13] deposeth further that he then saw the said Brend in the head of A Rabble to goe round the great Conduit[14] saying sound, sound.

Richard Cunningham Esquire high sheriff of the said City and County,[15] being yesterday in the execution of his office and labouring to keep his Majesties peace was by one Lyonell Williams heelmaker[16] assaulted and beaten as he deposeth.

William Arnold Grocer[17] deposeth that Mr Mayor being yesterday in St Peters churchyard to keep the King's peace, one George Trump tobacco pipemaker attempted to stabe him the said Mayor.

James Glyde one of the serjeants att mace[18] yesterday attending Mr Mayor, this Deponent was assaulted and beaten by one Samuell Paul, taylor. For which said offences the said Lyonell Williams, George Trump, and Samuell Paul were committed to prison for want of Bayle.

fo.198v.

The foresaid William Browne further saith that yesterday he saw one Samuell Paul of the said city Tayler to endeavour to rescue one Thomas Ellard the younger who was then taken into custody for his ill behaviour,[19] saying, sound, sound, let's rescue him.

Patrick Cunningham of the said City gent deposeth that yesterday he saw the foresaid Lyonell Williams after proclamation made, to assault the high sheriff and gave him a vyolent blow.

[before Thomas Chrispin Ar. deputy mayor 4 July 1688]

John Bayly of this City barber[20] deposeth that yesterday seeing Three persons committed to prison for being mutinous and in A Ryott the day precedent, heard one Sampson Mannington[21] to say that the Dene of Exeter would fetch them out agayne, And that if the said Dene had thought of such doeings, he would have risen the militia, being in his power soe to doe.[22]

Philipp Tomlyn[23] and George Rogers deposeth that John Twigge of this city, presman, Amy his wife and Mathew Galpen their servant[24] committed outrages and misdemeaned themselves in a mutinous manner att a bonfire made without the Westgate on Monday last ...

fo.199r.
John Heysom, James Pitts and Robert Brend committed to prison for want of sufficient Bayle to answear their offences att Sessions.

[before Thomas Chrispin Ar. deputy mayor 4 July 1688]
Richard Warren of the parish of St Sidwells sleamaker[25] being sworn saith that on Monday last he saw one Robert Brend of the said city feltmaker assembled with divers others on St Peters Churchyard (after proclamation made by the Sheriff for every one to depart) and heard the said Robert Brend to say—sound you popish rogues, speaking these words att the passing of his Majesty's Justices of the peace through the said Churchyard, And about 8 or 10 of the clock the same Evening, he saw the said Robert Brend in A riotous and tumultuous manner carry two faggots towards A Bonfire made before Oxford Inn[26] and cryed sound, sound.

John Trigg of this City weaver deposeth that he saw Robt Brend in a riotous and tumultuous manner bring A Furst Faggott towards the making of A Bonfire after the sheriff had made proclamation to depart, it being before Oxford Inn. And this deponent further saith that he saw Toby (late Porter of Eastgate) in a tumultuous and riotous manner to bee ayding and assisting at the making of a Bonfire before Oxford Inn, after the sheriff had made proclamation to depart.

John Hambley of this City Barber[27] deposeth that on Monday night last he saw in the high street of the said City about one hundred persons saying down with this window, meaning the window of this deponent and about a quarter of an hower thereafter returning said sound, sound, one and all, now for the Ma[yor? gap in text] about Eleaven of the Clock att night, after the sheriff had made proclamation to depart.

[before Thomas Atherton Ar. JP 4 July 1688]
John Atherton of this city gent being sworne saith that on Monday night last about nyne of the Clock he saw one James Tayler of the said city Grocer[28] in a tumultuous and riotous manner throw Faggotts to make a bonfire and being requested to forbear, he said, he would persist in it.

James Leigh of this city Grocer being sworne, saith, that on Monday night last he saw one William Carter of the said city goldsmith[29] in a violent and riotous manner assembled with severall others to make a bonfire and said he had brought faggots to that purpose after the proclamation to depart as aforesaid.

fo.199v. [before Thomas Chrispin Ar. deputy mayor, Hugh Westlake Ar. deputy recorder,[30] William Glyde,[31] Thomas Atherton, Joseph Mauditt[32] and John Starr, Ar.[33] JPs [no full date given]]

Henry Jackman of the city of *Exon*[34] being sworn deposeth that comeing in for water for the Engin[35] he heard Thomas Whitehaire of this city Vintner[36] and Philipp Robinson say Sound wee will stand one by the Legg of the other.

Joseph Trowman of the city of *Exon* carpenter[37] being sworn deposeth that Thomas Whitehair of the city of *Exon* Vintner and Philipp Robinson of the said city Cooke fell upon the Deponent And tooke him by the Coller And stroke him severall blows.

William Browne of this city of *Exon* shoemaker being sworne deposeth that he saw Richard Shobrooke,[38] Abraham Jennings[39] and James Wills throw sticks from the windows of John Myon [?] upon one John Dennis[40] who was imployed by his Majesty's Justices of the Peace to exercise the Engin.

Peter Prew of the city of *Exon* fuller[41] being sworne deposeth that Robert Chilcott of the said city Drugist[42] layd hands on Mr Blatchford being a Constable in the execution of his office and said here is nothing but a parcell of pitifull Taylors.[43]

The aforementioned Peter Prew deposeth that Thomas Robinson,[44] Phillip Robinson and Henry Humfryes[45] came to this Deponent in a rude manner and thrust him upp and downe and said Sound, stand by Church of England and Bishopps.

NOTES

1. John Miller, *Popery and Politics in England 1660–1688* (Cambridge, 1973), 259 cites the correspondence of the Florentine minister in London (BL Additional MSS 25376) as reporting that the Exeter magistrates who tried to put out the bonfires were in danger of being burned themselves.
2. J.R. Jones, *The Revolution of 1688 in England* (1972), 171–2; Narcissus Luttrell, *A Brief Relation of State Affairs* (Oxford, 1857), I, 443, 446, 450; George Duckett (ed.), *Penal Laws and Test Acts* (1882–3), II, 240.
3. For contrasting views of the respective strengths of Jefford's party and that of 'the Bishop, Dean and Chapter and their tenants and other Church of England men', see Duckett, *Penal Laws*, I, 381 and II, 231 and 240.
4. The best guides to Exeter's complex politics in this period are: Alan Brockett, *Nonconformity in Exeter 1650–1875* (Manchester, 1962); Robert Newton, *Eighteenth Century Exeter* (Exeter, 1984); M.G. Smith, *Fighting Joshua* (Redruth, 1985); Mark Goldie, 'James II and the Dissenters' Revenge', *Historical Research*, 66 (1993), 53–88.
5. Crispin, a fuller (freed 1647, master of his company in 1656–7, 1687–8, died 1689), was a leading Presbyterian. He was placed on the Corporation in November 1687 and like many other supporters of the new regime who may, perhaps, have been disfranchised in the previous years of Tory reaction he was freed again on 27 August 1688, as an alderman: A.W. Brink (ed.), *The Life of the Reverend Mr George Trosse* (Montreal, 1974), 129; Brockett, *Nonconformity*, 30–2, 36, 41, 44; Joyce Youings, *Tuckers Hall, Exeter* (Exeter, 1968), 79, 93–5, plate IX (portrait), 124–5, 138–9; Margery M. Rowe and A.M. Jackson (eds), *Exeter Freemen 1266–1967*, DCRS, Extra Series 1 (1973), 139, 177.
6. A mercer freed in 1658 and again 27 August 1688 as an alderman. Appointed to the Corporation in November 1687; on 6 July 1688 he became a deputy lieutenant as well: Rowe & Jackson, *Exeter Freemen*, 145, 177; *CSPD, 1687–9*, no. 1257.

7. Freed 27 August 1688; in 1702 a namesake was freed and sworn as an attorney: Rowe & Jackson, *Exeter Freemen*, 178, 209.
8. A chandler of that name was freed in 1681, and a cordwainer on 27 August 1688: Rowe & Jackson, *Exeter Freemen*, 173, 178.
9. Thomas Jefford, dyer (freed 27 August 1688), mayor by royal order from 27 November 1687 to 1 November 1688 and knighted by James II in late June 1688. Though not himself a recorded dissenter, he was clearly sympathetic to dissent and may have attended their meetings. As mayor he coordinated corporate support for James' policy of toleration, offered to support it in Parliament as a potential MP and sat on a commission of inquiry to recompense dissenters in late July 1688. In 1690 the Secretary of State, acting on information from Bishop Trelawney, ordered his apprehension and examination, presumably for Jacobitism: Goldie, 'James II', 75–6; Rowe & Jackson, *Exeter Freemen*, 177; *H.M.C. 71 Finch*, II, 294 and III, 379.
10. The riverside area outside the Westgate was a notoriously poor and unruly suburb, where the Mayor nevertheless had his main house, pending the completion of Great Duryard: Newton, *Eighteenth Century Exeter*, 3.
11. Fo. 209v: in August a 'Robert Brenn' was bailed for £40. A Robert Brend (no occupation given) had been freed in 1679: Rowe & Jackson, *Exeter Freemen*, 170.
12. The centuries-long dispute between the Cathedral and civic authorities over the jurisdiction of the Close had taken a new twist when the March 1688 charter explicitly gave the city JPs powers over all the liberties within the city. Dislike of this power may have heightened tempers both here and in St Sidwell's fee, outside Eastgate (see n. 26): M.E. Curtis, *Some Disputes between the City and the Cathedral Authorities of Exeter* (Manchester, 1932); *CSPD 1687–9*, nos. 841–2, 852, 855.
13. William Browne cordwainer was freed in 1658 and two men of that name and occupation were freed again on 27 August 1688; in 1680 one of them attended a conventicle: Rowe & Jackson, *Exeter Freemen*, 146, 178; Brockett, *Nonconformity*, 53.
14. Presumably the conduit at Carfax (the junction of High, North and South Streets), rather than the smaller conduit within the Close.
15. A clothier freed in 1673 and again as sheriff 27 August 1688; sheriff for 1687–8 and rechosen for 1688 on the King's order in letter of 27 August; deputy lieutenant 6 July 1688: Rowe & Jackson, *Exeter Freemen*, 159, 177; *CSPD 1687–9*, no. 1257.
16. Fo. 209v: bailed for £40.
17. Freed 1681, again in 1686 without fine and again 3 September 1688: Rowe & Jackson, *Exeter Freemen*, 174, 176, 180.
18. A chandler freed 27 August 1688: Rowe & Jackson, *Exeter Freemen*, 178.
19. Fo. 198r: before Thomas Chrispin deputy mayor on 2 July 1688, Thomas Ellard junior fuller was put on bail of £40 for an unnamed offence; his sureties were Robert Foster (a woolcomber) and Arthur Searle (an upholsterer). A fuller of that name was freed in 1673 and in 1671 he or a namesake had a house with 2 hearths in the Close: Rowe & Jackson, *Exeter Freemen*, 160; W.G. Hoskins (ed.), *Exeter in the Seventeenth Century* DCRS, N.S. 2 (1957), 70. Also bailed for £40 each at the same time were Henry Humfryes (see n. 45) and John Thomas, a fuller (possibly the clothier freed 'by grace of the mayor' in 1669: Rowe & Jackson, *Exeter Freemen*, 158).
20. Freed in 1673: Rowe & Jackson, *Exeter Freemen*, 163.
21. Fo. 200r: Sampson Manaton porter bailed for £20.
22. The Dean (1681–1701) was Richard Annesley, later Lord Altham. According to a letter of Bishop Trelawney of Bristol written on 16 August, when Bishop Lamplugh had proposed to have the declaration read by his clergy, the Dean sent 'him word that if he would betray the church he should not the cathedral, for he would rather be hanged at the doors of it, than the declaration should be read there or in any part

of his jurisdiction, which is large in the county. The gentry and clergy complained to me very much of the Bishop's giving a church to the mayor for his conventicle (in which the declaration was read)'. When the judges involved in the trial visited Exeter the bishop proposed to entertain them, but 'the Dean and chapter assured me they would withdraw their civility and not receive them either at the Church or at an entertainment as hath been customary': J. Simmons (ed.), 'Some Letters from the Bishops of Exeter 1668–88', *DCNQ*, XXII (1942–3), 168. If the Dean did, indeed, have any control over the militia, he lost it on 6 July when the new deputy lieutenants for the city were appointed.

23. Possibly the feltmaker freed in 1656, but more likely one of the two Philip Tamlyns freed on 27 August 1688, a haberdasher and a goldsmith, one of whom was sent by the Corporation to greet the Earl of Bath in February 1688: Rowe & Jackson, *Exeter Freemen*, 143, 178.
24. Fo. 198v: John Twigge presman [i.e. pressman] bailed for £100, and also stood bail for his wife and servant.
25. Freed as a sleymaker (maker of sleys, i.e. weaver's reeds) 27 August 1688 and again 1692: Rowe & Jackson, *Exeter Freemen*, 178, 189. Fo. 207r: on 20 August 1688, Richard Warren and Mary Cruse, spinster, both of St Sidwell's parish, accused James Tremlott, a St Sidwell's cooper, of threatening Warren 'that he would tear him in pieces whensoever he mett him and called him false forswearing Rogue' because 'he was a witness against Robert Brenn lately indicted for a notorious ryott'; Tremlott was bailed for £40.
26. The Oxford Inn was sited where the Taunton and London roads converged outside the East Gate: Newton, *Eighteenth Century Exeter*, 21. And thus just on the edge of St Sidwell's Fee (see n. 12).
27. Freed 3 September 1688 and again in 1691. Rowe & Jackson, *Exeter Freemen*, 180–1.
28. Freed 1694: Rowe & Jackson, *Exeter Freemen*, 190.
29. Freed 1689: Rowe & Jackson, *Exeter Freemen*, 180.
30. Freed 27 August 1688. A barrister and member of the London Green Ribbon Club who had been arrested after the Rye House Plot of 1683 and jailed in Exeter; deputy recorder in the new charter of March 1688; deputy lieutenant 6 July; a commissioner for the inquiry into dissenters' sufferings later that month: Rowe & Jackson, *Exeter Freemen*, 177; Goldie, 'James II', 75; *CSPD 1687–9*, no. 1257.
31. Merchant freed 1667. In 1690 Glyde was suspected of Jacobitism: Rowe & Jackson, *Exeter Freemen*, 155; *H.M.C. 71 Finch*, II, 294.
32. Grocer freed 1657, later also called a druggist (see Robert Chilcott below). Appointed to Corporation November 1687 and freed again 27 August 1688 as an alderman. His brother John was an ejected minister who in 1664 was living with their father Isaac, but as mayor in 1672 Isaac nevertheless prosecuted conventiclers: *Exeter Freemen*, 144, 175, 177; Brockett, *Nonconformity*, 24.
33. Grocer freed in 1656 or 1660; appointed to Corporation November 1687 and made an alderman; deputy lieutenant 6 July 1688. A dissenter whose son became a nonconformist minister at Topsham; 14 March 1687 he received a royal discharge for his dissenting offences: Rowe & Jackson, *Exeter Freemen*, 144, 148; Brockett, *Nonconformity*, 40, 48, 62; *CSPD 1686–7*, no. 1570; *CSPD 1687–9*, no. 1257.
34. Carpenter freed 27 August 1688 and again in 1691: Rowe & Jackson, *Exeter Freemen*, 179, 182.
35. The fire engine had been purchased from London in 1652 and repaired in 1665: H. Lloyd Parry, *The History of the Exeter Guildhall and the Life Within* (Exeter, 1936), 96.
36. Fo. 200r: Whitehaire bailed for £100. Freed as a grocer in 1673: Rowe & Jackson, *Exeter Freemen*, 160.
37. Freed 27 August 1688: Rowe & Jackson, *Exeter Freemen*, 179.

38. Fo. 200r: Richard Shobroke given bail of £40.
39. Fo. 200r: Abraham Jenings chirurgeon given bail of £5. Freed 1695: Rowe & Jackson, *Exeter Freemen*, 191.
40. Carpenter freed 1683 and again 27 August 1688. He was given a royal dispensation on 6 January 1687, presumably for dissent (or Catholicism): Rowe & Jackson, *Exeter Freemen*, 175, 178; *CSPD 1686–7*, no. 1312.
41. Freed 1689. Given a royal discharge, presumably for dissenting offences, on 14 March 1687; a John Prew was involved in the new Presbyterian chapel in 1687: Rowe & Jackson, *Exeter Freemen*, 180; *CSPD 1686–7*, no. 1570; Brockett, *Nonconformity*, 55.
42. Fo. 200r: bailed for £40. Freed 1683 as apprentice of Joseph Mauditt, before whom he was now appearing: Rowe & Jackson, *Exeter Freemen*, 175.
43. The insult was well-aimed. George Blachford tailor was freed 1673 and was named as an assistant in the Merchant Taylors company in its charter granted 3 July 1687: Rowe & Jackson, *Exeter Freemen*, 159; *CSPD 1687–9*, no. 117.
44. A cook of that name was freed in 1661 and a vintner in 1691: Rowe & Jackson, *Exeter Freemen*, 150, 188.
45. Fo. 198r: on 2 July 1688 Henry Humfryes 'bibliopola' [bookseller] was bailed for £40: see discussion of Thomas Ellard in n. 19. This may either be the bookseller/bookbinder freed in 1662 (with fees remitted because of poverty), or his son and apprentice freed 1670: in the 1671 Hearth Tax both are recorded in the Close, one in a house of two hearths and the other as one of the 'poor of the close': Rowe & Jackson, *Exeter Freemen*, 150, 158; Hoskins, *Seventeenth-Century Exeter*, 71.

Jonathan Barry

4. The Travel Journals of Elizabeth Ernst; North Devon in the 1840s

The following extracts are taken from one of the surviving travel journals of Elizabeth Ernst, the wife of Thomas Henry Ernst of Westcombe in the parish of Batcombe, Somerset. Thomas, a retired member of the Bengal civil service, married Elizabeth Strachey in 1819. She was the cousin of Henry (later Sir Henry) Strachey of Sutton Court with whom Thomas had been friendly since 1792 when they met in Bengal.

The Ernsts travelled frequently, both at home and abroad. In 1843 and 1845 they made two tours of Devon and Somerset, visiting, amongst other places, Plymouth, Exeter and Tiverton in August 1843, Lynton, Combe Martin and Watermouth in July 1845 and Ilfracombe, Barnstaple, Bideford and the Appledores in September 1845.

The first extract describes a visit to the circus in Tiverton—a spectacle, it appears, little to Mrs Ernst's taste. The second extract relates to some mine workings which Thomas visited while the couple were staying at Combe Martin. Elizabeth notes his remarks on production at the mine and adds a comment of her own on the condition of the local children. The third extract describes a day in Lynton spent visiting the Valley of Rocks followed by a day in Ilfracombe. Mrs Ernst was not impressed by the Britannia Inn there even though the Mayor of Liverpool had chosen to stay at it. On the following day the couple moved on to Bideford. Here, Elizabeth was struck by the appearance of the inhabitants, 'a comely race', and admired the workhouse children's drill under the Master, an ex-soldier. The journals are deposited in the Somerset Record Office and form part of a small estate collection.

SRO, DD/SWD 10/9, 11

9th [August 1843]   After breakfast Mr D & his Sons & my husband & Augusta went on Horseback & in the Car to Tiverton where they arrived in time to see Sands's entry into the town with an open Car containing a band of music drawn by ten cream colored horses, two abreast, & after passing all through the town they with some difficulty contrived to drive by an awkward winding turn through a narrow gateway into the yard of the Angel Inn. Mrs Daniel, Louisa, Miss Hall a Lady from Clifton, sister to Mr Webbe Hall the Agriculturist & myself joined the party at two O'clock at Mr Saunders's house adjoining the School, where Mrs Saunders a very pleasing woman was doing the honors. From thence we went to a large Pavilion where we saw a fine display of Horsemanship & gymnastic exercises—& were particularly struck (at least some of our party were) with the following performances, which my husband wished me to commemorate. Mr Sands standing upright supported on his shoulders a man as stout as himself & the latter first took upon his shoulders 'Master Buckley' who got upon the man's head, & afterwards turning head over heels, planted his head on that of his supporter, with his heels in the air, waving his feet about in a graceful manner, & whilst this was going on, the undermost man moved forward several steps with apparent ease & unconcern. Another feat of Mr Sands was this. Standing on two horses abreast, he took 'Master Buckley' first on his shoulders, and afterwards held him upon his outstretched palm of his right hand & whilst he was doing this, two loose horses running round the Circus, passed separately and together between the two horses on which Sands was standing. Afterwards whilst he was riding one of the horses, a man stood in his way holding up a Hoop covered with paper through which he darted whilst going at full speed & perched himself again on the horse. Amongst the Carpet leaps the most extraordinary was Sands, or a stout man like him, stretched on his back on a carpet, passing first with his hands & then with his feet a long heavy pole which he tossed to some height in the air & caught on the soles of his feet, perfectly balancing the pole in all his movements. Most of the performers made repeated somersets in the air, backwards & forwards & two of them continued these leaps without interruption thirty forty & even fifty times. I certainly never saw the like before & I must say that I hope I never shall, for I think the whole of it a fearful and disgusting sight.

[11th or 12th July] 1845   On our return to the Hotel at Combe Martin, E. went to see some Mines of some celebrity which he was told were tin, but he found to be lead with small portions of silver & antimony of which he brought away specimens. These mines are it seems worked by a private joint stock Company. The best parts of the Ore are separated chiefly by women, & sent to Bristol & other places to be smelted. The Overseer told E. that 30 or 40 people (men, women & children) are employed in the different processes of the Manufacture & that a tun of the picked ore is worth from twenty to twenty four pounds, & produced twenty ounces of silver, about the same proportion of Antimony & the rest chiefly lead. He also said that the people are constantly employed & get better wages than Agricultural labourers. But nothing can be more wretched than the appearance & habitations of the people of Combe Martin & we never saw a place with so many ragged & sickly looking children. Poor little things! They seemed the victims of hunger & disease.

9th [September 1845]   A busy day. E. walked before breakfast almost to the Valley of Rocks & about xi he & Hall & I took the same walk, along the beautiful bold Cliffs & leaving me on a large flat stone in the Valley, they ascended the fine insulated rock a little beyond me, hanging over the sea with convenient resting places at different elevations & from the top of the hill my husband waved his hat & handkerchief to me. They were soon joined by Charles who it seems had some difficulty in squeezing himself up a steep narrow flight of steps to the top, & was in some danger of being jammed in! About 4 o'clock I took another walk on the Cliff whilst Ernst & Hall were accomplishing a long meditated trip to a Summer house built by Mr Herries at the top of the Hill overhanging his grounds, & commanding *Linmouth* [Lynmouth], *Linton* [Lynton] and all the magnificent scenery stretching out to the sea. As the ascent to this Summer house is almost two miles, Hall had a Donkey to take her up, but it turned out such a wretched Animal that before she had got halfway up the hill, she was obliged to send it back & she was very near having a frightful fall almost at starting, on the back of her head, which was prevented by E. laying hold of her legs which were flying up.

10th [September 1845]   Left *Linton* [Lynton] at 10 and arrived at Ilfracombe between 1 & 2. Put up at the Britannia on the Quay at the bottom of the town—a seafaring bustling Inn, where it would never do to stop for more than a few hours, tho' the Landlord told us that the Mayor of Liverpool & his family had taken up their quarters there—and as far as we are concerned they are heartily welcome. From this Inn we found a convenient level walks through fields to the new approach to the Capston Hill, which has been lately made by a subscription of three or four hundred pounds & does great credit to the taste & public spirit of the Subscribers and the persons employed. They have executed the work admirably. The towering perpendicular cliff on one side of the walk, & the sea rushing over large masses of rock on the other, in the midst of which we saw Ladies lounging & reading at high water with foaming surf all around them, are really very fine. The ascent to the Capston by this approach is gradual & easy, and for the most part guarded by a firm parapet on the sides of the Cliff overlooking the sea.

Bideford—11th—to 19th [September 1845]   We found our rooms as comfortable as possible & furnished with some elegance—good fare, and attendance & everything clean & orderly. This is a very pretty place. The Hotel stands high, tho' not ½ way up the hill, & there is a steep ascent to it. From a Bow window in our sitting room there is a fine view over the roofs of houses, of the river & bridge (24 Arches) & of its winding course to Instow & the 2 Appledores. The Torridge here is ⅛th of a mile wide, & the level well paved Quay 1200 feet long. It is only 2 miles from the sea. Vessels of 300 tons can come & unload at it & the river is navigable for small craft to W. Gifford three miles beyond Bideford. The town is well built, has good streets & shops which are remarkably clean & bright. The people & particularly the children are a comely race—healthy & good looking—& there is more ease & comfort in the appearance of the lower classes than I have witnessed anywhere else. There are hardly any beggars! The air is pure & bracing & this place escaped the Cholera whilst it raged in other parts of Devonshire. I had suffered very much during the winter, spring & summer from pain in my back. To my no small surprise & I hope thankfulness I found one day here that the pain was gone!

We went one morning to the Union Workhouse and were much struck with all the arrangements there. It is a handsome building a good way up the hill & the Entrance is by an open balustrade in front of it, & very different from most of the Union Houses with a high wall as if a prison. The Master & Mistress seem to be admirably qualified for their situations—the former an old soldier, who served during the Peninsular war, and retired with a pension. His name is Sermon & he was a Sergeant Major of the 15th or 16th Lancers I think—& many years ago was on duty at Sandhurst College with his Company. We saw 40 children from 4 or 5 to 10 or 12 drilled & exercised by him. This performance was really excellent. Their little arms & legs were brought into full play by varied evolutions which they went through in concert, with due attention to the word of command—& they seemed to consider the exercise more like play, than a task.

Sue Berry

5. The Teaching of Honiton Lacemaking in the Early Twentieth Century

When compulsory elementary education was introduced in 1870 the decline of lace schools was inevitable. The attendance at school left little daylight time for lacemaking by young girls. A report in 1887 by Alan Cole of South Kensington Museum identified this decline. However, very little was achieved to rectify this until the Education Acts of 1902 when County Councils were given the responsibility of elementary and secondary education. A Lace sub-committee was formed and chaired by Mr Kennet-Were. Amongst their papers a report describes 'The condition of the Lace Industry and the best means of developing and organising it in East Devon'. This was sent to the Technical Committee of the County Council.

DRO, DCC/86/7/9

The Sub-Committee hope that the revival in the lace industry will not prove of a mere transitory nature, especially if steps are taken to give further instruction, not only in the art of lacemaking but also in the production of improved patterns. They are of opinion that the County Council should lend its aid in fostering and improving an industry which, in the past, has done so much to afford occupation for a large portion of the working classes.

This industry is, so to speak, endemic in the County; it is specially a cottage industry, which may afford additional earnings to the families of the country labourers; it requires no elaborate or expensive plant, and a pillow and set of sticks,[1] a few pins and a supply of good thread is nearly all that is necessary for the production of a very beautiful and costly material; and it affords a means of livelihood to many who would otherwise be dependent upon parochial relief.

They accordingly recommend
1. That a staff teacher should be appointed for the whole districts of East Devon, whose duty should be to give and to organise instruction in lacemaking, to procure, where necessary, competent teachers, or to establish classes for the better education of those who are at present, or are willing to become, teachers.
2. That the classes should be organised, if possible, as Evening schools under the regulations of the Board of Education, so as to earn grants from the Board.
3. That exhibitions of lace should be held at convenient centres and at suitable times, and that the County Council be invited to offer prizes for exhibits made by students, which may be recommended by independent judges.
4. That the management and superintendence of the scheme be placed in the hands of a special committee, and that an annual sum of £250 be placed at their disposal for this purpose.

The annual expenses of the scheme are estimated to be as follows:
1. Salary of Staff Instructess; about £100 per annum, with Travelling Allowances [say about £75]
2. Cost of materials about £25

It is impossible to estimate the total cost of local instruction, but the Sub-Committee are of the opinion that the salaries to be paid to local teachers will be about 4d to 6d per hour, and that one teacher will only be able to supervise six pupils or less. If the Board of Education consent to recognise the local classes and make a grant, it is estimated that this grant will be sufficient to cover the cost of the classes taken by the local instructors.

A letter, dated 26 May 1903, to a Miss Elton from Mr Young[2] illustrates the setting up of such classes:[3]

> Mr Ward has forwarded to me the letter you wrote to him about paying for the room for these classes. The Committee are prepared to make some payment, especially for the cleaning, but the funds allotted by the County Council are hardly sufficient to allow a charge for ordinary rent. As you know it is the practice of the Committee to expect local subscriptions or fees to cover the local expenses for rent etc. it is not desirable however that a fee should be charged for the lace classes, I think having regard to the position of the lace workers: there is therefore no local fund to draw on and it is hoped that the local expenses will be kept to as low as possible.
>
> I find that I have omitted in the press of the work to answer your earlier letter as to the management of these classes. The lace Committee directed Miss Ward[4] to communicate with the members of the Committee resident in the locality when making her arrangements and she therefore communicated with Lady Peek also, in arranging classes in Colyton. Owing to the changes produced by the recent Education Act some charges will be possibly made in the matter of the Local Committee previously organised in connection with the District Committee, but if meanwhile your local committee would interest themselves in the lace classes I am sure the Lace Committee would be indebted to them for their help.
>
> I shall be very glad if you will let me have a note as to what charge you think must be paid for the room and the caretaker.

The progress made in the lace classes is described in reports made by Miss Ward to the Lace Committee. In the minutes of a meeting held on Friday 10th May 1907 she reports on the state of the room at Broadclyst Institute 'it really is not fit to hold lace classes in, the dust is so thick on the tables and floor that it is very difficult to keep the lace clean'. This was followed up by a letter[5] to Miss Ward from the Hon. Secretary of the Broadclyst Institute, dated June 17 1907:

> The Committee of the above having had a complaint come before them as to the state of the room you use for the Lace class have considered the matter and find they are unable to do it at the price you pay.
>
> I am requested to say they will in future let it to you at 1/6 per meeting as they have had to rise the pay of the caretaker in consequence of your complaint and to ensure the room being kept clean.
>
> I must ask you to see that the members of your class do not run about on the seats as I hear they do sometimes and I notice that they leave pins about on the floor which are dangerous to anyone scrubbing it.

The final matter to be raised at the meeting concerned 'an exhibit of lace to be sent to the forthcoming Australian Exhibition on condition that no expenses are incurred by the County Council'. It is unfortunate that little support should be offered, especially due to the fact that only in the previous year a Gold Medal had been awarded to Devon County Council for the lace submitted at the Milan International Exhibition 1906.

NOTES

1. Sticks: lace bobbins, a type only used for Honiton Lace.
2. Mr Young, Education Officer, Devon County Council.
3. DRO, DCC/86/7/9.
4. Miss Gertrude Lee Ward, the staff instructress appointed by the Lace Sub-Committee to oversee the teachers of Honiton Lacemaking.
5. DRO, DCC/86/7/9.

Susan Bradshaw

6. Defence Preparations in Devon Against the Arrival of the Spanish Armada: 'So doth the state of this countrye reste quiet in orderlye readynes'

A wealth of evidence has survived in the Public Record Office which, together with a more modest collection in local repositories, sheds considerable light on defence preparations made in Devon in anticipation of the expected attack by the forces of the King Philip II of Spain in 1588.[1] Despite the extensive range of material which is available, it is not easy to choose a single document which encapsulates not only the high drama of the threat of the Armada invasion attempt, but also touches upon the kind of military preparations in Devon, a maritime county which, after all, ranked prominently in the crisis as one of the most vulnerable in England's 'front-line'. To find a document which conveys all this, and hints at the attitudes and the feelings towards the threat manifested in Devon during the months of anxious waiting, might seem impossible. However, on 7 December 1587, in response to the latest urgent request for information sent by the Privy Council, William Bourchier, third earl of Bath, Devon's young Lord Lieutenant, in collaboration with four of his deputy lieutenants, drafted a remarkable letter which mentions virtually all aspects of the crisis.[2] Their carefully chosen words were committed to paper in a small, neat secretary hand and the document was then signed with a flourish by the earl of Bath himself and his deputies Sir William Courtenay, Sir Robert Dennis, Sir John Gilbert and Mr George Cary.[3] As the writers note, they were replying to a letter sent from Westminster on 9 October. Thus their response had taken almost two months. While the delay was undoubtedly in part occasioned by the need to gather from across the county the information required by the Privy Council, it also indicates something of the friction which existed between the centre of affairs in Westminster and a periphery bombarded with an incessant barrage of inquiries and orders.

Much of the correspondence flowing between the Privy Council and the lords lieutenant of the front-line 'maritime' counties concerned, on the one hand, requests for accurate information about the physical defences erected to protect vulnerable havens against any enemy attempt to force a landing and, on the other hand, calls for certified surveys of the numbers of trained and untrained soldiers, together with the quantity and character of their weapons and equipment. An extremely precise check-list of items of information required by the Council was issued in early March, 1587.[4] But Devon's response, like that received from other counties, apparently failed to address a number of key points and the earl of Bath was asked to provide more details.[5] His lengthy reply, dated 10 April 1587, supplied the answer to some of their Lordships' questions, but important queries nonetheless remained. The earl craved the indulgence of the Privy Council in not supplying the names of those in Devon who had 'war experience as captains, lieutenants, ensigns or corporals'. The problem, he implied, was a matter of geography; it was not easy to gather such information in so large a county, the 'distance of the places being greate'.[6] Indeed, much of the earl's letter amounts to a litany of excuses and apologies, but he clearly relished his chance to point out that the reason why the county's return had failed to itemize the provision of 'carriages' for Devon's militia lay in the narrowness of the Westcountry lanes: 'this is likewise omitted in the certificat', wrote Bath, 'for that this countrie is alltogether unapt for caryadge with cartes or waynes'. Lord Burghley, however, was still dissatisfied, and the maritime counties were instructed to prepare new certificates. In Devon, yet another survey was duly undertaken and the certificate was ready by June.[7]

At this point the role of Sir Richard Grenville in making his official survey of South-Western defences began to make an impact. Grenville had been appointed to undertake this task by the Privy Council in March 1587.[8] As the note endorsed on the letter of 7 December makes clear, Sir Richard had already submitted a report by June. His involvement is in fact underlined in a detailed, annotated summary of defence preparations in Devon and Cornwall drawn up for the Privy Council that month.[9] This document notes that musters had been 'performed' and certificates drawn up and 'delivered to Sir Ric[hard] Grenvile to acquaint y^{or} L[ordships] with'. We also learn that in the absence of satisfactory information from Devon about the provision of 'cover' for soldiers and the measures which had been taken to 'impeache a landinge', the matter was to be referred to Grenville for further inspection. However, the precise extent of Sir Richard Grenville's role in planning and installing the defences of the South West has never been fully explored, though he has been associated with a map, probably drawn in 1587, of gun emplacements and military positions deployed around Plymouth Sound,[10] and a sketch map or 'plott' purporting to show how all the coasts of Devon and Cornwall were 'to bee fortyfied in 1588 against the landing of any enemy'.[11] It therefore seems likely that Devon's young and inexperienced Lord Lieutenant readily deferred to Grenville in the matter of local defence preparations.

On 9 October, in view of the deficiencies in the two returns submitted by Devon in March and June 1587, the Privy Council ordered the earl of Bath to prepare yet another certificate.[12] The 'one generall Role of certificate for the whole shire', referred to in the letter of 7 December, is probably the lengthy document in the State Papers which has been innaccurately dated to April 1588.[13] This exceptionally full survey answered the deficiencies complained of earlier by the Privy Council.

The acute vulnerability of England's south coast counties was recognized by the Queen in August 1587 when she instructed the earl of Warwick, Master of the Royal Ordnance, to send cannon and powder to augment local supplies.[14] In fact, Devon was to receive two sakers, two minions and two falcons, 'well-mounted uppon carriages wth wheeles shod wth iron, and furnisshed wth ladles, sponges and rammers, with all other necessaries incident for the travell and service where they are to be emploied'.[15] As the letter of 7 December makes clear (no doubt taking account of the difficulty of moving wheeled vehicles along the narrow lanes of the county), the Queen's ordnance and powder was to be conveyed to Devon by sea.

From February 1587 onwards, senior Privy Councillors became increasingly aware that 'places of descent' on the south coast required 'skonces, parrapets, trenches, and such other artificiall plotts and devises as ar[e] meete to be used for the anoyeaunce of the enimye, and the safetie of her ma^{tes} subietes'. But the terminology used in the orders sent from Westminster clearly engendered confusion in Devon. After all, the earl of Bath and his deputies were not experts in military engineering and they worried that their trenches and ordinary bulwarks may not have been what the Privy Council had in mind when it spoke of sconces and parapets. In a passage which betrays these local doubts and uncertainties, the letter of 7 December suggests that the advice of experts was needed, but was unavailable in Devon. Assistance was therefore requested.

The critical role of Plymouth in the defence of the realm is acknowledged. Indeed, special measures for the speedy relief of the port and haven had been both a national and a local preoccupation for months. Thus Grenville's work had focused particularly on the protection of Plymouth Sound. A garrison of soldiers, drawn from all four South-Western counties, was to be deployed to defend the town and reinforcements were placed on stand-by to march to the aid of Plymouth in the event of an enemy attack. There were even plans to set up road-blocks ('turn-pikes') on the roads from Plymouth to ensure that if the town fell to the enemy, their further progress inland might be impeded. Such detailed arrangements clearly added to the apprehension and fear felt in the county. The letter of 7 December refers to the receipt of news, despatched from London on 29 November, that Spanish forces had been 'discovered on the seas betweene *Ingland* and *Irland*'.[16] Although this was one of many false alarms, the growing realization in Devon that an invasion attempt was a certainty 'moved undoubted resolutions in the minds of all people'. However, the earl and his deputies offered the reassurance that the county nonetheless rested 'quiet in orderlye readynes'. It would stretch credulity too far to suppose that the Lord Lieutenant of Devon and his deputies were unaware of the real situation in the county at the time. Local evidence suggests, however, that in Plymouth at least there was frantic activity, and even a sense of panic amongst ordinary townspeople, which continued almost to the day that King Philip's formidable fleet was first engaged by Lord Howard and Sir Francis Drake off the Eddystone Reef on 21 July 1588.[17] By suggesting that Devon was quiet, orderly and ready, the earl probably judged that this was what the Queen and the Privy Council wanted to hear, though he must have known that he was bending the truth. Here, then, we have a fleeting glimpse of the complex relationship which existed between the core of government in Westminster and the crown's officials operating in Elizabethan England's peripheral counties.

PRO, SP12/206/25–6

Our dewtyes unto yor good Lordeshipps alwayes considered, wherras by yor Lo^{rps} le[tte]rs of the ixth daye of October laste paste to us directed, yor Lo^{rps} require to be advirtised what accompte her ma^{tie} maye make of the strength and forces of this countrie, and in like manner to be thoroughlie resolved what hath byn done for the accomplishement of the instructions sent downe with former le[tte]rs from yor L^{rps} conteyening sondrye spetiall matters of service both to impeache the landinge of the enimye and to hinder his intente of further recourse, wee have since the receite of yor saide le[tte]rs (herein firste mentioned) wth verye precise consideracon entered into a veiwe of all manner of armor and weapon together wth the habilitye of persons serviceable in this countrie, readye to be imployed uppon anye occation wherin her ma^{tie} shall comaunde (either for defence or outherwise) wch according to our duetyes wee doe herewhth signifye unto yor L^{rps} one generall Role of certificate for the whole Shire, with the pticuler devisions thereof, aswell of footemen as horsemen, and under what chardge and leading the same and everye of them are wth, for that p[ar]te hath byn observed and withall duetifull regarde so farr as the captaynes both in fidelitie, industrie, and resolute myndes have byn able and wilbe readye from tyme to tyme to accomplyshe.

And whereuppon further consideration taken of the aforesaide instructions wee fynde that amounge the reste there is required at the places of descent: skonces, parrapets, trenches, and such other artificiall plotts and devises as ar meete to be used for the anoyeaunce of the enimye, and the safetie of her ma^{tes} subietes (whereof wee hope yor L^{rps} have receaved intelligence by Sr Richarde Grenefilde longe since, to whose spetiall chardge by yor Lo^{rps} the same was referred). Even so have wee thoughte it owr duetyes to signifye unto yor Ho[nour]^{es} that for wantt of skillfull psons fitt for conducte, leadinge of an armye, and knowledge in making skonces and other fortifications, wee cannot yelde unto yor Ho[nour]^{es} suche sufficient and effectuall resolucon as is required in that behalfe. And therefore wee humblie desyre yor honorable regardes that some pson of good accompte and experience in theis late services (as to yor Lo^{rps} wisedomes shalbe thoughte necessarye) might be imployed here for the assistaunce of us and other gentlemen that are [de]taled herein. And albeit that wth suche exactnes as yor Lo^{rps} doe require, wee have not in theis spetiall poyntes done as therein is sett downe, yet wee have not neglected our duetyes to pforme by trenches and ordinarye bulworckes uppon the sea coaste to impeache the attempte and landinge of the enimye and all other things to hinder theire further passage. Your Lo^{rps} late l[ette]^{rs} of the xxixth of november laste, importinge some doubte that the kinge of Spaynes Armey shoulde be betweene the coaste of Englande and Irelande hath moved undoubted resolucons in the myndes of all people in this countrye togeather with our selves to pforme the p[ar]tes of loyeal subietes in eache waie that shall appertayne, expecting hourelye to receave anye direction or apparaunte cause that shoulde move us to pceede unto action, whereof as wee have not either here, or from yo[r] Lo[rps] receaved, anye further intelligence, so doth the state of this countrye reste quiet in orderlye readynes untill the occation be offered and therein have taken spetiall direction for the spedye releif of the Towne of Plymouth as yo[r] Lo[rps] have given comaundment. And lastelye wee maye not omitte to acknowlege unto her ma[tie] our most humble thanckes for her highnes gratious regarde of this countrie in pviding for the same wth pte of her owne store of ordinaunce and powder w[ch] wee understande is alreadye imbarqued to be transported thither, the use and expence whereof when it shall please god that it maye arryve heere, shalbe so ordered as the same oughte to be for the pfecte readynes and sure effecte of her ma[tes] service. And so wth desyre of yo[r] Lo[rps] favorable acceptaunce of theis our doinges, wee does moste humblie take our leaves. From *Exceter* the vij[th] of December 1587

Yo[r] LLp[s] to comaunde

[signed] W:Bathon
W Courteney Robart Denys
John Gilbert George Cary

[Dorse. referres to a report to be made by s[r] Ry Grenfield, but there is no mention in his report of the nomber of th'ablemen or how furnished neyether of pioners, lances, lighthors or petronels, but only of defects in the trained bandes upon a reviewe taken by him in Jun[e] 1587]

NOTES

1. Mark Brayshay, 'Plymouth's Coastal Defences in the Year of the Spanish Armada' *DAT*, 119 (1987), 169–96; 'Tudor artillery towers and their role in the defence of Plymouth 1588', *DH*, 35 (1987), 3–14.
2. PRO, SP12/206/25–6.
3. Joyce Youings, 'Bowmen, Billmen and Hackbutters: the Elizabethan Militia in the South West', in Robert Higham (ed.), *Security and Defence in South-West England before 1800* (Exeter, 1987), 60–1.
4. PRO, SP 12/199/75.
5. PRO, SP 12/209/1.
6. PRO, SP 12/209/79.
7. PRO, SP 12/202/37.
8. PRO, SP 12/199/19.
9. PRO, SP 12/204/58: 'Abstract of the proceedings of the deputy lieutenants in execucion of the orders sent from the C[ounci]l in the beginning of March last: Devon, Cornewal, June 1587'.
10. PRO, MPF/6. The map is endorsed: Sir Ric Grenvylle for the fortification of Plymmouth.
11. BL, Cotton MS Augustus I. ii. 6; Mark Brayshay, 'Plymouth's Coastal Defences', 181–7; Mark Brayshay, 'Spatial realities and cartographic distortions: Tudor and Stuart maps of Plymouth and its region', *Society of University Cartographers Bulletin*, 26, 2 (1992), 1–12.
12. A convenient summary of the Privy Council's struggle to obtain satisfactory information regarding defence preparations in the maritime counties is provided by John Bruce, *Report on the arrangements which were made for the internal defence of*

these Kingdoms when Spain, by its Armada, projected the invasion and conquest of England ..., State Papers Office (London, 17 May 1798) Appendix xix.
13. PRO, SP12/209/123.
14. John Roche (ed.), *Acts of the Privy Council*, New Series, xv, 1587–88 (1897), 280.
15. PRO, SP12/203/17–19.
16. *Acts*, 288 (see note 14).
17. PRO, SP12/212/81; Brayshay, 'Plymouth's Coastal Defences', 190–3.

Mark Brayshay

7. A Seventeenth-Century Survey of Hardwick Farm

The papers of the Parker Family, once of North Molton, but more recently of Boringdon and Saltram, Plympton St Mary, were deposited at Plymouth City Archives in 1953. Listing was finally completed in 1995. There are a number of surveys and rentals in the archive. This survey of 'Herdwick' Farm, now Hardwick, is deemed to be unfit for production. The document measures 18″ × 7″, and is folded once. It is in a neat hand, though with several alterations, indicated with scoring-through in the transcript. Hardwick Farm lies a mile ESE of Saltram House and immediately north of the A38. It is sheltered from the North by Dorsmouth and Amados Hills. Hardwick was acquired by George Parker, then of Boringdon, in 1721. This survey predates Parker ownership and is of the late seventeenth century. Among other things this survey is interesting for its noting of the apple pound.

WDRO, 69M/6/66 [UFP]

A survey ['of the eighth part of the whole parts divided or to be divided' crossed through] of ['all that' crossed through] the capital messuage Barton ffarme and demesne lands of *Herdwicke* lyeing within the parish five parts thereof the whole in eight parts divided or to be divided of Plympton St Mary in the County of Devon being the lands fee and inheritance of Thomas Periman Gent.

A survey ['of the eighth part of the' crossed through] capital
messuage or mansion house of *Herdwicke*, Dovehouse,
Barnes, stables, poundhouse and other out[houses],
Orchards and gardens, Woodparke, Broadparke,   yearly value
Crosseparke, Verbery, Roseparke, Torreparke, Culverparke
now the new orchard, The Warren,
Rudgeparke   8
Kilpeitt   ⅓

Westwood	14	
Willparke	6	
Jordansparks	16	

	li s d
Common of pasture and common of Turbary on Leighmore, Common of Estovers and Common of pasture in Torricombe Woods, The ['eighth parte' crossed through] way of the way leading from the Killmeadow near *Herdwicke* to Hamparke Corner and from thence northward to the Lower Yeat of Westwood 104 ⅓	100 50 00
['And alsoe' crossed through] The moyty or halfendtale or foure parts the whole in eight parts divided or to be divided of all that the aforesaid capital messuage Barton farme and demesne lands of *Herdwicke* aforesaid the ['lands' crossed through] fee and inheritance of the said Thomas Perriman, gent	li s d 050 00 00
And alsoe the eighth part the whole in eight parts divided or to be divided of all that the aforesaid capital messuage Barton ffarme and demesne lands of *Herdwicke* aforesaid ['for and dureing' crossed through] The ffee and inheritance of the said Thomas [Per]riman gent.	012 10 00
one other eighth part of the said farme to the said Thomas Perriman in lease for 99 years if two lives soe long live	012 10 00
Two other eighth parts of the said farme to the said Thomas Perriman	025 00
in lease for three lives absolute	100 00
The ffield under Westwood called Gists lands wholly Mr Perrimans 6:2	006–10
Timber and the sider or apple pound	

Paul Brough

8. A Brawl at a Shobrooke Parish Meeting, *c.*1758

An account by a participant in a brawl which started at a parish meeting in Shobrooke, near Crediton, is one item in a collection of papers found in the Old Rectory there which were deposited in the Devon Record Office in 1971.[1] A large number of these papers relate to the Dyer family and their landholdings in Shobrooke from the early sixteenth century and evidence from the account itself and Shobrooke parish records[2] points to the writer being a Thomas Dyer of Moor. He and the other people mentioned in the account all served as parish officers in the 1750s and 1760s, either as churchwardens or overseers of the poor or both, and would, therefore, have been some of the more substantial inhabitants of the village. According to the account, William Rowe and a Mr Brock were overseers of the poor at the time and this dates the event to either 1757–8 or 1760–1 when Rowe is recorded as holding this office with Moses Brock. William Rowe died in 1761 and was buried in Shobrooke, described in the parish register as 'lately clerk', on 9th February.[3] He was also a churchwarden in 1760–1 but the account for this year mentions his death and it is continued and completed by a Roger Rowe. It is tempting to think that his death may have been a consequence of the incident recorded but no proof of this has been found. In fact, as William Rowe was asking for 'the account' to be signed, this must presumably have related to a full year's finances and would, therefore, date the incident to 1758.

By the end of the seventeenth century, the parish poor relief system was well established and the payment of rates to fund it was generally accepted as a reasonable price to pay to care for the impotent poor, attempt to provide work for the able poor and, as a result, prevent social disorder. By 1700, the costs were recognized as significant but there is no evidence of any general resistance to payment of rates in the period up to 1750 although efforts, mostly unsuccessful, were made to reduce the burden on the ratepayer. However, annual national expenditure on poor relief doubled between 1750 and 1776 and this provided the impetus for the reforming movement which grew in pace in the second half of the eighteenth century. Rural poverty was a factor which contributed to the rising costs in this period and the ratepayers of a parish like Shobrooke might have seen a considerable rise in the amount of their assessed contributions as a result of this.[4] Unfortunately, no records of poor relief income and expenditure survive for this parish for the eighteenth century after 1707 and it is, therefore, difficult to ascertain whether, and, if so, how much, rising costs could have been an issue in this incident.

Thomas Dyer's statement refers to specific tensions between the participants, particularly William Rowe on the one side and Robert Skinner and John Brown on the other, and these may have been the dominant factors in the incident. Dealing with a reluctance by Skinner to pay the poor rates was a problem which all overseers would have had to face from ratepayers from time to time and would normally have been dealt with in a peaceful manner. As for John Brown, he refers to William Rowe being 'maintained' and to him and his family as being the cause of substantial financial loss to Brown and his family and this assertion, although perhaps exaggerated from the effects of too much beer, seems to reflect more than a dispute about the cost of poor relief in the parish. William Rowe may have been in financial difficulties towards the end of his life as, although he was an overseer of the poor in this period and a churchwarden for the years 1759 to 1761, the surviving churchwardens' accounts do not record him paying church rates after 1753. That he continued to serve as a parish officer and parish clerk right up to his death, suggests that any such personal problems did not affect his or the parish's attitude to his public responsibilities. However, they may have involved Brown and Skinner directly and tensions between individuals in a small community like Shobrooke in the mid-eighteenth century were likely to surface at any time and on any occasion.

DRO, 1049M/Z1

At a parish meeting held to hear and determine the complaint of the poore[5] after it being ended William Rowe desired Mr Skinner as well as the other parishioners that were present to signe the account which Mr Skinner refused. He was asked whither he had any objection to the account; he said no, but he would not signe it. Then William Rowe said I have something to say concerning Mr Skinner and I will speak it before all present: that Mr Skinner refuseth to pay me the poore rates. With that Mr Skinner threw himself in apassion and abused William Rowe greatly calling him all manner of pityfull rogues and raskels and charged him with forgery saying he could prove it against him; and likewise abused and called his father which was dead calling him old bunney[6] back with many such like expressions. Then Mr Skinner rose from the insaid of the table where he was siting and went out of the chamber and I bleeve went down stairs and staid some considerable time, then came up again and seated himself in his former place and threw out upon the table a receit which was for apoore rate, and desired Mr Brock the other overseer to signe it which he did, and received the money for the poore rate of Mr Skinner. Then I spoke [to] Mr Brock and told him it was not right of him to receive it for it was altering the custom of the parish and I bleeved it was more than he could justifie. Mr Brock said he did not think there was any thing amiss in what he had done for he would be accountable for it at the years end. After this Mr John Brown began to examine me what business it was of mine and to abuse me calling me fool and many other names and gieving me the lie in every thing I said and wherefore I did vindicate and uphold asuch fellow against them who maintained him. I told him I would not vindicate him nor no other man unless in aright cause. Then Mr Skinner rose and came out from the insaid of the table where he was sitting and struck William Rowe where he was on the outsaid several blows. With that William Rowe to defend himself str[uck] up Mr Skinners heels and he fell along the room. Mr Brown seeing this he stept to William Rowe and struck him ablowe or two in the breast and Mr Skinner and

Mr Brown fell upon William Rowe. After that I stept to them and parted them and exspected they would be quiet; but they both fell at him the second time and I parted them again as well as I could; but being so much vex I called them great logies[7] and asked them whither they was not ashamed both of them to fall upon such little fellow and said if they were minded to fight they should fight with me. With that Mr Skinner took his stock and buckell from of his neck and threw upon the table in the said room and flew to me as wilfull as possible and struck me back upon ajoynt stool that lay along the chamber; and I fell to anon power[8] in upon the window and Mr Skinner upon me, where I received ablack and bloody eye. Soon after I recoverd my self again I took hold of him by the coller of his coat and put him back to the other end of the room against the wall and struck him several blows. Then some person came to us and held me by my right arm and desired us to be quiet. Then I gave Mr Skinner atwick by his coller and he fell along the room and by his falling I recoverd my arm and struck him whither it was one blow or two after he fell I am not certain and he cried out once murder and I never struck him afterward. Mr Brock standing by said Gad he is not fit to goe against the French. Then I thought the brawl had been over but Mr Skinner seeing an oppertunity where William Rowe was standing against the table in the said room very enviously stept to him and struck up his heels. He rose and placed himself as before and Mr Brown went to him using some churlish words and struck up his heels likewise. I seeing this I thought th[ey] intended to go at it again which made me pull of my coat and wastcoat but being perswaded by Mr Brock to put them on again I did it without meddle any person. Soon after Mr Brock finding the company parting stept to the table and took up Mr Skinner stock and buckel and desired him to take it with him but he refused, and said he would sware that William Rowe and I had stollen it from him and so left it to the house.

Down Stairs

When we came down stairs I spoke to Mr Brock and William Rowe and asked them whither they would stop and drink a pint after hurry.[9] They both were willing and we seated our selves at the kitching table, Mr Brock and I at the head of the table and William Rowe on the insaid, and had apint of beer. Mr Skinner and Mr Brown finding we were designed to stay alittle longer they both came back and sote with us and drank with us for severall hours. But Mr Skinner and Mr Brown were very abusive. Mr Skinner calling and abusing of me after avery bad manner and sporting at me and saying I see Dyer hath gote ablack eye as well as my self and told me he should not mind my tissing up stairs if I had not gave him ablack eye, and charged me three time the same night for bugering of a sow. Mr Brock hearing me so often and vilely charged by him cryed out upon him, Fie on thee, Fie on thee, forbear. Robert Skinner wept bitterly. Then I presantly desired all presant to bear witness his words. Likewise Mr Brown abuseing and [call]ing of William Rowe, calling him all manner of little pityful rogues and raskels and telling him that he and his family were hundreds of pounds the worse for William Rowe and his family and threatened him to knock out his brains which very likely might have fallen upon him, for haveing avery large headed walking stick he held it up with both his hand as he stood upon the outsaid of the table and swore he would. If I had not very fortunately caught hold of the stick as the blow was falling I make no doubt but would so have happened.

NOTES

1. DRO, 1049M/Z1.
2. Particularly a churchwardens' account book, 1713–1800 (DRO, 1048A/PW 80), and rotas for holding Parish offices, 1719–1800 (DRO, 1048A/PW 82–86) on which the evidence for much of this commentary is based.
3. DRO, 1048A/PR 3, Shobrooke parish register.
4. J.A. Sharpe, *Early Modern England: A Social History, 1550–1760* (1987), 214–20; Paul Slack, *The English Poor Law, 1531–1782*, Studies in Economic and Social History (1990).
5. Some parishes held frequent vestries or appointed committees to adjudicate on applications for relief: Geoffrey W. Oxley, *Poor Relief in England and Wales 1601–1834* (Newton Abbot, 1974), 46, 47. As accounts were presented for signing at this meeting, this was more likely to be the annual vestry meeting.
6. A bunny is a lump, hump or swelling especially on the joints of animals: *A New English Dictionary*, edited by James A.H. Murray, Oxford, 1888.
7. Exact meaning uncertain.
8. 'anon power', meaning uncertain.
9. Meaning uncertain.

John Brunton

9. A Holiday in Sidmouth, June 1933

The following extracts are taken from a diary written and illustrated with photographs by a Mr P. C. Catlin while on holiday in Sidmouth in June 1933. Little is known of P. C. Catlin except that he came from Luton and spent a few summers touring the West Country. Sidmouth had developed in the nineteenth century from a small fishing village to a fashionable watering place, frequented by Royal and Distinguished visitors.[1] It was popular for its Baths but it had a natural beauty, an excellent climate and fertile soil which produced wonderful flower gardens and even the birds sang well into the winter months. In 1933 it was a holiday for the more discerning visitor who could amble through the countryside unimpeded by noisy traffic, public transport at his command, gossiping with friendly locals, and surveying the local flora and fauna the most important object of the day.[2] Evocative of another time, an almost forgotten peaceful and leisurely era between the wars.

DRO, 3621Z/Z6

Saturday, May 27th
I had to change at Seaton Junction into a local train, and again at Sidmouth Junction. The branch line down to the sea passed through very wild and pretty country, of high hills and deep gulleys overgrown with bracken and oak scrub, bluebells, pink campion, foxgloves and other delightful flowers, with occasional glimpses of the river Otter brawling over its pebbly shallows.

Sunday, May 28th.
I had some Devonshire cream with my tea today. Then it rained heavily for two hours. When it left off I took a walk up to the Roman Catholic Convent and then down to the Bickwell Valley, where the aristocracy of Sidmouth live. The gardens are gorgeous with rhododendrons, pink hawthorn and other flowering shrubs. In one garden I noticed a whole border about ten feet wide and thirty or more yards long, devoted entirely to various coloured aubretias. I also observed some fine clumps of lupins.
This road brought me down to the Royal Glen, which Queen Victoria visited as a young girl, and so on to the western end of the esplanade. I paused awhile to breathe in the sea air, and admire the towering Salcombe cliffs.

Monday, May 29th.
After tea I set off for Ladram Bay ... I found the cliff path was practically impossible, being practically on the edge, and overgrown with bushes. I therefore took a path through a wood of fir trees, which clothes the landward side of the peak, and here were some of the largest bluebells I have ever seen. The path was delightfully soft to the feet, owing to the accumulation of fallen pine needles. After the darkness of the wood, the bright blue sea, dancing in the sunlight, came as a great contrast. The path went down steeply to Ladram Bay, passing some fine hawthorn trees, loaded with masses of fragrant blossom, in the shelter of which thousands of pale primroses lifted their starry heads.

Wednesday, 31st May
I then made my way down towards the beach, but passing the 'Masons Arms' I called in for some tea. A very charming girl served me, and I commented on the lovely flowers in the room. There were seven vases on the table filled with magnificent oriental poppies, single yellow roses and other flowers. She agreed that the single yellow roses were quite a novelty, and I was going to suggest that she let me see the garden after I had had my tea; but unfortunately another customer came in.

Thursday, 1st June
This lane, leading up the side of Salcombe Hill, was gay with pink and red campion, the paler wild geranium, greater and lesser stitchwort, honeysuckle and of course ferns. Several thrushes were busy breaking the snail shells open on the stones, and they were so persistent that I was able to approach within a yard or two before they picked up the shell in their beaks and flew further on, only to repeat the performance when I again caught them up, until the shell was empty of its, to them, no doubt, succulent contents.

Friday, 9th June

At Hayes Barton a mile westward of East Budleigh was born in 1552, the famous Sir Walter Raleigh. It is now a farm, nestling in a pretty hollow of the hills, and is built in the usual Elizabethan style, E shaped, with projecting wings and pillared porch, and a thatched roof.

I went up the path between a row of espalier apple trees and a flower border, and rang the hand bell in the porch. The lady came after some delay and asked me to wait a few minutes, as 'she [I] had to see to the milk'. On her return she asked me to come in, and conducted me round the house. She was a very attractive lady ...

We then proceeded upstairs, through various bedrooms, to the one in which Sir Walter was born, as is proved by a letter written himself, which is preserved in the British Museum and of which a facsimile copy is shown to visitors at Hayes Barton ...

On returning downstairs I found it was drizzling slightly with rain, so I enquired whether they could provide me with tea. She said 'Yes, but I am going out to do some shopping', so I was about to depart, but she added, 'however, I will get you some tea before I go', and in two minutes she had the tea laid, and the teapot was only a minute later. 'There you are', she said, 'that's quick work, now I am going out, but you can help yourself, and do not hurry'. I heard her leaving some final instructions about the milk to 'Uncle' in the kitchen, and then off she went.

I proceeded to have my tea, and then 'Uncle' looked through the doorway and we soon got chatting about the farm, the weather and the crops and I found him a very entertaining talker, the weather and the crops being a congenial topic, although he spoke pure Devon and I had some difficulty in getting his meaning at times.

He was a tall broad shouldered handsome man, and when I had finished tea, shook hands with him. He showed me into the porch, where there were some newly-hatched ducklings in a basket, and he then showed me a woodpecker's nest in a hollow in a tree. This had been discovered, and the tree sawn in two sections, so by taking off the top, the nest and nestlings were exposed. The mother birds were continuing to feed them. In the corner under Sir Walter's room was a very fine Osmundi fern and on pointing this out to the farmer he said that he was in the habit of bringing home any good ferns he came across. Bidding him a very cordial goodbye I returned along the lane to East Budleigh.

The weather had cleared up, and I walked on to Otterton, where I crossed the Otter. The village is very unspoiled, and lacks the petrol pumps and advertising signs which disfigure so many villages. There are a good many thatched cottages and a little brook running down the side of the road.

The road rose up towards the cliffs encircling Ladram Bay, and hereabouts I noticed a blue iris growing wild in the hedge. After a stiff climb the road began to dip and soon I was overlooking the bay, with a pretty thatched cottage on the left, a narrow sandy gully leading to the tiny beach, one or two boats and on either side meadows of tall standing grass. I climbed down to the beach, which is very small and pebbly, and found several boys and girls disporting themselves in the water. The cliffs here are fretted into coves and huge pinnacles of rock, which have been severed from the mainland, and provide homes for the seagulls.

There is a very pleasant cliff walk to Budleigh Salterton, and above Orcombe Point there are very pretty views of the estuary. Here one faces the open sea. The afternoon was rather dull and misty, but there were occasional shafts of sunshine slanting down, and flooding the estuary with silvery light, against which the background of hills stood out sombre and imposing.

Monday June 12th

My last day. A lovely sunny morning, with snowy white clouds sailing slowly overhead, their shadows chasing each other across the hills and fields. I went to the top of Salcombe Hill, and sat down to feast my eyes on the lovely coastline, bathed in sunshine, and the houses of Sidmouth far below, surrounded by tree-clad hills. I walked a little way along a grassy path at the top, so as to look down on to Salcombe mouth and the headlands along to Beer, and then returned to the beach.

I walked down by the cliff path, returned to my lodgings, had my dinner, took a photo of Mr and Mrs Allender and Elinard (Ken is away this weekend), said goodbye to Mr Allender, and then went down for a last glimpse of the river.

NOTES

1. Vaughan Cornish, *Scenery of Sidmouth* (1940), 15.
2. Peter Orlando Hutchinson, *Sidmouth Historical Guide* (1926).

Margaret Burgess

10. One Last Chance: A Passage to New York, 1751

The following letter comes from a small collection of documents relating to the merchant Samuel Munckley which is to be found amongst the Smyth MSS held at Bristol Record Office. This particular document is one of four letters written to Munckley in Bristol by Herman Katenkamp in Exeter between 10 June and 4 December 1751. Little has at present been discovered about Katenkamp other than that he was clearly a business contact of Munckley's and involved in the Hamburg trade. The *Exeter Flying Post* tells us that he lived in Meeting-House Lane, Exeter, and that he died on Tuesday 30 September 1777 'after a lingering illness'.

Samuel Munckley was born around 1723 to a Presbyterian family in

Exeter. He first appears in Bristol's records in 1738/9, being bound apprentice to Richard Farr the Younger, merchant.[1] His father is named as Nicholas Munckley, deceased, a tucker late of the city of Exeter, and Samuel seems to have been well provided for, possibly by his half brother Sir John Duntze (who was a partner in a London bank and later a baronet), being able to command £300 bond money at the commencement of his term of apprenticeship. In 1746/7 he attained the freedom of the city by virtue of his completed apprenticeship to a burgess,[2] and began trading in a general way, not concentrating at this stage on any one particular market. It is in these early years that we find evidence of one slaving venture.[3] The lack of further evidence of this nature suggests that he was not directly involved with the trade, although he did develop a role as broker for the planters in the West Indies (who relied on the supply of slave labour), and also, as a partner in the Harford Bank between 1769 and 1774,[4] it seems likely that he may well have been banker to merchants who were involved in it.

In 1768 he became Master of the Society of Merchant Venturers, and upon leaving the bank in 1775, joined with fellow West India merchants Gibbs and Richards to form a partnership which would eventually evolve into the noted Bristol West India House of Gibbs, Bright and Co. In order to get the maximum return from the sugar which he was importing, he also at this time entered into a partnership in order to take over the Whitson Court sugar house, a noted Bristol sugar refinery with a long history.[5] Being so heavily involved in the West India trade it was natural that he should take part in the foundation of the West India Association, an exclusive society formed by like-minded merchants for the purpose of protecting their interests. In 1793, as the French Revolutionary War began, he appears to have retired from active business, although the city's accounts of town dues show Munckley and Co. continuing to trade at least to the end of the century.[6]

He maintained his Presbyterian connections, attending the chapel at Lewin's Mead which his master, Richard Farr, and many leading members of the mercantile community also attended.[7] It was in the chapel's burial ground at Brunswick Square that he was buried, 'in a vault under [the] west side of [the] Speaking House'[8] as might befit a former chapel treasurer, having died at his house in the prestigious Queen Square on a Saturday evening in July 1801, aged 77. During his working life Munckley had been known as 'the Chancellor' and was greatly respected amongst his peers for his sound judgement. It would seem unlikely that the same could be said for 'young Mr Wilcocks', the subject of this letter.

BRO, 32835 AC/MU 1(5)b

Exon 15 June 1751

I onely rec^d your fav^r of th^e 11 Inst Last wensday, but being out of Town, no answer could be given by the return, but since, I have consulte[d] with Old Mr Wilcocks concerning his sons affair & having well considere[d] every circumstance, we are come to a final resolution: that the Young Gentleman without anymore ado embark for New York, & to make him easy, all his desires to be comply'd with except his having anything out of the box which has been consignd to you & which he shall not have the use of till his arrival in America. I request therefore you will agree with the Captain for New York for his & wifes passage &c. at the most Reasonables[t] term you can, supply Young Mr W. besides with a Great Coat not exceedin[g] the Value of 1 Guinea & pay him his stipend from the day of his waiting first upon you to the day of his Embarkation, & towards any other littl[e] expences he may want his mother will furnish one Guinea, which I beg you will pay him likewise if he be really in earnest to go. His mother has likewise sent him as much Coffe & Tea by this days carrier as will almost supply a family during such a Voyage, & if after all you should find some neccessaries wanting, if of no considerable amount, please to supply the same & place it to my acc^o. for it is absolutely necessary t[hat he] should go & therefore £4 or £5 is not to be regarded, but you must be cautious, for he is not to be trusted: give him an inch he will take an Ell. As to his going to S^o Carolina, I cannot approve by reason of the length of Time, for if Hans in th^e Kelder should appear before, insuperable difficulites may then Occurr, which should by all means be avoided. Inclosed you have a L^r for Young W. & one for Mr John Rowe in Boston who has the proper orders to supply him with his Stipend in America. As New York is contiguous to Boston, I suppose Mr Rowe may have a Correspondent at New York to whome he will give proper directions, so you will be so good to con[vey] th[e] Box to Mr Rowe in such a manner as that he may have the dispos[al of] the same & accordingly you will put the key with the L^r & bill of Lading under a cover to said Mr Rowe & give the Capt. the charge of it that it may be forwarded to said Mr Rowe upon his arrival at New York by the speedyest & safest conveyance possible. I hope this will come in time to engage the passage for New York. If it should not, I know not what can be done, but if it do & the same is neglected by the Young Gent^l. he must then shift for himself. You will then stop his stipend, & I shall not give you any further trouble about him. When you shall favour me with y^r answer, be pleased to avoid making any mention about any thing paid him on acco. the mother, because the L^r will come to the Father's hands, & I shall not be able to rectifye anything as I shall be absent, intending next tuesday to set out on a long tour which I find absolutely necessary on acc^o. my health, & possibly I may have th^e pleasure ab^o. the beginning of next month to pay my personal comp^{ls} to return you my sincere thanks for the Trouble I have given you in this & to assure you how much I am

S^r Y^r most obliged h[um]le serv[ant]
Herman Katenkamp

I wrote y^o. Last munday, & confirm herwith y^r paying the £1:1 to W. upon the conditions then mentioned.

NOTES

1. BRO 04353(5), Bristol Apprentice Books.
2. BRO, 04359(10), Bristol Burgess Books.
3. David Richardson (ed.), *Bristol, Africa and the Eighteenth-Century Slave Trade to America: Volume 3, The Years of Decline, 1746–1769*, Bristol Record Society, XLII (1991), 10.
4. Charles Henry Cave, *A History of Banking in Bristol from 1750 to 1899* (Bristol, 1899), 92.
5. I.V. Hall, 'Whitson Court Sugar House, Bristol, 1665–1824', *Transactions of the Bristol and Glos. Archaeological Society*, 65 (1944), 1–97.
6. BRO, 04058(9), Bristol town duties, collectors' accounts.
7. O.M. Griffiths, 'Side Lights on the History of Presbyterian-Unitarianism from the Records of Lewin's Mead Chapel, Bristol', *Transactions of the Unitarian Historical Society*, VI no.2 (October 1936).
8. BRO, 39461/R/2(a), Lewin's Mead Chapel burial register.

Richard Burley

11. 'Remarkable Occurrences' Viewed from Exeter, 1754–1809

The following extracts are taken from the journal of Samuel Poole, an Exeter Dyer, which was deposited at the Devon Record Office in June 1994. Marked 'Remarkable Occurrences' on its cover, the volume contains notes on astronomy and a variety of references to events chiefly in and around Exeter in the latter part of the eighteenth century and the early years of the nineteenth, including unusual or extreme weather, ceremonial occasions, public hangings and the deaths of citizens, together with some rough accounts. Although erratically punctuated, the book is written in a clear and easily readable hand and offers a highly individual insight into the life of the city and one of its residents during the period in question. All spelling, punctuation and capitalization are as they appear in the original.

DRO, 5183M/Z1

1754 Oct 23d Mr Fryers Dye House was on Fire, and the water that runs t['h' inserted above]rough the island was lett run the night before, for the first time

1772 January 1st Dyed Mr George Bennets Clerk of the parishes of St Edmond 28 years and of St Mary Steps 20 years and on Jany 5th George Bennets his son was Decleared Clerk in his stead by the Revd John Stobback

1775 Tuesday Decr 12 a Dreadful fire broke out at the House of one Knight on Exbridge in this City which consumd the same with the House adjoining it was supposed near 20 persons was burnt to ashes 14 of whom arrived there the night before the house had been long a receipticle for vagrants it is supposed upwards of 30 persons was in the house when it first caught fire, supposed by melting of Brimstone to make matches

1782 July 29 Rebbecca Downing[1] was Hung & Burnt for poisining of her Master at Heavitree

18 Nov Died Lucretia the wife of John Bennets now commedian aged 34 years

1783 16th augst Lord Hood[2] came into this City

18 augst John Cunningham for the murder of John Pratt & John Grinslade for the murder of the Revd Mr Yard of Whiteway [Barton in the parish of Kingsteignton] & Rector of *Teigngraze* [Teigngrace] was Executed on *Halldown* [Haldon][3]

26 sept was Hung at *magdilen* [Magdalen] Gallows John Ashbolt & John Lee for a robbery near *Exweek* [Exwick] Bridge they where soldiers belonging to they 20 Regt of Foot

1784 8th Janry Died Mr John Rice Fuller of this City he was making merry with Lieut Colonel Simcoe[4] and some other Gentlemen at the Globe Tavern[5] he fell down & never spoke afterwards

This month January was the severest weather of Frost ['and snow' inserted below] ever remembered

1784 May 8th a fire broke out on Southernhay near the Hospital burnt several hours and consumed seven Houses[6]

1784 augst 4 Died Doctor Puddicombe of Topsham he was playing at Racketts on Southernhay and ['died' inserted above] away immediately

Septr 8 Mr Foster Builder of this City was thrown from his horse near the black boy turnpike was killed on the spot

Septr 8th Passed through this City the remains of Sir Eyre Coote[7] who died in the east Indias 16 months before was landed at Plymouth last week with his effects supposed to value 1 million sterling

1786 June 19th Mr St Croix went up in an air Balloon from the Castle Yard and floated in the air near one Hour it took its Course away to *Cadely* [Cadeleigh] where by accident it bursted and fell a distance of about 9 miles

Decr 11 Nathan Hole and his son was drowned in attempting to cross the River Exe near the lime kilns about 2 o Clock in the morning the water was very high the son was found by Danial Carter on the 18th nearly opposite where the Glasshouse formerly stood the father was washed up to the lower sluce on 26 January 1787 by the Tide

1787 Feby 26 The Westgate of this City was taken down[8]

1790 Feby 7th Died Henry Inglett Fortescue Esqr one of his Majesty Justice of the Peace for the County of Devon and Collecter of his Majestys Customs in the Port of Exon

april 11 There fell a Large Quanty of snow such as hindred the Post from traveling in all Parts of the Kingdom the snow on *Haldown* [Haldon] and neigboring field was not all gone until 22 april

1795 March 20 a Black was Hung on the new Drop for a murder he was the first that was hung at the new Goal

21 Octr 1805 admiral Lord Nelson[9] gained a compleat victory over the combined Fleets of France & Spain ['off Trafalgar' inserted above], wherein he lost his life on board the Victory his flag ship admiral Cuthbert Collingwood was second in Command took 19 & sunk one admiral Strachan took 4 about a fortnight afterward

1808 January 1st Mr Hallifax started for a Bett of one Hundred Guineas made by him and an officer of the 40th Regmt to walk 30 miles per day for 20 [unidentifiable word crossed through] Successive Days which he performed and finished on wednesday 20th Inst he came in about 3 o Clock in the afternoon to the Hotel amidst about Ten Thousand People he was made Lieutenant in the light Company of The 1st Lancanterkshire militia a short time before

1808 9 January a man, servant, to Mr Leigh near Countess Wear walk [unidentifiable word crossed through] on the road as Mr Halifax was then walking, which was on the *Topsam* [Topsham] road, from the one mile stone to the two, and Back again, he Bett one Guinea that he would walk 50 miles within 12 hours which he performed in 25 minitues less than the time given

1808 10th Febuary Died Mr John Mardon Shoe & Boot Maker of this city he died in a decline

1808 March Mr Hallifax of the 1st Lancanterkshire militia who walk 30 miles for 20 successive days on *Topsam* [Topsham] Road, started this day from the angel Inn Tiverton at half past four in the afternoon to walk 2 miles in every hour for one Hundred successive hours, which he performed on Saturday March 5th

20th Sunday Richd Porter Breaches Maker & Glover Cut his Throat in Bed with his wife was carried to hospitial on the 21 and died the 22d at 12 o Clock at night aged 44

July 12–13–& 14 was the hotest weather known in this City for 30 years particular the 14th the weather glass at 4 o Clock in the afternoon was up so high as Eighty one and a very severe storm of Thunder and Lightning on the Evening of the 14th as was ever known in this City but no damage was done

1808 Septr 9 Mrs Allen wife of the Revd R P Allen[10] who served Castle Street meeting strangeld herself with a Buckle Garter

1809 January 29 a very high wind & on monday the 30th the highest wind almost ever known it done great damage in many parts of this County particular at Cowick it blew down 101 trees on that Estate and one in the sherif ward in St Thomas the last Tree on the left hand ingoing up to the prison it was considered astonishing to blow down a tree in that place same time there was 59 Debters in that prison amongst them was 6 woman 53 men those men had 44 wives & 169 Children a scene of Distress Indeed this was a very wet and windy time for several weeks such weather at this time ['of the year' inserted below] was scarcely ever known

1809 Septr 28 This Day was celebrated the anniversary of 100 years of the Charity schools in this City, The Mayor which was Mr Gatty[11] Baker in St Sidwells & Corporations the Bishop and Clergy and many of the forty & other Gentlemen with the two hundred Charity Children met in & proceeded from the Guildhall to St Peters Church where a sermon was preachd by the Bishop Doctr Pelham[12] in support of the said Charity & a collection made at the Church Doors which amounted to [£48, '8' crossed through and replaced with '7'] £47 upwards than returnd to the Guildhall where a Dinner was provided for the Children & much to the honer of the Bishop who Presided at dinner & said Grace

25 Octr 1809 This Day his Majesty George the 3d enterd the 50th year of his Reign it was keep a Jubilee all over England Ireland & Scotland particular in this City of Exeter the Mayor & all the Corporative Bodies and the free masons of the different Lodges walk to St Peters Church where a most excellent sermon was preach'd on the occasion by the Bishop Dr Pelham from the 10 Chapter 1st Book of Samuel & 24 Verse and the people shouted & said God save the King—in the Cloth Hall Mr John Cook Sadler of this City gave a dinner to upwards of 160 poor persons of the parish of St Lawrance in the evening there was a great deal of fireworks in different Parts of the City.

NOTES

1. Rebecca Downing was a fifteen-year old girl from East Portlemouth who poisoned her master, a local man called Richard Jarvis to whom she had been apprenticed by her parish some seven years earlier, with a liquid preparation of arsenic, concealed in hot water. A vivid account of her sad story is given in a broadsheet held by the Westcountry Studies Library: WSL, 'The life, character, confession and dying behaviour of Rebecca Downing, burnt at Heavitree, July 29, 1782, for poisoning'.
2. Probably Samuel, first Viscount Hood (1724–1816), a distinguished Admiral who later entered Parliament (1784) and became a Lord of the Admiralty (1788–1793) and Governor of Greenwich (1796): *DNB*, I, 638.
3. *The Exeter Flying Post* of 29th May 1783 noted that the Reverend Yarde, who was 69 years old and had been Rector of Teigngrace for more than 36 years, had been robbed and clubbed to death on his farm the previous Saturday by a man, 'John Grenslade', who had previously been a servant of his but had been dismissed, and about whom Yarde had recently provided a detrimental character reference. In August he was tried and sentenced to death at Exeter Assizes before being hanged at Haldon.
4. Almost certainly John Graves Simcoe (1752–1806), first Governor of Upper Canada: *DNB*, I, 1202.
5. The Globe Tavern, later the Globe Hotel, stood in the Cathedral Yard facing the west front of the cathedral from the latter half of the seventeenth century until May 1942, when it was destroyed in Exeter's worst air-raid. Peter Thomas and Jacqueline Warren, *Aspects of Exeter* (Plymouth, 1980), 137.
6. *The Exeter Flying Post* of 13th May 1784 reported that: Sunday last about one in the morning, a most dreadful fire broke out at a Wheelwright's, without Southgate, adjoining Broad Southernhay Lane, which soon communicated itself ... and burnt with most amazing rapidity for some hours ...
7. Sir Eyre Coote, General (1726–1783), who died at Madras: *DNB*, I, 277.

8. This is a mystifying entry, as Hoskins states that the West Gate was, in fact, not demolished until 1819: W.G. Hoskins, *Two Thousand Years in Exeter* (Exeter, 1960), 89.
9. Horatio, Viscount Nelson (1758–1805): *DNB*, I, 934.
10. Reverend Allen was a prominent Exeter Nonconformist in the late eighteenth and early nineteenth centuries before resigning the leadership of the Castle Street Meeting in July 1819: Allan Brockett, *Nonconformity in Exeter, 1650–1875* (Manchester, 1962), 168–9.
11. Joseph Gattey, Mayor of Exeter in 1798–9 and 1808–9: Margery Rowe and J. Cochlin, *Mayors of Exeter* (Exeter, 1964), 18–19.
12. George Pelham (1766–1827), Bishop of Exeter, 1807–1820: *DNB*, I, 1022.

Brian Carpenter

12. The Glebe Terrier of Cheriton Bishop, 1680

Glebe Terriers were returns of the property of benefices, usually compiled by the incumbents in collaboration with their churchwardens and sometimes the more substantial parishioners. They were made in response to requests from diocesan bishops. Most terriers which survive in county and diocesan record collections range in date from the early seventeenth to the mid and later eighteenth century. A canon of Archbishop Parker of 1571 and another of 1603–4 required the compilation of terriers and laid down their form and content. The request for these terriers was the Anglican church's response to encroachment and threat of encroachment on church property arising out of the English Reformation.[1] The fact that dangers still existed a hundred years later is suggested by an order to ministers and churches of the Diocese of Gloucester of 1679, concerning the compilation of Glebe Terriers: it declared 'for as much as by sad experience it is found that the rights and revenues of the Reverend Clergy are diminished, invaded and much lessened by ... unjust customs and prevented composition ...'[2]

The requirements of Canon 87 of 1603–4 are wide-ranging 'All bishops within their several dioceses shall procure ... a true note and terrier of all the glebes, lands, meadows, gardens, orchards, houses, stocks, implements, tenements and portions of tithes lying out of their parishes ... to be taken by the view of honest men in every parish ... whereof the minister to be one.'[3] However, the content of terriers varies from one diocese to another and one period to another, according to the demands of specific bishops. They were usually required for an archdeacon's Visitation Court before an episcopal visitation—normally a primary visitation but sometimes also for a secondary one.

The main series of Terriers surviving for the diocese of Exeter follow this pattern. They are pre-visitation returns from the benefices of Devon and Cornwall and relate to visitations of 1601, 1613, 1679–80, 1726–27 and 1746. There are also a few for intermediate dates. They are lodged in the Record Offices of Devon and Cornwall respectively, having been deposited by the Diocesan Registrars and for Devon are indexed in the Diocesan Records catalogue Moger Supplement II, Index to Basket C, and cover approximately three hundred and seventy out of Devon's four hundred and fifty four ancient parishes. The information contained in these terriers varies and indicates what was considered important at different times. In many Exeter diocesan terriers of the early seventeenth century a primary concern was to describe parish boundaries, which suggests that even centuries after their establishment it was still necessary to re-proclaim them. By the time of the terriers compiled for Bishop Lamplough's visitation of 1680 (one of the fullest collections for the diocese of Exeter) the emphasis had shifted. There were two main preoccupations. One was to describe in detail the glebe lands; fields, meadows, orchards, gardens, their size and bounds and position in relation to other adjoining land. The second was to give a description of the parsonage house, also in considerable detail, together with its various outbuildings.

As in other Devonshire glebe terriers of this date, the information contained in that for Cheriton Bishop is restricted to descriptions of glebe lands and parsonage house, both given in some detail although not unusually so. Where it is unusual is the way it is presented. Most contemporary parsons used a broadly narrative style, with separate paragraphs for the different categories of information. Parson Rowe at Cheriton Bishop seems to have been a man who liked order and clarity and he arranged his information in neat columns with headings for the different details. In the first section he described his glebe land, with separate columns detailing plots, acreages and boundaries. In the second section he gave details of the parsonage house and associated buildings, with columns for rooms, walls and floors and wall finishes. The result is a particularly clear-cut picture of one Devon incumbant's house and land in the later seventeenth century.

The farmland of the benefice amounted to forty five and three quarter acres, all of it apparently in enclosed plots, whose size varied from twelve acres to half an acre. The larger enclosures were the 'parks' or fields which, in the context of Devon's convertible husbandry of the time, could be used for arable or stock as required. In addition, there were several small meadows for grazing and for the making of hay, and an orchard and a garden. There had obviously been some re-arrangement of the land, as four 'parks' had been created out of what had been only two fields, a garden had been made into a meadow, and a nursery had been taken out of one end of a field. This re-arrangement seems to be in line with what was happening in other Devon benefices in the later seventeenth and earlier eighteenth centuries, with change and experiment and the alteration of plots. Some rural incumbents were particularly enthusiastic about increasing the number and extent of their orchards but there was no hint of this at Cheriton Bishop. Two references in the description of its glebe mention a 'Ware pool': as no river of any size runs through the glebe this may refer to the weir of a former mill pool. The immediate area has been considerably altered by the dual carriageway of the A30 which runs to the north and by the new housing which now covers most of the glebe land. There were also references to two villages, Crockernwell and Cheriton 'town', and to the highway to Exeter.

The house described in the terrier for Cheriton Bishop was typical of the homes of many westcountry rural parsons at that time. The front part of it was a rectangular block running east and west: in it were the main living rooms—hall and parlour—situated on either side of the 'entry' or entrance passage. The hall had a small secondary room, 'the little house', opening off it, but the main domestic quarters were behind, to the south and included kitchen, 'pastry', and the larder where meat was salted. A cellar between the parlour and larder and pastry would have been a ground floor storage room, as in many Devon farmhouses. The bed chambers in the parsonage were limited to a large room over parlour and cellar and two little chambers over the entry between the hall and the parlour: the limited accommodation upstairs indicates that parson Rowe was living in a house which still had a medieval-style hall open to the roof timbers, as were a number of other westcountry incumbents in the late seventeenth century (and some even later). The Listed Building description for Cheriton Bishop parsonage, (which survives as the Old Rectory and is a II* building) describes at length the important medieval roof timbers, smoke-blackened and with trace of a louvre, which run from end to end of the front block of the house. This suggests the survival of an earlier simple priest's house which preceeded more extensive post-Reformation accommodation of which the domestic quarters were part.[4]

The parson's house was not only typical of other local parsonages; it would also have been very similar to the homes of many farmers in the South West. The only room not likely to be found in their houses was the study fitted in over the little room next to the hall. The building materials were also typical of Devon farmhouses of the period, with the lower part of the walls of stone and the upper part cob, reaching to the thatched roof. Beyond the house were outbuildings which reinforce the similarity; the large barn and the two 'shippings' or cow houses, as well as the stable for the parson's nag. The fact is that up to the late eighteenth or early nineteenth centuries the majority of westcountry parsons were parson-farmers with a strong bond of common interest linking them to their rural congregations, a bond only put at hazard by the contentious issue of tithes.

One feature of the house at Cheriton Bishop in 1680 which does stand out is the gatehouse. Many much larger and more important houses of the time were approached through gatehouses—it has been suggested that these sometimes served on 'Banqueting houses' where guests were entertained after dining.[5] How far does the gatehouse at Cheriton Bishop indicate a house (and perhaps an incumbent) of superior status? It was not unique among parsonage houses in the region: other terriers for Devon and Cornwall mention gatehouses. There is plenty of evidence for courts and enclosed yards attached to sixteenth and seventeenth century westcountry houses covering a wide social range including smaller gentry houses and farmhouses. These often included a front entrance court with high walls of stone or cob and with a strongly-defined entrance—a pillared ornamental gateway (as at Collacombe manor, Lamerton); a canopied gate (Radford farmhouse, Boyton) or a full-scale gatehouse (Trenethick Barton, Wendron). The description of Cheriton Bishop's parsonage 'gatehouse with a loft over it', with 'cob walls and the loft beamed and piggined' like the tallet over the stable, suggests a fairly modest structure, perhaps similar to one which gives access to a farmyard at Hatch, Loddiswell, which is an opening with a loft over incorporated into the farm buildings.

The parish lies to the north of the granite uplands of Dartmoor. Its name means the Churchtown of the Bishop: the bishop of Exeter held land in the parish and was patron of the church. The benefice was a Rectory, valued in the Kings Book at £22 and with a tithe rent charge, after the commutation of tithes in the nineteenth century, valued at £390; this puts it into the middling band for valuation in Devon incumbencies. The same goes for its size—4875 acres of undulating land. Richard Polwhele, writing a hundred years after the 1680 terrier gives an interesting picture of the parish:

> It consists of hills and valleys and is an inclosed parish: and every inclosure may be described as a little hill with a narrow valley at

the bottom of it. The stiff clay of the soil was in some parts full of springs which the farmers call 'goils'.[6]

The parish roads had been 'execrably bad' until recently but much improved in his time. As the Exeter–Okehampton road ran through the south part of the parish this had encouraged the establishment of a 'decent inn at Crockernwell where chaises have lately been kept as the Exeter–Okehampton stage is very long and tedious'. There were two villages in the parish, as in 1680; Crockenwell and the village 'called Cheriton town, according to the custom of the county', both 'built in the country style with mud or cob and covered with thatch'. The social structure was changing, of three former manors only one retained its seat when Polwhele was writing, but there were several estates belonging to 'yeomen or persons of a degree below gentlemen (as it would formerly have been expressed'). There were also a number of cottages scattered about the parish inhabited by husbandmen 'with the usual proportion of country tradesmen'. He described the church as 'a neat structure on an eminence, in good repair' with a hewn moorstone tower which 'if one except one or two towers in the north part of Devonshire we shall not see so good a tower in any country parish'. The parsonage house, which he also thought worthy of mention, probably had not changed much since 1680, as he described it as 'an old structure, situated on an eminence a short way from the church'. Two hundred years later than the Revd Polwhele and three centuries after the terrier, the rectory house (now the Old Rectory) of Cheriton Bishop still stands on its modest eminence and still retains the core of the house described in detail by Thomas Rowe.

The document is divided into two parts. Portions of the text which are missing are indicated by three full stops. The heading is '... true and perfect terrier of all th[e] Glebe fields, meadows, gardens and house belonging to th[e] Rectory and parsonage of Cheriton Bishop. As also how many Acres ... contain by common estimation And ... and with an account of th[e] several rooms and out houses belonging to [the] parsonage house of Cheriton Bishop aforesaid exhibited th[e] third day of September in th[e] year off Our Lord 1680'.

DRO, Exeter Diocesan Records, Cheriton Bishop glebe terrier, 1680

The first part is headed			
The names of the several parcels of land	The number of acres contained in them		How they are bounded
Item The [?]Chester parks formerly two now four fields	About nine Acres		Southward with th{e} Highway from Cheriton Bishop northward with Lungies tenement
Item The three corner park with a little Quillet against Lungies Meadow	About four Acres		Eastward with th{e} Land from Cheriton Cross tha{t} leads to {the} Town, westward with th{e} land tha{t} leads to Lungies
Item The Great Sanctuary with a little meadow at th{e} foot of it northward	About twelve Acres		Southward with th{e} Highway from Cheriton Cross tha{t} leads to Exeter, Eastward with Gorwen Tenement
Item The two middle Sanctuaries	About ten acres		Eastward with Gorwen Tenement …ward with th{e} Highway from Cheriton Cross tha{t} leads to the Town
Item The meadow called the old garden	About one Acre		North and west with the Highway from Cross tha{t} leads to th{e} Town
[Item] … meadows called the Browns parks	About three Acres		Eastward with Gorwen Tenement …ard with t{he} Highway from Cheriton Cross tha{t} leads to th{e} Town
Item The Graze park with a Nursery taken out of th{e} East end thereof	About four Acres		Eastward with Gorwen Tenement. north(ward] with two meadows called Grunden Hay
[Item] The Beafe meadow	About one Acre		Westward with th{e} Highwayt tha{t} leads … Cheriton Cross towards th{e} Town
Item One Little Meadow	About half an Acre		Northward with th{e} parish land, west… with the Highway against the Ware-pool

Item The Ware meadow with th^e Ware-pool adjoining to th^e Easter hedge thereof	About one Acre & quarter	Eastward with th^e Highway from Cher[iton] cross that leads to th^e Town, westward with Lungies Tenement
Item One Orchard	About thirty land-yards	Westward with th^e Highway tha^t [leads] th^e town from Cheriton Cross
Item One garden	About twenty land-yards	Northward and westward with …h way tha^t leads to th^e Ware-pool

The second part is headed

An Account of the Several Rooms belonging to the floors parsonage house

	Wt walls and floors	How plaisterd or d… etc.
First One large Hall on the west side of th^e Entry	Earthen floor & mud walls	with white lime
Item One room called th^e little house adjoining to th^e Hall	Earthen: stone & mud	with white lime
Item One parlour on the East side of th^e Entry	planched: partly stone, partly mud	with white lime
Item One kitchen on the south end of the house	Earthen: partly stone partly mud	with white lime so high as th^e p…ig
Item The Larder within the kitchen	Earthen: partly stone partly mud	with white lime so high as the p…ig
Item The pastry within th^e kitchen	Stone: partly stone, partly mud	with white lime
Item One cellar between th^e larder and pastry and th^e parlour	Earthen: mud	with white lime so high as th^e

Item One large Chamber over th^e parlour & cellar	—; partly mud and partly stone	with white lime
Item Two little chambers over the entry between th^e Hall and parlour	—: mud	with white lime
Item The study chamber over th^e Roome called th^e little house	—: mud	with white lime
Item The chamber over th^e larder and pastry	—: mud	with black mortar so high as …atch
Item The Stable containing three Bays of timber	earthen & stone; stone & mud	
Item The tallet over th^e stable	Beamed & piggined; mud	
Item The shipping adjoining to th^e stable pted with with wide studs of timber	Earthen: partly stone, partly mud	
Item The two chambers over th^e shiping	partly planched: mud	partly with white lime, partly with bla … ortar so high as th^e thatch
Item One gatehouse with a loft over it	beamed & piggined: mud	partly with white lime, partly wi … ck mortar so high as th^e thatch
Item The little Shippings	Earthen: mud	
Item One Large Barne	earthen & planched: stone & mud	

We believe the contents of th^e above written Terrier to be true. In witness whereof I have herein [sign] my hand th^e day and year above written

Tho: Rowe cur. *at this time* Thomas Noswouthy Thommas Tolly

NOTES

1. Richard Potts (ed.), *A Calendar of Cornish Glebe Terriers 1673–1735*, DCRS, N.S. 19 (1974). The introduction, VIII–X, includes a full discussion of the possible origins and provenance of Glebe Terriers.
2. M.G. Dickinson, *Gloucester Diocese Terriers* (Gloucester City Libraries Local History Pamphlet no.4, n.d.), quoting from Orders and Instructions to the Ministers and Churchwardens of the Diocese of Gloucester concerning the drawing up of glebe terriers, 1679.
3. Quoted in Potts, *Cornish Glebe Terriers*, ix.
4. A brief description of the house in a terrier of 1613 for Cheriton Bishop supports this suggestion.
5. For example at Lanhydrock House, Cornwall, built in the early seventeenth century.
6. Richard Polwhele, *History of Devonshire* (1793, republished Dorking 1977), II, 60–63.

Veronica Chesher

13. An Early Crew List from the Newfoundland Trade; The *Prosperous* of Appledore in 1739

This document is an early form of crew list: like the very much more numerous survivals under Victorian legislation it also was regulated by act of Parliament. It is of still greater interest in that it refers to the Newfoundland trade at the very end of an era in its development.[1]

The *Prosperous* of Appledore was a 'Fishing' ship, a vessel of between 70 and 100 tons, heavily manned in order to be self sufficient when fishing began in Newfoundland.[2] Once the mainstay of that fishery, by 1739 such craft were confined to North Devon and no longer an economic proposition. Later in that year war broke out with Spain closing the Newfoundland trade's most lucrative markets, a final blow to the 'Fishing' ships.[3] The agreement's erratic spelling and capitalization is in the handwriting of Christopher Chappell the ship's master and has been transcribed as it stands. The least recognizable words are given their modern form in a footnote: others are used in a special sense. 'Voyage' means enterprise, not a journey by sea.[4] 'Cargo' [Cargue] the goods carried by a vessel is distinguished from 'Fr[e]ight', the charge for carrying it. 'Tunnage' normally a customs duty on wine,[5] however seems to be used in a more general sense.

The agreement is made complex by the basic three cornered nature of the 'Fishing Voyage'. After an outward trip across the North Atlantic, the 'Fishing Ship' anchored in Newfoundland waters. On this occasion Placentia, until 1713 under French control, was to be used as a base.[6] Fishing, from the ship's boats and drying and salting of the catch proceeded until early autumn. The full crew were now no longer needed merely to sail the ship to those markets in the south of Europe where the dry 'stock fish' could be traded for wine and other products of the area. Surplus crew were to be left to find their own way home on a 'Sack' (provision)[7] ship, trading direct from Newfoundland to England.

Examination of the crew list shows a majority of names associated with Northam and Bideford or at least with North Devon. John Hocken or Hockin was surely a Cornishman. Robert Bartholate is the most intriguing name. Perhaps he was of Hugenot stock; some of them came to North Devon in the early years of the eighteenth century. The crew structure had the all powerful master at its apex: his mate, John Thorne, followed by a First Hand, three Second Hands and a Third Hand. There were fifteen other men on a monthly wage, and nine on a 'Standing Wages'—a fixed payment.[8] Six men do not seem to have joined the ship for either their names are deleted or they did not sign up. An addition to the contract signed away the men's shares in fish and in 'train' (fish) oil:– surely a symptom of the decline of the trade, for this feature had been for many years a notable feature of it. For those, presumably fishermen on 'Standing Wages', this presented a real hardship, especially if they had to pay their passage home. There must surely be some factor which made possible a wage of £2 for up to eight months work.

DRO, D2422 M/B1

A monthly Bill For the Ship *Prosperous* Chr. Chappell Mastr. James Chappell and Companey Sole Owners and by gods grace bound For Placentia In Newfoundland as Sune[9] as wind and weather will permit Then and at the Place Called the Cape or Else Wheare as the Master Shall Derecte to Bee Imployed In a fishing Voyage To Beegin and Leave of fishing at Such Time and Season as the sd. Master shall appoint and when The fishing Voyage Is Ended In Newfoundland sutch men as the Master Shall Directe are to Proceed with The Ship To any Market in Spaine Portugale or Ittilay and Such men as the Master Shall order home Are to Bee sent In Som Port in great Brittain where Monthly pay are to Continue untill there Arivele In Such a port as afore sd. Unless the sd. Master Shall Enter Into any other A Greement with the Marriners or any of them In Newfoundland or Else where.

Now It may Bee that the Sd. Chr. Chappell at the End of the Fishing voyage In Newfoundland afore Sd. will Bee ordered Home with Tunnage In the sd. Ship *Prosperous* or where the Cargue of fish is Discharged At amarket Engage To take a fright to a place within the Dominions of England holland France Portugall Spain or Ittilay and Eather Which home to England with Tunnage or Engageing Fright at Market are as Diricte.

And for the Monthly Pay Particularly Expressed In the Columens as Followeth ...

Mens Names	How mutch per Month	[Signature]
Chr. Chappell Mr	£3 - 10s	Chr.Chappell
Jno. Thorn Mate	£2 - 10s	Jno.Thorne
Willm.Chidley	£1 - 10s	Wm. Chidley
Willm. Allyen	£1 - 12s	William Alleyn
Richd.Briant	£1 - 10s	[mark] 2^d H[and]
Henry Paker	£2 -	[attempts to write]
Willm. Stoett	£1 - 10s	Wm. Stott
Richard Foard	£1 - 4s	Richard Ford
Willm.Marklay	£1 - 5s - 6d	[mark]
Jno.Adams	£1 - 10s	John Adams
Richard Servant	£1 - 5s	Richard Servan
Thomas Williams	£1 - 6s	Thomas Williams 2 yr [sic]
John Lowsmore	£1 - 5s	John Lousmo
Robert Bartholate	£1 - 10s	[mark] 3^d [Hand]
Jno.Yeo	£1 - 1s	[mark] [crossed through]
Willm. Barrew	£1 - 7s	[mark]
John Austin	£1. - 13s	John Austin
Peter Sainthill	£1 - 10s	Peter Sainthill
Edwd. [illegible]	£1 - 10s	[crossed through]
Nicholas Huxtable	£1 - 8s	Nicholas Huxtable 1^d H[and]
James Davies	£1 - 3s	James Davies
John Mock	£1 - 10s	John Mocke 2^d H[and]
Charles Ladman	£1 - 6s	Charles Ladman 2^d H[and]
John Hocken	£1 - 3s	John Hockin
Henry Peace	£1 - 2s	Henry Peace
Mens Names	Standing Wages	[Signature]
George Natt	£7 -	
Charles Hartnoll	£2 -	Cha.Hartnal
Willm. Power	£4 -	William Power [crossed through]
Homphry Brialey	£4 - 10s	Humphrey Brayley
John Webber	£3 - 15s	[mark]
John Joce	£4 - 15s	John Joce
John Lewes	£2 - 15s	John Lewis
John Colley	£4 -17 - 6d	John Cotkey [sic]
Thomas Charley	£3 - 2s - 6d	Thomas Charley
Thomas Night	£5 - 10s	Thomas Knight [sic]
John Sloley	£3 - 15s	
Richard Hoyle	£2 -	
John Mogford	£5 -	[mark]

Its Hereby Covenanted and Agreed By and Between the Afore Sd. Master and Marriners to Undertake by Gods Permission as Sune as the Said Master Shall Directe and weather Permit [sic] the Voyage afore Mentioned and for the wages afore Sd. Respectively Set Downe In Coluames For that Joyness where Each mans Name Is Set against his wages afore Sd. with the Munthley Pay and Standing wages For the whole voyage which Sd. Monthly pay and Standing Wages as well those that are sent home as them that geo a Broad In the Sd. Ship to Be Com due To bee paid at the Safe Delivery of the Sd. Ships Cargo of fish to Amarkit and Not Else Now Its further

[dorse. A Greed Between the Sd. Master and Marriners That whereas for times Past it has ben the Costom for Sailors to have a Shere of fish killed in Newfoundland and Traine oil when Sould that the Marriners afore Sd. are to have no Demand on Fish Trayne nor any other thing whatsoever but there monthly pay and Standing wages as afore Sd. and Pursuant to an act of Parliment wee Enter In to and Signe this as an agreement Betwene the Master and Marriners afore Sd. In Confirmation of which wee Due set our hands the Day and Date as followeth *apeldore* [Appledore] the 3d of March 1738/9. James Chappell Chr. Chappell]

NOTES

1. The most available accounts of the Newfoundland trade and Devon's involvement in it are by Dr Neville Oswald and by Dr David Starkey: Neville Oswald, 'Devon and the Cod Fishery of Newfoundland', *DAT* 115 (1983), 14–36; David J. Starkey, 'Devonians and the Newfoundland Trade', in Michael Duffy *et al.* (eds) *The New Maritime History of Devon* (London and Exeter, 1992), I, 163–71.
2. Starkey, 'Devonians', 164.
3. Starkey, 'Devonians', 167.
4. A sense still given in *Chambers Twentieth Century Dictionary, new Mid-Century Version* (Edinburgh and London, 1952).
5. Jacob, *Law Dictionary*. I am indebted to former DRO colleagues for this reference.
6. Newfoundland was ceded to Britain by the Treaty of Utrecht: J. Hampden Jackson (ed.), *A Short History of France* (Cambridge, 1959), 93.
7. Starkey, 'Devonians', 164.
8. Compare the later crew lists from 1770: Starkey, 'Devonians', 169 and references there given.
9. Some local vernacular and other spellings are not obvious: Sune = soon; Leave of = leave off; sd., Sd. (throughout) = said; Cargue = cargo; Fright = Freight; Columens, Coluames = columns; Joyness = joins; geo = go; Amarkit = a market; Shere = share; Due = do.

Michael Dickinson

14. 'Designed and executed by John Kendall AD 1818': Exeter Cathedral's New Reredos

In the history of church architecture the nineteenth century is remembered above all as the age of the Gothic Revival. Handsomely illustrated volumes published over the last thirty or forty years have documented and analysed the work of virtually every major architect active during Victoria's reign. In contrast, there have been very few studies of their predecessors, the pioneers who began the serious investigation of medieval building techniques and the evolution of architectural style. The Victorians themselves are, perhaps, partly responsible for this neglect. In their eyes the ecclesiastical architecture of the two centuries preceding their own times had no merits: it had no nobility of purpose and no understanding of the true principles of form and construction. The tendency of commentators to judge past events, tastes and opinions by their own contemporary standards is an easy trap in every age, and the viewpoint of the early ecclesiologists, fired with the enthusiasm of the newly converted, is not difficult to understand.

Interest in the Gothic style during the eighteenth century was literary rather than architectural. Ruins were Gothic: they graced the parklands of the nobility and provided the romantic setting of the horror novel. Roofless abbeys were the stuff of fashionable reading: the idea of studying their history and form was regarded as decidedly strange, and the notion of accurately copying them downright eccentric.

Only a few antiquaries and topographers really cared about recording or preserving even the ancient buildings that were still in use: indifference and neglect were far more common attitudes among the custodians of cathedrals and parish churches alike. The lack of interest was not total, however. Browne Willis' surveys of various cathedrals, published between 1727 and 1742, were followed by James Bentham's *History and Antiquities of the Conventual and Cathedral Church of Ely*, 1771, Richard Gough's *Sepulchral Monuments of Great Britain 1786–1799* and the Revd John Milner's *History and Survey of the Antiquities of Winchester* 1798–1801. The Society of Antiquaries, incorporated in 1751 and its publication *Archaeologia*, begun in 1770, did much to stimulate the exchange of ideas and information. Milner and Gough, both Fellows of the Society, encouraged the young John Carter's obvious talents as draughtsman and architect. Carter (1748–1817), son of a London marble carver, first became known through his drawings for the *Builders Magazine*, leading in 1780 to employment by the Society of Antiquaries as their draughtsman. In the same year he published the first of his influential architectural studies, *Specimens of Ancient Sculpture and Painting*, taken from buildings throughout Britain. Three major series followed, of which the surveys of cathedrals and abbeys, published by the Society of Antiquaries between 1795 and 1813 were of outstanding interest. *Some Account of the Cathedral Church of Exeter*, 1797, was the second of these surveys. Volumes on Bath, Durham, Gloucester and St Albans appeared between 1798 and

1813, but at the same time Carter, by then a highly respected FSA, was writing scathing attacks on contemporary cathedral restorations in the *Gentleman's Magazine.*

In contrast to the drastic modernizations and 'improvements' at Lichfield and Salisbury, so much criticized by John Carter, the building works at Exeter seem to have been confined almost entirely to essential repairs during the years between 1790 and 1820. The stonemason's bills seldom exceeded £100 a year and activity was centred on repairs to the West Front, renewal of windows and buttresses in the cloisters and the removal of redundant buildings in that area, new pinnacles and coping stones, refronting the Chapter House—all necessary and urgent tasks.

Why the Cathedral authorities should have decided on a new reredos as a major expense is not at all clear. The entry in the Chapter Act Book for 21 September 1811 merely stated that the altar screen was to be replaced, the cost would be defrayed from the timber fund and that the design by John Kendall would be submitted to all members of the Chapter for consideration.

Who was John Kendall? Dictionaries of architects have tentatively identified him as a pupil of James Paine, the London based designer of country houses, and have listed him as surveyor to the Dean and Chapter of Exeter, working on the Cathedral from about 1805 onwards. Examination of the Act Books and fabric accounts, however, identifies a locally grown talent, not a surveyor but a stonemason and active well before 1805. In 1765 Edward Kendall signed a lease on a workshop next to St Mary Major church.[1] The fabric accounts for 1765–1766 make it clear that he had succeeded James Meffen as the Dean and Chapter's stonemason.[2] Regular payments were made to him until, in the fabric accounts for 1792–1793, a separate entry records £3 3s paid to John Kendall. In the following two years similar small sums were paid, but in the 1795–1796 accounts the entries appear as 'executors of Edward Kendall £48 13s 4d' and 'John Kendall his bill £16 0s 0d'. Final confirmation of John Kendall's identity is given in the Act Book entry for 22 December 1796, which records that the Chapter 'approved John Kendall their Stone-mason in the room of Edward Kendall his late deceased father'.[3] In this office he continued until his own death in December 1829.

John Kendall had a natural skill at both design and practical construction. If he was a pupil of James Paine in his twenties, an exhibitor of plans at the Royal Academy prior to his employment as his father's assistant, it would explain the Chapter's confidence in his abilities. In their view he was well able to tackle both restoration and new work, without the oversight of a specially commissioned expert. Perhaps some of the clergy had seen some of Kendall's minutely observed and superbly executed pen and wash drawings of parts of the cathedral interior, done in 1805 and 1806, some of which were later to appear as illustrations in his treatise, *An Elucidation of the Principles of English Architecture, usually denominated Gothic*, published in 1818.[4] This was certainly a man with more than just a stonemason's practical skills. The book displays John Kendall's comprehensive knowledge of medieval architecture and his close interest in contemporary opinion concerning ancient buildings.

The furnishings of the choir in 1811 were much as they had been since the mid seventeenth century, apart from the addition of some comforts such as cushions and hangings. The plain back wall of the medieval altar screen, retained when the statues and central silver altarpiece were removed in the 1550's, had been painted over by William Cavell in 1638.[5] This enormous view of the triple entrances to an imaginary cathedral had as its centrepiece the figures of Moses and Aaron, supporting the tablets of the Decalogue. An engraving, made by William Cartwright in 1791, conveys some idea of the vastness of a painting, which at 34 feet wide and 20 feet high, still impressed visitors a century and a half after its completion.[6]

John Kendall had already been working on the Cathedral's west front for several years when the Chapter invited him to submit a plan and estimate for a new altar screen. Probably the idea was to commence the alterations whenever funds allowed and other urgent work had been completed: as it was, Kendall remained busy on the west front, cloisters and chapter house for another six years. Ralph Barnes, the chapter clerk, doubted whether Kendall was equal to the task of actually designing a new reredos, but his cautious letter suggests that he was not entirely in favour of any alteration to the existing cathedral interior.[7]

Senior members of the Chapter were nonetheless anxious to get the project under way. Once the estimate for the new screen had been submitted in September 1811, absent members were asked for their comments.[8] John Garnett, the Dean, who also had a living in Hampshire, wrote from Farleigh Wallop in enthusiastic approval, promising to obtain a drawing of part of the Winchester screen.[9] Hugh Percy, Exeter's youthful and ambitious Chancellor, reported from Bishopsbourne, one of the two Kentish benefices granted him by his wealthy father-in-law, the Archbishop of Canterbury. He had consulted the Archdeacon of Norfolk, John Oldershaw, who had forwarded the questions to a man 'noted for his knowledge and taste in Gothic Architecture'.[10] The response, from Thomas Kerrich, Fellow of the Society of Antiquaries and Principal Librarian of the University of Cambridge, lent weight to Kendall's proposals. Kerrich's replies to the Archdeacon's questions display a deep respect for the architecture of the past and a concern to avoid the rash destruction of anything ancient. Like his exact contemporary John Carter, whose volume on Exeter he had obviously studied, Kerrich had contributed many drawings to Richard Gough's topographical publications. After graduating in 1771 he had used his travelling scholarship to further his study of medieval architecture in France and Italy. Hundreds of his drawings were later passed to the British Museum, while many articles on Gothic buildings were published in *Archaeologia*. His comments on the proposed work at Exeter were based on extensive personal knowledge and careful observation. Many later church restorers would have done well to copy his own cautious principles.[11]

After a lapse of six years there does, in fact, seem to have been a momentary wavering in the Chapter's resolve. In August 1817 William Tucker offered to clean and varnish the existing altarpiece for one shilling per foot, telling the Precentor 'I shall consider it my duty to make as good work of the cleaning as any men in England can do'.[12] Four months later a young Totnes painter, William Brockedon, wrote in some detail to explain his plan for a new wall painting, entirely covering the seventeenth century work.[13] The proposal was courteously received but never seriously investigated.

The way was clear for John Kendall's screen to take shape. It consisted of an altarpiece filled by the tablets of the Commandments, flanked on either side by three vaulted bays. The whole screen was surmounted by an intricate and exuberant display of crocketed ogee gables, closely modelled on the early fourteenth century stonework of the adjacent sedilia.[14] The final details of the design were approved in March 1818,[15] the stonework was ready for fixing the following August and the whole structure, apart from some work on the floor, completed by the end of September 1818.[16] Blocks from the demolished medieval wall were, in the best traditions of the original builders, re-used in repairs until well into the present century. Kendall's own work lasted only long enough to appear in the earliest surviving photographs of the cathedral interior. Sir George Gilbert Scott's restoring zeal reduced it to rubble in 1874.

John Kendall continued his work on the cathedral for another ten years after the completion of the reredos. In this period he undertook the refurbishing of the chapter house to accommodate the cathedral library and restored the lady chapel to devotional use after the removal of the books. To his contemporaries, however, the reredos remained his major achievement. *Trewman's Exeter Flying-Post* death notices of 1 October 1829 contained an eloquent tribute:

> On Thursday [24 September] Mr J. Kendall statuary, aged 63, after a protracted illness, which he bore with greatest calmness and composure, leaving a wife and seven children to lament his death— To a superior genius were added the abilities of an artist: his work on the principles of English architecture and the design and execution of that splendid monument of his skill, the altar piece in the Cathedral, need only be mentioned to accompany his name with the meed of commendation due to it, and to record the loss of such a man in his native city.

D&C 7063/1 [Undated, following Chapter Meeting of 21 Sept 1811]

To the Revd the Dean & Chapter of Exeter

Sirs, I must allow the present Skreen has glaring faults and Absurdities but it has a Grandeur which the proposed alterations will not reach and probably the Voice will not be so well heard. I comply with the present proposal of taking it away on this condition only that one or more Plans or Designs shall be obtained from some skilfull Architect of allowed Taste and Judgment. Mr Kendall can execute but he is not equal to design and direct so great an alteration in so fine an ancient Building which can only be justified by the Superintendance of some approved Architect.

I am Sirs Your humble Servant, Ralph Barnes

D&C, 3577, 104 [21 Sept. 1811]

They resolved that it is highly desirable that the present Altar Screen be removed, and that a new Screen be substituted of the heighth of the Side Screens, of Stone, similar to the Internal ornamental architecture of the Church, and that the expence thereof, which has been estimated by Mr John Kendall Stonemason at £350, be defrayed out of the timber fund, and they directed that the proposed plan for this alteration be taken into consideration and that all the Members of the Chapter be consulted thereon, and they directed the Chapter Clerk to write to the absent members of the Chapter accordingly.

D&C, 7063/1

My dear Sir, Wallop Sept. 29th 1811

I was duly favor'd with your Letter of the 21st Ins^t and approve very much the proposed Improvement at the back of the Communion Table in the Cathedral at Exeter and agreeably to your suggestion have written to Winchester for a drawing of part of the stone screen there, which I hope shortly to receive & will forward to you the moment it comes to hand ... Believe me, Ever truly yours
   John Garnett

Ralph Barnes Esq

D&C, 7063/1 [To Ralph Barnes]

Bishopsbourne Decr 11th 1811

My dear Sir

...

I fear I shall not be able to send down to you the plan Kendall drew for me for a new Screen at the Altar, but as I suppose the Chapter will scarcely decide upon it at the Xmas audit, it may not be of any consequence. I have intrusted the drawing to Archdeacon Oldershaw to take the opinion of some scientific friends of his upon & at present he has not returned it. Kendalls valuation for putting up the new screen making good all the pavement tombs etc. amounted to £350, & he to have the old materials & engaging that the whole should be compleated within two months from the taking down of the present wall ...

My dear Sir, Yrs faithfully

Hugh Percy

Decr 13th I have just received the accompanying letters from Mr Oldershaw, which as they relate to the screen at the Altar I have forwarded for the Chapters inspection & the drawings shall be sent down as soon as I receive them.

Mr Kerrich is noted for his knowledge & taste in Gothic Architecture.

D&C, 7063/1

Cambridge Decr 3d 1811

Dear Sir,

If the flat wall, you mention, on which the ten Commandments are painted, be one of these abominable, blank, clumsy things, built up in later times, since all knowledge of Gothic Architecture has been lost, I should certainly say take it down; but I cannot well make out from Carter's Prints of Exeter Cathedral that it is so. If it is Gothic it should by no means be meddled with: We are, as yet too ignorant of the <u>Principles</u> of that Style of Architecture, to <u>Justify</u> our <u>destroying anything</u> that we find remaining.

But to leave this matter, as I cannot tell how the fact really is, & go to your Questions 1st To fill up the 2 fine Gothic Arches with a flat surface of wall or with anything however ornamented, I should hold to be most barbarous.

It would, according to my notion of the matter, be perfectly correct & proper to put up a Gothic Screen, which should be flat at top, & so low as not to hide the Capitals of the 3 pillars which support the 2 Arches.

The pattern of the Gothic <u>Feint Arches</u> and <u>Tracery</u> up on this Screen, might, I should think, with the greatest propriety, be copied from those of the Inclosure of the Choir on each side between the Stalls & the east end. To imitate the Stalls, or take them for a model in its decoration would surely be quite absurd. It will in some measure make part of the Inclosure, & should therefore agree rather with that, in style, than with the Stalls, Bishop's Throne, Seats, Desks, etc, which ought more properly to be considered as the Furniture of the Choir.

2d It is is settled that the Stalls are not to be imitated at all, in the decoration of this Screen; your 2d question wants no answer.

I do not quite understand, from the Drawings, where the new screen is to be placed. I hope it is not proposed to carry it back quite to the 2 Arches. I am clearly of opinion that it <u>ought to be built upon the foundation of the</u> wall, taken down, still leaving the space between it and the East end as it is: that surely should on no account be alter'd.

Such an alteration as this has lately been made in the Cathedral of Wells, & a low screen built at the East end of the Choir, which gives a view into the Lady Chapel, & Aisles, with their beautiful vaultings; and every body is charmed with the effect.

...

Dear Sir, Yours sincerely
T. Kerrich
The Revd Mr Oldershaw Harleston Norfolk

D&C, 7063/1

London 6 Poland St.
December 15th 1817

Sir,

The polite attention which I received from you, and the liberal view which you took of my communication to the Chapter, induce me to write to you with the sketch I now send, and request that you will oblige me by showing it at the audit & using the letter if it will answer any enquiries which may be made.

The sketch is on a scale of an inch to a foot with the present Altar Screen, 34 by 20, the screen is a little wider but all that is seen of it from the entrance to the Choir is 34 feet. I regret that the sketch I have now sent is not more finished, but I thought the day of audit was later, & deferred its commencement till last Tuesday, having been entirely engaged on a large picture of Christ raising the Widows Son, for the ensueing exhibition at the British Gallery. I have been employed night and day on the sketch since I heard that the audit would be on the 17th. Tho' unfinished I hope it will be perfectly understood. The colours have not been sufficiently dry to subdue & harmonise & the architecture has not been at all studied. You are aware perhaps that in a sketch, composition color & <u>chiaro scuro</u> are all that can be given, drawing character and expression, are only sought for and obtained, in the finished work. The foreground figures would be above 9 feet high, which on the scale of the picture would not appear larger than life. St Paul in the cartoon of Lystra is 10 feet high. In my former communication I offered to paint the picture for the <u>actual</u> expenses these would be principally incurred by a room materials & models (studies from the life). I have now an opportunity of engaging a very large room at such a rent, that I will insure the whole of the expenses <u>not to exceed £500</u> perhaps it would be considerably less it would employ me about 2 years.

As the picture from its size would cover the screen entirely, no contingent expenses would be incurred, as a frame would not be necessary. The incidents, characters & costume of the subject I have chosen (of a date long anterior to the Cathedral) would all accord with the grandeur of the situation of the subject. <u>St Peter's Repentance</u> is not only firmly adapted for a Christian Church but the principal incident in the life of the patron saint of the Cathedral.

I am eager in pursuit of professional reputation, with any other motive except my feelings as a Devonian, I should neither have made the offer to the Chapter or troubled you with this letter. I hope the Bishop will be at the audit as his Lordship entered into my proposal in a way most flattering to me.

I am ashamed of having taken up so much of your valuable time by this long letter but it will render unnecessary my writing directly to the Chapter as my former letter may be referred to. I regret that I am not rich enough to make an immediate offer of it to the Cathedral, but I shall be proud to date the professional rank to which I aspire from the encouragement of my native county.

I remain Sir, Your obliged obed' Sevt,
Wm Brockedon

I shall direct Mr Taylor the carver and gilder to call at your house for the sketch when the chapter has decided he will return it to me early enough to exhibit with my large picture.

To Ralph Barnes Esq

D&C, 3578 61 [Chapter Act Book 11 & 12 March 1818]

They resolved to accept the tender now made by Mr Kendall to execute and compleat the new Altar Screen agreeable to the directions at the last Audit and to the design and the execution of one compartment of the Screen now produced and inspected by the Chapter for the Sum of Five hundred Pounds. Mr Kendall taking to his own use the materials of the present Screen the same to be compleatly erected and finished by the twenty fifth day of October next.

And it was agreed that the work should be deposited in some convenient part of the Fabrick from time to time as the same be executed and that Mr Kendall should be paid by the following Installments—vizt Fifty Pounds has been already paid—Sixty Pounds shall be now paid on signing the Contract and Twenty Pounds shall be paid on the last day of every Month including the present Month of March and the last payment to be on the said twenty fifth day of October making together £270 and the remainder to be paid when the work is compleatly erected and finished to the full approbation of the Chapter and their Surveyor.

D&C, 3578, 83 [Chapter Act Book 25 April 1818]

Mr Kendall having reported that the New Altar Screen would be ready to be fixed by the third of August and that it should be compleated by the twenty ninth of September. They ordered that he should begin to take down the present screen and erect a new one on the third of August and that from that day the Choir shall be shut up and the Service discontinued except on Sundays for so long only as shall be absolutely necessary and thought most conducive to the speedy completion of the work, and Mr Kendall now engaged to use his utmost endeavour that the Service shall not be impeded for more than one month and during the time of the work they ordered a Screen of Framework and Green Baize to be erected so that the Baize might be removed on Workdays and put on clean on Sundays, to separate the work from the Choir.

D&C, 3578, 155 [Chapter Act Book 22, 23 December 1818]

They examined the Account delivered by Mr Kendall of the expence of the New Altar Screen with additional work as follows

	£ s d
The New Altar Screen as pr contract allowing £50 for the old materials	500
Taking down Back Wall & Monuments facing with Stone Ashler the Back of the Altar Screen and re-erecting the Monuments as by Estimate	181 0
Additional work in ornaments to the parapet on the East window	17 18 4
Taking up & relaying at 4 inches lower surface the Marble floor 426 feet at 6d & 20 New Marble Squares at 8/6 as by Estimate	19 3 0
Eight other New Squares and additional work at Base of Stalls & Tomb	6 5 11
[total]	561 8 3

Paid at several times by order to this day an account of the £500 Contract £425

They ordered Thirty pounds more to be paid on account of that Contract and Fifty pounds on account of the additional work—and the finishing of the work to be examined the whole being now completed except a little work at the end and replacing the Monuments at the Back

D&C, 3578, 186, 188 [Chapter Act Book, 20 March 1819]

They ordered Mr Kendalls Bill of Six pounds seven shillings for sundries at the Altar Screen to be paid—which together with the sum of Five hundred and sixty one pounds eight shillings and three pence audited and allowed at the last audit makes the total of Mr Kendalls work for the Screen and they ordered the balance of that account to be paid to him—there remaining only some work which he will finish this week at the side stalls.

They ordered that Mr Kendall be permitted to engrave on the stone at the end of the Altar Screen 'Designed and executed by John Kendall AD 1818'.

NOTES

1. D&C 3570, 184.
2. D&C 2776/3.
3. D&C 3580, 203.
4. The original drawings are mounted in a large folio, presented to the Dean by John Kendall's great grandson in 1935.
5. D&C 3557, 112.
6. Coloured engraving in Dean & Chapter Archives.
7. D&C 7063/1, Ralph Barnes to Dean.
8. D&C 3577, 104 Chapter Act Book.

9. D&C 7063/1, John Garnett to Ralph Barnes.
10. D&C 7063/1, Hugh Percy to Ralph Barnes.
11. D&C 7063/1, Thomas Kerrich to John Oldershaw.
12. D&C 4711/18, William Tucker to Dean.
13. D&C 7063/1, William Brockedon to Ralph Barnes.
14. D&C P2/3plan & elevation.
15. D&C 3578, 61.
16. D&C 3578, 83, 126, 155, 186, 188.

Angela Doughty

15. Discordant Notes or A Broken Consort; Exeter's Waits in 1631

A series of entries in the Exeter City Sessions book under the year 1631[1] sheds an unusual light on the activities of the city waits in the early 17th century. The waits already had a long history in Exeter. One is recorded as early as 1362–3;[2] there were two by 1395–6;[3] and in 1405–6 robes were provided for three.[4] In 1527–8 autumn liveries were provided for four waits,[5] and in 1602 two 'boys trained in music' were to be kept to join in with them.[6] How many waits were involved in the 1631 incident is not clear, though three are mentioned by name: Henrie Geale, John Bicklie the elder, and John Bicklie the younger.

Hoker[7] lists the instruments bought 'at the cities charges' as 'a doble curtall' (a kind of bassoon), 'a lyserden' (apparently a lizardine, a kind of serpent), 'too tenor hoyboyes' (a large oboe), 'a treble hoboyes', 'a cornet' (a wooden instrument blown like a trumpet), and 'a sett or case of fower recorders bought by Mr Nicholas Martyn'. There is mention also in 1602 of a set of 'vyalls' and other instruments.[8] Clearly the waits were versatile players, as was usual at the period. It is hard to tell whether their number were ever augmented; instrumental music in more than four parts would perhaps have been unusual, though the City of London had six waits at this time.

The 1631 depositions tell us incidentally what instruments the three waits were playing: a 'cornute', a 'tener hoboye', and the 'baze tenor'. The first two of these are easily identifiable from Hoker's list, but the third is more of a mystery. It may be that the two tenor hautboys were in fact of different sizes, one sounding lower than the other, or merely that one took the tenor part and the other the bass. Why the cornet was used instead of the treble hautboy is not obvious, though it is not impossible that Henrie Geale carried more than one instrument. In any case, the waits were clearly equipped with their outdoor instruments, rather than the quieter recorders or viols, which would have been played indoors.

In order to understand what the waits were doing playing their instruments around the city at two o'clock in the morning, we must turn back to Hoker,[9] who gives a list of their duties. They were to go before the watches and play on the eves of St John and St Peter; to play at the election of the new mayor; to play every morning from three o'clock onwards through the whole city between All Saints and Candlemas, on every day except Sundays, holy days, and Fridays; to play through the city in the morning on Christmas Day and Easter Day; to go at Christmas to the houses of the twenty-four and the stewards and officers to play; to attend on the mayor; and to attend the mayor to St Peter's Church on principal days.

The incident recorded took place on (Tuesday) 29 November 1631, during the period between All Saints and Candlemas, when the waits were to play throughout the city in the early morning (though they seem to have been a little ahead of the appointed time). This practice, and the reference to their going before the watches on the eves of St John and St Peter, reminds us of the origin of the waits as night watchmen who carried a horn to sound the alarm. The need for a watch during the long winter nights is attested by the number of other people who seem to have been about at the same time.

We know a little about the three waits mentioned in the sessions book. John Bickley (it is not clear which one) was elected a wait on 5 June 1623 in the place of Alexander Fortescue;[10] Henry Geale was admitted on 21 January 1630;[11] and on 19 April 1638 Gilbert Tothill was paid 12s 6d at the mayor's order 'towards the burying of the old Bicklye one of the waites.'[12] The other men mentioned are Thomas Mills and Edward Wood, both vintners; John Blackmore, an innkeeper; Mr Gowlding, Mr Bartlett, and Kellie, who are only mentioned as the owners of houses; Thomas Coles; and John Hayne, fuller. The diary, or more accurately household account book, of a John Hayne, beginning in 1631, survives in the Devon Record Office[13] and records payments to the waits in the early 1630s, but it does not mention this episode, and the two men may be unrelated.

The Sessions Book does not give much idea who started the trouble on 29 November, and, given the amount of alcohol consumed, it is likely that no one could remember. However, the Chamber Act Book for the period records that on 11 September 1634 John Bickley, one of the waits, was dismissed (this was presumably the younger John

Bickley, since the elder was described as a wait at his death) in consequence of 'divers complayntes ... att sundrie tymes' made against him, and that Gilbert Till was appointed in his place,[14] which suggests that the musicians may not have been faultless.

DRO, ECA Book 63, ff.50v–52r

Before Nicholas Martyn, esq., Mayor, Thomas Flaye, Ignatius Jurdain, & John Acland, esqs, 29th day of November 1631

Henrie Geale one of the waights of this Cittie informeth that this morninge he goeinge wth his consorts in their usuall course wth their musicke about the Cittie about Two of the clocke they mett wth one Thomas Mills A vintner & John Hayne fuller in Southgate streete neare Mr Gowldinges house, the said Mills & Hayne leadinge one another, And the said Mills came to John Bicklie thelder one of their Companie desiringe him to goe wth him the said Mills to drinke a cupp of wine unto whome the said Bicklie answeared he could not goe wth him for divers reasons but the said Mills his importunitie was such that he tooke the said Bicklie by the arme and leadd him awaye wth him to his house yet this informant and the rest of their Companie went on in their course a litle farther soe farr as Mr Bartletts house, but wantinge the said John Bicklie who carried the baze Tenor of their consortshipp they could not goe on in orderlie maner and thereuppon they went to the said Milles his house to call or seeke out the said Bicklie where they found him and the said Hayne: And the said Mills desired this informant and thother of his Companie to come into his house alsoe, and the said Mills called for wyne for them, and after a litle time spent wth their musicke this informant and his Companie were desirous to departe the house, but the said Mills went and made fast the dore and kept them in, & made them playe againe unto him and would by noe meanes suffer them to be gone And yet a litle afterwardes the said Hayne & Mills beganne to quarrell and fall out wth this informant and his Companye and the said Hayne tooke this informantes instrument (being a Cornute) and brake it and then the said Milles [blank space] a quarrell betweene them came and stroke this informant wth his fiste (askinge whie this informant did offer to strike the said Hayne, whereas this informant nor any other did ever offer any violence to him or intermedle wth him and yet the said Hayne did ['again' crossed through] most dangerouslie strike him againe wth a Tynin quart pott on the head that this informant did thinke he had broken the skull of his head

John Bicklie the younger another of the said waights seinge the said Henrie Geale to be thus abused by the said Milles and Hayne spoke unto them and demaunded of them what they meant then the said Hayne tooke upp a Tynyn quart pott and strocke the said Geale therewth Twice on the head soe that he was astonied and knewe not where he was as this informant conceived and then the said Milles tooke this informantes instrument beinge a tener hoboye and stroake him on the ground and brake the said instrument alsoe and wth a little peece that was lefte in his hand stroke this informant on his head and afterwardes havinge a naked knife in his hand did offer to thrust it into this informantes bodie but that he prevented it by strikinge it out of his hand, ['the' crossed through]

The said John Bicklie th'elder doth likewise informe that he and his Companie mett wth the said Milles and Hayne neere M[r] Gouldings dore in Southgate streete about 2 of the clocke in the morninge and that the said Milles inforced this informant to goe wth him to his house where this informantes Companie cominge to him he said Milles would not suffer them to departe the house againe but after some time spent there the said John Hayne tooke upp a ioyned stoole in his hand & offered to strike downe this informant wth it, And this informant further sayeth that he thinketh that the said Hayne had killed him if he had not prevented & avoided the said stroke of the said stoole

The said Mills beinge examined confesseth he was yesterday night about Eight of the clocke att the house of John Blackmore Inkeeper wth one Thomas Coles and did there Drinke a iugg of beare & from thence they went over to Edward Woods house A vintner and there mett wth John Hayne Fuller where they dranke beere againe all Three togeather, & paid monie for the same And this Examinate and the said Hayne continued there drinkinge Two or Three howers And as to the severall abuses offered by this Examinate unto the waights in his owne house he sayeth that the waights offered wronge unto the said Hayne, And thereuppon he this Examinate would have putt them foorth of his dores, but they would not begon, And as for any other offence he denyeth that he did any unto any of them

The said John Hayne beinge alsoe examined sayeth that the last night about Eighte of the clocke he was att Edward Woods house w[th]out Southgate and there stayed Two or Three howers and from thence he went to Kellies house and there the waights Did beate him, & pulled a handfull of his beard from his face, but would make no other answeare to the severall things laid to his charge

The Said Thomas Coles beinge examined confesseth he was wth the said Mills att John Blackmores house & there dranke beere togeather, and after was with the said Mills att Edward Woods house and there dranke beere & wine alsoe togeather, And that he this examinate did pay iid for beere att the said Edward Woods house

The said Edward Woode beinge alsoe examined confesseth that the said Thomas Mills Thomas Coles & John Hayne were att his house the last night & dranke some beere there but howe longe the said Mills & Hayne staied there this examinate knoweth not, but sayeth that he left them in his house when he went to Bedd

NOTES

1. DRO, ECA Book 63, ff 50v–52r, transcribed here by kind permission of Exeter City Council. I should like to thank my colleague Susan Laithwaite for drawing my attention to this.
2. H. Lloyd Parry, *The History of the Exeter Guildhall and the Life Within* (Exeter, 1936), 18.
3. Parry, *Exeter Guildhall*, 18.
4. Parry, *Exeter Guildhall*, 18.
5. Parry, *Exeter Guildhall*, 158.
6. Parry, *Exeter Guildhall*, 159.

7. W. J. Harte, J.W. Schopp, and H. Tapley-Soper (eds), *The Description of the Citie of Exeter by John Vowell alias Hoker*, DCRS, (1919), 946.
8. H. Lloyd Parry, *Exeter Guildhall*, 159.
9. *Ut supra*, 945–6.
10. J. M. Wasson (ed.), *Records of Early English Drama: Devon* (Toronto, 1986), 191, citing ECA Chamber Act Book 7.
11. Wasson, *Records*, 195.
12. Wasson, *Records*, 203, citing ECA Receiver's Accounts.
13. DRO, Z19/36/14.
14. Wasson, *Records*, 198, citing ECA Chamber Act Book 8.

John Draisey

16. The Channel Fleet in Torbay in 1800

Britain was kept safe from invasion during the wars against Napoleon by the blockade of the main French naval base at Brest by the Channel Fleet. At times of maximum danger a close blockade was mounted, the basis of which was to keep the Fleet off Ushant, as close in to Brest as possible and for as long as possible, in order to be able to intercept all movements into and out of that port. If severe weather forced the Fleet to seek shelter it took refuge in Torbay, the closest large British protected anchorage (Plymouth breakwater was only begun in 1812).[1] When the gales abated the Fleet left as fast as it could to resume station before the French could take advantage of its absence to leave port, but, while in Torbay, opportunity was taken to replenish the Fleet's water, victuals and stores to enable it to both to remain on station for as long as necessary and also to have sufficient supplies to pursue any escaping French squadron around the world (which meant storing with 3–5 months' supplies). In these circumstances the Fleet's arrival in Torbay was something like a pit stop in a modern grand prix motor race, with a frantic scramble to resupply before the weather changed and it was off again. To the perils of the elements in such a rush, were added the temptations offered by the local community—the Fleet in Torbay constituted the largest concentration of population and hence the biggest potential market in Devon, and efforts were made to sell or barter commodities of all sorts to its seamen. Such efforts particularly focussed on the watering depot at Brixham to which the ships sent their boats to refill with fresh water, and the Commander in Chief, Earl St Vincent, was continually complaining of the resulting 'scenes of drunkeness, obscenity, blasphemy, and consequent casualties (by the men fighting with each other and falling over precipices, which, to the disgrace of His Majesty's Navy, obtained heretofore, in watering the Fleet at Brixham ...'.[2] He sought to protect his crews by sending a marine guard in rotation from his ships, by instructing his officers to remain with their boats crews, and by orders such as the following. It was however a constant battle, slowly won, to try to restore discipline to a Channel Fleet still suffering the effect of the naval mutinies of 1797, and if bad weather prevented the marines from the duty guardship reaching Brixham in time, chaos quickly resulted![3] The order displays the meticulous attention to detail that made St Vincent the most efficient Admiral of his day, and shows a concern for the lives of his men and of the need for his officers to be responsible for their welfare that belies his reputation as a tough martinet. That a copy of this order to a Fleet in which Nelson did not serve should survive in the Nelson Papers indicates the degree of respect Britain's most famous sailor had for the Admiral who had fairly launched him in 1796–98 to the pinnacle of his career.

BL, Add Mss 34,940, fos174–5
Royal George off Ushant, 31 August 1800
Regulations respecting Boats to be observed by the Channel fleet, or any Detachment thereof, while in Torbay, and under the command of Admiral the Earl St Vincent.

In order to prevent as much as possible, the unfortunate accidents that too often happen, by Boats carrying an improper proportion of Sail, of which there is a very recent, and fatal instance in a cutter belonging to the Edgar, it is my direction, that no six oared cutter, Pinnace, Yawl or Jolly Boat, be allowed to have more than one sail in her (which ought to be placed far aft, or nearly a Midships) or an eight, ten, or twelve oared cutter more than a Fore sail and mizzen, and the respective Captains are desired to give positive orders to their officers, to be very careful, and prudent, in carrying sail in the Launches, which, for dispatch, may be permitted to have all their sails.—And as the very dreadful casualties have occured at Brixham, by part of drunken Boats crews falling over the Rocks, some breaking their Limbs, and others losing their Lives, it becomes my Duty, to enjoin, in the strongest manner, the Captains and Officers in the fleet, to give those poor unthinking Fellows as little opportunity as possible of committing irregularities by never sending a Boat on shore unnecessarily; and it is my positive direction, that no Boats remain on shore after sunset, unless the public service absolutely requires it, nor are they to be suffered at any time, to wait for Officers, on leave, servants at market etc., but a time must be fixed for them coming off, to which it is expected they will be very punctual, and meet the boat on her landing whose time for waiting on shore, on such occasions must be limited to a quarter of an hour, at the expiration of which time, the Petty Officer, sent in the Boat, is strictly required to put-off even if not one of the Officers he is sent for should be come down.

The necessity of this Regulation, will, on a moment's reflection, be obvious to every Officer, as he must be well aware, of the distresses occasioned by Boats Crews, wandering about the Beach, and the temptations that are constantly thrown in their way to sell their Clothes, for inflammatory Spirits, very frequently causing desertion, which, probably, never would have entered their imagination, had they not been idly, and improperly left on shore.

[signed] St Vincent.

To The respective Captains and Commanders.

NOTES

1. See M. Duffy, 'Devon and the Naval Strategy of the French Wars, 1689–1815', in M. Duffy *et al.*, eds, *The New Maritime History of Devon* (1992) I, 182–91.
2. BL, Add Mss 31,172, f.110v, St Vincent to Secretary of the Admiralty, 28 September 1800.
3. BL, Add Mss 31,172, f.108, 25 September 1800.

Michael Duffy

17. 'having altogeather forgotten his handwrytinge'; Two Early-Seventeenth-Century Letters and Clatworthy

The two letters from Hugh Clotworthy in Antrim to his brother Simon Clotworthy of Clatworthy in the parish of South Molton illustrate the remarkable resilience needed to survive as historical documents and also offer a vignette of life in Ireland and Devon in the early seventeenth century. The letters are from the Tremayne collection deposited at the Cornwall Record Office. The Tremayne family home in Cornwall was at Heligan in the parish of St Ewe, a place now more widely known for its 'Lost Gardens'.

Having taken two or three months to travel from Ireland to Devon the letters then had to rely on their survival for the rest of the journey to the twentieth century on a number of marriages and various moves from Clatworthy to Sydenham in Marystow, another Tremayne family home, to the attics of Heligan and eventually to Truro.

Here is not the place to go into the details of family descent of the Tremaynes; suffice it to say that it is a remarkable but often little noticed fact of archives, particularly local ones, that survival is almost exclusively dependent on a 'good' marriage. Having survived the journey the letters may be used to look back at the everyday life in Ireland and Devon.

In many ways letters are the most difficult of documents to index and it is perhaps for this reason that they are so often found in many record offices' lists as humble 'correspondence'. The following two letters offer a range of subjects from 'Antrim, life in' to 'whoredom, opinion of'. In between one may find 'affairs, marital', 'debts', 'forgery', 'falconry see also tiercel, mews', 'sea, passage, Ireland to Barnstaple, vagaries of', 'personalities', 'handwriting', 'relatives, opinions'. In fact we have in two letters the wide expanses of economic, family, military, social and transport history.

The letters have been transcribed but have not suffered the present fashion for 'modernisation' lest we altogether forget that having survived their journey they need to be read now as they were on the day they were first received.

CRO, T/(2) 231/2

To his most worthy Brother Symon Clotworthy Esq att his house att *Clot-Worthy* neere Southmolton In Devon there

Hugh Clotworthy to his brother

Deare Brother

I wraute unto you about 3 monthes sence by Robert Evans & as I heere hee hath had a very Cross passadge so as I thinke this letter will not be longe behinde him if this bearer Sr Hugh Pollards man have a speedy passadge In my letter by Robert Evans I wroute you howe combersome a gest you sent me his vises beinge so many that neyther then nor nowe am I able to relate.

Sence my beinge free from him, god hathe laide on other judgement uppon me by a most wicked villan that I thought had ben my kinsman, but am nowe perswaded otherwise. hee brought this letter inclosed as from my cosen Bartholomewe Clotworthy which I think is Counterfeited for I never heard of any childe that his breatheren had; If hee be his brothers sone, hee digenerates from our kindred; for I have not knowne any of our race so wicked as to defiell the house wherein he lyved with whoardome this villany being discovered to fre my house from such wickedness; I tourned him and his whoare out of my house who not beinge ashamed of his wickedness nowe lyvieth with the whoare wandringe from Ale house to Ale house; In a most beastly manner The whoare is Mollands wief and in the opinion of weoman shee is with childe if it be so I am sure it is none of Mollandes; The poore man Molland hath even broken his hart with greef. I comfort him so well as I can for in my opinion hee is an honest man;' this knave & whoare have disconted me; I trusted the knave upon my Cosen Clotworthies letter with many thinges and sence his departure I have founde him to have been most dishonest unto me though I am confident his service was worth him with me 20[li] yerly That I did for him uppon upon my Cosen Clothworthies letter if yt weare his letter as I truly think yt is not havinge altogether forgotten his hande wrytinge

Nowe deer Brother If hee were sent me by my Cosen Clotworthie & that I intertayned him as I have wrytten for his sacke I shall thancke my cosen Clotworthie if hee reiecte for my sake for doupteles hee is of a most basse and wicked disposition otherwise hee would neaver have so abused me that used him so well. I would have had them boycarted for their wickedness had yt ben so greate a blemishe to my name The knave and whoare as I heere qare gone for England I praye let them finde the favour they diserve from me att yor hands and so from all my freindes and I desire you in poore Mollandes name to be carefull that this damnable whoare possesses noe parte of Mollands goods; If it were possible for me to wayte the particulars of this knave and whorse basse wickedness they would be most lothsome to all people that have any feelings of god.

My good brother I have not seene my Cosen Thomas sence my last letter to you hee beinge inioyned to live with S[r] Arthur Bassetts Company in Conogh att least 140 tie miles from me so as his expence wilbe the greater wherefore I praye you in his behalf let me tast of your blessinge some lines for I assure you his carriadge and conversation is every waye licke a gent my Intertainment from the kinge is much lesned though I have a pattent for yt under the broadseale duringe my lief I purpose eare longe to be a peticioner to his Matie to have my pattent restored, for I knowe yt was the kinges meaninge yt should stand in force when hee gave yt me If the Kinge come for Skotlands as yt ys heere reported hee will this yeare godwillinge I willbe their to see what friendes I can finde. Besides the losse of this intertainment I have a greate Charge of Childeren 4 Boyes and 3 daughters the eldest not able to put on his clothes. These things considered I intreate you thinke on my Cosen Thomas for my abillety is not to doe as I have done. S[r] Hugh Pollards man toulde me yt [you] resolved to see thee partes this somer good Br [...] hold your resolution for I desire nothing moore I have as in my last letter I wraute you a Tossell of a goshaucke for you in the mewe I hartely wishe you have him for beinge an ydle falkener I feare what will become of him and howe to send him you I knowe not. I will expect directions from you to howe I shall delyver the haucke I have nothinge ells to wryte you only my self and wief remember our intriest and unfainded love to you or deere sister & all yours prayenge to god for all your happinesse in this world. And that in the world to come wee maye bee partakers of his glorious kingdome

your ever lovinge brother to dispose of, Hugh Clotworthy

My love to all my friendes I praye remember

CRO, T(2) 231/3

Worthy Brother

Your letter dated the last of June I reseaved by Mr Lygon the 12th of August

First touchinge the Rugges their are none made neare me by 120 tie miles; whence sence you wraute unto me I have had Callowes two severall times; But none so good as I would send you. Not-withstandinge If Mr Lygon had had shipinge for *Barnestaple* I would have sent you the best I had for the present but be you assured that I will send your Calowes the best I can get by the first convenience with some Aquavita which I must gett from *Waterfurd* for Carrickfergus yeldes none good

Molland had sent you a letter of Attorney by Mr Lygon I have not heard a longe time of Mollands wief nor that knave John Clotworthy. I am perswaded they are to geather and that shee wilbe home shortly for before this time shee hath emptied her gouge

Nowe for your Haucke Mr Lygon had seene her in the mewe she hath a feather or two to cast and as I am advised by my Cosen Winch that if shee should be carried sodenly; she will take hurt. In all mens opynioin shee is a faire haucke for my owne parte I have noe Judgement in her; But by the first Shipinge that come for *Barnestaple* I will send her you; and I thinke by Robert Evans; Mr Lygon was very much desirous to have carryed your haucke; but as I have wrytten I was advised to the Contrary; As for Smaldon I heard of some leande partes of his in Englande; which caused me to quite him; as lso on Barnard Lu[x]on that was my servant; I am hartely glad to heere of my Sisters recovery of her helth, which I hartely praye god to contynewe unto her; As for our Brother Lewes I have not herd of him, neyther doe I desire to see him, unles I might reape moore comfort by him; so in this kingdom hee is a most noted Cokoll as I lately wraute you by Barnard Lopton that servid my lo: Chichester, who I thincke hath not thryved by his service as hee might have done if hee had ben provident; I heere hee hath some things in England that hee purposith to sell; I could wishe that my Brother Lupton would stopp yt if that be in his power; for otherwise I feare hee wilbe chargeable to him hereafter.

In my lettre by Barnard Lupton I wraute you conserninge our Brother Lewes, And I shouldbe glad hee would take the course as in my lettre I have advised;

My Cosen Thomas was lately with me 3 or 4 dayes and is retorrned to Sr Arthur Bassetts company into Conogh; I could wishe you would alott him his [?]proportion, If you prupose he shall staye in this Countrey; for the deereness of land increasith dayly. I praye thinke of him for hee deserves to be thought of; So myself and wief remember our unfayned best wyshes to you our deere sister & all yours; prayeng god to blesse you with all hapines in this world, and that in the world to come wee maye be partakers of his kingdome; I most humbly take leave restinge

Antrim 13 of August Yor lovinge brother to dispose of Hugh Clotworthy

1617

the lo: Ridgewaie hath ben longe in my dept hee owes mee 3 or 4 hundred pounds; which hee hath promised to paye me att alhalentid next if hee breake with me; as I thincke hee will, I purpose to see you before Christmas;

Colin Edwards

18. The Closing and Reopening of a Chapter, 1646 and 1660

The passage from the act book of the meetings of the Dean and Chapter of Exeter records the official business of the chapter transacted at its regular meeting of 6 June 1646, the last minutes to be recorded before a complete lack of entries during the Interregnum. They are followed without even the break of a page by the minutes of the chapter's first meeting after the Restoration, held on 31 August 1660.

By 1646, Royalist resistance in the Civil War in the West had failed, and Exeter, in any case largely Parliamentarian at heart, was besieged and forced by Col. Fairfax and his troops to surrender on 13 April.[1] The Royalist cathedral chapter, which had managed to maintain some semblance of normal activity up to this time (although some of its members had already removed themselves from the city) was increasingly under pressure. At the end of May the confrontation came: though duly and properly summoned on a matter of urgent necessity to a meeting in the chapter house on 6 June, Dr Robert Hall, acting president of chapter in the absence of Dean William Peterson, found the chapter house already occupied by a session of the Parliamentary Committee for Exeter and Devon, so he moved the chapter meeting across the Close to a chamber in the residence of Dr Laurence Burnell, the Chancellor of the cathedral. Here an entirely validly constituted chapter (though being only three chapter members in number) met the demands of the Parliamentary Committee for the surrender of the documents of title and financial administrative records with a dignified refusal on the grounds of their illegality and also on the members' inability to go against their oaths to the harm of their successors. They proceeded in a normal manner to two pieces of routine business and closed with their usual formula for the continuity of their meetings until the following Michaelmas. There is no acknowledgement in the record of any official dissolution of the chapter; with no break, the next entry, dated 31 August 1660, only three months after the restoration of King Charles II, records that the old Dean, William Peterson, and the same Robert Hall, the Treasurer, in the due presence of a notary public, met to make a chapter whose first business was the admission with all due form and to give order for the installation into the prebendal dignity of Archdeacon of Barnstaple of James Smith, clerk. So the chapter of Exeter had never yet ceased to exist: a chapter had closed for some years, then reopened with the same Dean and Treasurer in office.

In spite of the refusal of the chapter to hand over its records, its estates and property were of course sequestered, though not until the next year. A sweeping act for the abolishing of deans and chapters, canons prebends and other offices belonging to any cathedral or collegiate church was passed in April 1649, and all their lands property and possessions of whatever kind were vested in named Parliamentary Trustees, just as Trustees for the lands of former bishops and archbishops had already been appointed in 1646.[2] Large consignments of archives were therefore transferred to these trustees, presenting an equally large problem in their handling and administration. A 'Regester' had been appointed in 1646 to keep the records in order—it was even suggested that he should catalogue them—and when the loads of records from cathedral chapters were added to those from dioceses, Guerney House in London was fitted up as an office and registry. But any firm control applied to the arrangements and the access by unauthorized searchers was soon lost, so much was mislaid or stolen; and by 1654, when the records were moved from Guerney House to the Excise Office in Broad Street in London, chaos reigned among the documents, tossed about and trodden underfoot as many of them were. When in November 1660 all sales of church lands during 'the late troubles' were made void, horrendous problems were encountered in sorting the documents and returning them to their rightful owners. Some part of the practical problems arising at the Restoration can be seen to have been archival ones.

Though many of the documents of the sequestered chapter of Exeter cathedral must have been among those transferred to London, the triumphant declaration of continuity in their central official record whereby the entry dated 31 August 1660 follows directly after the last entry for 1646 does demonstrate the practical point that the act book itself must have been physically available in Exeter in the chapter house ready for entries on that date. Someone must have hidden it away when the other records were confiscated—and since property transactions had frequently been entered in the minutes it is likely that it would have been demanded.

On the evidence of the record itself, the obvious candidate for such a deed of defiance is Dr Robert Hall, Treasurer of the cathedral from 1629 until his death in 1667, who was present at both meetings.[3] And all that is known about him makes it an even more likely identification. He was one of the clerical sons of Joseph Hall, bishop of Exeter from 1627 to 1641, and he owed his preferments, including the Treasurership, to his father, to whom he gave loyal and unremitting support; similarly, he was devoted to the cathedral, exemplified by his valuable bequests to it at his death. Though of course ejected from the treasurer's residence (which was sold by the Trustees in 1651) he remained resident in the locality, as from among his various preferments he managed to retain the rectory of Clyst Hydon, which he had acquired through his marriage to Rebecca Reynell, as it was in the Reynell patronage. Here he lived during the Interregnum, devoted to the good of his parish and the welfare of ejected clergy, being through his marriage part of a family network of gentry of more or less Presbyterian sympathies, which may have accorded some protection for his own position. His rectory could at the least provide a haven for some cathedral archives and perhaps valuables too, easily transportable back to Exeter when better times returned for him and the cathedral.

Robert Hall's testament[4] in its own way provides some corroboration of his interest in preserving records. It was drawn up shortly before his death in 1667, and among its provisions he stated 'I will and appoint that all those aunceint manuscripts and records which I have laid up in a chest or box standing now in my study at Exon be forthwith delivered to the deane and chapter to be by them carefully laid upp in their archives and places where their records are usually kept'. What these 'aunceint' records were it has up to now proved impossible to discover, though presumably he must have taken possession of them in 1646; and for what reason he should then have hesitated for seven years after the Restoration before directing their preservation in the chapter archives is very puzzling. Perhaps he had forgotten about them? That is not very likely in one who appears to have been meticulous in his arrangements. Perhaps he was still suspicious about the safety of the cathedral chapter's arrangements for its possessions, and could only bear to hand over what he regarded as in his own particular care when he was on the point of death? For whatever reason, this testamentary direction of his shows his attitude to his responsibilities as Treasurer, and strongly reinforces the suggestion that it was he who triumphantly produced the chapter act book in August 1660 to receive the entries recording the resumption of the activities of the cathedral chapter of Exeter.

D&C, 3558, Exeter Cathedral Chapter Act Book

[p69 Saturday 6 June 1646] *On that same day in the afternoon in a chamber in the house of Dr Burnell, Chancellor, in the presence of me Thomas Payne, clerk of the Exchequer, before the same Dr Burnell, Chancellor and President of chapter, Dr Hall, Treasurer, and Mr Bury, residentiary canons ... appeared: the rest however, that is, the Dean* [William Peterson] *Mr Cotton, Precentor, Mr Hall, Archdeacon of Cornwall Mr Cotton Archdeacon of Totnes and Dr Cox, did not appear, whom the said President and canons, forming a full chapter, pronounced to be contumacious and to be penalized for their contumacy, and then proceeded as follows.*

Whereas they understand that the Committees of the County of Devon and the City and County of Exeter have demaunded of their officers their books of accompts rentalls and writings and evidences belonging to the Deane and Chapter they have upon consideracion thereof advised and resolved for their owne parts not to withstande any ordinance of Parliament which shall come to their knowledge. But forasmuch as they cannot yet understand of any ordinance past making the lands and rents of this Deane and chapter lyable to sequestracion, and in case there were any such ordinance, they conceave themselves soe bound by their oathes taken at their first admission to their places that they cannot by any voluntary act doe any thing to the prejudice of the Deane and Chapter and their successors. Therefore they cannot resolve at present to give any order or authority to their officers to deliver such writings wherewith they are intrusted upon their oath.

On the nomination of Mr Robert Ford, clerk, master in arts, to the vicarage of Culmstocke [Culmstock] *vacant through the death of Mr Augustine Osborne, clerk, the last incumbent there, by Dr Burnell, in whose ballot the said vicarage belongs, they decreed that the presentation of the said Mr Ford to be sealed.*

Also on the intimation made by the Lord Dean that the vicarage of Guinnepp alias Wynnepp [Gwennap] *in whose ballot the said vicarage now belongs, was and is vacant through the death of Richard Harris, clerk, the last incumbent, they decreed that the presentation made there should be sealed. And they continued the chapter in statu quo on the following Saturday and thus from Saturday to Saturday until the following feast of Michaelmas.*

[signed] Laur. Burnell

Robert Hall

[p70] *Friday the thirty-first day of the month of August in the year of our Lord 1660 in the chapter house of the cathedral church of the blessed Peter of Exeter before the venerable men William Peterson STP Dean of the said cathedral church and Robert Hall STP Treasurer of the said cathedral church, in the presence of me Henry Lynscott notary public.*

On which day and place appeared personally the venerable man James Smyth, clerk, STB, and presented and exhibited the mandate of the most serene in Christ Prince and our lord Charles the second by the grace of God of England Scotland France and Ireland King, defender of the faith, dated the eleventh day of July last past, for his installation into a prebend or canonry founded in the said cathedral church, now vacant by the death of the venerable man William Cox STP and in the collation of the said lord King ...

NOTES

1. Mary Coate, 'Exeter in the Civil War and Interregnum', *DCNQ*, XVIII (1934–5), 338–52. But for a recent view that allegiances in Exeter were less clearly defined at this time, see Mark Stoyle, *Loyalty and Locality* (Exeter, 1994), 94–6.

2. On what follows, see Dorothy M.Owen, 'Bringing Home the Records: the Recovery of the Ely Chapter Muniments at the Restoration', *Archives*, VIII no.39, April 1968, 123–9.
3. Audrey Erskine, 'Dr and Mrs Robert Hall: a Ledger Stone Identified', *Friends of Exeter Cathedral Annual Report 64*, 1994, 11–13.
4. D&C, 3560, a contemporary copy of the testament is bound into the Act Book, unpaginated.
5. *a.pillula* [the balls] was the description of the practice of sharing by ballot a gift of the chapter rectories (which were of varying value) among the canons from time to time.

Audrey Erskine

19. Fishing in Cockington Documents

One of the most interesting of the family collections acquired by the Exeter City Record Office in the first part of this century is that of the Mallocks of Cockington.[1] An especially useful listing exists, with a title page as follows 'Calendar of Documents of the Mallock Family of Cockington: list submitted in part requirement for University of London Diploma in Archive Administration by M.M. Sparkes, May, 1959'.

The document chosen for transcription is an account roll from the manor of Cockington for 1439–40. In the thirteenth and fourteenth centuries reeves or other officers in charge of running a manor had a demanding schedule of work, accounting not only for income and expenditure in cash but also for the land (and its crops), labour and livestock of the demesne, down to the last chicken or peacock.[2] Later on, when lords tended to lease their demesnes rather than keep them in hand, reeves had less to do and their accounts can be measured in inches rather than feet. The Cockington account for 1439–40 is of this type, for by then the Carys, owners of the manor, had leased most of the demesne. Thus many of the entries in the account are of a routine nature: receipt of cash from rents, from sale of a heriot (best beast) and from the profits of seigneurial jurisdiction in the manor's court. Expenses set against this income included suit to the superior hundred court, minor administrative costs (e.g. purchase of parchment for the manorial rolls) and upkeep of buildings for, as the account tells us, the Carys used Cockington as a summer residence at this time. We learn that their buildings included a hall, probably a great hall open to the rafters, a chamber block probably under the same roof, a kitchen and, it seems, a gate-house.[3] There was also a stable and a mysterious building called 'le abbaye'.

Fifteenth-century manorial accounts sometimes also contain entries of a less routine nature relating to aspects of the local economy other than arable and livestock husbandry, either because the lord received payments from tenants engaged in these alternative activities or because he himself was involved in them. The Cockington account for 1439–40 is a good example, for it has some information on quarrying and cider-making and a good deal on fishing. Almost the very last entry in the account mentions a rent of 12d paid by John Bere for a quarry, doubtless (so the geological map suggests) a working for New Red Sandstone, like those at nearby Goodrington, at Kenn and at Whipton. Cockington's quarry was in the small-fry class: its rent in 1439–40 was only 12d, whereas the quarry at Kenn was let at 16s 8d in 1495–6 and Whipton produced stone for repair of Exeter's walls in the middle of the fourteenth century.[4] The first reference in the account to cider-making comes under the heading 'Issues of the manor' (i.e. miscellaneous items of income). 'Of issues of the cider press nothing this year' probably means that the Carys normally took a small toll from tenants for their use of their press, as did many other Devon lords, at Plymstock and South Pool for example;[5] but that no payments were received in 1439–40. One good reason for this may have been that the press was constantly in service for the lord's own use in the autumn of 1439.[6] In that year 6s was spent on payments to pickers (both men and women according to another account) during the harvest; 'the lord's vessels', presumably vats, were mended; straw was bought to lay between layers of apples in the press, as described by Celia Fiennes in the seventeenth century.[7] The Carys took great pride in their orchards, probably the 'Langegardyn' and 'Southgardyn' mentioned in the account: they were kept in hand long after the rest of the demesne was leased out and, another document tells us, they were partly re-planted in 1449.[8] No sales of cider are recorded in the account for 1439–40, so presumably the total vintage was consumed by the lord and his household.

There was another very good reason for the Cary family's residence at Cockington during the summer, namely the plentiful supplies of fish to be had off Livermead Sands; fishing is recorded here as early as 1327 and yields many references in documents contained in the Mallock collection.[9] In the account for 1439–40, under the heading 'Issues of the manor', 12s is received 'from the issue of the seine fishery'. Sometimes entries of this kind in accounts refer to payments made by tenants for permission to fish, as at Plympton and Yealmpton,[10] but the Cockington reference is probably to the lord's own fishing operation, for we are told that tithe and other expenses had been deducted. Further expenses are mentioned in the section headed 'Looking after the buildings' (in manorial accounts this heading often includes some miscellaneous expenditure) and in the following two sections, confirming the suggestion that the lord was operating his own fishery. The Carys had a boat at Livermead Sands and for this a rope and oars were bought in 1439–40. There are references in the account to a payment made to William More 'for drying and salting fish for the lord in summer', to purchase of a barrel 'for the lord's mackerel' and to purchase of salt at Dartmouth and elsewhere.[11] The document also hints at the organization of the Cary family's fishing which seems to have involved a partnership between some of Cockington's tenants and their lord, for both parties had a share in the buying of the seine nets. One can only hazard a guess at the precise details: perhaps the lord provided part of the expensive capital equipment (the boat and a share in the nets), used some of his tenants in the team-work which is necessary in handling large seines, and then allowed them a proportion of the catch. The nets were certainly large (a part share in a new one cost 10s in 1439–40) and could only have been managed by teams of fishers, as was the practice along the South Devon coast well into the present century.[12] Of the destination of the fish obtained by all this activity the account tells little. A small quantity was sold locally (the 12s from 'issues of the seine fishery' mentioned in the account) but some may have been traded elsewhere, perhaps in Somerset where the Carys had a winter residence—in which case the income would not have been included on the Cockington account. The fishery at Cockington is another example of a landlord's development of 'alternative' sources of income during the fifteenth century, a period when income from rents was not buoyant.[13] We can be sure too that some of the fish was consumed by the household. It was well salted, so no doubt thirst was quenched by the cider which is another of the preoccupations of this account of 1439–40.

In the following transcription the marginal sub-headings of the original have been set in upper case; sub-totals at the end of each section have been omitted. In the receipts section the repetitive 'for' (i.e. 'he answers for') has been omitted from the beginning of each entry. The account is quite easy to follow if the reader realizes that arrears from the previous year are counted as receipts (i.e. sums owing to the lord) and that rents not paid are counted as expenses (i.e. cash lost to the lord).

DRO, 48/13/4/1/2

Cokyngton. Account of John Piers bailiff there from the feast of Michaelmas in the eighteenth year of the reign of King Henry VI until the morrow of the same feast in the following year, the nineteenth year of the said king, for one entire year.

[Receipts]
Arrears. First he answers for £9 2s 7½ d of arrears in the last account of the preceding year as appears on the foot of his [preceding] *account.*

Rents of assize. 14s received of the rent of John Taillor paid at the four yearly terms for his free tenement in Cokyngton [held] *by charter. And 10s received from Isolda Gilberd widow of William Gilberd for certain lands in Lovyngtorr* [Loventor] *paid at the same terms. And 2s received from William Vagge for a parcel of demesne land in Cokyngton.*

Rents of assize of conventionary tenants. £22 2s 6d received of the rents of assize of the conventionary tenants of two parts [of the manor][14] *through examination of a rental made thereof. And 4s 9d, with 3d the price of one goose, received for the half ferling of land which Philip Mechyne formerly held in Cokyngton.*

Lease of the demense land. 119s 4d for the lease of the demesne land let this year to diverse tenants.

Lease of the mill. 10s received from John fflour for a water mill which he newly built, and he shall maintain and sustain it at his own costs and expenses in all things.

Issues of the manor. 16s 4d received from the meadow called Langemede this year and it should render 18s. Of the 20d [formerly received] *from the second hay crop this year nothing because it was sold with the meadow, above. Of pasture of the wood nothing this year. Of loppings and bark nothing this year. And 4s received from the pasture of Langegardyn over and above the hay taken against his* [the bailiff's] *visit with his servant. From Southgardyn nothing because the hay is taken for the lord's use. Of pannage for pigs nothing. Of issues of the cider press nothing this year. Of sale of cider nothing. And 12s received from the issue of the seine fishery this year up to the feast of All Saints, tithe and expenses thereof deducted. And 40s received from sale of wood this year. And 5s received from a treasure trove which is called a noble, and it is not worth more. And 4d received from the sale of two capons coming from a fine* [or fines] *of land. And 11s 6d received from one ox coming from the heriot of Richard Colle as* [appears] *in the court of the 19th year of King Henry VI. And 3s 4d ...* [entry unfinished]

Perquisites of court. 17s 3d received from the pleas and perquisites of five courts held there through the time of the account. 10d received from the censura rent[15] *as in the same* [courts].

Sum total of receipts with arrears: £44 15s 9½d.

[Expenses]
Defects of rent and other payments. Purchase of one pound of pepper and [its] *payment to the lord of Dertyngton* [Dartington] *for chief rent this year, 18d. Fine for the lord's suit there, 12d yearly. Payment made to the clerk of the court for*

entering the same fine, 3d. Fine for the lord's suit at the hundred court of Haytore [Haytor], *12d yearly. Payment made to the clerk of the court for entering the same fine, 2d. Defect of rent of Caggelane existing in the lord's hand, and it is totally decayed, 2s.*

Looking after the buildings. *Purchase of 400* [bundles of] ... [one word obscure] *straw for covering the house there (at 2s 4d per 100), 9s 4d. Hire of a thatcher for 6½ days thatching on the stable and le abbay there (taking 5d per day), 2s 8d. His servant hired for the same time, 15½d. Collecting twists, 3d. Making the bank around Langemede, by piece-work, 6s. Bonus, 1d. Hire of men by the day to hedge and enclose around the lord's wood there, by piece-work, 4s. Bonus 1d. Purchase of 1 bushel of salt for the lord's fish, 2s. Purchase of 2 bushels of salt on another occasion (each bushel 16d), 2s 8d. Carriage of the same from Dertemouth* [Dartmouth] *to Cokyngton, 3d. Purchase of three oars for the lord's boat, 3s. Purchase of one rope for the said boat, 4s. Purchase of one new net for the lord's use there, for the share which John Mey has, 10s. Purchase and repair of one net with Richard Jaan, 4s. Purchase of a rope for the same, 2s. Purchase of one seine rope for John Pyers, 2s. Hire of men to hedge around the lord's garden, 2s. Purchase of half a barrel in which to place mackerel for the lord, 8d. Purchase of half a bushel of salt for the same, 6d. Purchase of 300* [bundles of] *straw for covering the lord's house there, with carriage (each 100,2s), 6s. Payment both in bread and drink for the said carriage, 4d. Collecting two loads of twists, 3d. Hire of men for four days roofing on the said stable and le abbaye (taking 5d per day), 20d. Their servant hired for the same time (taking 2½d per day), 10d. Hire of one man to mow the lord's hay there in the garden, 8d. Turning over the same hay, collecting it up, stacking it in the field and carrying it to the house, 16d. Hire of one roofer*[16] *and his servant roofing on the hall, chamber, gate-house and kitchen, together with lime, nails and laths brought for the same, all in cash* ... [MS faded and obscure], *17s.*

Looking after the cider [? word faded] *and other necessary expenses. Collecting apples and fruit in the gardens, by piece-work, 6s. Purchase of six dozen hoops for binding the lord's vessels (each 8d), 4s. Purchase of 100* [bundles of] *straw for the cider press, 2s 4d. Hire of a hooper for 10 days binding the lord's vessels (taking 5d per day), 4s 2d. Hire of one man for six days cutting and laying down thorns and briars, taking 12d. Purchase of six clamps for the cider press, 12d. Hire of one man* [?looking after: MS faded] *10 pipes of cider, 3s. Tithe of the wood paid to the rector, 4s. Tallow bought for the cider press, 12d. Purchase of* ... [?a type of nail: MS faded], *2d.*

Expenses of the lord and steward and the fee of the bailiff. *Expenses of the lord and his servants staying at Cokyngton in the summer, 6s 8½d. Steward's expenses and his fee, 6s 8d. The accountant's stipend for the year, 13s 4d. Expenses of one chaplain coming to* ... [reading obscure] *and for other business there as appears by the lord's tally. Purchase of parchment for the court rolls and estreats and for writing the present account on, 4d. Payment made to William More for drying and salting fish for the lord in the summer, 20d. Payment made to the said William More for drawing in fish in the 12th year of Henry VI, by the lord's order, 18d.*

Cash deliveries. First paid to the lord by one indenture dated 16 September in the 18th year of the aforesaid king, for arrears of the preceding year, £8 10s 7d. Paid to the same lord for rents at Christmas by the hand of John Mulys by one tally, £6. Paid to the same lord for Easter rents by one tally by the had of John Venton, chaplain, £6. Paid to the same lord for rents at the nativity of St John the Baptist by the hand of the said John Venton, chaplain, £4 6s 8d.
Sum of all receipts and deliveries: £32 16s 10½d

And he [the bailiff] *owes £11 18s 11d. Of which allowed 3d for arrears* [? reading obscure] *Elizabeth Gilberd ...* [MS faint]. *And* [allowed] *to him 12d for of arrears* [? reading obscure] *of Edward Aputtore because he* [the bailiff] *is not able to distrain him within his bailwick as he says upon his oath. And 22½d for his expenses and his own clerk. And 2s 1d paid for expenses at the audit of William Bovy the lord's clerk and other servants staying there for two days and two nights. And £7 10s paid to the aforesaid William Bovy upon the audit of the account. And he owes £4 3s 9½d. And thereafter he is charged with 12d received from John Bere for the stone quarry. Sum £4 4s 9½d which he owes with 12s ½d of arrears of the preceding year, which he paid to the lord at his manor of Orchard in County Somerset and so he withdraws quit.*

NOTES

1. DRO, 48/13.
2. As in the detailed accounts used by Herbert P.R. Finberg, *Tavistock Abbey* (Cambridge, 1951).
3. The word translated here as 'gate-house' is *porta* which can also mean 'gate'. The former translation is preferred because of the reference to repair of the feature's roof. 'Porch' is another possibility.
4. BL, Add roll 13770 (Goodrington); DRO, C.R. 552 (Kenn); Audrey M. Erskine (ed.) *The Accounts of the Fabric of Exeter Cathedral, 1279–1353*, pt ii, DCRS 26 (1983), xv (Whipton).
5. DRO, 1258M/D/74/6; CRO, Arundell MSS, MA 277.
6. Or late summer, 1440: the account begins and ends at Michaelmas.
7. Celia Fiennes cited in Robin Stanes, *The Old Farm* (Exeter, 1990), 67.
8. DRO, 48/13/4/1/2, account of 28–9 Hen.VI.
9. Deryck Seymour, *Torre Abbey* (Exeter, 1977), 252; other examples of fishing in Cockington documents will be found in Harold S.A. Fox, *Village Origins: Medieval Fishers and Fishing Settlements along the South Devon Coastline* (forthcoming); Hilda H. Walker, 'Livermead Harbour, Torquay', *DAT* 99 (1967), 287–8.
10. DRO, C.R. 496; PRO, SC/6/1118/6.
11. The salt was probably of foreign origin, imported at Dartmouth. For this trade see Maryanne Kowaleski (ed.), *Local Customs Accounts of the Port of Exeter*, DCRS 36 (1993), 26.
12. Melvin Firestone, 'The traditional Start Bay crab fishery', *Folk Life* 20 (1982), 56–75 reprinted in part in M.G. Dickinson (ed.), *A Living from the Sea* (Exeter, 1987), 14–23.
13. Other south-western examples: Harold S.A. Fox, 'Devon and Cornwall' in *The Agrarian History of England and Wales*, iii, *1348–1500*, Edward Miller (ed.), (Cambridge, 1991), 738.

14. One third of the rental seems to have belonged temporarily to another party, possible a widow with dower.
15. A payment made by landless persons living on the manor.
16. The word is *tegulator*, strictly 'tiler'; elsewhere in the document the clerk uses it, and related words, where 'roofing' more generally is clearly meant.

H.S.A. Fox

20. The Sermon of Richard Saunders of Kentisbeare, 1651

Richard Saunders was intruded into the wealthy rectory of Kentisbeare in March 1647 replacing the royalist incumbent John Parsons. The latter was obliged to find alternative openings in Somerset but his eventual removal to Down St Mary can only be verified by his free resignation from there in 1661.[1]

Richard Saunders had an older brother Humphrey who had become rector of Holsworthy in 1632. Both Humphrey and Richard were to become convinced Presbyterians during and after the first Civil War. A third brother, Thomas, served as an officer in the Parliamentary army rising to the rank of Major by the end of 1650. It was he who was to become an important lay influence both at county level and also as M.P. from 1653 to 1658.[2] Brother Thomas died childless in 1660 so that his newly acquired wealth soon became scattered among relatives including Humphrey and Richard. Humphrey died in 1672 but the much younger Richard survived till 1692 thus living long enough to witness the beginning of a durable religious toleration in England. Edmund Calamy praised Richard as 'an excellent casuist'. More extensive tributes were seemingly added at a later date.[3]

Interest in the extracted sermon rests largely on the preacher's unenviable task of justifying secular authority as it existed in March 1651 (new style). In his preface to the reader Saunders admits some alteration to the sermon as he first delivered it. However, as there was but a gap of only two months between preaching the sermon at Exeter and sending it for publication the line of argument is likely to have been predominantly the same.

Religious enthusiasm in the mid-seventeenth century was eager to find the hand of God in contemporary events but despite some success for Protestant forces abroad there was also copious evidence that left the godly in considerable bewilderment. In England many Presbyterians were aghast at the summary execution of King Charles I yet felt obliged to co-operate at least for the time being with the victorious Army and its Rump Parliament. Faced with the challenge of preaching to Devon's de facto magistracy Saunders looked to Scripture as his overriding authority. To his credit he faced head on the problem of secular government as then constituted but he was frequently caught in a process of special pleading that might convince only those of his listeners who already wished to be persuaded.

Fairly recent research has pointed to the great difficulty in keeping Presbyterians and Independents apart. The latter had no formal organization which makes it hard to identify them anyway. The Exeter Assembly of 1655 to 1659, though predominantly Presbyterian, included not only some Independents but a few Anglicans also.[4] For most responsible clergy there remained the constant risk on the one hand of Church anarchy and on the other of being linked far too closely with a government both in Church and State that was of very dubious legitimacy. However, in early 1651 Saunders still believed there would soon be new Parliamentary elections to help resolve the crisis.

The quotations below form only about a tenth of the total publication yet they reveal the theoretical nature of the predicament facing all clergy, magistrates and people at the time. Unsurprisingly the Bible offered little real help. The New Testament was almost entirely composed by a Church eager to stay on the right side of the still mighty Roman Empire. The Old Testament, so much favoured by Puritans wishing to justify their own militarism, is lavish in fulsome praise for godly rulers while as passionately critical of the wicked and corrupt. If vengeance belonged to God surely the faithful could execute justice on His behalf. But what if the faithful had no agreed interpretation of current events?

In an age that has seen the spectacular growth of liberation theology the issues raised in this sermon can be shown to have relevance well beyond a limited period of the English Commonwealth almost three and a half centuries ago.

BL, E638

Plenary Possession makes a Lawfull Power or Subjection to Powers that are in being proved to be lawfull and necessary.

In a sermon preached before the Judges in Exeter March 23 1650 By Richard Saunders, Preacher of the Gospel at *Kentisbeer* in Devon.

Titus 3,1 Put them in minde to be subject to principalities and powers.

Printed for William Adderton and to be sold at his shop at the Three Golden Falcons in Duck Lane 1651.

To the Reader

In preaching of it my drift was to satisfy Conscience in a thing of generall concernment to all persons belonging to this Commonwealth. I confesse I was silent for a while ... but finding ... many consciences by this means ensnared I could not hold my peace. From my study in *Kentisbeer* 19 May 1651.

Romans 13, 1 Let every Soul be subject to the higher powers for there is no power but of God. The powers that be are ordained of God.

The Gospel meddles little with State matters: we find the Apostles very sparing in them: And what Paul speaks here he speaks as a Divine, not disputing of the Powers that were in Being whether they were lawfull or usurped (though there was room enough for such a dispute if it had been proper for him) but onely exhorting the Saints ...

They that are well acquainted with my Ministry and way of Preaching know I seldom ingage in State Divinity, the work of a Gospel Minister being to win souls to Christ and so reveal a spirituall Kingdome which is not of this world: but where Scripture speaks though but sparingly there may we speak too, so that we remember still what our main work is; especially when some emergent reasons provoke unto the same ...

Christ himself gave an example of this in that he himself payd tribute by way of acknowledgement of the Civil Order established Matt. 17,27 Not that he himselfe was to be accounted subject to any earthly power; for being made heir of all things he had a preheminance above all Kings and Princes of the earth: But this he did to give us an example of subjection unto those that are over us ...

He (Paul) gives satisfaction in one thing which has but little difficulty in it, viz. That lawful powers such as are rightly and regularly introduced, are to be submitted to; but he leaves us to seek about that which is far more difficult, yea even impossible in some cases for us to finde out and that is, what powers are lawfull, what not? How can Christians give judgement of those supreme Powers that they live under? What a worke should a Christian have to do, if he were to seeke out the originall Right of Supreme Governours by which they hold their power? Where should they have recourse for satisfaction? what rule should they proceed by? ...

Indeed there is nothing by which we may judge of a Power whether it be of God or no but onely this that it actuall is. If you say yes, the consent and choice of the people; I say that demonstrates what is the peoples will, not what is Gods will. We are commanded to be subject to Powers in the text not because the people choose them but because God ordaines them. Now by what can we know that a Power is ordained of God unless we make providences putting men in possession of power to be Gods way of ordaining Powers? ... God doth not now reveale himself by expresse word concerning this thing, how shall we know his will then? God giveth the Empires of the world to whom he wil. Thou canst not know who is ordained of God but onely by considering whom providence hath exalted as supreme. For as says Calvin As soon as ever the Lord hath lifted up any unto the Height of a supreme power, he doth witness to us that it is his will that he should reign.

Against this is argued from 2 Kings 11 thus, If possession makes a lawfull Power then Athalia was a lawfull Power and they did ill who did rise against her and crown Joash king. It had questionlesse been rebellion in them to thrust out her that had been in full possession for six years together; but we finde not that they did amisse in putting her off though she had been actually supreme for so long time that the right heir might be annointed King, therefore her being in actual possession did not make her a lawfull power, or a power to which the people were bound to be subject: and so by consequence, the like doth not now constitute a power to which the people owe subjection.

To which I answer Jehojada who contrived the deposing of Athaliah after six yeares reign was no private man but the chiefe Priest to whom it did belong ... to judge not onely church matters but State affairs too. God then ordained rulers by manifest word and command, and therefore such were onely to be acknowledged for lawfull Powers then as were thus appointed by God, in respect of which Athaliah was not but Joash was the rightful Prince. But now to us there is no such expresse way afforded to determine who should govern but there is an expresse way teaching us whom we should acknowledge and submit to, even the powers that are ...

But may not Christians resist an Usurper?

They may resist an Invadour or Usurper while he is invading and usurping his power; Yea I may say they ought; for so much do Christians ow unto the Powers in being over them, that they ought to oppose any that shall endeavour to dispossesse them of that power which God hath put into their hands so violating and disturbing the Civil Order that is established & fixed; But for Tyrants and Usurpers when they are in plenary possession, Christians may not oppose themselves against them. So Peter Martyr and others ...

Is not the late King with his heirs and successours dispossessed by God who gives and takes away rights of government according as seems good to him, by putting downe one and setting up another? The Parlament have declared the supreme power to be in themselves exclusively without a King or house of Lords and they are the Powers that now are.

If a man should promise to marry a certain woman before such a time and she in the interim be married to another he is not any longer bound by his promise. And is this not our case? hath not this State another head? is there not another power over us? and is there not a Gospel command enjoyning subjection to the Powers that be? either the obligation of former engagements must be at an end, or we must be bound to the violation of a Divine law; which can not be.

NOTES

1. Bodleian Library, Oxford W.MS.C.2.263; A.G. Matthews, *Calamy Revised* (Oxford, 1947), 554; DRO, Chanter 24, 17 Oct 1661.
2. Bodleian Library, Oxford, W.MS.C.2.231; Matthews, *Calamy*, 426; PRO, Probate 11/302 f 274; S.K. Roberts, *Recovery and Restoration in an English County* (Exeter, 1985), 27, 58, 161 albeit this source consistently calls him Humphrey Lawrence!
3. Society of Friends Library, London, Anon. *The West answering the North*, 85, 92, 107; E. Calamy, *An Account of the Ministers ... ejected or silenced at the Restoration* (1713), ii 245; Calamy, *Nonconformists Memorial* (1802), ii 45–8.

4. For example, J.S. Morrill, *Reactions to the English Civil War* (1982), 98; Ann Hughes, *Politics, Society and the Civil War in Warwickshire* (Cambridge, 1987), 309–12; Ian Gowers, 'The Clergy in Devon, 1641–62' in T. Gray, M. Rowe and A. Erskine (eds), *Tudor and Stuart Devon* (Exeter, 1992), 213, 214.

Ian Gowers

21. Stopping up the Market Place: Crock Street and Barnstaple's Potters in the Seventeenth Century

The following extracts, from Barnstaple Quarter Sessions Records for 1669–70, show the Court cracking down on local potters selling their wares in a narrow thoroughfare. The potters, whose views were not recorded, could well have argued that the lane had been their traditional market place, 'time out of mind', for records show its name, Crock Street, in use as early as 1344.[1] In the later seventeenth century, a period of expanding trade, more potters brought wares to set out in the narrow street, where countrymen buying earthenware pans and pitchers for kitchens and dairies in the rural hinterland, rubbed shoulders with mariners and porters taking pottery down to the bottom of the street where the West Gate opened on to the quay. Many ships, whether trading in the Bristol Channel, to Ireland, or to the colonies across the Atlantic, carried pottery, which was cheap to buy and in almost universal demand, to top up outward cargoes.[2] Crock Street, now beginning to be known as Cross Street, was the main link between the town centre and the quay, and therefore a popular pitch for other traders as well as potters. On market days, as people flocked to see what was on offer, and stopped to bargain, buy and chat, the narrow way became severely overcrowded, and the pottery laid out on the ground for sale probably did represent a hazard, as well as slowing down traffic. The matter was brought to the attention of the Court by the 'grand inquest', a jury empanelled to go around the town and report 'nuisances'. The justices (recorder, mayor, and previous year's mayor) then made an order which empowered them to act against subsequent offenders.

Four entries in the Court Record tell the story. The Order is in English. The others, here translated, are in 'dog' Latin, with some unusual equivalents; *urnarius* for potter, for example. English words and phrases are often inserted, as in *'firtilia vasa, Anglice* Earthen weares, *vocat* potts, pans and dishes'. The word 'cloam', used in the Order, is a dialect word, still in use in parts of Devon, for vessels made of clay.

NDRO, B1/3983

[p.114. Presentment by the jury on 11 October 1669] *Item they say and present that Joseph Westlade, Christopher Hannaford, Benjamin Smith and William Oliver on divers market days last past, did place certain earthen wares (in the place called Crock Street) for sale to the danger of the king's liege people in their passage.*

[p.115 An Order made at the same Court] Whereas complaint hath been made to this Court and it hath been presented by the grand inquest that the Potters within and which doe come to this Burrough and parish doe place their earthen weares and Potts in the Street called Crock Street (within this Burrough) to the hinderance of the king's leige people, and the hinderance of other things brought to the said Markett, for which the said street is a proper place and not for the Potters, It is ordered by this Court That all Potters, and others doe (from and after the nine and twentieth day of this present October) forbeare to place any Cloame, Earthen weares or Potts in the said street to be sold uppon paine of forfeiting of three shillings and fower pence for every time offending, And if any Potter or other person doe or shall place any Cloame, Earthen weares or Potts in the said street it shalbe lawful for any person or persons to remove the same.

[p.120 Presentment of 17 January 1669/70] *Item they present the potters, (vizt) William Oliver, Joseph Westlade of Fremington, Benjamin Smith and Christopher Hannaford for stopping up the Market place.*

[p.142 Court Record of 25 April 1670] *The Jury of our Lord King present and say that William Oliver of Barnstaple in the County of Devon, potter, on the twenty-second day of April in the twenty second year of the reign of our Lord King Charles the Second, by the grace of God King of England, Scotland, France and Ireland, Defender of the Faith, did place certain Earthen weares called potts, pans and dishes in the king's highway in Barnstaple aforesaid called Crosse Street alias Crock Street and permitted the same to remain in the same street during the space of six hours continuously to the harm of the town and the danger of all the liege subjects of the same king near the dwellings of those who walk between them against the peace of the said Lord King, his crown and dignity etc.*

And the said William came and admitted that he was guilty of the aforesaid premises as specified in the aforesaid Judgement; and furthermore was fined five shillings, which he, the aforesaid William, here in Court paid to Thomas Lugg, the Receiver of the said borough.

Similar entries in the same court record show that Christopher Hannaford was also fined five shillings, and Benjamin Smith three shillings and fourpence. Although the order specified three and fourpence as the amount of the fine, the two first-named potters, who were men of greater means, may have laid out more wares for sale. Joseph Westlade of Fremington apparently did not offend on this occasion; he may not have brought his wares in to Barnstaple.[3] The fines appear to have stopped the use of the street as the potters' market, for no more entries of this kind are found in the court records. The potters probably moved to the quay, where one soon had 'a little shop'.[4] Others no doubt set out their wares on the ground, a tradition which, as elderly residents remember, local potters followed on Barnstaple Quay until after the First World War.

NOTES

1. NDRO, B1, 410, Deed of 1344.
2. A. Grant, *North Devon Pottery: the Seventeenth Century* (Exeter, 1983), 88, *passim*.
3. NDRO, B1, 444, shows that Fremington men paid no tolls in Barnstaple markets, but Westlade could sometimes have sold his wares in Fremington, or shipped them out direct.
4. NDRO, B1, 3971, Rentals of 1670–83.

Alison Grant

22. William Lucombe and the Iron Oaks of Hillersden in 1796

The following letter and description was sent to Lord Dartmouth of Sandwell in Staffordshire in 1796. It relates the history of the 'Iron' and Lucombe oaks and accompanied a number of seedlings. Four days after the letter was written thirty-nine of the 'Iron' oaks were planted: '18 [in] the east corner by the seed room, roots cut; 12 [in the] south corner, tap roots cut; 5 on the border by the orchard door, roots not cut; 4 in pots [in the] greenhouse tap roots cut'.[1]

The letter demonstrates the eighteenth-century interest in new varieties of plants but of more immediate interest to garden historians of Devon is the information it reveals concerning Hillersden near Cullompton. Although the current house is more modern there are some remaining eighteenth-century features in the garden, including some mature Turkey oaks. These may well be the oaks discussed in the letter which were planted from Lucombe's Nursery more than two hundred years ago. The Lucombe oak (*Quercus* × Hispanica 'Lucombeana') was accidentally developed in Devon in about 1765 by William Lucombe[2] and may have been a cross of a Turkey oak (*Quercus cerris*) with a Cork oak (*Quercus suber*). Distinguished by its evergreen habit and vigorous growth it is also known for its propagator cutting down the original tree and storing the resulting planks under his bed for its eventual use as timber for his own coffin.[3] Three of what is thought to be the original graftings remain at Thomas Hall, University of Exeter.[4] However, the trees sent to Staffordshire were the more common Turkey oaks and the interest in them demonstrated by Lord Dartmouth and at Hillersden seems not to have been for ornamental reasons but for practical ones. The eighteenth-century experimental planting is revealed by this solitary documentary survival.

Stafford Record Office, D564/12/14/19

Mr Gisborne presents his Compliments to Lord Dartmouth & takes the pleasure of enclosing a short account of the Iron Oak; of which tree the person sent to receive Lady Dartmouth's very obliging present of pea-fowl brings some seedlings. Mr G. can answer for the accuracy of the particulars specified in that account, having received them immediately in answer to minute enquiries from Mr Babington, & the present Mr Lucombe who has succeeded his father in his business.

Mr & Mrs Gisborne beg to write in compliments to the family at Sandwell, & shall have very sincere pleasure in hearing of their good health.

Yoxall Lodge, November 24th, 1796

Iron Oaks

About fifty years since the late William Balle esquire of Mamhead House (now Lord Lisburne's) in Devonshire received from Turkey, by one of his own ships trading thither, a quantity of acorns. Some of these acorns he presented, under the name of Iron Oak Acorns, to Mr Lucombe, a nurseryman, in that neighbourhood. In a few years afterwards Mr Lucombe sold some of the young trees produced by these acorns to Mr Crewy,[5] who planted them at Hillersden House near Cullompton in the same county. Those trees were planted there in rows on a gravelly bank & inter-mixed with English Oaks, & a few other trees. All the trees now stand in rows ['twenty' crossed through] ten feet asunder & each tree is twenty feet from the next in the same row. By Mr Gisborne's desire, his brother-in-law Mr Babington, being resident at Hillersden House last year, accurately examined & measured a considerable number both of the English & of the Iron Oaks, indiscriminately taken, in order to ascertain the comparative growth of the two species. Of the English Oaks the average circumference, at three feet from the ground, was 3 feet 7⅓ inches. Of the Iron Oaks, at the same height from the ground, the average girth was 5 feet 4 inches. As the solid contents of circles are as the squares of their circumferences, the quantity of timber in a piece of the butt of the Iron Oak a foot in length would be to a particular piece of Iron Oak nearly as 4096 to 1877; or considerably more than double. And as the Iron Oaks appear to the eye manifestly to exceed the English Oaks in height as much as in thickness, &

likewise seem to carry up their thickness better than the latter, Mr B. is of [the] opinion that the Iron Oaks contain on an average five or six times the quantity of wood contained in the English Oaks.

Some of the Iron Oaks have been heretofore cut down & employed to make pales, gates &c, in the enclosures; & as far as the different trials purposely made afford ground for judging, the wood is not inferior to English Oak either in hardness, toughness or durability.

The seedling trees now sent to Lord Dartmouth are from acorns produced last year by the Iron Oaks at Hillersden. The Evergreen Oak known by the name of the Lucombe Oak was an accidental variety raised in Mr Lucombe's Nursery from an Acorn produced from an Iron Oak raised from one of the original Acorns given by Mr Ball, a full account of the Lucombe Oak is given in Dr Hunter's edition of Evelyn's *Sylva*.

NOTES

1. This is noted on an accompanying slip.
2. John Harvey, *Early Nurserymen* (1974), 72.
3. NCCPG (Devon Group), *The Magic Tree: Devon Garden Plants History and Conservation* (Exeter, 1989), 90.
4. John Caldwell and M.C.F. Proctor, *The Grounds and Gardens of the University of Exeter* (Exeter, 1969), 53.
5. The Cruwys family.

Todd Gray

23. The Bounds of Meavy Parish, 1613

Glebe terriers are a rich source of descriptions of parish bounds. The following item relating to Meavy parish on the south-western edge of Dartmoor is of special interest both on account of the detail it records and also because it throws light on several important matters of local historical and archaeological interest. The bounds as described nearly 400 years ago appear to coincide more or less precisely with those of the modern civil parish of Meavy, which can be followed on an Ordnance Survey 1:25,000 map.

The name of the starting point 'Gyes Crosse als Smallacombe Crosse' resolves once and for all a long-running debate as to whether or not historical references to Smallacombe Cross should be identified with Marchants Cross (SX 54626681). The former is now shown to have a quite separate location, in the vicinity of Ringmoor Cottage (SX 558666). Its alternative name 'Gees Cross' survived at least until *c.*1840 where it is recorded on the Sheepstor Tithe Map and Apportionment.

'Litterburne' is an otherwise unrecorded name for the stream running from Ringmoor Cottage to the River Meavy which it joins at SX 550670. 'Crekabyelake foote' is now under the waters of Burrator Reservoir at SX 55506868.[1] The point where the boundary meets the highway from Sheepstor to Walkhampton church is on a lane at SX 54986909. This portion of the lane is still known locally as Woodland Hill. 'Yannadon Crosse' would appear to be identified with modern Lowery Cross at SX 54876920 or else was sited at the highest point where the lane leads out onto Yennadon Down itself at SX 54786924.[2] The route from here was 'by an old Reve' towards Dousland and Lake, seemingly following the modern line of the parish boundary southwestwards along a continuous hedge. The description of this as a reave supports Andrew Fleming's suggestion that the parish hedgeline is on a prehistoric base.[3]

The 'bounde in the hie Waie at lake' must have been at SX 53206829, in Lake Lane where until recently there was a ford which was probably the 'Stoford' of the charter of Isabella de Fortibus of 1291.[4] The boundary then followed the stream to 'Churcheford' which is in Meavy Lane at SX 53026760. This bound point is also mentioned in 1291. 'Gratton yeat' (ie gate) is to be identified with modern Gratton Cross at SX 52436745. The route to the River Meavy follows the modern boundary and is interesting for its mention of both Higher and Lower Elfordtown and for the fact that the use of the dialectal 'y' in the name is the earliest record of this form, some 200 years before the previous known instance.[5]

The route along the ancient course of the river Meavy is self-explanatory. Palmers Yeat has not yet been identified but the newly erected 'bond stone' was presumably somewhere in the vicinity of Leebeer Wood (SX 527654) south of Hoo Meavy, where the boundaries of Bickleigh, Buckland Monachorum and Meavy meet, though the latter point today is on the river (SX 52656540) rather than on the hillside as implied by the seventeenth-century text.

The boundary then ran, as it does today, to the confluence of the Rivers Meavy and Plym, then up the course of the latter to 'Griddleford', a lost place name but which is probably to be identified with the ford at the confluence of the Legis Lake with the River Plym at SX 56656515. Another candidate would be the ford one mile further upstream below Ditsworthy Warren at SX 58206608, which is supported as an approximate location by the description of bounds of Yeasterhill tinwork in 1625 which mentions 'Wenford and Griddleford'.[6] At this point the surveyors lost their nerve and admitted that they could not be sure of the exact route of the boundary across 'certayne Commons', i.e. Ringmoor Down, to the starting point at Gyes Cross, apart from a general north-westerly direction (which supports identification of Griddleford with the lower ford). Their reason for imprecision is given as 'controversie & stryffe' which, incidentally, still exists today regarding the status of Ringmoor Down as a common and the ownership of land in the vicinity.

DRO, Exeter Diocesan Records, Meavy glebe terrier, 1613

Meavye: a note of the Boundes and limittes of the parishe aforesaid 1613

Begininge on the east side of the said parishe at or nere aboute a certen place called Gyes Crosse als *Smallacombe* Crosse abutting with the parishe of *Shipstorr* [Sheepstor], and thence liniallie downewards & Westwards, followinge the ancyent course of *Litterburne* till it fall into the Ryver of *Meavie*, and so ascendinge by the ancyent course of the said Ryver of *Meavie* Northwardes so far as *Crekabyelake* foote (And those bondes devyde the said parishes of *Meavie* & *Shipstorr*). Thence by a hedge ascendinge Westwards betwene Woodland & *Crekaby* and so forth upwards betwene *Woodlands* & *Lowrye* to the hie Waie leadinge from *Shipstorr* toward Walkhampton Churche, and so by that Waie to *Yannadon* [Yennadon] Crosse and from that Crosse by an old Reve downe the hill till it come to *Lake* grownde & *dowstyland* [Dousland], and thenceforth directlie downewards by a hedge till it come to a bounde in the hie Waie at *lake* leadinge from *Shipstorr* to Buckland monachorum (and those bonds devyde the parishes of *Meavie* & Walkhampton) and from that bounde downewards and southwards by the ancyent course of a [sic] Lake till it come to *Churcheford* lyinge in a Waie leadinge from *Meavie* to Buckland aforesaid and so Westward by the same Waie to a crosse lane at *Gratton yeat*, and thence Westward by a hedge, lyinge betwene Gratton and higher *Yelvertowne* [Elfordtown] untill it come so farre as Lower *Yelvertowne* and thence southwardes by a hedge lyinge betwene the growndes of Gratton & of Lower *Yelvertowne*, until it come to the Ryver of *Meavie*, and thence a longe descendinge south Westwards & southwards by the ancyent course of the said Ryver so far as a bond stone latelie set up, standinge in the hill over against *Palmers yeat* (and those bonds devyde the parishes of *Meavie* & buckland Monachorum) then descendinge as before by the said Ryver untill it mete with the Ryver of *Plim* (and that devydes *Meavie* & *Bickleighe*) And thence ascendinge eastwardes by the said Ryver of Plym to *Griddleford* or *Weyn*[?]*ford* or theraboutes (and that bond *Plim* devydes the parishes of *Meavye* & Shaugh) and thence Northwestward from the said Ryver, over certayne Commons to Gyes Crosse first above mencioned: But by What bondes from the said Ryver to Gyes Crosse we doe not certaynlie knowe, For ther hath of longe tyme bene & yet is controversie & stryffe betwene the Lords of those landes where the[y] do lye (and those boundes should devyde somewhat more betwene *Meavie* & *Shipstorr* aforesaid.

Aliter. *Meavie* parishe is bounded and abuttinge with the parishe of Shaugh on all the south syde the parishe of Bickleigh on the south west parte, Buckland

Monachorum on the West syde, the parishe of Walkhampton on the north syde and *Shipstor* on the Northeast & east partes.

the signe of Edward hedd Churchwarden

Isacke [?]Conyer churchwarden

NOTES

1. Tom Greeves, 'A Burrator Centenary—an Historical Context', *Dartmoor Magazine*, 31 (Summer 1993), 8.
2. In about 1750 the Revd Mr Crew, a native of Walkhampton, told Dean Milles of the site of a cross on 'little *Yanadon*': Bodleian MS Top.Devon.b.2/Milles/Parochial Returns L–Z fol.407/221a. Little Yennadon lies on the north, i.e. Walkhampton, side of the parish boundary.
3. Andrew Fleming, 'The Prehistoric landscape of Dartmoor, Part I, South Dartmoor', *Proc. Prehistoric Soc.*, 44 (1978), 114, & '... Part II, North and East Dartmoor', *Proc. Prehistoric Soc.*, 49 (1983), 238.
4. Stuart A. Moore & Percival Birkett, *A Short History of the Rights of Common upon the Forest of Dartmoor & the Commons of Devon* (Dartmoor Preservation Assoc. Publication No.1, Plymouth, 1890), 105. See also Della Hooke, *Pre-Conquest Charter-Bounds of Devon and Cornwall* (Woodbridge, 1994), 196–200, for the most recent interpretation of a charter of AD 1031 which describes bounds which coincide in part with those of 1613 and the present day, at least in the vicinity of Elfordtown, Lake and Yennadon Down.
5. Samuel Rowe, *The Panorama of Plymouth or Tourists Guide ...* (Plymouth, 1821), 270.
6. WDRO, 72/1034; Thomas A.P. Greeves, 'The Devon Tin Industry, 1450–1750; an archaeological and historical survey' (unpublished PhD thesis, University of Exeter, 1981), 387.

Tom Greeves

24. A Gentleman's Travel Journal on Dartmoor in 1856

The following extracts are taken from an unattributed author's journal of his sight-seeing excursions in Devon in 1856. Having travelled down from London with companions by train, the author spent eleven weeks exploring Dartmoor and its environs, whilst lodging at Westcott cottage near Chagford.[1] The journal shows his interest in natural history and archaeology. Whilst staying at Westcott, he became acquainted with George Waring Ormerod,[2] a solicitor in Chagford who agreed to show him archaeological sites of interest in the area. Chagford was noted as a focal point for natural historians and tourists alike, who were drawn to this particular beauty spot for a variety of reasons, as noted in Kelly's *Directory*:

> The scenery around Chagford is of a most romantic character. This portion of Dartmoor is much frequented in the summer by invalids, its dry and bracing air having been found very beneficial to people having a consumptive tendency. In the opinion of many eminent medical men the air in Chagford is the purest in England. It is also much frequented by tourist antiquarians, and the disciples of Izaack Walton; to the former it recommends itself by the romantic scenery with which it abounds, its mountain torrents rushing with impetuosity down their course from a succession of cascades and lines of silver light which cannot fail at once to delight the beholder. The most beautiful points of scenery are Whiddon Park, the Sharpetre Rock, Castor Rock, Mileton Hill, and the Holy-Street Mill. To the antiquarian it is also interesting on account of the many Druidical and other remains of ages long gone by, to be found as the Cromlech, Logan Stone, Via Sacra and Bowling Green in Rushford.[3]

As a 'tourist antiquarian', it is open to conjecture that the author may well have consulted some of the tourist guides available or even a route book of Devon to enable him to enjoy his visit. His excursions around Dartmoor's panorama are vividly observed, noting the vernacular architecture and local inhabitants' mannerisms. Daily outings were enjoyed by the author and his companions during an evidently hot summer combined with socializing, often using a donkey for transport.

DRO, Z19/36/23

Monday July 21   A bright sunny day M Sp & A Sp over Sandy Park Bridge, and up the road towards Drewsteignton. Left the donkey at the beginning of the Path on *Piddledon* [Piddledown] Heath; and, desiring the little boy to meet us at Fingle Bridges, proceeded along that beautiful walk. It is a narrow path, only wide enough for one, formed for the benefit of visitors, and was almost on a level (excepting at the E. end) along the north side of the deep ravine through which the Teign runs. You pass two projecting crags from which you look down almost perpendiculary upon the river Teign below and at the same time obtain pleasant views of the country to the west. For a space, the view is confined to this lovely valley; but presently the Country to the east begins to open out, and Fingle Bridge is seen far below towards which the descent is rapid ... [The entry concludes with both little boy and donkey failing to meet the author at the appointed hour and rendez-vous at Fingle Bridge, having become bored with waiting and not knowing where the bridge was.]

Saturday July 26   To Whiddon Park and there dawdled sometime, and pleased with it. About 10 pm Augusta and George arrived from their foreign travels, having been as far as Venice. Sat up much later usual listening to their account of what they had seen and met with.

Monday July 28   Set out at 2.20 for Kestor Rock by Way, Thorn & Yeo, where we crossed the South Teign in a beautiful valley, up the opposite hill by Frencham [?Frenchbeer] Farm to the end of the enclosures, then up the open hill to the right to Frencham [?Frenchbeer] Tor, Middle Tor and Kestor Rock, which three are in a line along the ridge of the hill. While sitting at the last, Mr Ormerod came up and pointed out the various Tors and objects in sight, describing the position of various places not seen. He then brought us down a romantic, rocky, rugged lane, to *Tincombe* [Teigncombe], and then by Holy Street Mill house, where we arrived about 8.20 after six hours spent amidst beautiful scenery. The thorn, however upon this rose was that MSp caught a violent pain in the face which prevents our going to *Hey* Tor tomorrow as intended ...

Wednesday July 30   Walked by Holy Street Bridge and Murchington to Gidley. While looking at the Castle, which is close to the church in the grounds of a private House (a wretched combination of lath plaster and sham windows) received an injunction from the occupier at an upstairs window, not to let the Donkey eat the roses. He would have been a clever animal to have found them out, even if he had been so minded! The remains of the castle are small; but the first specimen of a real castle, or strong tower, that we have seen in this Country. The lower part of a spiral staircase remains, ascending from the outside, but the inside was locked, and we had too much respect for our noses to ask the clergyman [crossed through] owner for the key.

Friday August 1   Bright and hot. The Robertsons from Woolston were to have come over to Chagford on monday and to have steud [stayed] over Tuesday' but this morning arrived a letter from Fanny Ramsey stating that they had just received news of the death of her brother John Robertson in Ceylon. It arose from the attack of a wild elephant after he had fired off his gun. We have heard no more particulars.

Wednesday Aug 13   By Holy Street to Gidleigh Park, a beautiful spot, well wooded with the North Teign running round the Lawn; but neglected and overgrown. What should be the residence, and ornamental cottage, is only half built and falling into ruin, no part of it being habitable. It belongs to the Revd W Whipham the Clergyman of *Gidley*, who lives at Holy street, where he is building and altering, as usual with him, having the Character of never finishing what he has begun, and of spoiling everything he muddles with. The view from the House is not extensive, but pleasing, and is unnecessarily contracted by the growth of its own trees; but expands as you ascend the hill towards the Village. Proceeded through to the grounds to the Folly, where we were met by a heavy shower of rain. Got behind a wall till it abated, and then took a hasty view from the Top. The clouds being very threatening, returned home the same way. This forenoon Mrs Grant and Rosa were sketching in Whiddon Park.

Friday Aug 15   The Hansons, with Miss Lloyd, came over from Okehampton to Whiddon Park to sketch. Joined them, and all dined under a tree. Mrs G went with us and Mr G came afterwards. Visited the Logan Stone, the

Ladies scaling the Park wall manfully, and crossing the river on a Ladder like witches on a Broom Stick. Mr H and I moved it slightly by the application of our shoulders; but he says that it may be moved to a greater extent by two persons getting on the top, and jumping on the end. Not much sketching. Half the party walked by Cranbrook Castle to Fingle Bridge and back along the bank of the Teign through the Moreton Woods. A fine day pleasantly spent.

Tuesday Sept 16   A long day: to *Gidley* Park whence Miss H. Aug [Augusta] and A scrambled up the south bank of the river penetrating through the valley with no small difficulty: met the rest of the part at the Tolman Stone at 2½ where we dined and Miss H took a sketch. Proceeded to the Longstone Pillar with its stone avenues; then to Kestor Rock, and home by Yeo and Thorn.

Comments on the local inhabitants show some bemused observations:

Thursday Sept 25   A confirmation at Chagford, about 200 confirmed 60 of whom belonged to this Parish; the rest from Drewsteignton, Moretonhampstead, and North Bovey. There was also a cattle Fair in the town, at which the farmers seemed to be as numerous as the sheep and yet created no obstacle to our passing through. Aug [Augusta] and A set out about 11½ to Kestor Rock to see Mr Ormerod's new discovery of a sacrificial rock basin there ...

Tuesday Sep 30   At 11.50 Aug [Augusta] & A set out for a walk. By the footpath on the north side of the Teign to Fingle Bridge. The Moreton woods had little changed in colour, but looking very beautiful in the varied lights and shades produced by detached clouds. I went up to the old earth work of Prestonbury. Beyond Fingle Bridge is a sort of continuation. After following this some time, all apperance of it vanishes and it becomes very rugged somewhat worn by the foot often very indistinct, passing over several precipitous craggs. At the last of these where the valley begins to open we descended to the bank of river, where we rested and refreshed. Harvest being over, some people were busy with a team of ten horses drawing the felled timber out of the wood where there is no room for wheels. Left the ten horses brought to a standstill and the men scratching their heads at a difficult pass, and proceeded to Weir Mill and Clifford Bridge ... We have had sundry hints that it is very Gothic to go to such an outlandish place as Chagford but have never reputed it. Our accommodation, though humble in character is thoroughly comfortable, and we are told that it is the best in the neighbourhood. So that, having no annoyance or even anxiety on that account, we have been left for outdoor enjoyment. The air is mild and pleasant and evidently healthy. In July it was very hot, but has never been close or relaxing. It was said to be hotter than for the last 30 years ...

Independently of the general beauty of the country, the abundant growth of everything is a great beauty in itself. When we arrived in July the hedges were splendidly bedecked with wild flowers in the greatest variety and abundance so that we almost forgave them the insulting manner in which they generally shut out the view on all sides ...

Of apple trees there are scarcely any. The crop has been a failure for several years, and the cyder which forms the usual drink of the labouring classes has been made from French apples. It is melancholy to see the numerous orchards with scarcely a busel [bushel] of apples in each. Our range has been blackcurrants, Raspberries, Hurtleberries and Blackberries.

It is a great comfort in this neighbourhood that there are no beggars and few dogs. Geese are abundant, but they generally go out of the way and are not so ill bred as to follow and hiss after you ...

About Chagford some of the fields are common in the winter months; and in September the gates are taken off when all the quadrupeds of the town are turned to enjoy the pasture. One day we suffered from this Republicanism (Sept 18) when our Donkey was missing and our intended walk consequently circumscribed. The owner however felt no uneasiness, concluding that it had only been borrowed for the day according to the custom of the country; and it duly appeared in its right place on the following morning without its being known where it had been.

Sheep stealing is said to have been very common in this neighbourhood but about two years [ago] a regular Policeman was established and the practice has been suppressed. Many clever attempts were made to get rid of him, by trying to make him drunk and involve him in scrapes by the evidence of parties to whom his presence was inconvenient; but they did not succeed and he holds his ground to the discomfiture of all his enemies.

NOTES

1. *Billings Directory of Devon 1857*, 96 shows Mr William Courtier resident of Westcott Cottage.
2. *DAT*, 23 (1891), obituary VI, 108–9. G.W. Ormerod was one of the founder members of the Association and Fellow of the Geological Society, having joned it at the first meeting in Exeter in 1862.
3. *Kelly's Directory* (1856), 59.

Josephine Halloran

25. Improvements to the Park of Castle Hill, Filleigh, and the Conversion of an Old Lime Kiln into a Mock Fort, 1769–70

What follows are three extracts from the correspondence between Matthew Fortescue, 2nd Baron Fortescue of Castle Hill (1719–85) and his agent, Mr H. Hilliard. They illustrate two aspects of Devon history in the eighteenth century. First, the desire of wealthy landowners to beautify their parks and grounds (the Fortescues owned over 20,000 acres in Devon in 1873); and second, the gradual decline of the old lime burning industry, which had done much to increase agricultural production from its first introduction into Devon about 1550, and throughout the following two centuries. Serious decline did not occur until the nineteenth century, but the old lime kiln at Castle Hill was an early casualty.[1] These lime kilns were circular structures built of stone, usually twelve to fifteen feet high and about ten feet in diameter. Limestone was fed in from the top and burnt into quick lime by a coal furnace at the base; they thus somewhat resembled miniature medieval castles. William Marshall, the celebrated agricultural improver on a tour of Devon, noticed a very deep quarry of black limestone at Castle Hill, which supplied the kiln.[2]

The Fortescue family had been settled at Castle Hill since 1454.[3] Matthew, Lord Fortescue had inherited the estate and the Barony (created in 1746) from his half-brother, who was also Earl Clinton, and who died unmarried in 1751.[4] Earl Clinton had retired from public life in the 1730s and devoted himself to rebuilding his mansion and laying out an elaborate park, designed by William Kent (1685–1748) described by Horace Walpole as the father of modern gardening.[5] Sweeping views centred on 'gothick ruins' were already a feature when Matthew, Lord Fortescue and Mr Hilliard elaborated their plans.

Matthew, Lord Fortescue was an influential Devon politician, who was High Steward of Barnstaple and sat in the House of Lords as a Whig from 1751 till his death in 1785. His wife, referred to in the letters, was Anne, neé Campbell, of Cawdor in County Nairn, Scotland. Their son, Hugh Fortescue (1753–1841) was created 1st Earl Fortescue in 1789. Anne, Lady Fortescue died at their London house in Wimpole Street in 1812, aged 81.[6]

DRO, 1262/M/E/29/17

1. Extract from a letter from H. Hilliard to Lord Fortescue from Castle Hill, Sunday, 26 November 1769.

The Weather has been rainy, and very tempestuous the latter part of the Week, and continues so. Our Business has been somewhat retarded by it. I have erected a Shed with Furz upon the Hill, and am filling it with lime for the Building in Holwell, and to-morrow intend beginning to carry some of the Stone from the Quarry. Some Preparations are making for the little Improvement of the old Lime Kiln—clearing the Rubbish, and picking up some Stone for it. It may have the Appearance of a Fort given to it, and will fall into several principal Points of View, when a few Bushes in a Hedge Row are cut down, which at present obstruct the View from the Platform. I shall do myself the Honour to send your Lordship a Sketch before I make the alteration.

Your Lordship's and my Lady's obliging Remembrance of us has our grateful Acknowledgements. My Wife joins her prayers with me for a happy Moment to my Lady, and for your Lordships Health and Happiness. I am, My Lord, Your Lordship's most dutifull Servant, H. Hilliard

2. Extract from reply of Lord Fortescue at Wimpole Street, 12 December 1769 to Hilliard

I have rec'd your last, and have taken notice of what you say in it ... the drawing for the intended addition to the old Lime Kiln came safely and I think it quite proper and suitable to the other part and I am certain will have the desired effect ...

I hope this will find you all well; I am, Mr Hilliard, Your sincere friend and Well Wisher, Fortescue

3. Extract from reply of Mr Hilliard, 5 January 1770

... I have the Pleasure to inform your Lordship that the Fort is finished, and has a formidable Appearance and I hope will answer your Lordship's Inspection. I have taken the Liberty to hang a port-Cullis in the Arch fronting the Meadow Park Wood which gives it a good Deal of Spirit. I found it necessary to stop up the other Arch; it being in the Angle threw the Building rather into confusion.

NOTES

1. Michael Havinden, 'Lime as a means of agricultural improvement: the Devon example' in C.W.Chalklin and M.A. Havinden (eds), *Rural Change and Urban Growth, 1500–1800* (1974), 104–34.
2. William Marshall, *The Rural Economy of the West of England* (1796) cited in R. Pearse Chope (ed.), *Early Tours in Devon and Cornwall* (Newton Abbot, 1967), 294–5.
3. W.G. Hoskins, *Devon* (1954), 397–8.
4. G.E.C. Vicary Gibbs and H.A. Doubleday (eds), *The Complete Peerage* (new ed. 1926), V, 560.
5. *Encyclopaedia Britannica* (1955), XIII, 327.
6. G.E.C. *et al.*, *Complete Peerage*, V, 560–3.

Michael Havinden

26. 'To cure the mind's wrong biass, Spleen, some recommend the bowling-green'

The game of bowls is inextricably linked with Devon in that most familiar tableau in the pageant of English history; as that county's most famous son displayed supreme calmness at Plymouth Hoe in the face of the Spanish Armada. The following document provides anecdotal evidence of the continuing popularity of the game, almost a century later. Something which was reflected by Mathew Green in his poem, *The Spleen*, published in 1737 from which the title to this piece is taken.

The poem, among the archives of the Troyte Bullock family of Zeals in the Wiltshire Record Office, was written probably in the 1660s by Bullen Reymes who, we may assume to have been its author, in view of its exuberant tone and gently mocking self-portrait. Reymes[1] was an intelligent and lively courtier and administrator whose career included service first in the household of the Duke of Buckingham and then in the English embassies in Paris and Venice. He saw action in the Civil War on the Royalist side and served the Crown in naval affairs after 1660. He was an acquaintance of Samuel Pepys and John Evelyn, who nominated him as a Fellow of the Royal Society.

His estates, centred on Whaddon in Dorset, ensured his loyalties to that county. However, his mother Mary, the daughter of William Petre, was born in Tor Newton house in Torbrian, which parish, together with the adjoining village of Ipplepen, provides the setting for the poem. The Petres sold the house in 1603 and moved to Petre Hayes near Exeter where Reymes was born in 1613. Reymes's personal papers and diaries reveal him to be a man of attractive qualities: sociable, warm-hearted and humorous, all of which are in evidence in this verse.

The lady to whom the poem was addressed remains unidentified although the clues in the final four lines at someone resident, at the time of writing, in Exeter and might enable a knowledgeable reader to suggest a name. Following the death of his wife, Mary, in 1661, Reymes developed a close friendship with Mrs Constance Pley, the wife of George Pley of Weymouth, and it is possibly for her that these affectionate and amusing lines were written.

WRO, 865/585

Verses on Tib & Tom
My service to you Lady I present
as vast as is the man by whom tis sent

Madam
We wonder much how Tib & Tom
can entertain you all this while at home
Whilst we at Ipplepin such Sports create
as bring us midnight, were we thinke it late:
then to our nests we goe and to our ease
Ale and the winter having charm'd the fleas.
After a good long draught and a short prayer
each morning we walke out to take ye ayre:
onely Tom grumbles for another cup
what? walke ere flickets or the sun be up?
come Cuz: one cup more, noe good Tom, quoth I
and forthwith to the bowling:greene we hye
the greene as smooth as Churchyard, wot you what?
where Bullen goes, he treads the hillocks flat
yet Peter Moreton sweares it is a shame
to give a fallowfield soe good a name
soe that to Com[2] and to Torbrian we
must sometimes goe for curiosity
here passing by the Church, sayth Bullen, come
good sirs, let's goe and see my Grandsire's[3] tomb
well, his agreed and having got his fill
of wall and dust he waddles up the hill
here Peter find's his errour now, forsooth,
he want's his former rubs, the ground's too smooth
let bunglers well consider, they shall find
a rub is theyre excuse and theyre best friend,
here bowling from high noone til it be even
we oftimes bring his twelvepence to eleven
the cheapest day he had yet, was the Fast
when a dull sermon & five psalmes did last
till two i'th afternoone and that day he
his zeale rewarded had wth shillings three
roome for a gamester, Mr Mowbray comes
not neare the Jack, for the first day he summes
six shillings lost and payd, we give noe tickett
at bowles, backgammon, cribbidg, coytes or picquett
when this our stomacks wee have sharpened well,
call here the Quartermaster, bid him tell
our Landlords here we dine, and there we sup,
if they refusd us we will eate them up.
Next you must know, to Dartmouth as I went
I found Tom's nagg, saised him, and home him sent.
There I procurd that you the next weeke shall
y^r bumbast stockins have and gloves wth all,
but for y^r drawers looke not yet, alass,
they'le not be made till after Michaelmas.
Perhaps I'le bring them wth me for till then

I dare not looke on Exeter again
Excuse my poetry, for now I have sayd all
but service to Sʳ John & Cousin Pleydall.

NOTES

1. The definitive account of Bullen Reymes is *The Conscientious Cavalier* by Helen A. Kaufman (1962).
2. Combe: possibly Combe Fishacre in Torbrian.
3. William Petre.

S.D. Hobbs

27. A Confession of his Drunkenness by George Boone of Bradninch, 1717

Among the voluminous records deposited in the Devon Record Office by the Society of Friends is an autograph by George Boone of Bradninch condemning his over-indulgence in drink and, consequent upon it, his infidelities.[1] It deserves comment for at least two reasons: firstly it throws light upon how the Society of Friends tried to ensure that those who associated themselves with them maintained certain standards of behaviour, and, secondly, it involves a person who, perhaps because of his lapses, emigrated to the Quaker haven of Pennsylvania. One of his grandsons, Daniel, born there became one of the folk heroes of American expansion westwards. Daniel, indeed, and his father Squire, are remembered in the parish church at Bradninch by a plaque fixed beside the gate to the churchyard, whilst in the wall of the north aisle there is a much larger inscribed panel, placed there by American descendants of the Boone family and the Society of Boonesborough, Richmond, Kentucky. It records the fact that the family went to Pennsylvania in 1717, but not that they were Quakers.

The practice of making individuals disassociate themselves from their former evil doing by writing what was called a paper of condemnation is found from the earliest days of Quaker history, although not all Friends approved of it. In Westmoreland, for example, these documents were gathered together in a special book from 1669 onwards, but two people, who finally left the Society, John Wilkinson and John Story, thought that these papers should only be recorded if the party concerned wanted that to be done, presumably as some sort of spur against relapse in future.[2] There is evidence that many groups of Quakers were concerned about too much drinking, and that sometimes those who over-indulged were made to read out their condemnations in the very places where they had tippled.[3] Not that Friends were total abstainers, indeed some kept inns, where they could excite criticisms. For example in 1705 Exeter Friends asked James Goodridge to stop selling 'brandy and strong liquors in his house at the bridge as it does tend to the dishonour of truth'.[4]

George Boone's life as a Friend before 1717 is only very partially known, since the first surviving minute book for Cullompton Monthly Meeting, the regional Meeting of which he was a member, begins in February 1718, some months after he had left for America.[5] The early Quaker records for births, marriages and deaths are clearly incomplete too.[6] A meeting of Friends seems to have been established in Bradninch as early as 1657, some years before George Boone was born, and to have still existed as late as 1696, but it is likely that around then any Quakers in the village would have gone to Cullompton for worship.[7] As will become clear, it looks as though George did not become a Friend until later, some time between 1702 and 1704. Most fortunately one of his grandsons, James, a schoolmaster in Pennsylvania, compiled a genealogy, revealing his interests as a mathematician when he brings in times of death, and longitude of the places where they occurred.[8]

His account states that George Boone was the third of that name, and that he was born at Stoke near Exeter, presumably Stoke Canon, in 1666, son of a blacksmith. He himself became a weaver and married Mary Maughridge who came from Bradninch, where she was born in 1669. The parish registers for Bradninch show that they married on 16 August 1689 and their first child, another George, was baptized on 20 July 1690, having been born, according to James Boone, on 13 July, a week before.[9] Presumably from the time of the marriage the couple lived in Bradninch. James's dates for the next four children can all be matched with entries in the register of baptisms there. Sarah, born 18 February 1691/2 was baptized 28 March: Squire, born 25 November 1696, baptized 25 December: Mary, born 23 September 1699, baptized 13 October: John, born 3 January 1701/2, baptized 30 January. His dates for the remaining four children, Joseph, born 5 April 1704, Benjamin 16 July 1706, James 7 July 1709, and Samuel, sometime later, can not be corroborated with the registers.[10] This strongly suggests that at some point after the birth of John and before that of Joseph, i.e. between late January 1701/2 and April 1704, George and Mary Boone had begun to count themselves as Quakers, and so ceased to have their children baptized. If this surmise is correct, it is not surprising that George Boone does not appear to have suffered from the penal laws against Friends and others which were repealed in 1689.[11] He became a convert in easier days, yet his problems with drink must have begun fairly soon after.

Some time before 1713 the three eldest children, George, Sarah and Squire, had made their way to Pennsylvania, where George appears to have been married that year.[12] He certainly occurs as a signatory of a letter preserved in Exeter from the Meeting of Men Friends at Abington to the northwest of Philadelphia, held on 31 August 1714 addressed to the Monthly Meeting of Friends at Cullompton.[13] The purpose of that letter was to commend a young man called Thomas Downing son of Thomas Downing of Bradninch. He had apparently left home, as the letter puts it 'from ould England to Pnnsilvania', without parental consent, and was now returning in response to his father's request. Thirty Friends signed the letter; one of them must be the younger George, since his signature is quite distinct from his father's on the document here edited.

The Boones were not the first Quaker settlers in Pennsylvania from villages north of Exeter. The earliest was James Chick, a carpenter, whose former employer asked Cullompton Monthly Meeting for a certificate in December 1683. In 1700 the same body sent statements to America that two members of the Hurford family, formerly living in Tiverton, had no marriage entanglements on this side of the ocean. Nearer still to the Boone's departure, Cullompton Monthly Meeting held at Spiceland in January 1713, provided a certificate for Joanna Meade, an unmarried woman, going westwards. The arrival of all of these people was recorded in Pennsylvania.[14] So the Boones could easily have known something about the conditions they might find.

According to the genealogy, the parents and the rest of the family left Bradninch on 17 August 1717, taking ship from Bristol and arriving in Philadelphia within a relatively short space. James Boone gives the date as 'September 29 Old-Stile, or October 10th New-Stile'. He says that they first went to Abington, the place from which the letter mentioned they had come from, but that very soon they moved to the area known as North Wales so-called because many Welsh Quakers had settled there. This was somewhat to the south of Abington.[15] His story is confirmed by the minutes of Gwynedd Monthly Meeting of 31 December 1717 which record that the older George Boone was there to present a 'certificate of his Good Life and Conversation from the Monthly [Meeting] att *Callumpton*, in Great Britain, which was read and well received'.[16] Such a certificate was a crucial document for any Friend wishing to move to an area where he might be otherwise relatively unknown, for it would at once provide him with a group who would support him and his family. In this particular case the records show how within four months of leaving home George Boone was putting down roots in new soil.

After about two years the family moved to Oley, where Sarah had already gone following her marriage, and there they stayed. This was not far from Reading, to the north of Gwynedd. Other records confirm this account. In 1718 George Boone was able to take possession of 400 acres of land in Oley and three years later petitioned Gwynedd Monthly Meeting to allow Friends in Oley to make their own burial ground at Oley and to build a Meeting House there.[17] In 1725 the Monthly Meeting allowed Oley friends to have their own Preparative Meeting (so-called because it 'prepared' the business for the Monthly Meeting) and next year the first log building for worship was put up.[18] In 1742, the number of settlers had grown to the point where the township had to be divided, and the place where the Boones lived was given the name of Exeter, because, as James Boone put it, 'they came from a Place near the City of Exeter'.

George Boone must have sobered down, since he lived on until 27 July 1744, when he was 78 years old, whilst his wife Mary predeceased him on 2 February, 1740/1, aged 72. Both were buried in the Friends Burial Ground next to the Meeting House, and when he died he had 8 children, 52 grandchildren and 10 great grandchildren. Not for nothing did his grandson comment 'in all 70, being as many Persons as the House of Jacob which came into Egypt [Genesis 47,27]'. It is nice to think that George would have known his grandson Daniel the future explorer of Kentucky, born in Oley in 1734, a son of Squire's. George could not, on the other hand, have known before he died that another grandchild, Ann, sister of the genealogist James, and born in 1737 was to marry into a family with one of the most famous names in American history, for she wed the brother of Abraham Lincoln's grandfather. Boones and Lincolns still lie side by side in the burial ground at Exeter. There we may leave George with an unanswerable riddle in two parts: to what degree did the decision to leave Bradninch and seek new pastures in America arise from a wish to leave behind memories of rowdy evenings in his local hostelry, and how far was his decision to make a clean breast of his wrongdoings to Friends connected with his wish to have a certificate attesting his 'Good Life and Conversation' before he set forth?

Paper, watermarked with a cross in a two-footed cupboard (also found on M120 of 1715): $c.195\,\text{mm} \times 305\,\text{mm}$, written on the front side of a sheet folded in four. Endorsed in roughly contemporary hand 'George Boone's Condemnation'. Two small holes towards top and bottom left for filing. I have not altered either spelling or punctuation since these have their own interest: *tharefore and thareunto*, for example, sound like attempts to express Devon vowels. Dating: Friends numbered the months starting with March, with which the legal year began until the change to New Style in 1753. Twelfth month is therefore February, and the 29th places the letter in 1716, a leap year. George Boone has however also put in 1717, because even before the adoption of the New Style many calculated the year's start from 1 January. The letter, therefore, was written in the February of the very year in which he emigrated, not six months before the family left for Pennsylvania.

DRO, 874 D/M 122

Dear Friends,

being fully sensable of my former transgressions and sins Against God and the Reproach that may and hath com upon truth for such grose Inormities I do tharefore after so long A time mak my humble confssion been compelled thareunto for wont of that true peace which my soul stands in need of, it hath being long laid upon me so to do and I can not pas it by with peace, for which cause to my shame and confusion of face I am constraind to make mention of this my transgression not without grief but with trouble and sorrow of heart for this my wickedness—which was keeping of evill company and drinking by which som times I became gulty of drunkenness to the dishonour of truth and shame to my self, yet to the honour of the Lord, I have thus to say for him he was all wayes with me cheecking and reprouing me for the same ['but' erased] he all wayes followed me with his repruf and his judgment were ['were' erased] in my soul so that trimbling hath taken hold of me many times, so that I haue been ready many times to say lord forgiue me and I hope I will do so no more, yet for wont of true wotchfulness and keeping close to my guide I have fallen into it again, and broken as it were couenant with the lord which was redy to pas it by and forgiue me. so not liuing in obedience to the lord I fell into Another grosse euill ['wh' erased] which I also confess to my great shame and sorow that I did so little regard the loue and tender mercies of the lord. but went on in Another gross sin. by which the honour due unto marage was lost, for the marage bed was defiled, Oh what shall I say lord wash me and clense me I beseech thee from these my great sins, for against thee haue I sinned and against the truth for thou art truth.

    This dear friends after so many years hauing born the indignation of the lord, and haue been as it were shut out of the camp by reson ot the great leprosie [cf. Leviticus 13,46] which did appear upon me I am drawn to make this my humble confession publikly unto you hoping I shall find some comfort and refreshment hear by, for blessed be the name of the lord hee hath not yet forsaken me;

Bradninch 29th of the 12th Month 1716 1717
[signed] George Boone

NOTES

1. I am grateful for help received in the Devon Record Office, the Library of the Society of Friends, Friends House, London, and the Quaker Library at Haverford College, Pennsylvania.
2. William C. Braithwaite, *The Second Period of Quakerism*, Second edition prepared by Henry J. Cadbury (Cambridge, 1961), 297, 301.
3. Braithwaite, *Second Period*, 595–6.
4. Allan Brockett, *Nonconformity in Exeter 1650–1875* (Manchester, 1962), 112.
5. DRO, 874 D/M14.
6. I have checked the microfilms of the registers in the Library at Friends House, London and found no entries for the Boones: the early entries for Cullompton Monthly Meeting are very sparse.
7. Hugh Peskett, *Guide to the Parish and Non-Parochial Registers of Devon and Cornwall 1538–1837*, DCRS, Extra Series II (1979), 220.
8. The original MS, now in the Library of Wisconsin State Historical Society, is reproduced in Hazel A. Spraker, *The Boone Family, a Genealogical History of the Descendants of George and Mary Boone* (Rutland, 1922). I have not seen this, but used an anoymous edition in *The Pennsylvania Magazine of History and Biography*, 21, 1897, 165–70. For James Boone see Amos Day Bradley, 'The mathematical notebooks of James Boone jr', *Scripta Mathematica, 6,* 1939, 219–27.
9. The registers are in the Devon Record Office. George's wife's maiden name is there given as Maggridge.
10. He was confused about Samuel, describing him as the youngest son, but not knowing the date of his birth. When Samuel died in 1745, James says that he was 'aged about 54 years' implying birth in 1691, which would mean birth before nearly all of his brothers and sisters.
11. I have not checked the original records, but note that he does not appear in the summary account provided by Joseph Besse, *Collection of the Sufferings of the People called Quakers, 1650–1689* (1753), i, 146–65.
12. Howard M.Jenkin, *Historical Collections relating to Gwynedd* (2nd ed. Philadelphia, 1897), 369. Jenkin does not cite his evidence, and it is just possible that the marriage occurred in England. If it had done so one would have expected James to have mentioned that George's wife travelled with him.
13. DRO, 874D/M119, dated '31st, VI month'.
14. Albert Cook Myers, *Quaker Arrivals at Philadelphia* (Philadelphia, 1902), 11–12, 27, 62–3. James Chick, or Cheek, was fined for absence from Anglican worship in 1680: Besse, *Sufferings*, i. 162.
15. See the map in H. Larry Ingle, *Quakers in Conflict, the Hicksite Reformation* (Knoxville, 1986), 170.
16. Jenkins, *Gwynedd*, 369, my emphasis.
17. Jenkins, *Gwynedd*, 81.
18. Information from a manuscript history of Philadelphia Yearly Meeting in the Library of Haverford College, Pennsylvania, 75–6. Another wooden house followed in 1736 and the present stone building in 1759.

Christopher Holdsworth

28. Landscape and Farming in the Mid-Nineteenth Century; Extracts from the Tithe Files of Two Moorland Edge Parishes—Holne (Dartmoor) and High Bray (Exmoor)

In August 1836 parliament passed the Tithe Commutation Act which brought to an end the much reviled and anachronistic method of supporting the established church by each farmer paying a tenth of the gross output of his farming enterprise to his local priest.[1] The tithe dues of each tithe district (usually a parish or township) were commuted for a money payment (tithe rent-charge) which was linked to annual changes in the price of wheat, barley and oats. To determine a fair value for the commutation of tithe dues, each district had to be valued to establish the total value of its rent-charge and then surveyed so that this total liability could be distributed (apportioned) among the various property owners. The results of these inquiries and activities are recorded in the well-known and much used tithe maps and apportionments of the mid-nineteenth century.[2] Less well-known and less used are the parish tithe files kept for each tithe district in England and Wales and now preserved in the Public Record Office as Class 1R18. These files contain the local papers generated by the process of commutation: minutes of meetings, copies of notices and, where tithe commutation proceeded by voluntary agreement of land owners and tithe owners rather than by imposition of a compulsory award by the Tithe Commissioners, a report written by one of the Tithe Commission's local agents or assistant tithe commissioners. These take the form of printed 'questionnaires' in which the local agents recorded information on local farming to enable them to assess whether the rent-charge as agreed was fair to both tithe payers and tithe owners. Though some of these reports are based on impressions of livestock numbers and quality and estimates of crop acreages and yields, their value lies in the fact that they were made by men with wide experience of farming practices in different physical environments and economic circumstances. Assistant tithe commissioners were uniquely placed to assess local farming practices in a broader, comparative context. James Jerwood who wrote the two reports from which extracts are printed below, visited some 122 parishes in Devon and wrote a total of 214 reports for the Tithe Commission on farming in Cornwall, Devon, Somerset, Dorset and Wiltshire between 1838 and 1845.[3]

Farming at the margins of cultivation in upland Britain was uncertain and unrewarding for land owners; this comes out clearly in these two descriptions of farming on the edge of Dartmoor and Exmoor respectively. Tithe owners often took a rather more optimistic view of the agricultural potential of such places in an attempt to maximize the amount of rent-charge for which tithe might be commuted. This is what the bishop of Exeter contended in his representations to assistant tithe commissioner James Jerwood during the commutations of Holne and High Bray: that moorland reclamation was both likely in the future and potentially profitable. It is clear that such arguments found little support from the assistant tithe commissioner; indeed what he saw at Holne and High Bray stimulated him to write what are among his most highly coloured, perjorative assessments of the natural productivity of farmland in the whole county.

PRO, 1R18 1323 (Holne)

This is a parish of considerable extent and some of the land would evidently bear improvement, but I am very sure that much of the land which is now occasionally cultivated does not remunerate the farmer for the trouble. At present it would be quite visionary to form my supposition as when any part of the common will be so improved as to affect the tithe owners' interest—I should say never. The bishop remarks that 'the common land is extensive and will be found to be of considerable value in natural productive quality'. The bishop is quite right with regard to extent, but it is not easy to account for the bishop's belief in the value of its 'natural productive quality'—unless stones and sterility be valuable. The common is a continuation of Dartmoor—the farmers allege that during the summer months when portions of the common produce some grass the cattle at that time grazing on Dartmoor enter it like locusts and eat it all up. Its extent renders the probability of its ever being fenced from the forest very small indeed and unless this could be done the landowners assert that the common is absolutely worthless. The common land is quite noted for its wild and romantic scenery, but the scenery alone will not feed cattle, nor would it very well pay were the tithe of it taken in kind.

James Jerwood, 27th July 1838

PRO, 1R18 1326 (High Bray)

Much of the land is not intrinsically very poor; but it is 12 miles from their chief market Barnstaple, and about the same distance from manure—and the roads are hilly. Their principal manure is lime and the cost of manuring an acre with that article is £4 10s. Wheat averages 14 or 15 bushels per acre; take it at 15 bushels and its price 7s per bushel;—an acre is worth £5 5s, the tithe on this is about 10s 6d, so that for the first crop the farmer gets <u>4s 6d</u> per acre <u>and the straw</u> to pay his rent, rates and taxes etc.;—when all these disbursements have been made the remainder, of course, is to remunerate him for his trouble, and may properly be termed the <u>farmer's profits</u> or <u>third rent</u>;—this being the case, they plough only about 12 acres per hundred of the arable. The course of tillage in this parish is the best, but the farmers cannot pay their rents by tilling the land; their chief dependence rests on grazing; the object of landowners, therefore, is to improve the pasture land. The bishop seems to apprehend that the common land may hereafter be cultivated. I have already made some remarks on the cost per acre of the land which has been cultivated in consequence of its distance from lime etc.; the common is still further from it. Plots of land adjoining the common have been broken up but at a dead loss to the farmer;— as pasture it was worth something, but the converting it into arable rendered the land valueless. Unless, therefore, the site of the common could be entirely changed, the great expense that would attend the attempt to make it arable and the utter worthlessness of the land after such a visionary scheme had been carried into effect are quite sufficient, I should suppose, to allay any apprehension of its ever being cultivated.

James Jerwood, 18 October 1838

NOTES

1. R.J.P. Kain and H.C. Prince, *The Tithe Surveys of the Mid-Nineteenth Century* (Cambridge, 1985); E.J. Evans, *The Contentious Tithe: The Tithe Problem and English Agriculture, 1750–1850* (1986).
2. R.J.P. Kain and R.R. Oliver, *The Tithe Maps of England and Wales: A Cartographic Analysis and County-by-County Catalogue* (Cambridge, 1995).
3. R.J.P. Kain, *An Atlas and Index of the Tithe Files of Mid-Nineteenth-Century England and Wales* (Cambridge, 1985), 12, 211–13; R.J.P. Kain, *A Socio-Economic Survey of Land Use: The 1836 National Tithe Files Database* (Marlborough, 1995, handbook and CD ROM disk).

Roger J.P. Kain

29. An Exeter Man Renounces the Freedom of the City, May 1312

The two court extracts translated below recount how Robert Belechere, a member of the élite freedom organization of the city of Exeter, renounced his freedom membership in protest over the borough court's attempt to discipline him for forestalling fish. Although forestalling— the purchase of goods by middlemen before the market opened in order to sell them later—is a common retailing practise nowadays, it was frowned upon in the middle ages because it inevitably raised prices for consumers. Exeter authorities, like civic officials elsewhere in medieval England, tried to discourage the practise by hauling offenders before a judicial inquest and fining them. Unfortunately, Robert Belechere refused to submit to the city's inquest on forestalling, so he was arrested and then convicted not only for withdrawing from the inquest, but also for defaming the Mayor and for causing such a scene in court that the proceedings had to be cancelled. Robert defamed the Mayor by accusing him of making Robert forfeit £100. The exact nature of this forfeit is not made clear, but the amount may have been the value Robert placed on the combined sum he lost from compensating his pledges,[1] paying a fine, the fish he may have forfeited, and the benefits of the freedom membership he no longer possessed. It is, however, also likely that Robert grossly inflated the amount to reinforce how injured he felt by the court's actions. Although Robert's contemptuous behaviour towards the Mayor and the court was punished by the withdrawal of his freedom privileges, the second court extract focuses mainly on Robert's own surrender of these privileges, as indicated by the marginal heading of the extract and by the recitation of Robert's actual words of renunciation. The solemnity of this renunciation was reinforced by the naming of 93 witnesses,[2] a list without precedent in the Exeter court rolls.

The case is interesting for several reasons. For one, it points to the on-going efforts of the Exeter authorities on behalf of consumers to restrict the activities of middlemen who forestalled fish coming to town.[3] The borough court repeatedly declared this practise harmful to both city and county consumers as well as detrimental to 'the estate of the freedom', an accusation that emphasized the freedom's responsibility to guard against this trading offence. The case thus also illustrates how the disciplinary mechanisms at the disposal of the city operated through the city freedom, an exclusive organization whose members enjoyed certain economic, political, and legal privileges; these included the right to trade at retail, toll exemptions, essoining and other prerogatives in the city court, the ability to vote in city elections, and eligibility for the city's top offices.[4]

The list of 93 witnesses attached to the renunciation is also of special interest because it allows us to check the coverage of the earliest freedom entries extant for medieval Exeter, which have been compiled and edited by Margery M. Rowe and Andrew Jackson from enrolments on the dorses of the Mayor's court rolls. Just over half of the witnesses appear in the printed freedom entries: 36 had entered by 1312, the date of the court case (their names are asterisked (*) in the extract printed below), 4 entered in the years after 1312,[5] and another 14 appeared in a context (such as their sons succeeding to freedom membership) that indicates that they also enjoyed freedom membership.[6] An additional

11 do not appear in the surviving freedom entries, but their membership is attested by other evidence, such as the offices they held or their exemption from port customs.[7] This means that at least 70 per cent of the witnesses can be shown to have belonged to the freedom. It is highly likely, moreover, that all of the remaining 28 witnesses were also members of the freedom; many may have appeared in the freedom entries recorded in those Mayor's court rolls which no longer survive, namely the rolls for 1266/7 to 1284/5, and the crucial years of 1292/3 through 1294/5. And some may have never had their entries recorded; we know that as many as 20 per cent of the entries (according to one survey), especially those by succession, were likely to go unrecorded.[8] The witness list is thus also valuable because it identifies a number of otherwise unknown freedom members whose entries were never properly enrolled.

The presence of so many freedom members at the renunciation of Robert Belechere's freedom privileges signals how seriously the freedom treated its responsibilities and role in the governing of the city at this time. Indeed, the witnesses included many of the city's most substantial citizens; no fewer than 44 per cent (41) belonged to the ruling oligarchy, while another 14 per cent (13) held lesser civic offices such as alderman, bailiff, and gatekeeper.[9] At least nine of the witnesses, moreover, were known fishmongers;[10] including them as witnesses to Robert's exclusion from the freedom for forestalling fish would clearly have reinforced the message the city authorities wanted to send.

The effectiveness of the freedom's enforcement, however, was beginning to wane in the early fourteenth century as the population grew and trade became more complex.[11] In 1302, the Mayor's tourn court was introduced; the court assumed jurisdiction over market-related infringements, but increasingly dealt with trading offences like forestalling by charging offenders a small annual fine that became tantamount to a licensing fee.[12] Certainly the freedom's effectiveness in halting Robert Belechere's forestalling activities met with only limited success since Robert continued to be presented and fined for forestalling fish.[13] In fact, Robert must have been readmitted to the freedom because he served in the office of city elector in 1324 and 1325, a position for which freedom membership was a prerequisite. Robert's wealth and position in Exeter most likely eased his way back into acceptance. In the 1327 and 1332 lay subsidies, for example, Robert ranked among the city's top 15 per cent of taxpayers, while his activities as a wine importer also point to his substantial commercial position.[14] This same wealth and position in the city were also what probably allowed Robert to rebuff the city's inquest and claim that he did not need the freedom; his renunciation has the ring of a rich and confident man who felt he had little to lose by turning his back on the city's primary economic and political institution. While his actions could be interpreted as those of an especially provocative character, they may also hint at the declining prestige and power of the freedom organization in Exeter at a time when the city's population and trade were growing.[15]

I. DRO, Exeter Mayor's Court Roll 1311/12, m. 30d (22 May 1312)

Robert Belechere, Alured de Crydyton, Walter Broun and William Vyke were attached to answer why, against the estate of the freedom of the city of Exeter and to the grave damage of the whole Commonalty of Exeter and the whole county of Devon, they went outside the city in order to intercept fishers bringing fish to the said city to sell and purchased this fish by forestalling the proper hour and location so that they made the fish more expensive in the city than the fishers would have if the fish were still in their hands. And the said William Wyke does not come so he is distrained, etc.[16] And the said Robert Belechere, Alured, and Walter come and say that they never purchased any fish coming to the city by means of forestalling the sanctioned hour and location except in the proper way and with respect to what is permitted to them according to the use and custom of the city, and regarding this they submit to an inquisition. And the said Robert Belechere, opposing this charge, withdrew after he had submitted to the inquisition, so his pledges for standing for the inquiry, Thomas Nottegrey and Gilbert de Nymet, are in mercy etc.[17] And because of his default he is to be arrested for an inquest. And the jurors, namely Henry Potel, Walter de Radeslo, Gilbert de Toryton, Richard le Grant, John Busse, William Bouffet, Adam le Spycer, Walter Sqwyer, Richard de Spaxton, William de Carswell, Thomas le Barber and Ralph de Nywton mercer, say on their oath that the aforesaid Robert, Alured and Walter Broun are forestallers for buying fish outside the proper hour and location, against the estate of the freedom, etc.. So the liberties of Alured and Walter are taken into the hands of the Mayor, etc.. And the aforesaid Robert is distrained so he may be judged before the Mayor because he left before the inquisition was taken, in contempt of the court. And the jurors, asked if there were other forestallers, say on their oath that William Vyke, William Chapel, Roger de Berbylaunde, Richard de Ellehey, Roger de Henton, Maurice Fisshare, Nicholas le Hopere, Walter Pylche, Robert Page and John Berepouwe similiarly are forestallers of fish. So they are attached that they may respond before the Mayor.[18]

II. DRO, Exeter Mayor's Court Roll, 1311/12, m. 31d (29 May 1312)
Renunciation of the Freedom of Robert Belechere[19]

Robert Belechere was attached to respond to the Mayor and Commonalty because, in the last court session, in the presence of the lords Dean, Precentor, and Archdeacon of Exeter, and Archdeacon of Totnes and other worthy persons, he falsely charged the Mayor of unjustly making Robert forfeit £100, in clear defamation of the Mayor and in contempt of the court. And also in answering to this, that the same Robert, whose disorder incited many from the Commonalty and inflicted various outrages in contempt of the Mayor and of the whole Commonalty, upset and disturbed the court itself so much that the court had to totally cease and the crown pleas, which should have been settled at that time, were left to be decided, to the injury of the freedom of the city of Exeter and to the great detriment and harm of the whole Commonalty.

And the aforesaid Robert comes and, when questioned and interrogated if he concealed from the said Mayor and said Commonalty the aforesaid outrages and troublesome disturbance and whether it is fitting for him to make amends for contempt, says absolutely no repeatedly, in contempt of the Mayor of the whole Commonalty and of the court; at first accused by the Mayor, now in open court he falsely and maliciously with wilful defamation accuses the Mayor rather than clearing himself of contempt for these other charges. So, according to the custom of the court, freedom members are forbidden ever to buy from him or to sell to him within the freedom or for him to use his freedom in any way until he clears himself etc. Robert, however, comes and says that this sort of prohibition is not in any way necessary for his freedom; so he says, 'I surrender the freedom which I have in this city from you the lord Mayor and Commonalty, claiming nothing from the same in the future', in the presence of those written below: Roger Beyvyn, William de Gatepath, Thomas de Langedon clerk, Thomas Fartheyn, Oliver de la Spynee,* John Dyrwyne, William de Carswell,* John le Perour,* Philip Denebaud,* William le Keu of Bridford, John de Smalecombe,* Peter Soth, Robert de Doune, Matthew Skinner [Pellipario], William Skinner* [Pellipario] of Northyetestret [Northgate Street], Ralph de Nyweton* cordwainer, Pagan le Bruere,* Walter Sqwyer, Henry Potel,* John Davyd, Walter Jugement, James Prudomme, Richard Caperun, John Gerveis, Geoffrey Strange, Henry Lovecok, Joel de Bradecrofte, Walter de Radeslo,* Geoffrey Cobyn, Henry Knyght,* Walter Broun,* Robert Knyght,* John Garlaund, Alured de Cridyton,* John Tug, Robert Pees,* William Corvyset,* John le Ercediakene,* Walter Seward, Henry de Gatepathe,* Gilbert de Nimet,* Robert le Parchemener, Thomas Nottegrei, William Vyke,* Walter Fartheyn, William Hamelyn, Ralph de Porte,* Thomas le Spycer, John David cordwainer, Jordan le Smyth, William de Cadycote,* Richard of Tyverton,* Robert Holye, Walter de Asschebrutel, Gregory de Metton, Robert le Taverner, John Palmere* baker, Richard Russel, Henry le Gurdlere, Alured de Chuddeleye, John de Fenton,* Thomas le Barber, Richard de Elleueheye, Elias Hardy, Thomas atte Porche, Richard Fos,* Nicholas de Betteburghe,* Robert Rogemound, Richard de Spaxton,* Walter Plente,* Thomas Pyleman, Robert Busse, Robert Pees,[20] William[21] Botour, John le Whetene, William Classh, John le Gurdlere, Thomas Wysdom, Roger de Langacre, Henry de Wyndesore, Walter atte More, John Horn junior,* Walter Persoun,* John le Yunge, Nicholas le Skynnere, Nicholas Waleis,* Thomas Britoun, John Soth junior,* Roger Kympe, Roger le Mercer,* Richard le Mey, Peter Beyvyn,* John Berepouwe,* William atte Welle[22] le Skynner and others then present there. And because the same Robert relinquishes his freedom[23] freely and willingly to the same Mayor and Commonalty it is decided that he should be wholly excluded from all benefits and profits henceforth arising in the future.[24]

NOTES

1. His two pledges were fined when Robert failed to show up at the inquest; it was not uncommon in such instances for the pledges to sue the defendant for the cost of the fine and damages.
2. The list includes the names of 94 witnesses, but Robert Pees was named twice.
3. The endemic problem of fish forestallers in Exeter is discussed in Maryanne Kowaleski, *Local Markets and Regional Trade in Medieval Exeter* (Cambridge, 1995), 307–10. For the general problem of forestalling, a common practise of middlemen, see Richard Britnell, 'Forstall, Forestalling and the Statute of Forestallers', *English Historical Review*, 102 (1987), 89–102.
4. Margery M. Rowe and Andrew Jackson (eds), *Exeter Freemen 1266–1967*, DCRS, extra series 1 (1973), xviii–xx; Kowaleski, *Local Markets*, 95–104.
5. Richard Caperun in 1313, Walter More in 1314, Walter Fartheyn in 1322, and Thomas le Barber in 1328.
6. Rowe and Jackson, *Exeter Freemen*, 1–25, *passim*. William de Gatepath, Matthew Skinner, John Davyd, Henry Lovecok, Joel de Bradecrofte, Thomas le Spycer, Robert le Taverner, Richard Russel, and Henry de Wyndesore had sons who entered the freedom by succession or at the instance of their father. The following were also clearly members since they sponsored other candidates for membership: Thomas Fartheyn, Peter Soth, Walter Jugement, William Hamelyn, Thomas atte Porche.
7. Those holding the offices of elector or above had to belong to the freedom (Kowaleski, *Local Markets*, 101–03); the municipal elections were enrolled annually on the dorses of the first membranes of the Mayor's court rolls. Those holding these offices but not named in the freedom entries are William le Keu of Bridford, Robert de Doune, Walter Sqwyer, John Gerveis, Geoffrey Strange, Henry le Gurdlere, and Robert Rogemound. Importers who paid no port customs and were not named in the extant freedom entries are John Dyrwyne, Elias Hardy, John le Yunge, and Nicholas le Skynnere; see Maryanne Kowaleski (ed.), *The Local Customs Accounts of the Port of Exeter, 1266–1321*, DCRS, N.S. 36 (1993).
8. Rowe and Jackson, *Exeter Freemen*, xiv.
9. The annual election returns were recorded on the dorses of the first two membranes of each Mayor's court roll. For the hierarchy of offices in the oligarchy see Kowaleski, *Local Markets*, 101–04.
10. John Berepouwe, William Botour, Walter Broun, Richard Caperun, Alured de Cridyton, Richard Ellenheye, Roger Kympe, William Vyke, and Henry de Wyndesore.
11. Rowe and Jackson, *Exeter Freemen*, xiii; Kowaleski, *Local Markets*, 180–95, 338–9.
12. The early lists of forestallers of fish were similar to those translated here; they rarely included more than ten names, the charges were recited in some detail, presentments occurred more than once a year, and fines could be stiff. By the late fourteenth century, however, the lists typically included 50 or more names, the charges were limited to a short formulaic statement and presented only once a year, and the fines were standardized at about 3d each.
13. DRO, Exeter Mayor's court rolls 1323/4, m. 8d; 1324/5, m. 4d; 1328/9, m. 2d.
14. He paid 5s in 1327, when only 13 of 84 taxpayers paid more; see PRO E179/95/6. In 1332, he paid 6s 8d, an amount surpassed by only 13 of 119 Exeter taxpayers; see Audrey M. Erskine (ed.), *The Devonshire Lay Subsidy of 1332*, DCRS, N.S. 14 (1969), 109–10. He also imported wine on two occasions, another indication of his wealth and commerical activity; see Kowaleski, *Local Customs*, 114, 118.
15. Kowaleski, *Local Markets*, 81–6, 92, 238–45.
16. *Monday, distrained* is written in the right-hand margin at this point.
17. *in mercy, 6d* is written in the right-hand margin at this point.

18. *Monday, attached* is written in the right-hand margin at this point.
19. This heading is written in large letters in the right hand margin at the top of the entry.
20. This is the second time Robert Pees is recorded in the list.
21. *Robert* is crossed out and *William* inserted above.
22. *atte Welle* is inserted above the line after *William*.
23. *his freedom* is written above the line.
24. *Judgment* is written in large letters in the right-hand margin across from the last two lines.

Maryanne Kowaleski

30. A Dutch Officer in Moretonhampstead, c.1807

Among a collection of papers presented to the Exeter City Library in 1935 are four letters written in the mid nineteenth century by a Monsieur Bronovo of Hellwort Sluys in Holland to John Ponsford of Moretonhampstead. The third and fourth letters describe Bronovo's life in Holland, but the first two contain his reminiscences of Moretonhampstead and paint a vivid picture of his life as a prisoner on parole during the Napoleonic Wars. At the time of his capture, Bronovo was a lieutenant in the Dutch Royal Navy, and was fighting against the British because Napoleon's brother Louis was then king of Holland. Bronovo's first letter is dated 7th March 1847 and was sent to Moretonhampstead in the hope that some of his old friends would still be alive and remember him. The letter was answered by John Ponsford, the agent responsible for the prisoners, and Bronovo's subsequent letters are addressed to him.

In the forty years between his capture and the writing of the first letter, Bronovo had a successful career and a happy family life. After his departure from Moretonhampstead, he travelled to the Dutch colony of Surinam where he married a young widow whom he had known from his school days. They returned to Holland where they had two children, a boy and a girl, and eventually Bronovo was appointed Colonel, and Director of the Navy. His wife, 'my dear Betsy', died in 1840 and possibly this event, and his own approaching old age, led him to reminisce with affection about the time he had spent in Moretonhampstead as young man.

The letters reveal that this brief period was a particularly happy time for him. He fitted easily into the social life of the younger inhabitants of the town and he certainly enjoyed flirting with the local girls. Possibly, living in an English town as a complete stranger gave him a freedom which he would not have enjoyed at home. Although Bronovo mentions that restrictions were placed on the movements of the Dutch officers, these do not seem to have been rigorously applied, and he enjoyed acting in pantomimes, excursions into the surrounding countryside and even trips to Exeter. He names about thirty other Dutch officers who were on parole in Moretonhampstead with him, and such a number, with the French officers as well, must have made a big impact on a small Devon town. However, only one of the Dutch men, Papendrecht, known as Papie, is, said to have 'made very much trouble in the Town', due to his liking for grog and his visits to the Red Lion. For officers willing to socialize with the local people, time must have passed pleasantly enough; otherwise, there was only alcohol to relieve the boredom and frustration. The following is an extract from that first letter of 7th March 1847. I have retained Bronovo's spellings, but altered his punctuation where the text seems to require it.

DRO, unnumbered letters in Misc. papers, accounts & letters relating to DD 35399-643, Box 6665

My Dear Friends!

Nearly forty years ago, a young Leutenant about 19 years of age, belonging to the Dutch Royal Navy, was on his parole prisonier, at *Moreton Hampstaed Devonschire*, his name was Bronovo, he got his rooms at the house of Mr Pearce opposit tot the Union Inn, farmer Scott. He engraved his name with large letters on the panis of the little parlour. He was acting in the Pantomimes as Arlequin, and his Colombine was the nice Susan Soper. D'ont some one of the familly, or other famillies, at *Moreton Hampstaed*, yet in live, remember him; That Gentleman am I.

Houw often, dit I think to my good freinds of *Moreton Hampstaed*, and spoke of them Hundred tims a year, I recollectet the many Civilites I received there of the Lovely family Ponsfort, and others, what trouble we caused to the most gallent Sir John Ponsfort[1] our Agent, and how Gentiel he resed us always, showing his noble character, truly we should be very ungratefull, for ever forgithing such behaviour.

Since that time, I have passed twelve times the Britisch Chanel, and always I wished, that the Wind would oblige me to run in to Plymouth, only with the prospect, to go at *Moreton Hampstaed*, too see my good freinds, but alas, all tims fair wind. Very often, too I intended to make a Journey, but various Circonstancis dit prevent it. Nevertheless, I was still curious to Know some thing about my old freinds of whom I suppos, a great many will alreaydy have left this world.

One of our Steam Vessels, is going to Falmouth, and I profit of that opportunity, to give you some Informations about me. I hope that one or other of my good freinds, will do me the pleasure to answer me. To show you that I remember all what passed in the time I was at *Moreton Hampstaed*, I'll ask you How is Miss Betsy Brock, they told me she was married to a Navy Captain, is she Happy, I wish such may be the Case, she was a nice Creature, and Certainly will be a good woman for her husband, and a good mother for her Children, when she is still alive, ask her of she remembers, that by my taking leave of her, she said

>   Hark I hear my father storming
>   Hark I hear my Mother sigh
>   I must go farewell for Ever
>   Graces be they god ally

How are William, and George Brock,[2] Do Dey remembre our hunting party. How is the good and amaible family Potekim,[3] are they all happy! How is Miss Mary Ponsford, and her younger sister,[4] she was always Gentil, and kind. How is Mr Luc Ponsford. How is Mr en Misses Marten; they treatet all the Gentlemens so most Civil. How is Miss Mary Ann Whitfeld, How is Miss Mary Brechemont,[5] How is Mr en Misses Winshed, and Misses Cristoffels. I rember, how we made sweet hay, and the agreable nut day with Capt. van der Zonde; our Journey at Blake Stone Rock, our walk to the factory and our Mille Stone,[6] which I then, very often forgot, but the good Mr J.Ponsford, never made any reflection. Frequently my Dear Mr Ponsford, I was at Exeter, and though you Knew it, you never take notice of it. We did not Care if the Boys Cried us, Gentlemens mind your quarters. When the prissonners bel was ringing, you meet us upon the street, and it was all well. How are all the girls who were playing in the Pantomimes, Susan Supper, Mary Osborn, Saley!!, Mary Sheers. How is it gone with Miss S.Bath, and Mother and Capt. Johnson, are they married—at last, How is the Daughter of the methodist Clergemen, she got a pretty figure, is t'not! She frequented much Mr and Miss Martin s'houze, you will remember her. Is the sentry on his own place. I remember there was in the neighbourghood a Corn field, one Day the Cryer of the town, was Crying out— Gentlemen are request, to not spoil the Corn by night. I Remember the song in the Church, and the Clergeman whit al his Dogs, arrived whit spurs on his boots in to Church—and the old Cryer; Crying Amen.

How is Mr Alewyn and his wife,[7] at the White Hart! How is our Hankok.[8] I was very often in to that butifull tree befour his Door—and how is the good Mr and Misses Paerce. I was there all the time I was at *Moreton Hampstaed*. The Child she got at that time, shall be at present a man or woman of 41 years.[9] How long, and what there is not happened since that time. How many left us since—our Theater was I beleve, at Mis Harvy. Is she alive. How goes the Bookshop, and is the Daughter Suse I beleve, alive—and married. I never Heard of Hubert who married Miss Tar. Is he alive, or not. Tell to Mr Parce that I meet a Dutch Major of our Army, Mr Du Pui, who has told me, that he lodget in my room, and read my name on the Windows. I read in the English Papers that the fire[10] made a great Confusion at *Moreton Hampstaed*. I hope, it has done not much harem, nor Caused great Loss, for I always wished the best for that Town, where I enjoyed so much pleasirs. I meet here with a Leutenant of the English Navy Called Smith, who was in 1808 at the Bording School of Mr Tukker. How de matters in General go at *Moreton Hampstaed*, are the peoples Confortable or not. I hope they may be happy, is there some trade or other bussnis. Pray, give my best well wishes to all those who remember me.

NOTES

1. John Ponsford, eldest son of William Ponsford, a Moretonhampstead surgeon, and Ann his wife, neé Luke.
2. William and George Bragg. William married Mary Ponsford, John's sister.
3. James Puddicombe, another Moretonhampstead surgeon.
4. Ann Ponsford, died 1836, aged 40.
5. Mary Bridgeman.
6. The mile stone, beyond which prisoners should not go.
7. James and Mary Alway.
8. John Hancock, landlord of the Dolphin Inn.
9. The only Pearce baptism recorded in the parish register at this time is that of Mary, on 15.2.1808. If this is the right child, the implication is that Bronovo had left Moretonhampstead before February 1808.
10. The fire of 1845.

Susan Laithwaite

31. A Common Culture?: The Inventory of Michael Harte, Bookseller of Exeter, 1615

The inventory of Michael Harte of Exeter is that of a substantial provincial bookseller of the early seventeenth century.[1] It is one of only thirteen recorded for English provincial towns outside Oxford and Cambridge during the seventeenth century and, as both were of a similar size, it invites comparison with that of John Foster of York compiled the following year. But while Foster had succeeded to a well-established York business run by his uncle Anthony, Harte was the son of an Exeter shoemaker and went to London to learn his trade.[2] He was apprenticed to John Windet, citizen and stationer of

London on 29 September 1585 and was turned over to Andrew Maunsell and then to Robert Dexter when he succeeded Maunsell at the sign of the Brazen Serpent in about 1590. He was admitted freeman of the Stationers Company on 5 October 1592 and the following year his name appeared in the imprint of George Gifford's *Dialogue concerning witches and witchcraft*. However he soon after returned to Exeter, becoming a freeman of Exeter by succession on 31 December 1593. He obtained a licence dated 20 November 1596 to marry Rebecca Harding and the wedding took place on 16 January 1596/7 in the church of St Petrock. His business was in the parish of St Martin where he is recorded in subsidies from 1595 onward. Two children are recorded in the parish register of St Martin: Joan, baptized on 7 October 1600 and Michael, baptized on 15 December 1601. One apprentice is also recorded: John Moungwell, who became a freeman of Exeter in 1604/5 and was one of those who drew up Harte's inventory in 1615. As Moungwell was active as a bookseller in his own right until the 1650s, one can therefore place some credence in the values assigned to the stock. Harte's burial is recorded in the registers of St Martin for 12 November 1615. The inventory was drawn up for the Exeter Court of Orphans on 9 December 1615. Michael's son, also named Michael, was subsequently free of the city on 2 December 1622 but is not recorded as an active member of the book trade.[3]

One could wish that John Moungwell, John Warren and George Prouze had not lost interest in listing individual titles so soon. In the case of the York inventory some three quarters of the 3373 copies listed can be individually identified, a total of some 750 different titles. Nevertheless some analysis is possible and some comparisons can be drawn. In the following paragraphs figures for Foster's inventory are given in parentheses.

For statistical purposes the parcels of books in Harte's inventory have been assumed to contain ten items each, a reasonable estimate based on comparison of prices. With this assumption we arrive at a total of 4558 volumes for Harte's stock (Foster 3373) with a total value of £103 8s 2d (Foster £144 16s 4d), 71 per cent of the total value of the inventory including household goods, which amounted to £165 14s 11d (Foster 88 per cent of £163/15/8d). Rather more than half the number, 2572 volumes, were shelved in the shop, although their value at £47 was less than half the total value of his stock. The most valuable items, a total of 923 volumes assessed at £44 7s 6d, including all those individually listed, were stored in the hall, while the remaining 1063, worth a mere £12·8d were in the warehouse. A fuller analysis is given in table 1.

Table 1. Numbers and value of Harte's stock by location and format

	Hall Vol	Value			Warehouse Vol	Value			Shop Vol	Value			Total Vol	Value		
Folios	56	14	5	2	53	1	10	0	136	12	10	0	245	28	5	2
Quartos	230	18	1	8	400	6	10	0	247	7	10	0	877	32	1	8
Octavos	560	11	0	1	590	3	10	0	1035	15	12	4	2185	30	2	4
12s & 16s	0			0	0			0	323	3	10	0	323	3	10	0
Misc.	77	1	0	8	20	0	10	8	831*	7	17	8	928	9	9	0
Totals	923	44	7	6	1063	12	0	8	2572	47	0	0	4558	103	8	2

* Excludes maps.

Like Foster, Harte also undertook bookbinding and his equipment, worth 12s 2d (Foster £8 6s 6d) was stored in the shop. Perhaps because of the more perfunctory nature of Harte's inventory, his volumes, at an average unit value of 5.4d, were consistently valued much lower than Foster's (10.3d), although full comparisons are difficult because of the different forms of binding, whether gilt, vellum, stitched or in quires, but the different sizes and unit values of the various formats of stock in the two inventories are best summarized in the following table. Prices are given in old pence.

Table 2. Proportions of volumes and value of Harte's stock by format with unit values.

Format	Volumes Per cent Harte	Foster	Value Per cent Harte	Foster	Unit value Old pence Harte	Foster
Folio	5.4	4.4	27.3	30.1	27.7	70.6
Quarto	19.2	19.5	31.0	30.0	8.8	15.9
Octavo	47.9	60.8	29.1	29.3	3.3	5.0
12s & 16s	7.1	10.5	3.4	8.3	2.6	8.1
Miscellaneous	20.4	4.8	9.2	2.3	2.4	4.8
Total/average	100.0	100.0	100.0	100.0	5.4	10.3

The currency of Harte's stock is difficult to assess as the dates of the editions are not recorded. In the identifications in table 3 the date of the latest editions recorded by the *Short-title catalogue*[4] before Harte's death are given. It would seem that editions of about two thirds of the titles which can be identified had appeared in the five years before

Harte's death. Over that period only about 2331 titles are recorded as having been published in Great Britain in the *Short-title catalogue*.[5] With a stock of 4558 volumes, even if many, such as psalms and schoolbooks, are duplicates Harte should have had a wide-ranging and up-to-date stock, perhaps some 1000 different titles, if duplication is similar to Foster's. There is a little evidence of foreign books such as the Galen (item 1), the Pineda (item 11), the Caesarius (item 17), the Hebrew Bible (item 26) and a parcel of French books (item 66) but Foster too only had seven per cent of continental books. There are also several entries referring to old books (items 1, 21, 43, 46-48, 65, 71 and 77).

Harte's subject coverage would seem to be broadly similar to Foster's. Religious works figure large, with prayer books, psalms and commentaries on the Bible. Religious works made up 28.8 per cent of Forster's stock. Schoolbooks both old and new are listed in Harte's inventory (items 42, 43 and 70), and this is a category which made up 27.8 per cent of Foster's stock. Of the 30 titles that can be identified in Harte's inventory, almost half find probable counterparts in Foster's stock.

So are we talking about a common culture? While there is much in common, there is some suggestion of a difference in emphasis. Harte's stock shows a significant interest in other countries in the histories of Spain, France and Venice. As well as the French dictionary there are translations of Montaigne and La Primaudaye. Perhaps this reflects an interest in foreign lands generated by Exeter's position as a major port. The contrast can perhaps be epitomized by the works of Thomas Blundeville in each inventory. While Foster stocks his work on horsemanship,[6] Harte's inventory lists his *Exercises* which, in its second part, contains a description of Mercator's globes and Drake's circumnavigation. Harte seems to be responding to a community which, while it shared much with the rest of the country, nevertheless maintained some cultural distinctiveness.

Table 3. Notes on the first 37 items (* indicates the same or similar title in Foster's inventory, STC refers to the *Short-title catalogue* number, and BLC to the British Library catalogue.)

Item	Title	STC no
1.*?	Galen. No folio English editions noted in STC. Quarto editions 1521–85	11531–7
2.*	Willet, Andrew. *Synopsis papismi*. 4th ed. 1613	25699
3.	Mayerne, Turquet Louis de. *The generall historie of Spaine*. 1613	17747

Table 3 *continued.*

Item	Title	STC no
4.	The historie of France. The four first bookes. 1595	11276
5.	Fougasses, Thomas de. The general history of Venice. 1612	11207
6.	Greenham, Richard. The works. 5th ed. 1612	12318
7.*	Babington, Gervase. The workes. 1615.	1077–8
8.*	Willet, Andrew. An harmonie upon the first [second] booke of Samuel. 1614.	25679–80
9.	Willet, Andrew. Hexapla: that is a six-fold commentarie upon the epistle to the Romanes. 1611.	25690
10.	Cotgrave, Randal. A dictionarie of the French and English tongues. 1611	5830
11.	Pineda, Joannes ed. ... ad suos in Salomonem commentarios ... New ed. Mainz, 1613.	BLC
12.	Bible (insufficient detail to identify)	—
13.*?	Jewel, John. Works. 1611	14580
14.*?	Vermigli, Pietro Martire. (Various folio editions 1564–83)	24667–72
15.	Walther, Rudolph. (Title not apparent in STC, Prof D.R. Woolf suggests 25013)	
16.*	Dallington, Sir Robert. Aphorisms civill and militarie. 1613	6197
17.*	Caesarius, Joannes. Dialectica (or other continental editions on rhetoric)	BLC
18.	Bodin, Jean. The six bookes of a commonweale. 1606.	3193
19.*	Montaigne, Michel de. Essayes written in French. 1613	18042
20–25.	(Insufficient detail)	
26.	Bible. Hebrew (no English edition traced in STC, various continental eds.)	BLC
27.	Zanchius, Hieronymus. Speculum christianum. 1614. Octavo edition.	26121a7?
28.*?	Ursinus, Zacharias. Summe of christian religion. 1611.	24537
29.	Smith, Henry. Sermons. Quarto. 1614.	22729
30.	Cowper, William. Three heavenly treatises upon the eight chapter to the Romanes. Octavo. 1612	5936
31.*	King, John. Lectures upon Jonas delivered at Yorke ... 1594. 1611	14979
32.*	Marlorat, Augustine. Propheticae. 1574.	17409
33.*	La Primaudaye, Pierre. The French academie. 1601, 1605	15239–40
34.	Blundeville, Thomas. Exercises. 4th ed. 1613.	3149
35.	Downame, John. The christian warfare. 2nd ed. 1608.	7134
36.	Downame, George. Defence of the sermon preached at the consecration of the Bishop of Bath. 1611.	7115
37.*	Dod, John & Cleaver, Robert. Briefe explanation of the whole booke of the proverbes of Salomon. 1615.	5378

DRO, ECA/Book144, 129–34

The Inventory of all the goods of Michaell Hart deceased taken and appraised the Nynth day of December 1615 by John Mongwill John Warren and Georg Prouz sen

Bookes in the Hall

1	*First* 1 gallens Workes in fo old	xxv s
2	it 2 Willetts Sinopses in fo:	xxvi s
3	it 2 Spannishe histories in fo:	xxiiii s
4	it 1 French historie in fo:	xi s
5	it 1 History of Venys in fo:	vii s
6	it iii Greenhams Workes in fo:	xviii s
7	it 1 Babintons Workes in fo:	vii s vi d
8	it 1 Willett vppon Samuell in fo	iiii s vi d
9	it ii Willetts vppon the Romans	xi s
10	it 1 French Dixsnary in fo:	vi s vi d
11	it 1 Penedam in Solimomons	vii s
12	it 1 Church bible	xxx s
13	it 2 Jewells workes in fo	xxiiii s
14	it iii wolloms of Peeter Marters workes in fo:	xiii s iiii d
15	it 1 gualter uppon the Corinthes	v s
16	it 1 Dallingtons Aphorismes in fo:	iiii s
17	it 2 Sezaries ii wolloms in fo:	x s
18	it 1 Boddyms Derepublica in fo:	iiii s
19	it 1 Tagnes Esses in fo	iiii s
20	it 27 old fo: bookes	xl s
21	it 1 old latten bible in 6 parts	iii s iiii d
22	it 12 peecs & v perfitt bookes	x s
23	it 60 books in 4°	vii li x s
24	it 40 bookes in 4°	iii li
25	it 100 bookes in 4°	iiii li iii s iiii d
26	it 1 Hebrew bible in 4°	vi s
27	it 1 Zanchy Tractacions in 4°	iiii s
28	it ii Vrcineus Catthesme in 4°	ix s
29	it 1 Smithes Sermons whole	v s
30	it 1 Cooper vppon the Romans	iiii s vi d
31	it 3 king vppon Jonas in 4°	vii s vi d
32	it 1 Maloonett vppon the profitts	iii s vi d
33	it 1 second & 3 parts of the French Ackedemea	iiii s
34	it iii Blundivills exercises 4°	vii s vi d
35	it ii xpian warfares 2 & 3 parts	v s vi d
36	it iii Downhams Defenses in 4°	iiii s vi d
37	it ii Dod vppon proverbes in 4°	iiii s
38	it ix books in 4°	xiii s iiii d
39	it 200 bookes in 8° in parchemt	v li

40	it 20 bookes in 8° in parchemt	xx s
41	it 160 bookes smale in viii°	xx s
42	it 60 new schoole bookes in viii°	xl s
43	it 120 old schoole bookes in viii°	xl s
44	it 40 small stitch bookes	vi s viii d
45	it 2 bundles of Stitch bookes	iiii s
	Sum	xlv li is vi d

The bookes in the warehouse behynd the Shoppe

46	*First* 53 old bookes in fo:	xxx s
47	it 100 old bookes in iiii°	xxx s
48	it 100 old bookes in viii°	x s
49	it 30 bundles of Stitch books 4°	v li
50	it 1 parcell of psalmes & geneoligy	v s
51	it 1 parcell of unperfit bookes & waste papers	v s viii d
52	it 49 bundells of stitch bookes in viii°	iii li
	Sum	xii li viii d

The bookes in the Shopp

53	*First* 20 bookes in fo	iii li x s
54	it 64 bookes in fo	vi li viii s
55	it 52 bookes in fo	lii s
56	it 100 bookes in iiii°	xlvi s viii d
57	it 1 shelfe Cont 80 bookes in viii°	xxvi s viii d
58	it 340 bookes in viii°	iii li
59	it 40 bookes in viii°	xl s
60	it 50 bookes in viii°	xv s
61	it 100 bookes in 4°	v li
62	it 147 bookes in iiii°	l s
63	it 100 bookes in viii°	xxxiii s iiii d
64	it 260 bookes in viii°	xliii s iiii d
65	it 2 old lating bibles	ii s
66	it 1 parcell of French books	x s
67	it 400 bookes in a presse	l s
68	it160 bookes in viii°	iiii li x s
69	it 310 bookes	l s
70	it 18 School books	xii s viii d
71	it 143 old books in 16°	xx s
72	it 5 prayer books gilt over	viii s
73	it 5 bookes in viii° veller and filts	iiii s
74	it 27 bookes veller and filts	xviii s
75	it 16 bookes in xii°	xx s
76	it 164 books in xii°	xxx s
77	it a parcell of old Mapps	xii d
78	it a parcell of wast paper	ii s

79	it 54 Stitch bookes in the Chest	v s
80	it 4 unperfitt & one perfit psalmes in quiers	ii s
81	it 1 old parchmt S[kin?] and a Shepes Skynn	iiii s
82	it for Inkhornes and quill	sxii d
83	it 2 pr of old Skales	xviii d
84	it 1 nest of boxes 2 old deskes	iii s iv d
85	it in Claspes bosses & pots of brasse	xviii d
86	it the Chest in the Shopp	x s
87	it 1 Cutten presse wth the plow	iiii s vi d
88	it 1 presse pynn of Iron	viii d
89	it 1 Sowing presse	xviii d
90	it for the Shelves in the Shopp	x s
91	it for the borde of thenterclose behind the Shopp	ii s
	Sum	li li xix s viii d

The houshold stuffe in the kitchin

First 95 li of pewter	iii li iii s iiii d
it 28 li of Brasse	xviii s viii d
it 2 little brasse potts	v s
it 1 morter	viii d
it 1 warming pann	iii s
it 2 old brasse Skeends and ii brasse ladles	xx d
it 2 Andirons with brasse Topps	iii s
it 1 Dryping pann	ii s
it 5 broches	iiii s
it 1 litle pr of Andirons & two pair of Doggs	ii s vi d
it 2 pr of pott hooks 4 Crooks	iii s
it 1 old pr of Tongs & a fleshook	ix d
it a parcell of old Iron	xii d
it 1 Amery	vi s viii d
it 1 parcell of Cloame & Cupps	iiii s
it for Trenchers Trencherkniffes & two Rolers	ii s
it 4 Timber boales	iii s
it 1 beating hammer & a stoane	ii s
it 2 litle Table bords	iiii s
it for Shelves windowes & bords	vi s
Sum	vi li xvi s iiii d

In the litle Buttery

First 1 old Amery	ii s vi d
it in wooden vessell	ii s vi d
it 1 old Chare	vi d

it for thenterclose of the
  Buttery & the Shelves   x s
it 2 Dores   ii s
  Sum   xvii s vi d

Household stuffe in the Hall

Item one Cubbord   xv s
it 1 latten basen & Ewer   xv s
it 4 glasses 1 little erthen pott   xii d
it 5 pictures & a mapp   vi s viii d
it 1 Galleaver with a Flask &
  Titch box & a Dagg without lock
  or Snappance   vi s viii d
it iii Chares iii low stooles   ix s
it 6 Joyne stooles   v s
it 1 Stayne Clothe   iiii s
it 5 green Cushins   iiii s
  Sum   lvi s iiii d

In the Chamber over the Hall

Item one Tablebord   iii s iiii d
it 1 wecker Chare   xii d
it 1 Trunke   iii s iiii d
it 1 great Trunk Chest   vi s viii d
it 1 bedd ii bolsters 4 pillowes   iii li ii s iii d
it 1 Old Doust bed 1 pr of blancketts   viii s
it 1 bed ii bolsters 1 pyllow
  of Flox   xiii s iiii d
it 1 old Arris Coidlitt 1 Arris
  Carpett   iiii s vi d
it 2 other old Coidlitts   iii s
it 2 Ruggs   viii s
it 2 pr of Curtaines 1 old   xviii s
  Sum   vi li xi s v d

More in the said Chamber

First ii Dornex Carpetts   v s vi d
it ii Cloakes   xxx s
it ii Sutes of Apparrell
  1 Dublett & Jerkyn   xxx s
it 1 pr of Stockins 1 pr of
  Busgins & one wastecoat   ii s vi d
it 1 Redd Capp 1 Rideing hood   xviii d
it 1 ounce 3/4 of Silver old   vii s
it 6 bands 3 Capps 1 pr of
  Cuffes ii handkerchers   x s vi d
it ii Shirtes   vi s

it iii pr of Sheets	xv s
it 6 bord Clothes	xvi s
it 7 pilloties	xx s
it 2 dozin Napkins & 1 Towell	x s vi d
it 2 remnants of old black stuffe	xii d
it 4 Carrick Dishes	xviii d
it for brushes	xii d
it 1 looking glasse 5 other glasses	xvi d
it for flaskitts & baskitts	ii s
it 1 Trendlebedsteed	ii s
it 1 hatt & band wth Siphers	iiii s
it for the painted Cloth	xviii s
Sum	ix li v s iiii d

In the Last in the said Chamber

First 1 standing bedsteed	xviii s
it 1 Trendlebed steed	ii s
it 6 old Coffers & boxes	vii s
it for old Hampers	xii d
it 1 pr of old bootes	xii d
it 1 old stool & a bord wth a brandiz wch was at the house at *Dawlishe* [Dawlish]	iiii s
it 1 Trowell	xi d
it for the lease of halfe the Shopp	iii li
it in reddy money	v s vi d
it in Doubtfull Debts	xx iiii li xvi s ix d
Sum Total	Clxv li xiiii s xi d

NOTES

1. The inventory is in the Devon Record Office, Exeter Court of Orphans records. Attention was drawn to it by W.G. Hoskins 'An Exeter bookseller's stock in 1615', *DCNQ* 21 (1940), 36–7. The numbers 1 to 91 have been added to the first items in the inventory to facilitate reference in the commentary.
2. A detailed analysis of Foster's inventory is given by John Barnard and Maureen Bell in *The early seventeenth-century book trade and John Foster's inventory of 1616*. Leeds Philosophical and Literary Society, 1994.
3. The main facts of Harte's life are given by Ian Maxted in *The Devon book trades: a biographical dictionary* (Exeter, 1991), 78.
4. *A short-title catalogue of books printed in England, Scotland, & Ireland and of English books printed abroad 1475–1640* (Bibliographical Society, 1976–91).
5. Maureen Bell and John Barnard, 'Provisional count of STC titles 1475–1640', *Publishing history*, 31 (1992), 54.
6. *The fower chiefyst offices belongyng to horsemanshippe*, Six editions 1565–1609. STC 3152–57.

Ian Maxted

32. The Social Tone of Torquay in the 1920s

The following editorial appeared in the *Torquay Times* on Friday 6 July 1923. It was typical of a number of editorials written in that newspaper during the 1920s, a decade of considerable upheaval in the seaside resort of Torquay. From its origins as a small fishing community, during the nineteenth century Torquay had developed into a major health and retirement centre, its period of greatest expansion in this century being between the 1840s and 1860s. Consolidating this expansion, the local authority provided several impressive tourism facilities later in the century, particularly during 1900–1914, the most notable being the White Pavilion overlooking the inner harbour. By the end of the First World War these facilities, its favourable climate and growing reputation for fashion had made Torquay one of Britain's premier seaside resorts, attracting not only recuperating invalids but also fashionable tourists.[1]

However, it was the interwar decades which proved most critical in the shaping of the modern resort of Torquay. The First World War and its aftermath saw far-reaching changes in British society, changes which were reflected in its holiday industry and in the 'twenties and 'thirties people indulged in the modern forms of leisure on an unprecedented scale. Indeed, the growth rate in the mass entertainment sector from 1931 to 1939 was 49 per cent, a figure far exceeding those in other economic sectors.[2] This boom saw a huge expansion in the country's seaside industry and Torquay was one of the most prominent beneficiaries. Between 1921 and 1931 its population increased by 17 per cent, largely as a result of its flourishing tourism industry but also as a result of the continuing influx of retired people into the town.[3]

It is these tensions between the holiday industry and the retired residents which are reflected in this editorial of July 1923. The summers of 1919 and 1920 had been spectacularly successful in Torquay as throughout the UK, but the economic collapse of 1921 began a more difficult period for the resort. The mid-'twenties were years of some conflict within the resort as the local authority, the tourism industry and residential groups clashed over the 'social tone' of the town. The key question was, should the town try to attract lower middle and working class visitors who would bring a greater volume of trade or should it appeal to greater numbers of 'fashionable' visitors who, although fewer in number, spent more per head? The attraction of the former entailed providing more lively entertainments, similar to those provided at resorts such as Brighton, and, to a much greater extent, at

Blackpool, entertainments scathingly described by the editorial as 'beach minstrelsy'. The attraction of middle classes visitors, on the other hand, was seen to revolve around providing a winter orchestra, good quality theatre, picturesque gardens and the correct 'tone'.

This argument became very heated and polarized during the later 'twenties when the conflict centred around a number of key issues including the provision of Sunday train facilities to allow working class tourists to visit Torquay. A motion to apply to the Great Western Railway to provide such excursions was defeated by 17 votes to 12 by Torquay's Borough Council, a clear victory for those favouring the retention of a high social tone.[4] Yet, the character of Torquay was gradually changing in these years, mainly as a result of an increasing democratization of holiday-making, improved communication links and also, a desire within the town's powerful tourism industry to attract a broader spectrum of visitors. Thus, despite the continued fight of those who did not want to 'vulgarise Torquay for the tripper element', they were swimming against the tide.[5] The 1920s and 1930s saw the beginning of the end of Torquay's 'gentry' era and start of its rise as a more 'popular' tourist resort. Certainly by the outbreak of World War Two the resort was firmly on the road towards attracting a more popular clientele, a move which was to ensure its continued growth and success in post-war Britain.

Torquay Central Library, *Torquay Times*, 6 July 1923

Don't Brightonise Torquay

There is, we fear, a tendency on the part of certain officials and others to introduce into Torquay a class of attractions which, however laudable the motive, will not conduce to the popularity of the town. Torquay is not Brighton, neither is it Blackpool. It stands upon a different plan to these watering places, a higher one, if we may venture to make the assertion. Brighton and Blackpool are cosmopolitan—Torquay is not. The two former places depend for their very existence upon shoals of trippers down for the day, or maybe two or three days, whose ideas of a seaside holiday are comprised in beach minstrelsy, side shows, an occasional dip in the briny, donkey rides, boating, excursions, and especially any form of amusement which the municipality may provide in the shape of a battle of flowers (which would probably degenerate into a glorified confetti fete), a carnival, gymkana, and similar undertakings. We can understand readily enough that, to dwellers in some crowded cities and towns far from the seaside such provisions for relaxation and enjoyment is welcomed and appreciated and we are glad that it is so. But we do not want this sort of thing in Torquay. Torquay's peculiar claim for the holidaymaker is that it provides as few other seaside towns do, a restful place for the jaded toiler in busy manufacturing towns, a place where he can bask in the sun by the seaside or recline in the shady nooks around the coast line, enjoy a morning dip, go boating or fishing and vary his programme by excursions inland by char-a-banc or motor. What he does not want, and what he will protest against, are itinerant minstrels, donkey boys, swings and roundabouts, so-called carnivals or fetes, or gymkanas, or whatever fancy name the promotors choose to give them. He probably comes to Torquay to be free from these distractions and if on the contrary he finds them in full swing, he will pack up his tent and go elsewhere. Let Torquay be content with its unrivalled natural beauties, its Pavilion, gardens, band, theatre and picture houses and leave carnivals and gymkanas and such like [sic] pleasures to Brighton and Blackpool, who could scarcely exist without them. Torquay needs no artificial attractions to bring holidaymakers to its precincts.

NOTES

1. See J.R. Pike, 'The Development of Torquay as a Holiday Resort: a lecture given to the Workers' Education Association in 1966' (Torquay, 1971).
2. J. Walvin, *A Social History of the Popular Seaside Holiday: Beside the Seaside* (1978), 107.
3. N.J. Morgan, 'Perceptions, Patterns and Policies of Tourism: the development of the Devon seaside resorts during the twentieth century with special reference to Torquay and Ilfracombe' (unpublished PhD thesis, University of Exeter, 1991), chapter four.
4. Torquay Municipal Borough Council Quarterly, Monthly and Special Committee, 6 May 1927 Torquay Central Library.
5. *Torquay Times*, editorial 9 Aug. 1929.

Nigel Morgan

33. 'It was only a copy of the Doomsday book...'; William Wynne's Travels through Devon in 1755

William Wynne was born in 1692, the eldest son of Owen Wynne of Gwenfynnyd in Anglesey, and Dorothy, daughter of Francis Luttrell. After attending Jesus College, Oxford, he became a barrister, a Sergeant at Law, and a judge on the Welsh circuit. Through his mother's family he inherited Luttrell properties in Cornwall, and he was connected by marriage with the Stackhouse family of Probus and St Erme.[1] In July–September 1755 he travelled from his home in Chelsea to Cornwall and back, and kept a diary. The visit seems to have been partly on business, to visit the Cornish properties, partly a family excursion: his wife, son, daughter and servant accompanied him in his coach and four.

CRO, PD 220

... We left the County of Dorset, and got to Axminster, the first town in Devonshire, in about 4 hours, though not above 12 miles from Bridport, and lay there.

Axminster is but a small village though the Hundred has its name from thence. It lyes on the river *Ax*, and was the place of a bloody battell, between the Saxons and Danes, after which the King (Athelstan) in a thankfull remembrance of his victory erected a Minster here with 7 priests to pray for the sons of those that were slain, whence it was called Axminster. It has a small market and a fair yearly on St Johns day.

Next day being 30th we left Axminster and went over high downs leaving Sir John Pool's seat on the left and several other seats on the right in the bottoms, and got to Honiton in two hours and half being about 9 miles. It is [a] large stragling town, tis a Market and a Corporate town consisting of a Mayor and Aldermen and sends two Members to Parliament. It was burnt down the same year with Blandford, but is now mostly rebuilt. Its chief trade is in woollen goods and Lace. From hence to Exeter is between 16 and 17 miles and about 4 hours drive through a vill called *Clist* [Clyst] Honiton from the bridge built over the River *Clist*.

We spent all day 31st at Exeter, which is a very large antient City well furnished with plentifull Markets for all sorts of provisions. It is a Corporation consisting of Mayor and Aldermen. It sends two members to Parliament. This City was made a County by Henry 8th. There are many streets but they are very old and shabby buildings and very narrow and steep in some parts Especially those leading to the key and the bridge. The four principal streets meet abt the Middle of the City at a large handsome conduit, corruptly called Carfax, but perhaps more properly Quartervoys [Quadrivium]. The High Street and Close are much the best. There is at the entrance into the City at East End a large Lock hospital or Lazaret, and a large County hospital or Workhouse for the poor lately built.

Exeter in process of time has had several names. In Antonines Itinerary tis called Isca Damoniorum, by the Saxons Exoncester from the great river *Ex* and Cester being the common addition to places of strength that had castles and garrisons, called also Monkton from the multitude of Monasterys and monks residing there. The Brittains called it Caeriske, from Caer a city, or Caer Ruth, of the red soil on which it stands, or Pencaer, a head or capital city.

The Cathedral is very antient and large, dedicated to St Peter, but little done of late years towards the repair. It is built of a reddish soft mouldring stone which lyes in great abundance in most of the hills about the City and upon violent rains discolors all the rivers, roads and streets. The west end is adorned with a multitude of figures big and little, but being all of that sort of stone have lost their beauty. There is a Dean, Canons residentiary and prebends, Chantor, Treasurer, and 4 archdeacons who have their respective houses, but the Deans is a very indifferent one and <u>very</u> bad situation, so is the Bishops palace, though the only house out of many now remaining to the Bishops of the See, stiffled almost with a deal of bad close buildings, and I believe most of the prebendal houses are the same.

In the Cathedral there are a great many Monuments antient and modern, of the several Bishops and others. The organ is reckoned the largest in England, the greatest pipes being 15 inches diameter, two of them were just sounded at my request. There are 5 great leaden pipes detached from the rest of the organ, and fixed against a large pillar on each side of the main body of the organ, wich alone is as large as in any other Cathedral, with a smaller organ below the rest, fronting the Quire.

I had heard much of a Doomsday book, said to be in the possession of the Dean and Chapter, and enquired after it, but could not find any one that could give an account of it. I enquired at the Deanery and saw the Deans study and lodgings on purpose but he being absent could get no information about it. I lookd into their Library but could find nothing like it. On my return from Cornwall enquired of the Deputy Register, who told me that he apprehended it was only a copy of the Doomsday book as far as it related to the Church estates, and was not to be seen without some of the Chapter, but kept in the Library, and so could not meet with it. But it is referrd to as an antient peice of authority by Borlase, 323, 5, 9, 354, but the Dean afterward told me that he had it with him in London to show to the Antiquary society and that he beleived it to be the original as far as it went but not the whole of what was kept in the Exchequer.

In the Library there are a good many books, but slovenly kept, it is in the upper part of the Cathedral above the altar, and I suppose was antiently a Chappel called Our Ladye Chappel, and Sir John Doderidge and his Lady lie there at full length with an inscription.

The City is walled round and has a ruined Castle called Rugmond from red castle, famous for its antiquity and scituation, of great extent, in part of which there is a church and gaol and the assizes are held for the county, and round the walls are very good publick and pleasant walks, and 4 City Gates.

[Inserted at this point in the diary is an entry dated 1763] The Assizes of the city is held at the Guildhall which is a handsome room. The Crown Court at the Castle is very indifferent. I sat there as Judge of Assize in July 1763 and experienced the inconvenience of this City being a County for myself, for I was obliged to go thither to swear witnesses and discharge the Grand Jury and sat 3 hours and upwards while they found some bills for misdeameanours after all the other business was over. The Cathedral being new paving and repairing the Assize Sermon was preached before us in the West end. In taking up the pavement near the Altar they found the body of Bishop Birton temp. Ed. 2, in a stone coffin, in June '63, and with it his ring which [is] a saphire set in gold, and a paten and smal chalice silver guilt and the host and wine probably in it when buried, and some remains of his pastoral staff, but being of perishable materials quite mouldred. Some ornaments appeared on it in colours. Dr Mills the present Dean showd it to us with whom we breakfasted in his large room where the Prince of Orange met the Gentlemen of the country upon his landing, and may be said to be the Commencement of the Revolution.

Continuing the journey in 1755 the Wynnes travelled to Okehampton along a 'turnpike road greatly mended, as it did before much want it'; they stayed overnight at Bridestow ('a tolerable inn'), reaching

Cornwall over Polson Bridge on 2 August. They returned *via* Callington to Tavistock by 'a very indifferent way for any coach, miry and stony, through a small village whose name I have forgot', and travelled on to Plymouth staying overnight at Tavistock.

There are many nearer ways to Plymouth without coming to this place but we were advised that they were not passable for a Coach, and the ferrys very dangerous and the passage almost a League over, so we thought it the safest to go about as we did. The passage is called Cremble or Tremble, as it frequently makes people do, who venture over it.

Plymouth Dock, from the river Ply[m], was in the memory of some people but a small barton or farm of £50 per ann., but by the present improvements and buildings on it is a large spacious place and produces to its owner Sir Jo. St Aubins at least £3000 a year, good rents and well paid, it was left him by his uncle the late Sir Wm. Morice, whose father by his influence and understanding with the public officers, procured this Dock to be built on his estate.

It is situated on the solid rocks, all the pavement and walks from office to office, and some of the staircases, are at a vast expense levelled and cut out of the rocks.

It is almost opposite to Mount *Edgecome* [Edgcumbe] and has a full view of it. The Commissioner and all other officers belonging to the Dock have here their respective houses such as Master Builder, Clerk of the Cheque, Clerk of the Stores etc., and makes a handsome row of houses and on a high terrace overlooking the Dock. Men of War of the 1st rate are here built and repaired. The *Magnanime* a French ship of 74 guns was here repairing and almost ready for service, it was taken in the late war from the French and has but two tier of guns and not the lower tier as ours have. There was other Men of War repairing, and a new Yatch for the Commissioner and a tender or two on the stocks a-building.

We saw the Rope rooms, which is one above stairs 340 yards long, where persons at the end appear very little and diminutive, and another room below, and other offices where they are tarrd and pitch and tarr made and boyled for the uses of the Navy.

The Mast room deserves also a particular remark. There was an old Mast hung up that in the late War was shot thro' and tho' and yet brought the Man of War home safe, and kept as a memorial, which ship it belonged to I have forgot. Another thing remarkable was that at the end of a fir mast a watch was held close and I stood at the other end with my ear close to it and heard it tick, though of a vast length, and was for the main mast of a 2nd rate Man of War.

The boat room, and as I was informed every Man of War had 5 boats of different dimensions belonging them; then we saw the sail room, and sails of most of the maritime powers, and were told every Man of War had Ensigns and flags of almost all other nations to delude the Ennemy; and the Armory for small Arms, and all sort of shot, Grapeshot of all scizes etc., and the standard pattern of the officers of the Marines clothing.

We were next carried to the Ordinance Office and were shown the Gunns belonging to the *Magnanime* and many other Men of War, with their respective bulletts lying by them, and a large Magazine of powder, which had copper doors, and every nail about it of Copper, and no iron about it, and several Lighters always ready to receive the ship stores as there was occasion to carry to the Men of War. There were the hulls of 10 or 12 Men of War lyeing in the Sound, reported fit for Service. to be repaired and put in Commission as ordered.

In the evening we went to the town of Plymouth 2 miles from the Dock, where we lay for the 3rd night. Next day Saturday 19th we went to the fort. The Gate of it is towards the town, it comands the town and Country round for some miles and secures the harbours, and faces the mouth of the Channell, so that no Ship that comes near the town is out of its reach. The whole fort is about a mile in compass. The walls of it are built of Marble or Moor Stone and most of them 3 foot broad. Many Canon are planted on the walls, and some Mortars with their respective balls lying by them and a Drawbridge and portcullis at the Entrance.

There is a house for the Governor, Deputy Governor, Captain of the Independent Company here, Engineer and other Officers, Storehouses for amunitions and Stables for horses, and a Chappel, and the whole is built on a rocky hill. One point of the Fort secures the Sea, another the Country, and another the town, and several Cisterns and receivoirs for water. This fort was begun in the year 1666, for in the rebellion the town of Plymouth was against the King, and he could never take it, but this Fort does so overlook and awe the town, that it can make no resistance and can batter down the town and Church in a few hours, and no Ships can annoy it on the Sea Side, for besides the extraordinary thickness of the walls and number of Guns planted there, the rocks at the bottom are a natural fence, and would split any Ships that should attempt to Land there.

Besides this there is a New battery of Canon called Legoniers Battery from the then Governor, about 40 pounders each and about 20 in number, and another large new battery of Canon in St Nicholas Island opposite to the fort, which contains between 3 and 4 acres and is strengthened by Nature as well as Art, subject to the commander of the Fort, and a Garrison relieved every day from the Fort; and a fine Terrace Walk all round the Fort, and [we] had all due Civilities there from Capt. Williams, Comander of the invalid Company, and from his son, who is the Engineer of the Fort.

The Town is a Corporation consisting of a Mayor and Aldermen and has a good market 3 days in the week and has plenty of flesh, fish and fowl. The Town is not walled in, the buildings chiefly of stone, and the streets paved, but slippery and bad walking. There is a Conduit and Channels of Water in the principal Streets brought in by Sir Francis Drake who was said to be born here. There are several Inns or taverns for entertainment but very dear. There are 2 Churches, and one of them has a very high tower, and to this town there are 2 large havens in one or other of which ships may ride safely as they are consigned Easterly or Westerly, and has a good Key and seldom without several Merchant ships there. It is also a burgess town and sends 2 members to Parliament.

After this we ferried over an arm of the sea about half a mile, the water being low, to Mount *Edgecomb*, and were let in at a garden door and walked up the hill towards the house, which is a large old square regular stone building with bastions at each Corner, and stands about the middle of the Hill, and a terrace under it the length of the house. Lord gave us leve to see the inside of his house, treated us with wine and desired us to dine, which we declined. There is a saloon, 3 or 4 parlors, and other rooms on a floor, and good Lodgings rooms above, which had every way immense Views, but the Chief Curiosity of the inside was a variety of Marble pillars, Chimney peices and tables of Moorstone, all raised from his L'ships own estates, and while we were entertained within, his L'dship of his own accord ordered his chair and two horses and his Coachman to ride the foremost horse to escort us round his walks and sloops [slopes] and walks that hang as it were over the Sea, which every way afforded us such views and prospects of Sea and Land as are not to be truely described.

There we saw the Dock and all its works at once, the Fort and town of Plymouth, Island of St Nicholas, the Sound, several hulls of Men of War, tenders, 2 Men of War 60 Guns under full sail, and between 30 and 40 French merchantmen brought as prisoners into the Sound, and several great rocks in the sea, and large prospects of Cornwall and Devon. It being a little hazy I could not see the *Edyston* lighthouse, which was said to be 4 Leagues off in the Sea, but very visible (as they said) in a clear bright day.

Being fully satisfied, we were carried over his park to the Sea Side, where we ferryed over to the opposite shore, the water being then very high, and safely landed. There are several sorts of ferry boats there and thereabouts for Coaches, horses or foot passengers, not flatbottomed but built high, that will bear tossing, but there was one that had about a dozen people that was pulled across by ropes from side to side. Ours was only a high boat with seats, and 3 oars to ourselves of the better sort and fit only for foot passengers.

NOTE

1. Colin Edwards, 'A visit to Cornwall in 1755', *JRIC* (1981), 338–49.

Christine North

34. Three Early Devon Wills

Wills provide one of the historian's most useful sources, illuminating family history and biography, funerals and religion, friendship and charity, life-styles and possessions. Three great collections of them survive, relating to Devon before the Reformation. The Mayor's Court Rolls of Exeter, now in the Devon Record Office at Exeter, contain some 564 registered copies of wills between 1257 and 1557.[1] These belong chiefly to Exeter citizens and usually reproduce only the parts of the document which conveyed property, though some of the later wills are recorded in full. The wills registered in the Prerogative Court of Canterbury, now held in the Public Record Office (London), begin in the late fourteenth century.[2] They were made by testators with property in more than one diocese and consequently tend to be confined to the wealthy, except on the borders of Devon with Dorset and Somerset where lesser folk are also represented. The wills registered in the courts of the bishop of Exeter and his archdeacons begin in about the 1530s, or rather began then, because they were destroyed during the bombing of Exeter in 1942. Fortunately, copious extracts were taken from them before that event by two local scholars—Olive Moger and Sir Oswyn Murray—whose extracts are preserved in the Westcountry Studies Library at Exeter.[3]

There are also a good many stray wills. They occur among the deposits in the Devon Record Office at Exeter, in the archives of Exeter Cathedral, and in other places.[4] Hard to track down, they need to be listed and, preferably, transcribed and published. Pending that desirable outcome, this article prints three of them, none of which is likely to be well known to local historians. The first occurs among the papers of the Walrond family of Bradfield (Uffculme), deposited in the Devon Record Office. It is in Latin and contains several odd words and spellings, which require ingenuity to translate. The second is also in Latin and is the only medieval Devon will, as far as I know, in the manuscript collections of the British Library. The third is in English and belongs to the Public Record Office, but it is not one of the registered wills from the Prerogative Court of Canterbury which are now available, and widely used, on microfilm. Rather, it belongs to a box of individual copies of wills from the same court but with a different reference, and its production requires special notice.

The first will was made by a gentleman, John Ufflete of Woolfardisworthy East, who was evidently an important resident of that parish and patron of its church. He married the daughter of Martin de Fyschacre, a landowner in the South Hams, and came to hold further property in that part of Devon including the patronage of Moreleigh church. His wife evidently predeceased him, and he mentions two of their children: Isabel and his heir Edmund, who married into the Walrond family, a fact which explains the presence of the will among their papers.[5] His bequests of armour, silver plate and kitchen vessels indicate the life-style of a member of his class. He also arranged for a superior kind of burial in church rather than, as usual, outside. The place he chose for this, the 'chapel' of St Mary, Woolfardisworthy, is most likely to mean a Lady chapel attached to the parish church, because the church itself (which was fully parochial) would not have been described as a chapel. No bequest was made to the rector of Woolfardisworthy;

instead, Ufflete put his trust in William Stockhay, who was the rector of nearby Puddington.

The author of the second will, John Schute of Westacott in Ashreigney, looks like a yeoman or husbandman rather than a gentleman, in view of the modest nature of his legacies and his willingness to be buried in the churchyard. He mentions both his parochial rector, Joce Blackaller, and the chaplain who evidently deputed for Blackaller as a curate. The will includes a valuable reference to the architecture of Ashreigney church. Apparently, this church also possessed a Lady chapel, entered through an arch from the main part of the church, probably on the north side of the chancel or nave. The arch was provided with a 'beam', probably to bear lights in honour of the Virgin. Shute relied on his wife to carry out his will and to provide for his three children: a reminder of the important role which women played in family life, especially in widowhood. This is a role of which we hear little in the ordinary way of things.

Our third testator seems to have occupied a status between those of Shute and Ufflete: that of a prosperous yeoman in the parish of Churchstanton, which was part of Devon until 1896 and remained in the diocese of Exeter until as late as 1971. William Richards 'junior' is recorded in 1524 as one of the two wealthiest inhabitants of Churchstanton, when he was assessed for taxation purposes as having goods worth £26 13s. 4d. The other wealthiest was William Richards 'senior' with the same assessment, presumably the elder brother mentioned in the will.[6] The fact that the two brothers bore the same name, as did two of the younger William's daughters, reflects the fact that children's names were often chosen not by the parents but by the senior godparent at the baptism who conferred his or her own name. John Shute mentions a godson who was also called John. Richards's will accords with the evidence of the taxation list, with its references to servants and its monetary bequests totalling over £50. He evidently died relatively early in life, since he left a large family of young children to be provided for, and like Shute he relied on his wife to take his place as head of the family. Of wider interest, his will preserves the unique evidence that Churchstanton church was dedicated to the Virgin Mary in the middle ages. The present dedication to St Paul dates only from the eighteenth century and was evidently a guess of that period. Richards's bequests show that the church, like most others at the time, contained various images and lights burning before them, the lights probably being supported by 'stores' or funds to which contributions could be made. Finally, the will reveals something of its maker's horizons, stretching out from Churchstanton on either side of the county border to Otterford, Upottery and West Buckland, and down to Wellington—the local market town.

It only remains to add that the texts of the wills have been translated into English (modern English in the last case), and that the use of capital letters and punctuation is also modern. Surnames, however, remain in the original form, as do some place-names, personal names and Latin terms (shown in bold italics) where these seem worth recording.

1. The Will of John Ufflete of Woolfardisworthy East, 1416

DRO, 1926B/W/W20c

In the name of God, amen. I, John Ufflete, being of sound mind and good memory, the seventh day of May in the year of our Lord 1416, make my will in this manner. First, I bequeath my soul to God and my body to be buried in the chapel of Blessed Mary of **Wolfordysworthy**. *Also, I bequeath to John Proues one hauberk [lorica] with one breastplate, and one sword with one shield. Also, I bequeath to Edmund my son one yoke horse. Also, I bequeath to Isabel my daughter one silver cup and one gilt nut* [coconut cup] *with a cover, and one maser* [maple-wood bowl]. *Also, I bequeath to the wife of John Fyllegh one gilt girdle of silk and one gold ring. Also, I bequeath to Alice Nywelond two brass pots and two dishes [***parassid'***] of pewter, and five pottingers [***potageres***] and four saucers [***sawseres***], two peels and three brass pans, and two bowls and one cover, with two pairs of blue* [word missing] *and one cloak, a griddle and one candlestick of latten, and two cooking pots of iron [**ferr' de ferro**], and one mattress and two cadr* [coverlets or beds], *and one tripod and three vats,* [and] *twenty sheep of either sex, under the condition that the said Alice does not carry away or steal anything without licence of the executors, and if it happens that the said Alice should carry away any goods of the said John, I will and grant that she have nothing of the said goods bequeathed to her. Also, I bequeath to Sir William Stockehay one black gown. Also, I bequeath the residue of all my goods not bequeathed above to Edmund my son* [and] *Joan his wife to dispose for my soul as they see best. Also, I appoint, ordain, make and constitute Edmund my son and Sir William Stockehay my executors.*

[Endorsement: *The present will was proved before us, John Orum, archdeacon of Barnstaple, and the administration was committed to Sir William Hokhey* [sic], *rector of Puddington, on the 13th day of the month of September, the year of our Lord 1416.*]

2. The Will of John Shute of Westacott in Ashreigney, 1437

BL, Additional Charter 25,912

In the name of God, amen. The twenty-fifth day of the month of January in the fifteenth year of the reign of King Henry the Sixth [1437], *I, John Shute of* **Westecote**, *being of whole mind and sound memory, make my will in this* *manner. First, I bequeath my soul to Almighty God and my body to be buried in the cemetery of the parish church of Ayshe Regny. Also, I bequeath to Sir Joce, rector of the place there, for my tithes forgotten and badly tithed, 12d. Also, I leave to Sir John Frelard chaplain there to celebrate for my soul, 6d. Also, I leave to the work of making the beam on the north arch of St Mary of the same church, newly constructed, 6d. Also, I bequeath to John Byllyng, my godson, a lamb. Also, I bequeath to John, son of John Lake of Doun, one lamb. Also, I bequeath to Richard, son of the same, one lamb. Also, I bequeath to Elizabeth, daughter of the same John Lake, one lamb. Also, I bequeath to Margaret, daughter of the same John, one lamb. Also, I bequeath all my goods and chattels, after my funeral expenses have been completed and my debts fully paid, to the ordinance of Agnes my wife to be divided into three equal parts, of which two parts are to remain to the said Agnes my wife, that she may dispose from them for the health of my soul, and the third part of the said goods and chattels in equal portions at the disposition of the aforesaid Alice is to be divided between John my son the younger and Joan and Isabel my daughters. For the execution of this present testament, I ordain and make the aforesaid Agnes my wife executrix, so that she may dispose* [my goods] *for the health of my soul, as she will not fear to respond before the Highest Judge. Dated as above.*

3. The Will of William Richards of Churchstanton, 1532 (Modernized spelling of the original English)

PRO, PROB 10/5

In the name of God, amen. The second day of February in the year of our lord God 1531 [1532, modern style], I, William Richarddes the younger of Churchstanton within the diocese of Exeter, laud be to God, whole of mind and of perfect remembrance, make my testament and last will in manner and form as followeth. First, I bequeath my soul to God Almighty, to his blessed mother Saint Mary and to all the celestial company of heaven, [and] my [body] to be buried within the church of Our Lady in Churchstanton aforesaid. Item, I give and bequeath to the High Cross light, Our Lady light, St Katherine light and to the lamp light within the said church, to every of them one sheep apiece. Item, to [the] light of St Bride chapel, one sheep. Item, I bequeath to the churches of Otterford, Upottery, West Buckland and Wellington, to every of them 3s. 4d. apiece. Item, I bequeath to my son Thomas £6 13s. 4d., to my son William £6 13s. 4d., to my son Humphrey £6 13s. 4d., to my daughter Joan the elder £6 13s. 4d., to my daughter *Bregett* £6 13s. 4d., to my daughter *Tomsine* £6 13s. 4d., to my daughter *Dorothe* £6 13s. 4d., and to my daughter Joan the younger £6 13s. 4d. And if any of my said children decease or [i.e. before] they come to a lawful age and discretion, that then their part of the foresaid bequest so dueth to remain to them that overliveth, equally to be divided amongst them, and if all my said children do decease before they come to a lawful age and discretion, that then I wish that the said legacies to them before bequest wholly to remain to *Emmotte* my wife, she to dispose it for the wealth of my soul after her best discretion. Item, I bequeath to every of my godchildren now being alive, 12d. apiece. Item, to every of my servants now being in my service, one ewe sheep and one lamb. Item, I will that *Emmotte* my wife shall have, hold and enjoy all my purchase lands which I have in Churchstanton and in Upottery within the county of Devonshire during the term of her natural life towards the finding of my said children, and after her decease the said lands to remain wholly to my son Thomas and to his heirs as in fee for ever more. The residue of all my goods and debts to me owing, my funeral expenses and debts paid which I do owe, my legacies afore except, the residue I give and bequeath it to *Emmotte* my wife whom I do ordain and make my very true and whole executrix, she to do for the wealth of my soul as she thinketh best after her discretion. To this I ordain and make my brother William Rychardes and my brother Thomas Rychardes to be overseers of this my last will to be truly fulfilled and performed. Thus *testijs* Sir David Moure my curate, Thomas Courte, John Sparke, John Haydon, Thomas Mager and John Grobham with others.

NOTES

1. There is a handlist of these wills in the Devon Record Office.
2. PRO, Probate Court of Canterbury, PROB 11.
3. There is an additional set of Olive Moger's transcripts in the Devon Record Office at Exeter.
4. The handlist of wills mentioned in note 1 includes a list of Exeter wills in the archives of Exeter Cathedral.
5. For Edmund Ufflete, see his inquisition post mortem, 14 October 1426, in PRO, C 139/29, no 47; there is an English transcript in WSL, Inquisitions Post Mortem (Devon and Cornwall), 16 vols., vol. xv.
6. T.L. Stoate (ed.), *Devon Lay Subsidy Rolls 1524–7* (Almondsbury, 1977), 38–9.

Nicholas Orme

35. An Angel at Castle Street: Extracts from the Autograph Book of Nurse Georgina Blatwayt, when Nursing at No. 5 Temporary Hospital, Castle Street, Exeter

The following autographs were dedicated to Nurse Blatwayt and the staff of No. 5 V.A.O. Temporary Hospital, from sometime before April 1915 until mid 1916. Georgina Sophia Blatwayt[1] was the daughter of Georgina Mary Weekes, part of the Lega-Weekes family, whose home was at Willestrew, Tavistock.[2] She served as a V.A.D. (Voluntary Aid

Detachment) nurse at several Temporary Hospitals; College Hostel (No. 5), Streatham Hall, and Cader Idris, and appears to have been at No. 5 for just over a year. The building began life as 'The Vineyard' a pleasant Georgian house with a fine garden. In 1906 it was acquired by the University College of the South West of England (now University of Exeter) as a student residence known as College Hostel.[3] The military requisitioned it as No. 5 Hospital in 1915 until 1919, when it was renamed Bradninch Hall after the House and Place of the same. As a student residence it held sixty students sharing rooms, as a hospital, two hundred and thirteen beds were shoe-horned in. It has retained its name and is located across from the Devon Record Office.

Number Five must have been a skilled surgical hospital, rather than the more usual convalescent home, judging from Pte. Young's many successful operations,[4] perhaps it specialized in specific injuries, as you would expect men from such diverse areas of the country to be sent nearer home or were they brought direct from France to Plymouth and Exeter.

The collecting of autographs between staff and patients in the form of poems and drawings, may have led to the publication of the hospital magazines. Relationships were fleeting and it was important to keep up moral. They were a mixture of news, poems, experiences and good humoured rivallry between local hospitals, with cricket matches and competitions. 'Rhubarb' repeatedly crops up as having been the bane of their lives; and their love of junket: 'The Everlasting—Patients may come and patients may go, But rhubarb goes on for ever'.[5]

The Editors' introduction to the first magazine[6] explains their purpose:

> This being a War Hospital, there is not one of us here who is not here solely as a result of or in direct response to, the call of Duty. But that is no reason why we should not endeavour to extract all the brightness and humour we can out of the incidents that present themselves day by day in the necessarily restricted life we are bound to live in Hospital. The World is a rough enough place for most of us, and the war is not likely to make it any the less so, therefore let us make the most of this little oasis in the desert.

The messages, drawings and poems written for Nurse Blatwayt, although somewhat comic and sentimental, hold poignant details. For the 'Tommy' or 'Tar' these jottings may have been their only opportunity to document their personal experiences of the Great War. All original spelling and grammar have been retained.

DRO, 1516M add F/2
Blessed is he that sitteth on a pin.
For he shall surely rise.
R. Joyson 9th Blackwatch. Wounded at Loos 25/9/15

He thought he knew

Moses was a good man
Of children he had seven
He thought he'd hire a donkey cart
And drive them all to heaven.

But strange to say he lost his way
Although he knew it well
He overturned the donkey cart
And tippen them all in H-11

Charles Farley 4th Wore Regt.
Wounded on the landing at the Dardanelles in a rowing boat on 25/4/15

Having felt it my duty at the commencement of the war to do something for my King & Country although been 40 years when I did it quite cheerfully for 9 months at the Front from which sights are two bad to describe midst shot and shell I was taken ill and had to be sent to dear Old Blightie where I am pleased to say that from the kind hearted nurses I had the greatest of kindness shown to me and I therefore wish the owner of this album good health prosperity and happiness whilst life shall last Respectfully yours the above.

No.2037 Ptge. J.J.Barnbary 25th Field Ambulance R.A.M.C.,
B.E. Force France 8th Division

Landed in France on 9th March 1915 came 'Through' the Second Battle of Ypres without a scratch June 10th 'Relieved' 3rd Dragoon Guards out of the 'Death Trap' my Friend John Mulholland got Killed next 'Day' I could not Bury Him till it got 'Dark' and many a Look I took at 'Him' as he Lay Cold at our Feet. Shifted to Hooplines two Days later 'Lost' another Pal there 'Ginger' Gray. Went Sick on 21st July Landed in 'England' 17th Aug. I respect the Officials of this Hospital and am very Greatfull to the Nurses and Sisters for their Kindness to me During sojourn under their Care.

No. 17526 Pte. Wm. Logue 2nd Batt. Royal Irish Fuseliers

Some people write for money
Others write for fame
I write to be remembered
Therefore I write my name

Pte. H.Offer 12st R.W.Fusiliers. Wounded on Sept 25th Nr. Loos.
With thanks to Nurse Blathwaite for her kindness while at No.6 ward.

Lives of great men all remind us
We can make our lives sublime
And departing leave behind us
Foot prints in the sands of time.

Kind hearts are gardens
King thoughts are the roots
Kind words are the blossom
Kind deeds are the fruits.

No. 68850 Bomb.B. Ladd R.H.A. 29th Division 4/10/1915

Whatever is, is Best

I know as my life grows older, And my eyes have clearer sight,
That under each rank Wrong somewhere, There lies the root of Right.
That each sorrow has its purpose, By sorrows oft unguessed;
But sure as the sun brings morning, Whatever is, is Best.

I know there are no errors, In the great eternal plan,
And all things work together For the final work of man.
And I know when my soul speeds onward, In the grand eternal quest,
I shall say as I look earthward—Whatever is, is Best.

No. 16890 Pte. A.Adams 1st Northamptonshire Regt.
Wounded at Loos. Feb. 19th 1916

Once there lived a Billican.
Who held more in his Beak,
than his Bellican.
He could eat enough, to last him a week
I don't know how the Hell, e, can.

Don't be angry with me <u>Nurse</u>

Grenadier Woollard J.R. 17th Royal Fusiliers
4th April 1916

True Friends are like Diamonds—
—Precious and rare,
But new friends are like Autumn leaves—
—found everywhere.

11th Bt'n Ry'l Sussex R'gt Pte. H.Stark May 29th 1916

Still Smiling. Driver H. Hawton A.I.C. thrown from a horse and smashed my right leg. Thanks to Nurse Blaithwaite for her kindness to me on Ward 10. November 19th 1915.

NOTES

1. DRO, 1516M add F/1 (1915–1916), Georgina Sophia Blatwayt, Temporary Hospitals.
2. DRO, Weeks of Willestrew, Estate, 1516M add.
3. Brian W. Clapp, *The First World War and the University Movement* (Exeter, 1982), 31, 47, 69, 82, 197.
4. The book includes a copy of the notice of the death of Pte. Young.
5. DRO, Buller Estate, 2065M add/F284, 325–46.
6. WSL, No.5 VAO Hospital Exeter Magazine, (July 1916) SB/EXE/820.5/No.F.

Deborah Phillips

36. Revd John Jago and his Survey of Tavistock of 1784; Demographic Changes, 1741–1871 and their Association with Mining Developments

The small community of Tavistock in south west Devon is situated some fourteen miles north of Plymouth and thirty-five miles west of Exeter between the rivers Tamar and Tavy. Although its early importance owed much to the establishment of Tavistock Abbey and the creation of a market, its prosperity was boosted, first by the Dartmoor tin trade and subsequently, by the growth of cloth making. By the mid-eighteenth century a mixture of specialist trades and commercial activities underpinned by a range of agricultural pursuits characterized this essentially pre-industrial settlement. However, less than a century later, the town and its hinterland had been transformed, becoming the centre of an extensive mining area with Devon Great Consols as the leading producer of copper in Western Europe. This review is primarily concerned with identifying the principal demographic adjustments that took place within the borough and parish of Tavistock during the period 1741 to 1871 which is made possible by a unique survey completed by the vicar of Tavistock in 1784 and the parish registers.

The process of population change is a finely attuned mechanism responsive to economic and social circumstances and characteristics. Variations in vital rates, births, marriages and deaths and the ebb and flow of migration combine to create a particular demographic regime. As Hoskins considered Tavistock was the only place in Devon to experience the industrial revolution, the area provides a special opportunity of considering the effects of such a transformation upon a traditional market town and its rural hinterland.

The investigation of such a complex phenomenon depends upon the collation, presentation and interpretation of information from appropriate sources. Data was drawn from the Tavistock Parish Registers, records belonging to a number of non-conformist groups and the Civil Registers of Births, Marriages and Deaths. These documents provided a running record of vital events that enabled many of the fundamental characteristics of demographic behaviour to be revealed. The availability of information on births/baptisms, marriages and deaths/burials allowed the broad contours of population change to be identified.[1]

The careful integration and juxtaposition of ecclesiastical and civil records not only helped to safeguard the accuracy and reliability of the data but also to substantiate the validity of individual returns. The derivation of nine year moving averages enabled overall trends in baptisms/births, burials/deaths and marriages together with the inter-relationships between vital events to be delineated. At the same time the assessment of the relative contribution of natural and mechanical change together with the role of individual demographic components facilitated more detailed understanding of the complex interaction between population and underlying socio-economic conditions.

At the outset of the period under review there were approximately 70–75 baptisms a year and this relatively low level was maintained until the mid-1770s when numbers began to rise slowly. By the close of the eighteenth century there had been a sharp acceleration and an era of rapid increase was inaugurated with baptisms reaching 200 in the early 1820s. Although subsequently there was a slight setback, growth was renewed after 1835. This second upsurge took registrations to over 300, however, the momentum could not be sustained and by the 1860s numbers were declining, the upward trend had been reversed.

In general, mortality trends were subject to less dramatic fluctuations. Initially burials exceeded baptisms, however, modest improvements from the late-1760s reduced figures from 80–90 to less than 70. This amelioration was relatively short-lived and the closing years of the eighteenth century marked the onset of a long term rise in interments. Overall numbers increased steadily reaching over 100 in the late-1820s. The adverse trends continued throughout the 1830s and 1840s with burials/deaths reaching a peak of 200 in the late-1850s. However, more favourable patterns characterized the closing years of the period as mortality declined.

Marriage was the most stable of the demographic components and for most of the eighteenth century the average number of weddings was remarkably constant, varying only slightly above and below 27. This pattern was interrupted in the 1790s and by 1805 the number of marriages had risen to 40. This upturn corresponded closely with mining developments in Tavistock and adjoining parishes. However, the momentum was not sustained and by 1815 most of the gains had been wiped out. Nevertheless, numbers did not quite fall back to previous levels and within a few years the upward trend resumed. From the 1830s onwards there was a steady increase in the average number of marriages and following a more pronounced acceleration in the late-1840s, figures peaked around 1855. Once again these adjustments may be linked with contemporaneous developments in the mining industry.

An assessment of the relationship or comparative movement of these demographic variables may be instructive. While a lagged response can usually be expected between movements in marriages and subsequent changes in fertility, there would appear to be little evidence of this in Tavistock during much of the eighteenth century. Apart from a weak association between the two variables in the late-1750s, the generally upward trend in baptisms in the last quarter of the century was not related to a corresponding rise in marriages. However, the sharp acceleration in the early years of the nineteenth century may be attributed to a previous increase in marriages. Furthermore, fluctuations also appeared to coincide, although it is the direction rather than the extent of the changes that can be interrelated.

At first baptism and burial trends appeared to be negatively correlated, with falling mortality levels associated with steady or slightly increasing fertility. By the end of the eighteenth century both these variables began to move in sympathy. These reciprocal movements were then sustained for the remainder of the period under review. The trends would suggest a significant shift in demographic patterns and relationships, with the end of the eighteenth century as the transition point.

A simple comparison of the annual number of events recorded over two nine year periods centred on 1745 and 1865 showed that births increased from 73 to 259, deaths from 89 to 194 and marriages from 25 to 52. These figures produced growth ratios of 3.55, 2.18 and 2.08 which were symptomatic of gross changes in the key demographic variables. At the same time the increases give a rough indication of the order of magnitude of population growth.

In conjunction with the assessment of overall changes in baptisms and burials, differences between these events may be calculated to obtain basic estimates of natural change. While the period 1741 to 1770 may be characterized as an era of natural decrease, as burials exceeded births/baptisms, these negative trends were overturned subsequently as small but consistent gains heralded a period of unprecedented growth. These trends coincide with those outlined by Barham who noted 'The marked excess of baptisms over burials commenced in 1786, and increased progressively afterwards'.[2] Whereas gains of over 2,000 were registered between 1810 and 1837, more moderate increases (704) in the 1840s were followed by a dramatic acceleration in growth (1,385) as the pace of change quickened. Undoubtedly this upsurge was related to the prosperity engendered by mining and the concomitant influx of young miners and their families as well as inherent population characteristics. In the same way the smaller annual increments registered during the 1860s underlined the impact of the economic recession created by the mining depression.

On the basis of the evidence it is likely that the 1780s marked the advent of a sustained increase in the population of Tavistock. Moreover, the timing and extent of subsequent changes were influenced by the nature of local economic developments, especially mining. Population will rise or fall according to the balance between a range of demographic variables including migration. Changing employment opportunities in Tavistock and its environs encouraged population transfers. The availability of data drawn from a local enumeration of 1784 together with results from the census provided the basis for a review of the relative importance of natural change and migration. However, an outline of the special significance of the local survey must be considered first.

During the latter part of the eighteenth century conflicting assessments of the scale and direction of population change in England and Wales became a matter of natural concern as claims and counterclaims were put forward by a number of workers. Among the contributors to this debate was the Reverend John Howlett, vicar of Dunmow and Great Badow, who wrote extensively on population issues. Howlett used a variety of methods in an attempt to estimate the total population of England and Wales around 1780.[3] Among the data which he obtained were the results of a survey undertaken by the vicar of Tavistock the Reverend John Jago.

DRO, 482A add2/PR1

From an actual Survey taken by John Jago Vicar at the request of the Revd, Mr John Howlett in the year 1784 it appears that there were in the Borough and Parish of Tavistock the following number of Inhabitants Houses & Families, viz

	Inhabitants	Houses	Families
In the Borough	2899	441	610
East Division	286	54	54
North West Division	222	35	38
South West Division	210	39	46
Total	3117	569	748

[signed] John Jago Vicar

Exclusive of Houses & Gardens in the Town of Tavistock and the highways throughout the parish the contents are—the site of the abbey 172 acres, 0 roods 33 perches, arable & pasture land 9505[a.] 3[r.] 2[p.], coppice wood and timber 1187[a.] 1[r.] 21[p.], commons 3122[a.] 1[r.] 38[p.], total 13987[a.] 3[r.] 39[p.]. Or twenty one square miles & 547 acres 3 roods 32 perches.

The availability of this information constitutes a valuable benchmark in advance of the first census results. Table 1 sets out these figures together with those obtained from successive census reports.

Although population grew continuously from 1784–1861, the pace of change varied considerably with marked increases being recorded from 1801–11 and 1841–51, periods of notable mining expansion. However, in the last decade this trend was reversed and there was a net loss of over 1,100.

Using the figures of natural increase derived from the parish registers the relative contributions of natural and mechanical change can be identified (Table 2). While natural change was the key factor before 1801, in the following ten years net migration became increasingly important. These may be designated the years of early mining expansion and the opening and prosecution of mines like Wheal Crowndale

Table 1. Selected Statistics on Population Change Tavistock, 1784–1871

Year	Population	Change	% Change
1784	3,117		
1801	3,420	303	9.7
1811	4,723	1,303	38.1
1821	5,483	760	16.1
1831	5,602	119	2.2
1841	6,272	670	12.0
1851	8,147	1,875	29.9
1861	8,965	818	10.0
1871	7,781	−1,184	−13.2

Table 2. Components of Population Change in Tavistock, 1784–1870

Period	Total Change	Natural Change	Balance (Net Migration)
1784–1801	303	604	–301
1801–1810	1,303	739	564
1811–1820	760	930	–170
1821–1830	119	768	–649
1831–1840	670	880	–210
1841–1850	1,875	747	1,128
1851–1860	818	1,288	–470
1861–1870	–1,184	769	–1,953

and Wheal Crebor encouraged a substantial influx of people. The success of these early ventures attracted skilled labour from the neighbouring county of Cornwall. As early as 1799 the *Sherborne Mercury* reported that a few miners from St Agnes had absconded leaving their families destitute and were thought to be working in mines around Tavistock.[4] Moreover, entries in the Methodist baptism register during this period testified to the presence of families from St Agnes, and other Cornish parishes including Gwennap, Redruth and Wendron. The adverse effects of economic difficulties and mine closures influenced subsequent trends, most notably during the 1820s when potential growth was checked by out-migration.

There can be little doubt that in the years before civil registration the momentum of natural increase was both enhanced and restrained by significant transfers of population associated with expanding economic opportunities and the harsh realities of depression and mining collapse. In 1827 Wilson, the Duke of Bedford's agent commented 'We are still oppressed with people out of employ'.[5] A few years later, in 1832, the situation was summed up thus 'the greatest of all misfortunes for the labouring classes is that their number should greatly exceed the means of employing them ... This is the state of Tavistock at present'.[6]

The expansion of employment opportunities following the opening of Devon Great Consols encouraged more positive developments and contributed to the substantial migration gains recorded in the 1840s. Population grew more slowly in the period 1851-60, as high rates of natural increase were tempered by out-migration, a factor which became even more important in the following decade, as miners and their families were forced to find alternative employment. Commenting on the results of the 1871 Census the *Tavistock Gazette* noted:

A marked decrease of the population has been shown. This is accounted for by the fact that for many years past the mining interest in the locality has been stagnated and hence the great emigration of large numbers of the working population, but for this circumstance the whole district would have exhibited a considerable increase.[7]

Clearly the twin pressures of economic pull and push were operating during this period, causing fundamental demographic adjustments.

The availability of a series of estimates of total population, including the local enumeration carried out by Jago and subsequent census returns, were used to calculate crude baptism, burial or marriage rates. Such indices may be defined as the number of baptisms, burials or marriages in a given year expressed as a percentage of the population, or more usually, as a rate per thousand of that population.

Marriage rates in the pre-civil registration period were characterized by small scale but frequent fluctuations. In general levels rarely rose above ten or fell below five in any one year. Despite the relatively even tenor of the rates there were perceptible shifts and variations. Until the 1780s the general pattern had been uncertain and characterized by short term changes. A short period of stability followed before a marked upturn raised the figures to a peak of 14.4 in the early years of the nineteenth century. However, levels fell back quite quickly and by the 1810s the earlier pattern of uncertainty had re-asserted itself.

The years of highest nuptiality coincided with the opening of mines such as Wheal Crowndale and Crebor and the expansion of copper production. These developments raised levels of employment, increasing the demand for labour and encouraging an influx of workers from adjoining mining areas. Such trends have long been associated with changes in marriage patterns for as Young noted 'marriages are early and numerous in proportion to the amount of employment'.[8] Subsequently financial uncertainty and the effects of the post-war economic depression contributed to the difficulties facing local mine companies and as the momentum of the early years of boom receded, marriage rates declined.

The validity of this relationship between marriage rates and employment opportunities was upheld by experience in the post-civil registration period when both ecclesiastical and civil ceremonies were combined to give a more accurate representation of marriage patterns. At first the characteristic trend of erratic movements was maintained but the opening of Devon Great Consols in the mid-1840s disrupted this customary pattern and precipitated an increase in the figures. Rates remained steady, at about eight or nine, for most of the 1850s, falling only slightly in the closing years of the decade. This downward trend persisted, with a temporary interruption in 1864, until the end of the period. By the late-1860s and early-1870s the marriage rate had declined to its lowest level.

There were much greater oscillations in the baptism rate, with figures varying from as little as 15.9 in 1742, a year of particularly high mortality, to just over 40 in the early years of the nineteenth century. In the period up to 1780 rates moved somewhat erratically albeit within a restricted range of between 22 and 27. Subsequently there were steady but sustained increases with the highest figures being recorded in 1808 and 1811. Although rates then fell back slightly, they remained consistently above the pre-1780 levels with only one temporary interruption.

The availability of information from non-parochial baptismal registers provided the means of verifying these adjustments. From the outset the impact of under-registration was apparent as the uncertain movements of the early years were repeated at higher levels, with rates varying from 24 to 29. In addition, the onset of steady growth commenced a little earlier, the turning point being reached in the 1770s. Figures of over 30 were regularly recorded throughout the 1780s and 1790s and in 1791 the rate reached 40.8. Even these levels were superseded in the opening years of the nineteenth century, when there was a further acceleration in growth, a series of high points occurring in 1803, 1807, 1808 and 1811. Although this upward surge wavered and then fell back overall momentum was sustained. During the 1820s and 1830s rates generally fluctuated between 32 and 38, some seven or eight points ahead of the parochial figures. Despite these refinements fundamental shifts and basic trends were confirmed.

The transfer to civil as opposed to ecclesiastical sources produced no major discontinuity in fertility trends. After a slight hiatus in 1837 there was a close correspondence between baptism and birth rates. In the period up to 1849 there was little overall variation with figures ranging from 33 to 38. A sharp decline in 1849, the year of the cholera outbreak, proved to be a temporary aberration, for the following year the rate not only recovered but reached 40, a level unequalled for almost thirty years. In general higher fertility rates were maintained throughout the 1850s, only to fall back slightly in the early 1860s and more sharply in the closing years of the period. In 1871 the figure was 24.3, one of the lowest recorded for a century. These fluctuations, together with the complementary adjustments in nuptiality, underline the interaction of demographic and economic change, most notably the crucial role of developments in the mining industry.

In overall terms burials showed the greatest variation. The sharpest contrasts occurred in the 1740s, 1750s and 1760s when periodic mortality crises associated with outbreaks of typhus or smallpox created sudden and dramatic increases in burial rates. In particular, 1742, 1756 and 1764 showed rates well above the usual level of between 20 and 30. In the second part of the eighteenth century Tavistock shared in the decreasing incidence of epidemics reported throughout England and the disappearance of earlier surges of mortality was the most conspicuous local feature. There were few changes in either scale or direction until the second decade of the nineteenth century when a new pattern of greatly reduced mortality was established. In general burial rates were much lower, ranging from 17 to 25. The downward trend was confirmed by data collated from the civil registers of deaths.

Apart from a few unhealthy years most notably 1842, 1849 and 1864 death rates were remarkably stable and until the mid-1860s hovered around the 20 to 25 mark. By scrutinizing the causes of death the diseases which took such a heavy toll of lives during these periodic crises can be identified. In 1842 scarlet fever and typhus were major contributors. Scarlet fever recurred in 1855, 1863 and 1864. While Howe notes that 1863 was the year of highest mortality from scarlet fever nationwide,[9] in Tavistock the greatest numbers of deaths were registered in the autumn of 1864. In contrast the excesses of 1849 were associated with cholera for Tavistock shared in the serious outbreak which ravaged so many places throughout Britain. Indeed the town was noted as a 'principal centre' and a total of 140 cases were reported.[10] After Plymouth and its environs this area had the highest mortality from cholera in Devon. While the 1849 cholera epidemic was an isolated event, there were other diseases constantly present which took a substantial toll. Fatalities from typhus and typhoid persisted throughout the 1850s and 1860s. Among the predisposing conditions contributing to both typhus and the spread of scarlet fever were poverty, undernourishment and overcrowding. The loss of life from these and other causes was an obvious manifestation of fundamental problems including poor housing, inadequate supplies of water, insanitary conditions and deprivation. As the mining recession deepened, emigration together with housing and sanitary improvements contributed to a reduction in mortality levels and death rates fell.

This analysis of aggregative patterns has provided mutually reinforcing evidence of overall patterns of demographic change in Tavistock during a period of economic and social transformation. The simple delineation of basic patterns and general trends has been complemented by more detailed assessment of the differential contributions of key components including nuptiality, fertility and mortality. Despite an apparently spontaneous transition from stagnation to growth during the second half of the eighteenth century, mining developments contributed to both the timing and extent of subsequent changes. Mining was the catalyst and for a short time the small town shared conditions as squalid as those experienced by much larger communities in the Midlands and North. However, with the collapse of the industry and emigration of population, environmental and social conditions improved. Nevertheless, the pressures and prosperity created by mining left a permanent imprint on the fabric and layout of the town with the rows of labourers' cottages, market complex and remodelled town centre as the major legacies of the mid-nineteenth century boom.

NOTES

1. Although the first entries in the Tavistock Parish Register were recorded in 1614, for the purpose of this review it was sufficient to consider information extracted for a more limited period commencing in 1741 and ending in 1871. This ensured coverage of the early phases of copper mining in the 1800s as well as the mid-century boom. At the same time it facilitated comparisons with the preceding agrarian economy.
2. C. Barham, 'Remarks on the Abstract of the Parish Registers of Tavistock, Devon', *Journal of the Statistical Society of London* (1841), IV, 34–49 (p.45).
3. D.V. Glass, *Numbering the People: The Eighteenth-Century Population Controversy and the Development of Census and Vital Statistics in Britain* (Farnborough, 1973).
4. Extract from *Sherborne Mercury*, 1799.
5. DRO, L1258/M/SS/C/DL/37, letter of 25 March 1827.
6. DRO, L1258/M/SS/C/DL/92, letter of 16 January 1832.
7. *Tavistock Gazette*, 21 April 1871.
8. A. Young, *A Six Months Tour through the North of England* (1770), IV, 561.
9. G.M. Howe, *Man Environment and Disease in Britain: A Medical Geography of Britain through the Ages* (Newton Abbot, 1972), 191.
10. C. Creighton, *A History of Epidemics in Britain* (2nd edition, 1965), II, 844.

M.C. Phillips

37. Mother Hubbard and Housekeeping at Kitley in 1869

Every English schoolchild used to know the story of Old Mother Hubbard. Some Devon children (even now) know that the nursery rhyme was written early in the nineteenth century to amuse the children of Kitley House in the parish of Yealmpton in South Devon, and concerned the old housekeeper—Mother Hubbard. Half a century after the verses were published one of her successors was presented with a set of written instructions by the master of the house. They illuminate the comforts and limitations of a life in service, underscore its segregation and stratification within a rigid hierarchy, and hint at the central role the country house played in the local community.

The Bastards, an ancient Devon family of Norman descent, acquired Kitley by marriage with a Pollexfen heiress, around 1700. An early-Georgian remodelling of the Tudor house was superseded by a reconstruction in neo-Tudor style by George Stanley Repton, c.1820–25.[1] Part of Repton's work involved hiding from view the basement storeys behind grass ramps and terraces, and building a new range over the back door to which access was gained via a concealed pathway. In this the architect was pursuing the increasingly popular nineteenth-century practise of protecting the proprietor and his family from the gaze of the domestic staff.[2]

Baldwin John Pollexfen Bastard was one month short of his thirty-ninth birthday when he drew up his 'Rules for Guidance of Housekeeper' in 1869. A substantial member of the gentry, he had been High Sheriff of Devonshire in 1865, and was a Deputy Lieutenant and Justice of the Peace. He had married Frances Jane Rodney in 1861 but the couple did not have children and the estate was inherited eventually by his brother.[3] The census for 1861 (bearing in mind its limitations as a 'snapshot') does not show that the Bastard's possessed a particularly large staff: Housekeeper, Butler, two Housemaids, Kitchen Maid, Dairy Maid, Scullery Maid, Coachman, Footman, Page and Helper—a total of eleven. Ten years later, ten servants are listed, with no mention of a Housekeeper; whether she was temporarily absent or the position had been dispensed with altogether is not revealed.[4]

Whichever, in 1869 her responsibilities were considerable. To her fell much of the burden in maintaining the decorum of the establishment, discouraging 'followers' and 'unnecessary conversation or unseemly jesting', and ensuring that the sexes were scrupulously segregated into their own territories. In common with most Victorian houses of this type, the Bastard's establishment was a demonstrably 'moral' one, with morning and evening prayers and attendance at the Parish Church on Sundays.

The supervision of the household accounts, too, would have been a most important task. Above all, whether in dealings with tradesmen, with applicants for charitable relief, or with the lower servants, the Housekeeper would have been the chief point of contact between the master and mistress and those who relied upon them for assistance, business or employment. She was, in a sense, the hinge upon which the green baize door swung.

WDRO, 540/14/6

Rules for Guidance of Housekeeper. Kitley 1869. Feb 11.

Rising   Under servants are expected to rise not later than 6 am. Breakfast at 8—to be finished by 8.1/2.

Boy's duties   Boy (or man employed temporarily) to sweep the Servants' Hall daily—clean the knives—wash copper and brass—lay cloth for hall breakfast and dinner—carry up wood and coals and go errands.

Meals   All Servants—home or strange—to dine together at 1.—and sup together at 9pm in Servants' Hall—Grace to be said before and after meat by the Housekeeper—in her absence, by the eldest Servant present—As soon as Grace after is said, the livery Servants will carry down the meat to the Larder, and all the Maidservants will retire at once to their room. When the quarter bell rings before dinner, all Servants are expected to prepare for that meal—the boy will lay the cloth and the proper Servants will proceed to the kitchen to carry up the meal—which is to be on table by 1 precisely. All Servants are expected to sit down punctually at that hour decently dressed. No unnecessary conversation or unseemly jesting to be permitted.

Family Prayers   All indoor Servants will attend Family Prayers in the morning, and all Servants those at 10pm. All will retire quietly to rest immediately after Evening Prayers—

Retiring to Rest   Men sleeping out will leave the house at once and the Butler will carefully lock outer and inner doors after them—bringing up the key of the outer door to be suspended in the best Entrance Hall.—

House Bell   The House Bell to be rung as follows—

Week Days	Sundays
8am	8am
12 noon	1. o'clock
1/4 to 1	9. p.m.
1. o'clock	
9 p.m.	

Divine Service   Also half an hour before the parlour dinner and at the parlour dinner hour—according to the time ordered—and on Sundays, half an hour before Divine Service in the morning and afternoon—when as many Servants as can be spared will be ready to proceed to their Parish Church at Yealmpton—and are expected to be punctual in their arrival there.

Maidservants   No females to be permitted to frequent the Pantry or Servants Hall—and no Men allowed in the Kitchen (unless on an errand of business) nor in the Still room or Maids Sitting room on any pretence whatever. Messages to be delivered at the door without entering.

Leave of Absence   No female Servants permitted to leave the house, except with theknowledge of the Housekeeper—and no followers or friends to be introduced into the house by any Servants unless with the express permission of Mr and Mrs Bastard.

Strangers on Errands All persons coming to the house on business to be shewn to the room appropriated to them in an orderly manner by one of the Servants—and all messages to be given at the back door without entering, unless requiring to wait an answer—

Rooms Tenant Farmers etc. to be shewn to the Steward's Room—Female Tenants to the Housekeepers' Room—Strange Servants, Labourers etc to the Hall.—

Entrance Door The Back door to be kept locked during Servants meal hours—also during the hours of Divine Service—

Relief to Sick and Poor The Housekeeper will acquaint her mistress with all applications for charitable relief made by the sick and poor of the neighbourhood before complying with their requirements—and will allow nothing to be given away at the door on any pretence whatever without her sanction. The names of persons in receipt of relief to be entered from time to time in a book kept for that purpose.

Accounts The Housekeeper will have charge of all household accounts—and will call in and examine weekly all Tradesmen's Books—those of the Butchers being compared with and proved by the Tickets which are to be brought in regularly with the meat—and the latter weighed as soon as brought.—

Orders to Tradesmen No Orders to be given to Tradesmen, workmen, or the like, by anyone but the Housekeeper or Butler—unless by express desire of Mr or Mrs Bastard.

The Housekeeper will appeal to her Master or Mistress for their countenance and support whensoever required, to enable her to carry out these instructions effectively.

B[aldwin]. J[ohn]. P[ollexfen]. B[astard].

NOTES

1. Christopher Hussey, *English Country Houses, Late Georgian* (1958), 168–74.
2. Jill Franklin 'The Victorian Country House' in G. E. Mingay (ed.), *The Victorian Countryside* (1981), II, 407.
3. *Burkes Landed Gentry* (1952 edn).
4. WSL, microfilms of 1861 and 1871 censuses.

Steven Pugsley

38. Devon Justices of the Peace, 1643–60

The commission of the peace is one of the most useful benchmarks of status of the provincial gentry in the early modern period. Many county studies, particularly of the civil war period, have drawn on comings and goings on the bench of magistrates as an index of changes in political loyalty and allegiance, as well as a measure of gentry standing in the shires. It is now many years since T.G. Barnes and Hassell Smith[1] produced a thorough survey of sources that can be used to compile a list of magistrates for any county in England and Wales, but no comprehensive list of Devon JPs for the mid-seventeenth century has before appeared in print.

The names that follow may be reminiscent of Beachcomber's lists of Huntingdonshire cabmen, or suggest an extended chorus of 'Widecombe Fair', but if used appropriately can be extremely useful to historians of politics, local administration and county society. It is important to stress at the outset, as many commentators have done, that the commission of the peace cannot be considered to be a list of active magistrates in the county. For an accurate guide to who among the justices were activists, the researcher must turn to the rich archive of the court of quarter sessions which met four times a year at Exeter. The order books and sessions papers contain ample evidence of the work of the magistrates, both on the bench itself and when they acted alone or with a small group in privy or petty sessions.

The reader cannot assume, either, that in the turbulent decades of the 1640s, 50s and 60s, a name of an individual on the commission meant complete political loyalty to the regime which had nominated him. The commission of the peace was a tool in the work of building up support, as well as a prestigious roll of honour, and sometimes the government made mistakes.

The final, and perhaps most obvious caveat to be noted is that many honorary nominations were made, of individuals who had no obvious connection with the county and who never visited Devon, let alone acted as magistrates there. In analysing the commissions for social status, there is a case for excluding such persons from account,[2] but in presenting this information as an edited source, it is important to include them, since they formed an important part of every early modern commission. To omit them might not be poor historical writing, but would certainly be bad record editing. Moreover, the order of precedence in commissions of the peace is of some considerable significance as a guide to an individual's standing among his peers as well as among those who nominated him, as was his inclusion or exclusion from the quorum, the 'inner circle' of prestige on the bench. No attempt has been made here to provide biographies of the men named in the commissions of the peace, although the details of many can be traced through the index and notes of a study of Devon in this period.[3]

Original commissions of the peace are the most accurate and reliable guides to what the Chancery Crown Office which produced them intended, and Crown Office entry books and *libri pacis* provided officials with working copies of the commissions they had despatched. Enrolments on the patent rolls are considered to be the least reliable source, often having been made carelessly, and for form's sake only; docquet books recorded changes in the commissions as they were made.

The following lists are an attempt to provide a complete picture of additions and omissions, entrances and exits, in the commissions of the peace for the county of Devon. Names for the city and county of Exeter, and for other corporate boroughs, will not be found here. Some lists have been reproduced in their entirety; to save pointless repetition, changes have been noted as they appear in other lists or docquet book entries. The Crown Office docquet books have been used to provide accurate dates for the inclusion or exclusion of individuals. Names of justices have been given in the order in which they appear in the commissions of the peace and the *libri pacis*. In the contemporary lists the spellings of both forenames and surnames are erratic and inconsistent. Here, forenames have been rendered in modern form, but the same consistency cannot be claimed in the case of surnames, where the original has mostly been reproduced. Where place names are given, they appear here as in the original. The nominating authority has been included to help readers identify the political changes which took place in the decades under consideration.

Asterisks indicate those of the quorum, and the name of the leading local justice charged with safekeeping of the records of quarter sessions, the *custos rotulorum*, has been given where known. Italics have been reserved for editorial annotations and archaic spelling of place names. The layout roughly follows the practice in J.R.S. Phillips, *The Justices of the Peace in Wales and Monmouthshire 1541 to 1689* (Cardiff, 1975), to which the reader is referred for a fuller discussion of the records and their value.[4]

1643: 30 May (Charles I). DRO DQS 28/1

*Edward, Lord Littleton, Keeper of Great Seal; *James, Duke of Richmond and Lennox; *Thomas, Earl of Arundel and Surrey; *Earl of Bath; *Thomas, Viscount Savile; *Edward, Viscount Chichester; *Lucius, Viscount Falkland; *Sir Peter Wich knt.; *Edward Nicholas knt.; *Robert Foster, knt, KB; *Edward Symour knt and bart; *Thomas Hele bart; *Amias Ameredith bart; *Gregory Norton, bart; *Richard Sydenham, knt; *Popham Southcott knt; *Thomas Hele knt; *Ferdinando Gorges knt; *Francis Fulford, knt; Edmund Southcott knt; *Richard Reynell *of* Ogwell, knt; *Thomas Reynell knt; *John Chichester of Hall knt; *Nicholas Slanning knt; *William Poole knt; *Edmund Fortescue knt; *Peter Ball knt; George Parry DCL; *John Ackland; *Arthur

Bassett; *Henry Rolle; *Edward Seymour; *Arthur Champernowne; *John Fortescue *of Fallopit* [Fallapit]; *Gregory Huckmore; *Thomas Monck; *Henry Aishford; *William Carey; Henry Carey; *Richard Culme; John Courtenay; John Gifford; James Welshe; John Peters; John Willoughby; Richard Cholmeley; *Peter Sainthill; *Humphrey Prouse; *Edmund Arscott; William Richards; *William Tothill; George Southcott; Roger Mallack; Richard Cabell; Francis Bluett; John Harris *of* Hayne; John Haris *of* Radford; Walter Hele *of* Lympstone; John Wye *of* Silverton; William Morrish; Richard Blagg; Edmund Yeard; Edmund Bampfield; Mathew Halse; Edward Tremayne; George Yeo

1643: 25 September, DRO, DQS 28/2

Add: John Berkley knt; Peter Ball attorney; John *not* William Morrish

Omit: Lucius, Viscount Falkland; Nicholas Slanning knt.

Gregory Norton *omitted from the quorum*.

1647: 6 March (Long Parliament), DRO, DQS 28/3

*Algernon, Earl of Northumberland; *Earl of Kent; *Earl of Pembroke and Montgomery; *Earl of Bath; *Edward, Earl of Manchester; *John, Lord Roberts; *William Lenthall; *John Godbold; *Oliver St John; *John Wylde; *Henry Rolle; *Francis Drake; *John Poole; *John Bampfield; *John Northcott; *John Davy barts; *Walter Earle knt; *Samuel Rolle knt; *Edmund Fowell knt; *Gregory Norton knt; *Nicholas Martin knt; *Henry Rosewell knt; *John Young knt; *Oliver St John, solicitor general; *Samuel Browne; *Edmund Prideaux; *Henry Walrond; *Walter Young; John Bampfield; Hugh Fortescue; *William Fry; *John Drake *of* Ash; *John Maynard; George Chudleigh; *Arthur Upton; Edmund Arscott; Robert Savery; John Bury *of* Bury; *John Harris *of* Hayne; *Robert Duke of Otterton; Thomas Reynell *of* Ogwell; Josias Calmady; *Edward Davyes; Ellis Crimes; *Francis Rowse; John Waddon; John Rolle; *Edmund Fowell; *John Beare; Peter Specott; *Henry Worth; *John Fortescue of Buckland; Thomas Hatch; *John Woolacombe; Robert Shapcott; Christopher Martin *of Plimpton* [Plympton]; *Christopher Savery *of* Shilston; Walter Yarde; Hugh Trevilian; *John Champneys; *Peter Bevis; *Henry Henley; *John Elford; Arthur Perryman; Thomas Drake; Roland Whiddon; John Kelly; *Robert Rolle; *George Prestwood senior; *William Morris; *John Quick; William Bastard; William Putt; William Northcott; Richard Duck; Henry Coplestone; William Fowell; *John Doddridge; John Tyrling *of Aulscomb* [Awliscombe]; Christopher Wood *of* Northtawton esqrs.

Edmund Prideaux custos

1647: 26 July (Long Parliament). DRO, DQS 28/4

Omit: Oliver St John

John Bampfield, George Chudleigh, Edmund Arscott. Robert Savery, John Waddon, John Rolle, John Bery, Christopher Martin, Hugh Trevilian. Josias Calmady *added to the quorum*.

1649: 30 June [*wrongly dated 1659 on dorse*] (Commonwealth). DRO, DQS 28/5

*William Lenthall; *Thomas Fairfax; *John Bradshaw; *Bulstrode Whitelocke; *John Lisle; *Richard Keble; *Algernon, Earl of Northumberland; *Philip, Earl of Pembroke and Montgomery; *William, Earl of Salisbury; *Henry Rolle, judge of Upper Bench; *John Wilde, judge of Common Pleas; *Alexander Rigby; *Edmund Prideaux, attorney general; *Francis Drake bart; *John Poole bart; *John Bampfield bart; *John Davy bart; *Gregory Norton bart; *Henry Rosewell knt; *John Young knt; *Henry Walrond; *Walter Young; *John Bampfield; *Hugh Fortescue; *William Fry; *John Drake of Ash; *George Chudleigh; *Arthur Upton; *Edmund Arscott; *Robert Savery; *John Bury of Bury; *Robert Duke of Otterton; *Thomas Reynell of Ogwell; *Josias Calmady; *Francis Rous; *John Rolle; *Thomas Boone; *Matthew Hele; *John Carew; *Henry Pollexfen; *John Beare; *Peter Specott; *Henry Worth; *John Fortescue of Buckland; Thomas Hatch; John Woolacombe; *Christopher Martin of *Plimpton*; *Christopher Savery *of Shiston* [Shilston]; Walter Yard; *Hugh Trevillian; *John Champneys; *Peter Bevis; Arthur Fortescue; *Henry Henley; *John Elford; Arthur Perryman; Thomas Drake; Roland Whiddon; John Kelly; *Robert Rolle; *George Prestwood senior; *William Morris; *John Quicke; *William Bastard; Henry Coplestone; William Fowell; John Tyrling *of Aulscombe*; Christopher Wood of Northtawton esqrs.

Edmund Prideaux custos

1650: 7 March. PRO, C231/6, p.178

Add: Sir Nicholas Martin knt; William Putt; Edmund Fowell;—Fortescue of Buckland

1650: 23 July. DRO, DQS 28/6

Add: *Oliver Cromwell; *Robert Nicholas; *Nicholas Martin knt; *William P:utt; *Edmund Fowell; *Francis Glanville; *Robert Dillon; *Robert Hatch; *Henry Walter; *John Desbrow; *Thomas Saunders; *Philip Croker; Philip Denis; Richard Coles; Philip Skippon; Maurice Rolles; John Doble; Robert Cockram; Richard Vicary; William Woollacombe esqrs.

Omit: Thomas Fairfax; John Bampfield; Henry Walrond; Walter Young; Peter Specott

[John Fortescue of Buckland *omitted from the quorum.*]
[Thomas Drake, Christopher Wood *added to the quorum.*]
Edmund Prideaux custos

1650: 20 August. PRO, C231/6, p.200

Add: William Morrice

1651: 15 February. PRO, C231/6, p.206

Add: Robert Rolle; Josias Calmady; Francis Glanville; Thomas Reynell; John Quicke

1651: 3 July. DRO, DQS 28/8

Omit: Alexander Rigby
Add: John Bampfield
Thomas Hatch *omitted from the quorum*
Roland Whiddon *added to the quorum.*
Edmund Prideaux custos

1652: 9 March. DRO, DQS 28/7

Omit: John Bampfield
Arthur Perryman *added to the quorum.*
Edmund Prideaux custos

1652: 11 May. DRO, DQS 28/9

John Rolle *described as* 'of Bickton'.

1652: 29 July. PRO, C231/6, p.243

Add: John Davy junior; Robert Bennett; Anthony Rouse; John Tuckfield; John Fowell

1653: before April. Cambridge University Library, Dd 8/1

Add: *Henry, Lord Herbert of Raglan; *Edward Atkins, Judge of the Common Bench; John Davy junior; *Anthony Rouse; John Tuckfield; John Copleston
Omit: Sir Gregory Norton
Hugh Trevilian *added to the quorum*

1653: 26 September (Nominated Assembly). DRO, DQS 28/10

*Oliver Cromwell; *Richard Keble; *Bulstrode Whitelocke; *John Lisle; *Henry Rolle, judge of Upper Bench; *Oliver St John; *John Wilde, judge of Common Pleas; *Edward Atkyns; Robert Nicholas; *Edmund Prideaux, attorney general; *Francis Drake bart; *John Disbrowe; *John Davy bart; *John Young knt; *Robert Rolle; *Francis Rous; *William Fry; *Arthur Upton; *John Drake; *John Woolacombe; *John Champneys; *John Fortescue; John Arscott; Edmund Prideaux of *Holdsworthy* [Holsworthy]; John Bury the younger; John Whichalse; Lionel Beecher; Philip Dennis; Arthur Fortescue; *James Erisey; William Venner; *William Maurice; William Fowell; Joseph Hunkin; Shilston Calmady; Christopher Cloubury; *John Elford; Henry Hatsell; *Edmund Fowell; *Christopher Martin; *John Carew; *Christopher Savery; *Servington Savery; *Philip Skippon; *Henry Henley; *Anthony Rous; William Bastard; *John Beare; *Thomas Reynell of Ogwell; *Rowland Whiddon; John Copleston; *John Quick; John Rowe; Richard Sweete; *Thomas Drake; *William Putt; William Woolcombe; John Marshall; *Thomas Bampfield;

Gideon Sherman of *Neeston* [Knightstone]; *John Tyrling; *John Searle; *Thomas Saunders; John Blundell; *Edmund Arscott of Tetcott; *Robert Bennett; *John Blackmore; Robert Crewes esqrs
John Disbrowe custos

1654: 4 March (Protectorate of Oliver Cromwell). DRO, DQS 28/11

Omit: Oliver Cromwell; Henry Rolle; John Wilde; Edward Atkins; Francis Rouse; William Venner; Christopher Clobury; Robert Crewes

Add: *William Lenthall; *John Glyn; *John Bradshaw; *Sir Henry Rosewell; *Hugh Fortescue; *Robert Duke of Otterton; *Thomas Boone; Henry Pollexfen; Arthur Perryman; Christopher Wood; Richard Viccary; John Hales; Henry Crewes

William Fowell, Joseph Hunkin *added to the quorum*.
Servington Savery, John Searle *omitted from the quorum*.

1654: 23 July. PRO, C231/6, p.294

Add: Baron Thorpe, judge of assize; Henry, Lord Herbert

1655: 10 March. PRO, C231/6, p.305

Add: Robert Nicholas, Judge of assize

1655: 25 July. PRO, C231/6, p.314

Add: Chief Justice Glynne; Justice Hale

1656: 20 March. PRO, C231/6, p.329

Add: Sir Coplestone Bampfield bart; Sir John Davy; William Fortescue of Buckland Filleigh; John Rolle of Bickton; Henry Walter; Henry Worth; Robert Hatch; Philip Francis; William Braddon

1656: 25 July. PRO, C231/6, p.345

Add: Chief Baron Steele; Baron Nicholas

1656/7. PRO, C193/13/6

*Nathaniel Fiennes; *John Lisle, commissioner of the great seal; *Bulstrode Whitelocke knt; Thomas Widdrington knt; *Edward Montague; *William Sydenham, commissioners of Treasury; *Henry, Lord Herbert; *John Disbrowe; *Francis Rous; *Philip Skippon; *John Thurloe; *John Glynn; *William Lenthall; *Oliver St John; *William Steele, Chief Baron of the Exchequer; *Peter Warburton, judge of the Upper Bench; *Robert Nicholas, judge of the Exchequer; *Richard Newdigate; *John Bradshaw; *Edmund Prideaux, attorney general; *Sir Francis Drake; *Sir Coplestone Bampfield; *Sir John Davy bart; *Sir John Coplestone; *Sir John Blackmore knt; *Sir

Henry Rosewell; *Sir John Young; *Hugh Fortescue; *Robert Rolle; *William Fry; *Arthur Upton; *John Drake; *John Wollacombe; *John Champneys; *John Fortescue; *John Arscott; *Edmund Prideaux of Holsworthy; *John Bury junior; *John Whitchalse; *Lionel Beecher; *Robert Duke; *Philip Dennis; *Arthur Fortescue; *James Erisey; *William Morrice; *William Fowell; *Joseph Hunkin; Shilston Calmady; *John Elford; Thomas Boone; Henry Hatsell; *Edmund Fowell; Henry Pollexfen; *Christopher Martin; *John Carew; *Christopher Savery; Servington Savery; *Henry Henley; *Anthony Rouse; Arthur Perryman; Christopher Wood; William Bastard; *John Beare; *Thomas Reynell; *Rowland Whiddon; John Coplestone; *John Quick; *William Fortescue of Buckland Filleigh; John Rowe; *John Rolle of Bickton; Richard Sweete; *Thomas Drake; *William Putt; William Wollacomb; John Marshall; *Thomas Bampfield; Gideon Sherman; *John Tyrling; John Searle; *Thomas Saunders; John Blundell; Richard Viccary; John Hales; *Edmund Arscott of Tetcott; *Robert Bennett; *John Blackmore; Henry Crewes; Henry Walter; Henry Worth; Robert Hatch; Francis Glanville; Edward Wise; Philip Francis; Thomas Southcott of Buckland; Joseph Hunkin; William Braddon; Richard Coffin; John Davy of Canon Teign; Nicholas Duck of Mount Radford; Henry Northleigh; John Fowell

John Disbrowe custos

1657: 16 June. PRO, C231/6, p.366

Add: Edward Ceely

1657: 26 July. PRO, C231/6, p.372

Add: Henry Northleigh; John Fowell

1658: 7 January. PRO, C231/6, p.382

Add: Sir John Coplestone; Sir John Blackmore

1658: 23 July. PRO, C231/6, p.401

Add: Sir John Northcote

1659: 10 March (Protectorate of Richard Cromwell). PRO, C231/6, p.420

Add: John Champneys; John Arscott; William Fowell; Joseph Hunkin

1659: 8 July (Restored Commonwealth). DRO, DQS 28/12

*William Lenthall; *John Bradshaw; *Thomas Tyrrell; *John Fountain sergeant-at-law, commissioners of the great seal; *John Disbrowe; *Robert Nicholas; *Richard Newdigate; *Robert Rolle; *Edmund Prideaux; *Sir Copletone Bampfield; *Sir John Davy; *Sir John Northcott barts; *John Blackmore; *William Fry; *Arthur Upton; John Drake; John Woollacombe; *John Champneys; John Arscott; *Robert Duke; *William Morris; William

Fowell; Joseph Hunkin; Sir Edmund Fowell knt; John Elford; *Thomas Boone; *Henry Hatsell; *Edmund Fowell; *Christopher Martin; *Servington Savery; Christopher Wood; *William Bastard; *John Coplestone; *Robert Bennett; *Sir Francis Drake knt; *John Beare; *Thomas Reynell; *John Quicke; William Fortescue of Buckland *Filly* [Filleigh]; *John Rolle; Thomas Drake; *William Putt; *Thomas Bampfield; John Tyrling; John Searle; *John Blundell; John Hales; Edmund Arscott of *Tidcott*; Henry Walter; Henry Worth; *Edward Wyse; *Thomas Southcott of Buckland; *Richard Coffin; John Davys of *Kinnoteen* [Canon Teign]; Nicholas Ducke; Roger Trobridge of Trobridge; *Walter Young; *Matthew Heele; Thomas Gibbons; James Pearse of Exon esqrs

John Disbrowe custos

1660: 13 August (Charles II). PRO, C231/7, p.26

Add: William Putt; William Morrice; Thomas Reynell: Robert Duke

1660: 20 August. PRO, C231/7, p.29

Add: John Kellond; John Stawell; William Bogan

1660: 11 September. PRO, C231/7, p.38

Add: John Fowell; Thomas Beare

1661. BL, MS Egerton 2557

*Earl of Clarendon; *Earl of Southampton; *Duke of Albemarle; *Earl of Ormonde; *Lindsay; *Earl of Manchester; *Earl of Bath; *Earl of Donegal; *Sir William Morrice knt; *Sir Robert Foster; *Sir Thomas Tyrrell; *Sir Peter Prideaux bart; *Sir Hugh Pollard bart; *Sir Edward Seymour bart; *Sir William Courtenay bart; *Sir Thomas Hele bart; *Courtenay Poole bart; *Sir Coplestone Bampfield bart; *Sir John Northcott bart; *Sir John Davy bart; Sir John Chichester bart; Sir Francis Drake bart; *Sir John Drake bart; *Sir John Grenvile knt; *Sir Edmund Fowell knt; *Sir John Chichester knt; *Sir John Young knt; *Sir Richard Prideaux knt; Sir Thomas Stucley knt; William Strode knt; John Rolle; *William Putt; *Arthur Bassett; Edward Wise; William Strode; Josias Calmady; *William Martin; Henry Ayshford;[5] *John Courtenay; *Thomas Southcott; Robert Fortescue; *Francis Drewe; *Robert Cary; John Willoughby; William Morrice; *John Stowell; *Thomas Reynell; Matthew Hele; *John Gifford of Brightley; *William Fry; *Arthur Upton; John Fowell; *Henry Northleigh; Richard Cabell; Henry Worth; *Richard Coffin; *John Arscott; John Bury of Colleton; Thomas Carew of Haccombe; *Thomas Drake; Nicholas Duck; *Edward Tremayne; William Bastard; *Thomas Wood; John Woollacomb; Robert Duke; Henry Ford; Henry Walter; *Thomas Bampfield; *John Champneys; *John Davy of Canonteign; *John Hale; *Christopher Clobury; *Edward Walrond; *John Kelland; *William Bogan; Thomas Beare

Duke of Albemarle custos

NOTES

1. T.G.Barnes, A.Hassell Smith, 'Justices of the Peace from 1588 to 1688—A Revised List of Sources', *Bulletin of the Institute of Historical Research, XXXII* (1959).
2. As in S.K. Roberts, *Recovery and Restoration in an English County: Devon Local Administration 1646–1670* (Exeter, 1985), 28.
3. Roberts, *Recovery*.
4. The documents that have been consulted and compared in order to compile these lists are: DRO, DQS 28/1–12 (original commissions of the peace, 1640–60); Cambridge Univ. Lib., Dd 8/1, BL, MS Stowe 577, MS Egerton 2557, Add. MS 3678 f.42, PRO, C193/13/3, C193/13/4, C193/13/5, C193/13/6, C220/9/4, C193/12/3 (Crown Office entry books and *libri pacis*); PRO, C66/2986, C66/3022, C66/3074 (enrolled commissions of the peace); PRO, C231/6 [formerly IND 4213], PRO C231/7 [formerly IND 4214] (Crown Office docquet books 1644–60 and 1660–79).
5. *marked* 'mort' in MS.

Stephen K. Roberts

39. A Family at Risk: The Thornes of Cruwys Morchard in 1793

On 13 February 1775, William Thorne, a farmer of Lower Yeadbury, married Catherine Way by licence in their parish church of Cruwys Morchard. A daughter, Mary, was baptized on 7 December and another daughter, Joan, on 8 April 1776. Catherine was buried on 30 July 1778. Left alone to bring up a young family, William felt he needed to marry again; having found Catherine Way congenial he saw nothing objectionable in her sister, Sarah. The couple were married by licence on 19 January 1780. In the register Sarah started to sign her name 'Thorne' then crossed it out and wrote 'way'. In the emotion of the moment it is a mistake a bride has been known to make even today but one may suspect that she was already taken for William's wife especially as their son, William, had been baptized on 3 October 1779. A further four sons and a daughter were born between 1781 and 1791.[1]

In 1791, William Thorne was elected an overseer of the poor by the annual vestry meeting. If he hoped for a quiet half year in office he was to be disappointed. His neighbours were outraged by the behaviour of a farmer in the next-door parish of Cheriton Fitzpaine called Daniel Tremblett: he got a local girl pregnant. Unwilling to acknowledge and maintain the child himself and reluctant to see the expense of doing so fall upon himself and his fellow ratepayers of Cheriton Fitzpaine, he forced the young woman to marry a mental defective from Cruwys Morchard by the name of John Gosling.

Tremblett was as sly as he was callous and Cruwys Morchard folk wanted justice. The vestry insisted that Thorne prosecute Tremblett at the Exeter Assizes.[2] Tremblett was found guilty and ordered to pay a fine of £50 and was sentenced to six months in prison. It was an exemplary punishment and Thorne considered it was too harsh. He petitioned the judge, successfully, to reduce the prison term by half.

Thorne's magnanimity did nothing to mollify Tremblett; he wanted his money back and hit upon a stratagem entirely in character. He began a prosecution against Thorne and his wife in the Exeter Consistory Court in September 1793 for incest while letting it be known that he would withdraw from the prosecution if Thorne repaid him the £50.

Marriage with deceased wife's sister was listed among the prohibited degrees of kindred and affinity. It still appears in the table printed at the back of editions of the Book of Common Prayer and Canon 99 of the Canons Ecclesiastical of 1604 provided that a copy of the Table was to be displayed publicly in every parish church. Marriage to a wife's sister ceased to be illegal in 1907 but, even today, a parish priest is under no obligation to solemnize such a marriage.[3] At this period, indeed until 1857, only an ecclesiastical court could pronounce on the validity or invalidity of a marriage. Because the relationship of William and Sarah Thorne was well-known, because the law did not permit the couple to marry, a serious sexual offence had been and was being committed. Tremblett was entitled to act as a voluntary promoter of the office of the judge, the procedure followed in the church courts in cases of criminal prosecution, because, although the couple's relationship had nothing to do with Tremblett personally, yet it was an offence both serious and notorious and anyone might initiate proceedings on the grounds of public spiritedness provided only that he gave security to pay the costs of the prosecution.

No one at the time harboured any doubts as to Tremblett's real motive; everyone was well aware what a sentence of nullity would mean for the couple and their seven children (a second daughter had been born on 1 January 1793). It was a vexatious suit but James Carrington, the Chancellor of the Diocese, did not consider he had any discretion in refusing to allow his office to be promoted. As we shall see shortly, one of the leading ecclesiastical lawyers in the country was of the same opinion.

A voluntary promotion of the office required use of the full or plenary procedure so both parties had to retain proctors; Geare appearing for Tremblett and Kemp for Thorne. These two men belonged to the last generation of full-time qualified practitioners in ecclesiastical and canon law to work in the Exeter church courts. They had acquired their professional knowledge in the course of a seven year apprenticeship. If any point of law arose on which they were unsure they could choose to pay a fee and seek an advocate's opinion. The twenty five Advocates belonging to Doctors' Commons, in London, represented the cream of the ecclesiastical legal profession. Requests for opinions were parcelled out in rotation to the Advocates and Kemp's request on behalf of his client was passed to Sir William Scott.

Later ennobled as Baron Stowell, Scott was one of the greatest civil and canon lawyers this country has ever produced. His judgments are still cited as precedents in law books down to the present day. In 1793, he had already begun his illustrious career as Chancellor of the diocese of London where he presided over the Bishop's Consistory Court from 1788 until he retired in 1820.[4] Having outlined the circumstances, Kemp asked if the Court would be justified in dismissing the case with costs. Scott's reply was as adamant as it was (uncharacteristically) brief. No length of time can legalize the marriage. If the fact be proved the Court had no choice but to pronounce a nullity and by the law of the land was bound to do so. If the fact of the marriage was proved the Court had no liberty, to dismiss the parties; be the motive of the promoter ever so spiteful the Court could not act contrary to law.[5]

The case had begun on 13 September 1793 when the citation was returned and both proctors exhibited their proxies. On 27 September, Geare submitted a set of articles (the formal charge). Having sought and received his advocate's opinion, Kemp entered a plea of not guilty on 25 October. The judge assigned to Geare his term probatory. This was the period of time in which he had to produce his evidence to substantiate his articles and, according to the practice of the Exeter Court, was limited to six weeks.

Geare's first move was to demand the personal answer of the defendant. This was good practice because the defendant might decide to confess to all or to a part of the charges; if he took the latter course, there was need to prove only the articles he denied. Thorn was not obliged to incriminate himself and he confessed to nothing. This set Geare the task of finding credible witnesses. The parish register was a key piece of evidence and Geare asked for a monition to be sent to the parish clerk of Cruwys Morchard to produce it. The rector who had officiated at both marriages had died in 1791 but this mattered less than in former times because, by the provisions of section 15 of the Marriage Act (1753) (26 Geo.2, *cap*.33), all entries had to include not only the date and the names of the parties but also the signatures (or marks) of the couple, the name of the officiating minister and the names of two witnesses. Geare needed to find at least two credible witnesses to depose that Catherine and Sarah had been sisters.

It was not easy to find witnesses; Cruwys Morchard folk seem to have suffered a bout of collective amnesia and were unwilling to come forward. Geare produced three witnesses in February and a further three in May at which point Kemp, protesting at the irregular delay of 28 weeks, sought and obtained the conclusion of the probatory term.

Once the judge had ordered the publication of the depositions, no further witnesses could be called unless new evidence came to light or new allegations were made. Now Kemp had the prosecution case in front of him and he pointed out the inconsistences of the witnesses knowing that this was his strongest card. He could argue that Geare had failed to prove his articles. He called no witnesses because his client was purely on the defensive but he could try to influence the new Chancellor, Ralph Barnes (Carrington having died in January 1794), by forcing Tremblett to give in personal answers.

By this time it was August; the case had dragged on for ten months and what Tremblett must have believed to be an open and shut case with only one possible outcome was looking decidedly less so. He agreed to go to arbitration; the arbiter produced an acceptable agreement so Geare announced on 21 November that his client was withdrawing from the case. The judge dismissed Thorne and ordered each party to pay their own costs. The Thornes' marriage and the legitimacy of their children was assured.

Vital though it was to the parties concerned, this purely local affair was of little more than passing interest. It demonstrates the flexibility of canonical jurisprudence; that the spirit was more important than the letter and that the peace of the parish community and the well-being of its members carried more weight than any single breach of the moral code. From this point of view this story is just one example among many and adds nothing fresh to our understanding. On one point of canon law, however, this incident in Cruwys Morchard does have a wider significance.

The promotion of the office was at the discretion of the ecclesiastical judge; all were agreed on this, because situations could, and did, arise when the party seeking to promote the office had no right in law to do so. But did the judge's discretionary power extend as far as to refuse to lend his office in a criminal suit?

A key concession in the passage of the Church Discipline Act (1840) was a safeguard against prosecution. Every diocesan bishop was given the right to veto any prosecution of a clergyman. This veto is retained in the present law dealing with clergy discipline. After 1840, it was argued that the bishop's veto did no more than to confirm a discretion given by ancient canon law. This became the view of the majority but some remained unconvinced. The members of the Royal Commission on the Ecclesiastical Courts, which reported in 1883, were not unanimous on this point. Several submitted minority reports; two of the ecclesiastical lawyers wanted to see the bishop's veto restricted in cases which involved ritual or doctrine and the Lord Chief Justice, Lord Coleridge, wrote:

> I am unable to concur in the recommendation ... that the bishop's assent should be made a condition precedent to the taking of proceedings ... against a clergyman. I believe that practically this is a power claimed and exercised by bishops for the first time since the Church Discipline Act ... But since the Reformation, though the fiction of permission was kept up by the forms of the court, yet it was a fiction only, and the practice was, as declared by the highest authority, Lord Stowell, for the assent to be given as a matter of course if the bishop were made safe as to costs.[6]

Coleridge cited Stowell in support of his interpretation. Members of the Archbishops' Commission on the Ecclesiastical Courts, quoted Stowell in support of the exact opposite. They were more explicit than Coleridge and referred to Stowell's judgment in *Maidman v. Malpas* (1794), 1 Hag. Con. 205 in support of their contention that an ecclesiastical judge 'had a very limited power of refusing leave; but it is from this power of refusal, *which the judge had in criminal suits* [my italics] that the modern bishop's veto in clergy discipline cases has developed.'[7]

The Archbishops' Commission took Stowell's remarks completely out of context. This can be seen by comparing his comments in the judgment of 1794 with the one he delivered in *Duke of Portland v. Dr Bingham* (1792), 1 Hag. Con.157, in which he made a clear distinction between the voluntary promoter of the office in a criminal suit and the promoter in a civil cause:

> There are other interests indeed in which every man partakes, such as that of maintaining public order etc. These are clear, direct and universal, and will entitle anyone to institute proceedings to preserve that order. But such proceedings must be *ad publicam vindictam*, and by criminal articles exhibited in due form ...[8]

The value of the Cruwys Morchard case, coming one year after this judgment of 1792 is to confirm that this was indeed Stowell's understanding of the law and that the judge (and therefore the bishop) had no discretion to withhold his office in cases where the offence was criminal.

D&C, AE/IV/2/16
Case

In the year 1775 William Thorn of *Crewnys*—Morchard in the County of Devon was married to Catherine Way of the same place Spinster, and of such marriage is issue one child, shortly after the birth of which Catherine Thorn departed this life leaving, as is alleged, a sister, (Sarah Way) to whom the said William Thorn was married in 1780, and which said William and Sarah Thorn are now living and have issue 7 children. Thorn was Overseer of the Poor of Crewys—Morchard aforesaid in 1791, and directed by the Parishioners to proceed against Daniel Tremblett of Cheriton Fitzpaine in the County aforesaid, for that he (Tremblett) in order to prevent a Base Child's being Chargeable to the Parish (in which he had Estates) prevail'd on the Woman to marry an Idiot of Crewys—Morchard. Tremblett was found guilty of this Offence and sentenced to pay a fine of £50 and Six Months Imprisonment, but afterwards at the particular request of Thorn, who petitioned the Judge for a mitigation of the Punishment, three months of such Imprisonment were remitted; notwithstanding which and the proceedings against Tremblett being an Act of the Parishioners and not Thorn's, Tremblett hath Articles against him in the Ecc. court for an Incestuous Marriage and refuseth to withdraw the Proceedings unless he is repaid the aforesaid fine of £50 but it being considered by all that are acquainted with the Parties, that the Promovent's motives for proceeding in this Suit, are revenge and in order to extort Money from the Defendant.

Your Opinion is requested upon the following Queries:

After 12 years can the Ecc. Court proceed to punish the Man for such Marriage and Bastardize the Issue, or if (admitting proof of the Marriage) the Court would not be justified in dismissing him with costs, considering the Suit as litigious and vexatious.

No length of Time can legalize a Marriage of this Sort; and if the Fact be proved, the Ecclesiastical Court can do no otherwise than pronounce the Marriage to be null and void, for it is so by the Law of the Land, which the Eccl. Court is bound to carry into Effect. It has no liberty to dismiss the Parties, if the Fact of the Marriage is proved, and the motives of the Prosecutor, be they ever so improper will not justify the Court in acting contrary to Law.

Wm. Scott [Doctors] Coms. 16th Octr.1793

NOTES

1. *The Report of the Commissioners concerning Charites* (Exeter, 1826), 113; DRO, Cruwys Morchard parish registers.
2. DRO, 1092/A/PO4, Cruwys Morchard Overseers' Accounts Easter to Michaelmas 1791.
3. The requirement to display the Table of Degrees ceased after 1946. For the right of a clergyman to refuse to perform such a marriage see *Halsbury's Laws of England* (3rd. edn), XIII, para. 809 (e).

4. For a life of Scott see *Dictionary of National Biography*. Also H.J. Bourguignon, *Sir William Scott, Lord Stowell* (London 1987).
5. D&C, AE/IV/2/16; DRO, CC 853 (c). Unfortunately, the cause papers do not appear to have survived.
6. Parliamentary Reports, Ecclesiastical Courts Commission (1883), lxii & lxiii.
7. *The Ecclesiastical Courts: Principles of Reconstruction* (London, 1954), 14.
8. English Reports 161 (1 Hag. Con. 159) at 510.

Michael Smith

40. Theresa Parker of Saltram, 1745–75

In the Leeds District Archives depository of the West Yorkshire Archive Service are two collections containing unpublished items relating to Theresa Parker, who was mistress of Saltram, Plympton St Mary, between 1769 and 1775.[1] A bundle of letters from Theresa and her sister, Anne, to their brother, Frederick, is amongst the Vyner family papers (Theresa's daughter, Mary, having married Henry Vyner of Gautby, Lincs.), while other letters and documents relating to Theresa are among the deposited papers belonging to Newby Hall, Ripon.

Theresa (or Therese as she is referred to in all these documents and as she always signed herself) was the second daughter of the diplomat, Thomas Robinson, 1st Baron Grantham (1695–1770). Between 1730 and 1748 he was ambassador at Vienna, where Theresa was born on 1 January 1745. Her godmother was the Empress Maria Theresa, after whom she was named. The family led a cosmopolitan life but its roots were firmly in Yorkshire. Lord Grantham had been M.P. for Thirsk (1727–30), his father, Sir William Robinson, had built Newby Park, near Topcliffe, and his mother was Mary Aislabie of Studley Park. Theresa's mother was Frances, third daughter of Thomas Worsley of Hovingham, near York. Newby Park, subsequently known as Baldersby Park, is not to be confused with Newby Hall which did not come into the possession of the Robinsons until 1792, when it was bequeathed to Theresa's nephew, Thomas.

The marriage of Theresa to John Parker of Saltram took place on 18 May 1769 at Twickenham, and lasted but a few years; she died aged only thirty on 22 December 1775 and is buried at Plympton St Mary. On all the evidence the marriage combined personal affection with due deference to considerations of social status and inheritance. By 1769 Saltram was already an estate of some substance and the house of considerable note, having been enlarged and enhanced, both outside and in, by John Parker's parents, especially his mother, Lady Catherine, a woman of ambitious artistic discernment. To Saltram Theresa brought added wealth and titled connections.

The letters in the Vyner collection reveal an apparently happy young wife, with many interests. Joshua Reynolds, a close friend of John Parker, whose paintings of Theresa alone and of her with her infant son still hang at Saltram, eulogized her in an obituary for her beauty and character and her skill and 'exact judgment' in the fine arts. She shared this interest in the arts with her husband and her two brothers. Her letters to her younger brother, Frederick (Fritz), in the Vyner papers reflect her interest in the gardens at Saltram, and in paintings and decorations in the house. On 17 September 1769, for instance, she asked Fritz to 'be so good as to call at Zucchis & let us have your opinion of the Paintings he has finished for the Library',[2] a reference to Antonio Zucchi, who painted the roundels in the saloon or 'great room' at Saltram. In 1770 she asked her brother to procure a border of 220 yards for her apartment 'of the narrowest sort as the Rooms are low', and to 'buy me a good Guittar',[3] and it was during her time at Saltram that Robert Adam completed the first phase of his work there. It is perhaps significant that both Adam and Zucchi were engaged by William Weddell in his enlarging and enhancing of Newby Hall in the late 1760s.

The letters in the Vyner collection record a full life of travelling, visiting other county houses, entertaining visitors, rides in 'the Phaeton', 'going upon the water', walking and playing billiards. They reflect, too, Theresa's interest (also shared with her husband) in horse riding and in horse racing, mentioning attendance at races at Bodmin, Exeter, Bridgwater and Barnstaple. Thus in June 1769, a month after her marriage, she wrote 'We set off tomorrow for Bodmin and hope to return on Thursday after having seen our four horses win'.[4] In August of the same year she wrote from Bridgwater (which she referred to as 'this vile place', and as 'a sad melancholy place Flat & no Prospect') 'I had the mortification of seeing Virage lose on Tuesday by half a length'.[5] Her letters contain, too, some observations on the Devon climate. Soon after her arrival at Saltram in 1769, for instance, she wrote 'I cannot say much for the weather here ... we have had only one day without rain & were so unfortunate as to have it rain without ceasing when we went to Mount Edgecumbe', and in January, 1771 she remarked 'We are all cover'd with Snow to a degree that surprises the people of this Country, but is really no more than what Nanny & I saw in Yorkshire in the Month of April'.[6] 'Nanny' was her sister, Anne.

The most important of the Newby Hall documents is a marriage settlement dated 13 May 1769. In addition there is a bond connected with the settlement, some letters of 1763 containing references to Theresa, medical reports on her in the same year, a couple of letters written by her and a receipt book belonging to her husband, John Parker. The marriage settlement is too lengthy to reproduce here, but consists mainly of a settlement on Theresa (in the event of her future husband predeceasing her) of houses and lands in Chudleigh, Devon (including Bath Place) and in the Somerset parish of Durston (including Buckland and Buckland Farm), as well as a sum of money, all of which had been previously and similarly settled on John Parker's first wife, Frances, who had died at Naples on their wedding tour in 1764. Details of the lands and properties include information on tenants. The document also includes arrangements for settling money on children other than an eldest son, and details of a bond, reproduced below.

Letters in 1763 to Lord Grantham from his agent, from Theresa to her father, and from Grantham to his sister, refer to Theresa's precarious state of health at that time, when she was eighteen years of age. A medical report (November 1763) refers to her having arrived in Yorkshire from London in May 1763 with a 'thin habit of a body with a quick and limited pulse and a continual hectic fever', a cough and glandular swellings on both sides of her neck, one 'not less than a pullets Egg'. A doctor's letter of advice dated 20 May 1763 is reproduced below. In June her father wrote to his sister that 'my little Therese is at present ... much better' and refers to his daughter as 'well mounted' and 'an excellent little horsewoman'. But further letters reveal that fever and swellings returned and blood continued to be taken from her. By November, however, though some swellings remained, she had greatly improved. She herself wrote to her father on 15 November 1763 from Studley, Yorkshire 'I continue very well, we have tolerable fine weather, and get a Ride pretty often'. On 18 December she wrote again to her father 'I am at present really very well and I think likely to continue so since ... I am not so apt to catch cold as I was'.[7] In a letter in the Vyner collection from Theresa to her brother Frederick, dated 13 December 1763, she reported that the lump on the right side had 'entirely vanished'.[8] No further information as to the eventual outcome is recorded, but at the time of her marriage four and a half years later, there is no indication of ill health.

A letter in the Vyner collection, reproduced below, suggests, however, the likelihood of early miscarrriages, and the matter of ill health did preoccupy her, especially after the birth of her son, John (Jack). Her husband, John Parker, ever solicitous for his wife's health displayed some cynicism as to the efficiency of contemporary medicine, which was proved to be only too well-founded when Theresa died in

1775, some three months after the birth of their second child, a daughter, Theresa (a portrait of whom, by Gainsborough, is in the Huntington Library, California).[9] John Parker outlived Theresa, becoming 1st Baron Boringdon in the 1780s and dying at Saltram in 1788. It had pleased Theresa that her husband came to place great trust in her brothers and her sister. Her unmarried sister, Anne, came to live at Saltram to look after the children after Theresa's death and her brother, Fritz, acted as executor to the Saltram estate on the death of John Parker.[10]

West Yorkshire Archive Service (Leeds), Newby Hall, 2750

[dorse. 'Lord Grantham and Honble Thomas Robinson to John Parker Esqr: Bond for £6000 payable at Lord Grantham's Death']

Know all Men by these Presents That we The Right Honourable Thomas Lord Grantham Baron of Grantham in the County of Lincoln Knight of the most honourable Order of the Bath and the Honourable Thomas Robinson of Whitehall in the Liberty of Westminster in the County of Middlesex Esquire Eldest Son and heir apparent of the said Thomas Lord Grantham are held firmly bound to John Parker of Saltram in the County of Devon Esquire in the sum of Twelve Thousand Pounds of good and lawful mony of Great Britain to be paid to the said John Parker or his certain Attorney Executors Administrators or Assigns For which payment to be well and faithfully made we bind ourselves and each of us by himself for the whole and in gross our and each of our Heirs Executors and Administrators firmly by these Presents Sealed with our Seals Dated this thirteenth day of May in the ninth year of the Reign of our Sovereign Lord George the Third by the grace of God of Great Britain France and Ireland King Defender of the Faith and so forth and in the year of our Lord One thousand and seven hundred and Sixty nine.

Whereas A Marriage is agreed upon and intended with the Permission of Almighty God soon to be had and Solemnized between the said John Parker and the Honourable Therese Robinson Spinster one of the Daughters of the said Thomas Lord Grantham Upon Treaty whereof it was agreed amongst other things Between the said Thomas Lord Grantham and the said John Parker That the said Thomas Lord Grantham should give the sum of Six Thousand Pounds as and for the Marriage Portion of the said Therese Robinson his Daughter to be paid to the said John Parker his Executors Administrators or Assigns by the Heirs Executors or Administrators of the said Thomas Lord Grantham within one year after his Decease with Interest for the same at the rate of Four pounds per Centum per annum to be computed from his decease and that for the more Effective securing of the payment of the said sum of Six thousand pounds to the said John Parker his Executors Administrators or Assigns at the time and in manner aforesaid he the said Thomas Lord Grantham and the said Thomas Robinson should Enter into a Bond or Obligation to the said John Parker in the penal sum of Twelve Thousand Pounds.

Now the Condition of the above written Obligation is such That if the said Marriage intended between the said John Parker and the said Therese Robinson shall take Effect and the above bounden Thomas Robinson his heirs Executors or Administrators or the heirs Executors or Administrators of the said Thomas Lord Grantham do and shall in such case within one year after the decease of the said Thomas Lord Grantham well and truly pay or cause to be paid unto the said John Parker his Executors Administrators or Assigns the full sum of Six Thousand pounds of lawful mony of Great Britain with Interest for the same at and after the rate of Four pounds per Centum per annum to be computed from and immediately after the decease of the said Thomas Lord Grantham without fraud or further delay Then the above written Obligation to be Void and of no Effect otherwise to be and remain in full force and Virtue.

Sealed and Delivered being first duly stampt by the above named Thomas Lord Grantham and Thomas Robinson in the presence of

Jn. Radcliffe) [signatures] Grantham) [signatures]
John Lancaster) Thomas Robinson)

[Seals of Lord Grantham and Thomas Robinson]

[Lord Grantham died in 1770 but the receipt book of John Parker, found with the above bond, records payment to John Parker of interest on the £6,000 each year from 1773 to 1780, and loose documents enclosed in the receipt book record the payment of the £6,000 in full in August 1780.]

West Yorkshire Archive Service (Leeds), Newby Hall, 2838

Medical report relating to Therese Robinson, dated 20 May 1763

It will be proper for Miss Robinson to take half a pint of ass's milk every morning and to ride out after breakfast. The dinner may be made of any sort of fish or butcher's meat or poultry dress'd in a plain manner. All high sauces must be avoided & it would be better to abstain wholly from wine. Greens & roots & fruit may all be used with moderation. All meat must be avoided at supper. The powder here directed should be continued all the summer, & the draught should be taken after it, whenever there is an unusual degree of heat perceived by Miss Robinson; at other times it may be taken with a little water. If her stomack bears it well there wil be no impropriety in repeating the ass's milk in the evening. Such a quantity of sea water should be taken twice a week, as will give three motions, unless any failure of her stomack or strength make it necessary to omit the use of it for a week or two. Once in six weeks it will be right to take away five ounces of blood, & at any other time if the cough or heat be extraordinarily troublesome.

West Yorkshire Archive Service (Leeds), Vyner, 6015/14479

Dear Fritz, Saltram, Friday July 6th 1770

The great Share you all have the Goodness to take in whatever concerns my Happiness made me a little too hasty in informing you of a circumstance which

I thought might contribute towards it, & the same reason makes me now more sorry to acquaint you that the Care & Prudence I boasted of so much in my former Letter, has not prevented just such an accident as happen'd to me last year, when you came down to Saltram—Mr Parkers kindness & attention to me upon this, & every other occasion is a Comfort & Satisfaction I feel so sensibly, that he must excuse my mentioning it. I am now as well as can possibly be expected, & recover fast ...

Therese Parker

NOTES

1. The Newby Hall records are cited and reproduced by kind permission of Mr Robin Compton of Newby Hall. My thanks are due to Mr Michael Collinson, formerly Leeds City Archivist, for drawing my attention to them. The Vyner papers cited and reproduced are the property of the West Yorkshire Archive Service, and I thank Dr Todd Gray of the University of Exeter for drawing my attention to them. I am grateful, too, for the assistance of Mr William Connor, Principal District Archivist, Leeds District Archives, and his staff, in whose care all these records now reside.
2. Vyner, 6015/14476.
3. Vyner, 6015/14478; 14480.
4. Vyner, 6015/14474.
5. Vyner, 6015/14475.
6. Vyner, 6015/14474; 14484.
7. Newby Hall, 2838.
8. Vyner, 6015/14452
9. *DAT*, 115 (1983), 1.
10. The introduction above draws on *DNB*; E.I.F. Musgrave, *Newby Hall*, revised by E.R.F. and R. Compton (1974); Robin Fedden and Rosemary Joekes, *The National Trust Guide* (1977 edn), 176–8; D. Dodd, *Saltram, Devon* (National Trust, 1994 edn); R. Fletcher, *The Parkers at Saltram 1769–89* (1970).

W.B. Stephens

41. 'The Counterfeit King': Popular Reaction to the Accession of King James I, 1603

The death of Queen Elizabeth I in the early hours of the morning of 24 March, 1603, after a reign which had lasted for almost half a century, was a potentially cataclysmic event. Elizabeth had never married, she left no heirs and the man whom she had named to succeed her was almost unknown to her English subjects. With the advantage of hindsight, it is easy to assume that the peaceful accession of James VI of

Scotland to the English throne was inevitable, but at the time there were few who would have been so sanguine.

The English Crown had not always descended in a regular succession —as septuagenerians who had lived through the ten-day reign of Queen Jane Gray in 1553 could still testify—and chronicles of earlier periods were replete with accounts of disputed successions leading to bloody civil wars. To be sure, there was a general consensus among the political nation in 1603 that James VI should become King.[1] Nobody was sure quite how this goal was to be achieved, however, or on whose terms, and inevitably there were fears that secret conspirators might be plotting to install a rival claimant. As a result tension built up across the realm, reaching almost unbearable heights in March 1603, as the old Queen lay struggling between life and death. Fears of some sort of emeute or insurrection were particularly strong in the capital, and the young Lady Clifford—who lived in London throughout the tense period surrounding the Queen's death—later recalled that 'about the 21st or 22nd of March, my Aunt of Warwick sent my mother word about 9 a clock at night ... that she should remove to Austin Friars, her house, for fear of some commotions'.[2]

In the event the predicted disturbances failed to materialize but, as the great councillors of England assembled together two or three days later in the immediate aftermath of the Queen's death, fear of such 'commotions' must have been prominent in their minds. There was bound to be popular prejudice against the accession of a foreigner— Scottish people were regarded with scorn and contempt by many of the inhabitants of England at this time—and, to make matters worse, it was clearly going to be many weeks before James himself could make his way south in order to take up his new responsibilities. Under these exceptionally difficult circumstances, it was up to the Queen's former councillors to proclaim the new regime and to ensure that the capital— and indeed the country as a whole—remained quiet. Fortunately, they proved equal to the challenge.

Around 10 am on the morning of 24 March, 'the Council and divers noblemen, having been a while in consultation, proclaimed King James to be King of England, France and Ireland, beginning at Whitehall on the green, where Sir Robert Cecil, the secretary read the proclamation'.[3] The assembled dignitaries then processed to Cheapside, where the proclamation was read out again 'with great joy and triumph'.[4] Having proclaimed the new King in the suburbs, the councillors finally prepared to enter the city of London itself. Arriving before Ludgate, which had been locked and barred on the orders of the Lord Mayor, the Lord Treasurer, Buckhurst, knocked at the gate. There then followed a formal interchange which, although largely ceremonial in its intent, nevertheless hinted at the atmosphere of strained unease which still prevailed in the city.

Upon Buckhurst's knock, we are told:

> the Lord Mayor being there with the Aldermen and the City in arms asked them what they meant to do. The Lords desired the Lord Mayor to open the gates for that, their Queen being dead, they would proclaim the King. The Lord Mayor answered that he would know what King before they should come in, for, said he, 'If you will proclaim any King but he that is right, indeed you shall not come in'. Then they said that they would proclaim James. Then said the Lord Mayor, 'I am very well contented, for he is my master, liege lord and King' ... then the Lord Mayor, being well guarded let them come in, and with great joy they went to the broad place before [St] Pauls and there proclaimed the King.[5]

Thus began the reign of King James, and Londoners greeted the peaceful accession of their new monarch with immense relief. The proclamation was heard, a chronicler recalled:

> with great expectation and silent joy, but no great shouting. To the astonishment of all men, there [was] no tumult, nor contradiction, nor disorder in the city; everyman going about his business as readily and securely as though there had been no change, nor any news ever heard of competitors, so that the people, finding the just fear of forty years for want of a known succession to be dissolved in a minute, [did] ... rejoice ... and at night they showed it by bonfires and ringing of bells.[6]

A similar picture of joy, mixed with heartfelt relief, appears in al the surviving sources. Londoners were 'not a little glad to see their long-feared danger so cleerely prevented' wrote one contemporary, while Lady Clifford agreed, noting that 'this peaceful coming in of the King was unexpected of all parts of the people'.[7] A Scottish chronicler was equally delighted 'His Majestie obteyned the peaceable possession of that kingdome by the speciall providence of the Almightie God', he later wrote, 'beyond the expectation of many, when nothing was looked for but warr on all syds'.[8]

By the evening of 24 March Londoners could breathe again—but across much of the rest of the kingdom fear and anxiety still reigned supreme. This was certainly true of the far South West. Even as James I was being proclaimed in the capital, the third Earl of Bath—North Devon's only resident peer—was writing to Secretary Cecil from his mansion near Barnstaple, begging for news of Queen Elizabeth's health. 'I received your letters ... containing the sorrowful news of her Majesty's continued indisposition ... on the morning of the 24th', wrote Bath, going on to assure Cecil that, in the case of the Queen's death, he would be 'ready to yield assent and best furtherance to any thing which you and the rest of the nobility shall think meet for the common good'.[9] 'I trust you will find me of avail in these remote parts for the prevention of disorders and the preservation of peace', Bath went on, revealing that, in Devon just as much as in London, there were fears of imminent trouble.[10]

Once James had been safely proclaimed and the capital secured, the Council hurried to put local governors like Bath out of their misery. A contemporary noted that 'great care and diligence was used to give notice of ... [James's accession] unto justices of counties, [and] rulers of ... cities' and scores of letters were sent out across the kingdom, ordering local governors to proclaim the new King at once.[11] On 27 March James was proclaimed at York, and next day at Bristol.[12] By 31 March, at the latest, the news had reached North Devon too.[13] The King's accession was greeted with as much relief in the provinces as it had been in London, and everywhere public celebrations took place to mark the event.[14] However, James was still in Scotland and, as the Earl of Bath (like many others) realized, there might yet be a fatal slip twixt cup and lip. 'In these times', Bath wrote in a letter to Cecil, 'such as I am ... (that live so far off) ... [must] seek how to inform and carry ourselves in the well ordering of things to the behoof of his majesty that now is ... [and therefore] I entreat the continuance of your kind advertisment therein'.[15]

Bath's desire to be kept informed of political events suggests that, even if his anxieties concerning the succession had abated somewhat, they had not yet entirely disappeared. The fact that the Earl and other Devon JPs later felt it necessary to read out a proclamation in Cullompton Church, expressly forbidding 'disorders' in the wake of the late Queen's death, tends to point the same way.[16] Local governors would not be able to feel completely secure until James had taken up the reins of power in London, in fact—and, bearing this in mind, it is hardly surprising that all eyes turned towards Scotland during April 1603, as the new king made the slow journey southwards in order to take up his inheritance. Having set out along the highroad to England on 5 April, James was at York by the 16th and at Stamford, in Lincolnshire, by the 23rd.[17] It was at this climatic moment—as the royal entourage drew near to its ultimate destination and the thoughts of the political nation dwelt on little else but the new monarch and his doings—that the inhabitants of the East Devon village of Silverton were startled by an outlandish visitor.

The document reproduced below tells the story in detail. Broadly speaking what happened was that, on or around 27 April, a certain Thomas Follett arrived in Silverton and attempted to pass himself off as the new King of England. His reasons for doing so remain completely obscure. Possibly Follett was a confidence trickster who had adopted the royal identity in the hope of gulling simple passers-by (it will be noted that he asked one of those who later testified against him for money, and another for bread and drink). Yet surely no one in full possession of their senses, no matter how poor or hungry, would have risked a charge of treason by impersonating the King, when it would have been so much more easy—and so much more convincing—to have adopted some other persona? Was Follett mad then, or drunk: or even possibly both? The vigour with which he hammered at Mrs Morrishe's cottage door and the fantastical nature of the statements attributed to him certainly suggest as much. So does the fact that, when Follett was later brought before the Devon Grand Jury, the jurors—who could hardly have ignored any genuine attempt to impersonate the King— decided to discharge him, dismissing his case as 'ignoramus'.[18] It is worth noting, too, that someone (possibly Bishop William Cotton, the justice before whom Follett was originally brought) later scrawled the words 'the Counterfett Kinge' on the back of the depositions.[19] The slightly tongue-in-cheek tone of this comment again suggests that Follett was seen as a source of amusement, rather than as a genuine villain.

Some confusion surrounds the question of where Follett lived. When his case came before the Grand Jury he was described as 'Thomas Follett ... de Silverton ... sayler', but the depositions make it clear that he was not a Silverton man.[20] Had he been so the individuals whom he had accosted would surely have recognized him—and he himself would never have 'missed his way' on the road. Instead it seems sensible to credit the original deposition, which described him as 'Thomas Follett of the Abbey of *Torr*' [Torre Abbey, near Torquay]. Torquay was an important maritime centre during the seventeenth century and a much more likely place than Silverton for a sailor to dwell in (though why Follett should have resided in the Abbey itself remains a mystery— could the old building conceivably have been used as some sort of institution or hospital for the mentally disturbed?).

Mad or not, Follett was clearly in tune with the times. His description of himself as ruler of 'England, Ireland, Scotland and Fraunce' shows he was familiar with the new royal style—and indicates that the recent plethora of proclamations had worked their way deep into the popular consciousness. When Follett asked Thomas Satchfeeld about the 'state of the contrye', moreover, 'and demaunded of hym whether he thought that Scottes should be welcom amongst them' he was doing little more than to repeat the question which members of the political elite had been anxiously asking themselves ever since James had first been mooted as Queen Elizabeth's successor. What is more, Follett clearly appreciated the anxiety about the future, and the desperate need for reassurance, which was currently afflicting men and women at every level of English society. His parting words to Thomas Satchfeeld as he strode off down the hill towards Silverton—that 'all thinges should be as they weare, and all thinges should be well'—must have sounded (as they were clearly meant to sound) like a royal benediction. So Follett may well have gladdened the odd heart during his madcap progress. And although the reign of the 'counterfett king' was to last no more than a few hours, it left a marvellous, and enduring, image behind it—that of King James I of England and Scotland, penniless, hungry and footsore, toiling down the lonely lanes between Butterleigh and Silverton in search of his new kingdom.

DRO, DQS Bundles, Box 11

The examinacon of Johan Morrishe taken before the Reverend father in God the L[ord] Bishop of Exon the 27th of Aprill 1603 concerning certen verry lewed abuses & misdemaynoures of one Thomas Follett of the abbey of *Torr*.

First she sayth that the sayd Follet came to her mothers house in the p[ar]ishe of *Silferton* & knocked att the dore & nobody did answer hym by reason that he did extraordinarely beate at the dore. Wheruppon he went uppon the backe syde of the house & did clymbe over a cobbe wall & then came to the backe windowe & cal'd for brede and drincke w[hi]ch she the sayd Johan gave hym, then she demaunded of hym where he did dwell, he answered in England, Ireland, Scotland, & Fraunce, & further sayd that all they had was his, & that he was Kinge of England, & so departed peaceablye.

The examinacon of Thomas Satchfeeld taken the same daye agaynst the sayd p[ar]ty.

First he sayth that the sayd Follett did overtake hym uppon the waye betwixt Tiverton & *Butterley* [Butterleigh] & enquyred of hym of the state of the contrye, sayinge he was a Scott & demaunded of hym whether he thought that Scottes should be welcom amongst them: to the w[hi]ch this deponent aunswered that he made no doubt thereof, then he further demaunded whether he knewe the Kinge yf he sawe hyme, to w[hi]ch question he answered that he could nott knowe the Kinge, for that he never sawe hym, then the sayd Follett beinge by this deponent sett into his waye w[hi]ch he had missed of before, he demaunded whether he had anye money in his pursse, he answered noe, then sayd Follett, you shall have money of me, sayinge he was his Kinge, & sayd further that all thinges should be as they weare, & all thinges should be well, & so dep[ar]ted peaceably.

NOTES

1. C. Russell, *The Crisis of Parliaments* (1988), 255–6.
2. D.J.H. Clifford (ed.), *The Diaries of Lady Anne Clifford* (Stroud, 1994), 21.
3. G.B. Harrison (ed.), *A Jacobean Journal, 1603–06* (1946), 1.
4. Harrison, *Journal* and Clifford, *Diaries*, 21.
5. Harrison, *Journal*, 1.
6. Harrison, *Journal*, 3.
7. J. Nichols, *Processes, Processions and Magnificent Festivities of King James I* (1828), 26; Clifford, *Diaries*, 21.
8. Nichols, *Processes*, 25.
9. *HMC, Salisbury MSS*, XII, 702.
10. *HMC, Salisbury MSS*, XII, 702.
11. Nichols, *Processes*, 27. One such letter, dated 25 March, still survives from the Council to the civic authorities of Exeter, see *HMC, Report on the Records of the City of Exeter* (1916), 73.
12. Nichols, *Processes*, 28, 31.
13. *HMC, Salisbury MSS*, V, 21.
14. D. Cressy, *Bonfires and Bells: National Memory and the Protestant Calendar in Elizabethan and Stuart England* (1989), 57.
15. *HMC, Salisbury MSS*, V, 21.
16. DRO, DQS Bundles, Box 11.
17. Harrison, *Journal*, 11, 14, 16.
18. DRO, DQS Bundles, Box 11.
19. That Cotton took the original examination reflects his position as the leading local justice. The bishop owned a rich manor in Silverton and spent much of his time there, see I. Cassidy, 'The Episcopate of William Cotton, Bishop of Exeter, 1595–1621' (D.Phil. thesis, Oxford, 1963), 11–12.
20. DRO, DQS Bundles, Box 11.

M.J. Stoyle

42. 'Holy Enterprises': Victorian Folk Religion at Chagford

Victorian Devon presented the would-be chapel-goer with a choice of five major Methodist denominations. Ironically the one that was smallest nationally was the second strongest locally, the Bible Christian Connexion.[1] In 1907 it contributed its 32,000 members to a union with another two of the five denominations. Then the grander union of 1932 brought all the denominations into the Methodist Church but if a plaque in the gable of a Devon chapel bears a legend like 'BC 1884' it is infallible proof of the chapel's origin.

The Bible Christian denomination began in 1815 in the border parishes of North West Devon and North East Cornwall and its heartland was always South West England. During its independent life of ninety two years the denomination moved on from uncertain origins, when itinerant preachers declaimed on North Devon's village greens, through a middle period of expansion and independence to a closing period, when it was clear that the future lay as part of a national Methodist Church. Its strength like its origins was always in the countryside, with chapels in village after village or even on waste land at the road side. As the 1907 Union drew closer its national leaders emphasized that the Bible Christians were indeed a proper Methodist denomination. The reality was that its strength was strongly regionalized and the whole denomination had a homely feel about it, being remembered nostalgically as an extended family. With its local, village-based, amateur character complete with humble chapels and humble congregations it was the nearest thing to a folk religion that Victorian Devon possessed.

Like all Methodists, the Bible Christians were great generators of records and between them the Devon and Cornwall Record Offices have by far the richest collections in existence of Bible Christian chapel and circuit records. Nowhere were the Bible Christians so strong as in the South West, for here the Bible Christians were second only to the Wesleyan Methodists and in much of North West Devon they were unchallenged.[2] The Bible Christians established a typical circuit around Chagford on the edge of Dartmoor and their hard pressed and financially fragile work in this remote rural area is clearly revealed by their records. The surviving records of the Chagford Circuit are in the Devon Record Office[3] and include its Circuit Book for the 1860s, firmly within their middle period. At that time the circuit comprised eleven congregations on the north eastern margin of Dartmoor some with their own chapels, some using rented premises. Lewis Court was minister here in the closing years of the denomination and wrote nostalgically about the local influence of the Bible Christians:

> There is scarcely a field in this locality, scarcely a yard of the King's highway, scarcely a house, but has been consecrated by the prayers and holy enterprises of devout souls. May we none of us be ashamed to meet them when with us they stand before the great White Throne.[4]

These 'holy enterprises' were closely associated with money, reckoned in ha'pences not pounds. For years the Chagford Circuit or Mission depended for its running expenses upon a pitfully small annual grant from the Denomination's Missionary Committee. In 1889 the Chagford Mission became self supporting but over the years it had received a total of £1096 8s 4d [£1096.42p] in grants from the Mission Committee.[5] The two 'Circuit Stewards' or lay officers had the thankless task each quarter of getting in the money from the congregations and inevitably bore a proportion of the deficiency themselves. The entries in the Circuit Book are largely the accounts quarter by quarter relating to housing and maintaining the preachers. Each quarter the congregations that sent contributions are listed, often with their memberships. In the year ended June 1865 the Circuit raised a total of £40.1.3 ½d [£40.6p] but spent £96.19.0d [£96.95p]. It received a grant of £45 and 'By special effort' managed to scrape together the remaining £11.17.8 ½d [£11.89p].

Each quarter a few resolutions are included and a selection of these between 1860 and 1867 is given below. At this time there was a total of some 165 members in the churches but congregations would have been considerably bigger than the formal membership. Generally there were two ministers, helped by local preachers, who maintained the work of Sunday and weeknight preaching as well as trying to open new preaching places. There was, too, the perpetual begging for contributions for this or that. The recurring concerns of the Chagford Bible Christians are well reflected in the resolutions. Some are mundane, asking the national Committee for repeated subventions or, in a spirit of self help, organizing teas towards the ever present debt. Other resolutions are cast in a more heroic mould, conscientiously examining and recommending young men for the Christian ministry. This selection sets the undoubtedly holy enterprises of this folk religion against its uncompromising remote, rural background of relative poverty.

It would be a strange religious group that did not develop its own jargon and typical Methodist organizational names occur throughout the resolutions. A 'Circuit' is a group of congregations or 'Societies' with one or more 'Ministers' (or 'Pastors' or 'Preachers'). But a circuit could also be called a 'Station' (because ministers were 'stationed' there) or even a 'Mission' if, like Chagford, it was dependent upon central subsidy. In the resolutions Chagford is described as all three! Circuits were grouped into 'Districts' and the Districts into a 'Connexion' (i.e. a body in which everyone is linked together) over which the final authority was the annual 'Conference'. Resolutions are couched in the forced rather pious style that was so typical. Ministers 'laboured' and were 'afflicted'. Requests were 'earnest' and statements 'respectful'.

To set the Chagford Bible Christians in geographical context, in June 1865 the list of congregations and their memberships was: Chagford 14; Providence 33; Hittisleigh 50; Gooseford [Farm] 15; Langdown 6; Lettaford 13; Challacombe 6; Crockernwell 0; South Zeal 10; Spreyton and St Cherris 17.

DRO, 2200D/2

The Circuit Book of the Chagford Bible Christian Circuit: A Selection of Resolutions 1860 to 1867

20 June 1860[6]
Resolution 1 Resolved that Br[other]. [William][7] Beer's and Br. [William] Seage's and Br. [Anthony] Gill's certificates be filled up in the usal [sic] way being satisfactory.[8]

Resl. 2 That we accept the statement given as being the spiritual state of [the] Mission.[9]

Resl. 3 We think as this station is enlarging it would be desirable for us to have two preachers and that the Act. [accounts] be forwarded to the [Denomination's Missionary] Committee as before and we believe our receipts will increase.

26 December 1860
Resolved that Br. James Crocker and Joseph Moore be elected Circuit Stewards for the year ensuing.[10]

26 March 1861
Resl. 1 That we express our thankfulness to the Missionary Committee for the favours we have received from them and earnestly beg that if we are left to ourselves we should want the sum of fifty two pounds to meet the deficiency of two preachers for the year ensuing.

20 June 1861
Resl. 3rd That considering our means as a body and that there was an increase a few years since we do not think it desirable to increase the salarys of our Preachers at present.

2 October 1861
Resl. 1 That the itinerant ministers and Cr. [Circuit] Stewards be requested to write immediately to the Committe to request an increase of grant as we find it impossible to meet our several disbursements under present circumstances.

Resl. 2 That there be held at Providence [chapel] on the 15th October a thanksgiving tea in behalf of the Circuit debt.

26 March 1862
Resl. 1st. That we express our thankfulness to the Missionary Committee for the favours already received and earnestly beg that they will grant us the same sum forty five pounds for the year ensuing.

25 June 1862
Resl. 3 That under present circumstances we cannot undertake to do any thing in a public way towards the Jubilee Fund.[11]

Resl. 4 That we most earnestly request the Missionary Committee to assist us in the erection of a chapel at South Zeal as expressed in the [report of the] spiritual state of the Mission.

29 September 1862
Resl. 1 That Br. William Wesley Finch hereby signify his intention to offer himself at our next Quarterly Meeting for the Itinerant [i.e. full time] Ministry among us.

Resl. 2 That there shall be held at Providence on Tuesday Oct.14th a thanksgiving service and tea the proceeds of which are to be applied to the liquidation of the circuit debt.

Resl. 3 That a horse hire collection be made in each place of worship in the circuit once this plan[12] for the purpose of assisting such brethren as have no other means than that of walking to their appointments.[13] That the said Brethren be not allowed a horse when their appointments are within six miles except in extraordinary cases and that the secretary be requested to lay his accounts before the Quarterly Meeting twice a year for inspection.

16 December 1862 Special Quarterly Meeting
Resl. 1 That we accept the offer of Mrs W.Brock's house and appurtances at Providence Place in the Parish of *Throwley* [Throwleigh] in the County of Devon as the future residence of the Bible Christian minister at a yearly rental not exceeding £4.10.0 [£4.50] with a proper proportion of the [illeg]. Possession to be taken at Lady Day next 1863.

Resl. 2 That this meeting depute the Itinerant ministers and circuit stewards to prepare and give due notice to the present proprietor of the house now in occupation of the Bible Christian minister of their intention to quit at Lady Day next 1863.

26 December 1862
Resl. 1 That Br. Wm. Wesley Finch having passed with much credit to himself and satisfaction to the quarterly meeting the usual examination and that he being of good report in character, piety and preaching among his kinsfolk and brethren himself being also convinced that he is divinely called to labour in a more extended sphere we most earnestly and affectionately recommend him to the notice of the next district meeting and conference as a candidate for the itinerant Bible Christian ministry.[14]

Resl. 2 That as there is distress of a most soulstirring character in the manufacturing districts in consequence of the American War we advise that a public collection be made in each place of worship in this circuit in aid of our suffering brethren.

26 March 1863
Resl. 2 That we hereby express our thankfulness to the Missionary Committee for favours already received and earnestly beg that they will grant us the sum of forty five pounds for the ensuing year.

23 June 1863
Resl. 3 That under present circumstances we cannot engage to do anything in a public way towards the Jubilee Fund.

Resl. 4 That we thankfully accept the grant of £42 made to us by the Missionary Society for the year ensuing.

Resl. 5 That we again most earnestly request the assistance of the Missionary Committee in the erection of a chapel at South Zeal.

28 December 1863
Resl. 1 That in consideration of there being a deficiency in the funds of the station we appoint that a society's [sic] meeting be held throughout the circuit and that the circuit stewards attend and bring the matter before the different societies.

29 March 1864
Resl. 2 That the Missionary Committee be requested to favour us with £5 as a supplementary grant for the present year in consequence of Br. [John] Kemeys salary and board being very much higher than that of a young man.[15] And that £50 be the grant for the year ensuing.

22 June 1864
Resl. 3 That as Br. Kemeys age and infirmity unfit him for the work of the mission we request that a young able man be appointed with Br. Denis for the ensuing year.[16]

Resl. 5 That we hope to make and [sic] effort for the Jubilee Fund next year.

12 July 1864 Special Quarterly Meeting
Resl. 1 That having considered the Res. 6th of the district meeting.[17] respecting the working of this station the coming year. We beg most respectfully to state to the Missionary Committee and conference That we cannot see how this mission can be worked efficiently with one preacher, and we therefore hope that the conference will send us an able young man with Br. [William] Dennis according to the res. of our Midsummer quarterly meeting.[18] And we would therefore record our gratitude for the £45 granted by the district meeting for the ensuing year and pray that the blessings of God may rest upon and abide with the entire connexion.

26 December 1864
Resl. 3 That Mr William Hill having passed with much credit to himself and satisfaction to the quarterly meeting the usual examination we most earnestly and affectionately recommend him to the district meeting and conference as a suitable candidate for the itinerant ministry among us.

[Appended note] Who was born at Murchington in the Parish of Throwleigh August 23rd 1844 and has been an approved local preacher for the last two years.[19]

29 March 1865
Resl. 5 The friends at Chagford having purchased an harmonium and tune books by free contribution at a cost of £16.17.3 [£16.86p] desire that notice

thereof be made in the circuit book declaring that it is therefore the sole property of the society and congregation worshipping at Zion Chapel.[20]

26 December 1865
Resl. 1 That the Brethren Wm. Webber and Wm. Perryman[21] be the circuit stewards for the coming year.

Resl. 3 That Br. W.Hill having again passed the usual examinations ... we most earnestly and affectionately recommend him ... as a suitable candidate for the itinerant ministry.[22]

20 June 1866
Resl. 1 That having reconsidered our application to the Missionary Society for £50 as a grant for the ensuing year, we hope the Committee will grant us £47 as we cannot see our way clear to do with less than that sum. We are willing to do our best with other circuits.

Resl. 6 That having increased our responsibilities by building new chapels we earnestly request that the Stng. Com.[23] will favour us by sending the right man for the coming year.

1 October 1866
Resl. 2 That thanksgiving services be held in this circuit and where a tea is provided the proceeds thereof shall be applied to meet the deficiency and where no tea is provided a collection shall be made instead for the same purpose.

26 December 1866
Resl. 2 That the circuit deficiency be made up by appealing to the various societies. Each society to pay its proportionate share.

19 June 1867
Resl. 2 That the preachers receive their certificates unqualified with the exception of Br.[William] Hopper's health.

Resl. 3 That we deeply sympathize with our Pastor [William Hopper] in his protracted affliction and fervently pray if it be God's will that his health may be restored, that he may be able to labour for many years longer in the ministry. We also desire to record our appreciation of his services which have been very valuable though performed under much bodily affliction.[24]

Resl. 7 That we recommend Geo. Adams Joslin as a candidate for the itinerant ministry among us subject to the approval of the Ringsash quarterly meeting.[25]

NOTES

1. For general history of the denomination see T. Shaw, *The Bible Christians 1815–1907* (1965) and M.J.L. Wickes, *The Westcountry Preachers; A New History of the Bible Christian Church (1815–1907)* (Hartland, 1987).
2. For a list of chapels in Devon and map of circuits see R. Thorne, 'The Last Bible Christians; Their Church in Devon in 1907', *DAT*, 107 (1975), 47–75.
3. DRO, 2200D.

4. L.H. Court, *The History of the Bible Christian Methodist Church in the Chagford Circuit* (Crediton, 1904), 44.
5. Court, *History*, 18.
6. Dates are of Quarterly Meetings.
7. Information regarding preachers' names, date and careers is derived from the alphabetical listing in O.A.B. Beckerlegge, *United Methodist Ministers and Their Circuits* (1968).
8. Each year Circuits had to certify the satisfactory work and character of their Ministers.
9. Each year the Pastor, i.e. senior minister, made a written report of the spiritual state of the circuit, generally a review of the year's work. These are not recorded in the Chagford records.
10. Circuit Stewards are the Circuit's senior lay officers with particular responsibility for the finances.
11. Marking the founding of the denomination in 1815.
12. i.e. this quarter. The 'plan' is a quarterly schedule of preaching services.
13. i.e. to the chapels where they were scheduled to conduct worship.
14. Finch entered ministry in 1864 and went as a minister to Australia in 1865.
15. He entered ministry in 1827 and retired in autumn 1864.
16. Edmund Turner came, aged 27. He stayed until 1866.
17. The minutes have not survived.
18. i.e. June 1864.
19. See 26 December 1865.
20. This is unconstitutional as Methodist property is owned by the denomination and not by individual congregations, even where the latter paid for it for their own use. The intention is to discourage the circuit officers from selling them to raise funds.
21. Court, L.H., *Some Dartmoor Saints and Shrines. Studies in Experimental Religion Among the Homely Folk.* (1927, Chapter VIII 'A Brother Minor of the Moorland'. William Perryman of Yeo was a well known local figure.
22. William Holman Hill entered ministry in 1866. He died in 1927.
23. The Stationing Committee allocates ministers.
24. Hopper was at Chagford from 1866 to 1868 and during this time had two assistant ministers W.H. Smith (aged 26) and R. Kelley (aged 27). Hopper retired in 1868 aged 54 and died in 1888.
25. Joslin entered ministry in 1867 and left in 1880.

Roger F.S. Thorne

43. An Enclosure Dispute at Lynton in 1854

The public letter which follows was circulated in Lynton and Lynmouth in January 1854. It was written by Charles Bailey, a local landowner. The letter was intended to reassure the inhabitants of the small coastal resort, who were greatly concerned about his proposal that all the remaining common land in the parish should be enclosed. It exemplifies the problems and anxieties caused by the process of enclosure. The unusual feature of this enclosure, however, was that part of the common land involved was the famous Valley of Rocks.

To understand the reasons for the local concern it is necessary to go back to the late eighteenth century when a few tourists began to arrive in Lynton. The Valley of Rocks was the principal attraction. These first visitors made the long and difficult journey over Exmoor because they wanted to see this gigantic dry valley and its remarkable rock formations. It also had several stone circles which many considered to be the work of prehistoric man. In 1789 the Revd John Swete visited the valley and in his journal recorded seeing 'several circles, large masses of stone, in diameter above forty feet' which he thought had 'been appropriated to the uses of the Druids'.[1] In 1799 Robert Southey considered the Valley of Rocks to be 'one of the greatest wonders in the west of England'.[2] The influx of visitors caused Lynton to develop a small tourist industry, with hotels and lodging-houses being opened in the village.

The late eighteenth century was also a period when many of the English 'wastes' which had been held in common were being divided among local landholders in proportion to their holdings. Usually what happened was that one or two of the biggest landowners would draw up a scheme for enclosure and would petition Parliament to introduce a Bill. This would usually lead to an Act of Enclosure. Commissioners then allotted the land. Occasionally enclosure would result from a private agreement between most of the landholders with rights on a common. Enclosures were often resisted by small landholders, who lost their rights to graze stock on the commons but received only a relatively small parcel of land, which they could not easily afford to fence or wall.

It was in this period that the enclosure of a small but important part of the Lynton commons was first mooted. William Lock, a Lynmouth merchant, had purchased the manor of Lynton in 1792. Soon afterwards he announced his intention to enclose part of the Valley of Rocks. He claimed that all he wanted was to wall off a large rabbit warren for his private use. The other landholders refused to give their consent, partly because they resented him taking a portion of the commons but more particularly because they feared he would cultivate the land and thus make the valley less attractive to tourists.[3]

In 1799 William Lock assigned his manorial rights to his son John Lock. In 1800 John Lock persuaded most of the people with rights on the Lynton commons to sign or put their mark to a private agreement to divide the land.[4] In the following year the commons were shared out by independent arbitrators. John Lock made sure he was allotted the eastern part of the Valley of Rocks and almost at once he enclosed part of it. Many thought his stone walls desecrated the wild grandeur of the valley. In 1802 T.H. Williams, an artist, visited the valley and complained that the eye was 'offended by a quadrangular wall ... lately erected' on which nothing grew to 'relieve the sight from so disgusting an object'.[5]

In addition John Lock ensured that he was allocated most of the common land near Lynton. He must have realized that, with tourists arriving in increasing numbers, there were profits to be made in enclosing and selling land for development. The letter we are considering looks back to these sales some fifty years earlier and singles out one in particular. This was the sale of a building plot overlooking the sea to William Sanford, a landed gentleman from Somerset.[6] In this one deal John Lock recouped most of the money his father had given for the entire manor.

Few of the other landholders exercised their right to enclose the land awarded to them in 1801, probably because the land they were awarded was barely worth the cost of enclosing it, and it was made clear that if they enclosed they would lose their right to turn out stock on the remainder of the commons. They were angry to find that even though John Lock had enclosed 90 of the 150 acres awarded to him, he still continued to graze just as many animals on the remainder of the commons.

After John Lock had made his enclosures, the arbitration agreement of 1801 was lost sight of until 1850. Then it was discovered by accident by Charles Bailey at a time when he became engaged in a dispute with the manor authorities over his proposal that the remaining Lynton commons should be enclosed.

Charles Bailey was a London-based land agent who worked for noblemen and members of the gentry. His business prospered and he decided to create a country estate of his own. In 1841 he bought Ley and Six Acre, two large farms in the parish of Lynton, situated immediately to the west of the Valley of Rocks.[7] After demolishing the old farmhouse at Ley, he supervized the construction of a fine country house on the site. He gave his new property the somewhat pretentious name of Lee Abbey.

In his capacity as a land agent, Charles Bailey was responsible for the enclosure of many commons, and this was why in 1844 he was called to give evidence to the Parliamentary Select Committee on Commons Inclosure. There he strongly advocated the enclosure of the remaining English commons, arguing that this would make it possible to improve the land and enhance its value.[8] The findings of this Select Committee led to the General Enclosure Act of 1845 which made the process of enclosing commons much easier.

Charles Bailey also gave evidence to this Select Committee about the prevalence of scab among the sheep that grazed on the North Devon commons. Scab is a highly contagious disease which attacks the skin of sheep. It is spread by parasitic mites and causes intense itching. He claimed that in North Devon some 'little farmers' deliberately encouraged the spread of scab among their sheep, knowing that this would cause more prudent farmers to keep their flocks off the commons to prevent them contracting the disease.[9]

As the owner of farms in the parish of Lynton, Charles Bailey was entitled to grazing rights on the local commons, but he became increasingly concerned that his sheep were contracting scab there. In March 1850 he suggested to the manor authorities that the remaining common land should be enclosed. By this time John Lock was dead. His sister Mary had become lady of the major, but effective control was in the hands of her husband, the Revd Thomas Roe. For three years Charles Bailey tried to persuade him to agree to the enclosure of the commons, but he had no success.

Charles Bailey was not a man to give up easily. Late in 1853 he managed to persuade a number of local landholders to sign a petition to the Enclosure Commissioners seeking sanction for a division of the Lynton commons. In January 1854 an Assistant Commissioner held public meetings at the Valley of Rocks Hotel in Lynton to consider the proposals.[10] Many and loud were the objections. Hoteliers, lodging-house keepers and other tradespeople attended the public meetings and made it clear they were bitterly opposed to the proposals. They thought Charles Bailey was planning to lay claim to the western part of the Valley of Rocks, fence it off and deny the public access to it.[11]

Charles Bailey circulated his public letter to try and convince the inhabitants that, unlike John Lock, some fifty years earlier, he had no intention of enclosing any part of the Valley of Rocks or any adjacent walks, but wanted 'to preserve them to the public from the despoiling hand of man'. He suggested that this could best be done by having the valley 'set out for public recreation'. In saying this no doubt he had in mind that in 1834 Parliament had agreed 'that in all Inclosure Bills provision be made for leaving an open space sufficient for the purposes of exercise and recreation of the neighbouring population'.[12]

However, Charles Bailey argued that, as the lords of the manor had already enclosed the bigger part of the land allotted to them in the 1801 arbitration, it was only fair that he should be allowed to enclose the portion of the commons that had been allotted by the same agreement to the farms he now owned.

Charles Bailey's letter also refers to the stone circles that early tourists had described. He claimed that the lord of the major had caused 'immense Druidical stones and circles' to be taken away for use as gateposts. What the original purpose of these stones was, and whether they were removed by order of the lord of the manor, it is impossible for us now to determine. All we can say with certainty is that some early nineteenth century topographical prints show a circle of stones at the foot of Castle Rock in the Valley of Rocks,[13] but these stones are not there today.

After the hearings at the Valley of Rocks Hotel the Assistant Commissioner went away to consider the case. In March 1854 came the news that he had decided the agreement of 1800 was a valid one and that, if the majority of those with rights on the commons so wished, then the remainder of the 'waste' could be enclosed.[14] The Revd and Mrs Roe would not accept the decision and decided to take the unusual step of instituting legal proceedings against the Enclosure Commissioners. The case was heard in March 1855. The Roe family won because it was held that, as owners of the manor, they had a right to object to any enclosure of the commons.[15] The Revd and Mrs Roe had prevented the enclosure, but they did not benefit from their victory. Thomas Roe died in January 1855, even before the case was heard, and his wife died in September.

The manor then passed to Mrs Roe's son, John Colwell Roe. His attitude was different. He decided to allow the remaining commons to be enclosed. In September 1856 a meeting of the Enclosure Commissioners was held at the Valley of Rocks Hotel.[16] Agreement was reached on a fair division of the remaining commons. All parties accepted that the Valley of Rocks should be left unenclosed. By 1860 stone walls were being erected across the uplands surrounding Lynton[17] and it was not long before work began to convert heather and gorse moors into more productive fields. The Valley of Rocks remained an open area of outstanding natural beauty, which still today gives enormous pleasure to its many visitors. The stone wall erected by John Lock is still there, but it has mellowed with age. Now it is considered such an attractive feature that the Council recently restored it.

DRO, 52/14/2/6

The Division of the Lynton Commons: A Statement to the Inhabitants and Visitors of Lynton, North Devon, by Charles Bailey

Many misrepresentations having been made and industriously circulated, to impress you with a belief that I am seeking to destroy the romantic and beautiful scenery of the Valley of Rocks; and, as this impression was manifested at the recent meeting, held at Lynton, by the Assistant Commissioner for the Inclosure of Common Lands, by the presentation of a petition, signed by many of you, against the 'Inclosure' of the 'Valley of Rocks', under misconception of my intentions, I am induced to lay before you what follows.

Those misrepresentations were made, doubtlessly, for the purpose of improperly continuing the dominion and control of the Valley of Rocks in the hands of those who have misused it for the last fifty years, and have committed and encouraged the commission of multitudes of acts: such as, the building of ugly stone walls and fences, the opening of quarries, and, worse than either, the removal of the immense Druidical stones and circles, and the rocks which formed its peculiar and striking interest and beauty, for the purpose of selling them for gateposts.

Although the petition was withdrawn, after I had been permitted to make known to the meeting what I had written to the Rev. Thomas Roe ... and after I had offered to purchase, at its full value, Mr Roe's wretchedly ugly inclosure, called the 'Warren' in the valley, and to level the walls, and dedicate the land for the amusement and recreation of the inhabitants; yet, it is right towards you, and towards me, that this should be known, and that your minds should be disabused of the calumnies, which it is but too plain have been cast upon me.

Previous to the year 1849, my tenants informed me, that the open commons of Lynton had become almost useless to them, owing to the numerous scabbed sheep that were turned upon them, and particularly by persons who had no rights of pasturage. My own flock, on the Lynton commons, had also been infected with the disease ...

I thought the most reasonable and best mode of preventing the spread of the disease, and so securing for the inhabitants and visitors of Lynton wholesome mutton, would be to effect a division of the commons, and thereby enable each proprietor to have the care, control, and advantage of his own flock ...

Until late in the spring of 1850, I had never the slightest knowledge, or even an idea, that an allotment and division of the commons had been made by three gentlemen of the neighbourhood, as arbitrators, in the year 1801, under the agreement dated the 25th July, 1800, entered into and signed by the late Mr Lock, the Lord of the Manor, and all the commoners of that day ...

The application I made to the Commissioners, ... was in effect to complete the measure in accordance with the agreement of 1800.

Mr. Roe's predecessors, Mr William Lock and Mr John Lock, received most ample compensation for all their manorial and other rights under that agreement, and have inclosed and sold, and granted leases for lives and for terms of years, and let to their tenants building sites and other lands in the most beautiful situations at Lynton, to a very large extent, all taken by them under that agreement. In one case, Mr Lock received the large sum of £1180 for about 10 acres, for a building site and ornamental grounds, part of the common land allotted to him. This was, in fact, nearly the whole of his father's purchase money of the manor, for which he gave Messrs. Short £1300, in the year 1792.

It is not discoverable, that either of the Lords of the Manor down to the present time ever expended a shilling in making roads or paths, or accommodation of any kind, either for the inhabitants of Lynton, or its visitors, whilst I know I may freely appeal to you, whether I have not liberally dedicated both my time and money to that end.

Should the Inclosure Commissioners issue their Provisional Order for the proceeding with this measure, it will now remain for you to decide which of the two, Mr Roe or myself, is likely to be the preserver of the western end of the Valley of Rocks, of which I am the owner; whilst the question for the consideration and judgement of the other owners of the farms and lands, included in the agreement of 1800, will be:

Whether they will sign the Provisional Order, and again second these proceedings, as enough of them did the application to the Commissioners?

Or, whether they will oppose the proceedings, and thereby subject themselves to the harassing and vexation of my only alternative—an expensive Chancery suit?

I have only to add, that, much as I should lament such a step, I do not feel myself either called upon, or at liberty, to abandon my property, if I can obtain it through no other means.

Charles Bailey, Stratford Place, London. Jany. 26th, 1854.

NOTES

1. DRO, 564/M, J. Swete, 'Picturesque Sketches of Devon' (1792), I, 159.
2. C.C. Southey, *Life and Correspondence of Robert Southey* (1849), II, 23. Early tourists are discussed in John F. Travis, *The Rise of the Devon Seaside Resorts, 1750–1900* (1993), 51–2.
3. DRO, 564/M, XII, 144. For a full account of the conflict between the lords of the manor and the inhabitants see John Travis, *An Illustrated History of Lynton and Lynmouth, 1770–1914* (1995). Chs. 2,3.
4. An appendix to the letter includes a copy of this agreement and a list of those who put their names on it.
5. T.H. Williams, *Picturesque Excursions in Devonshire and Cornwall* (1804), 33–4.
6. Lynton Cottage Hotel, Lynton, 'Title-Deeds'. The house that Mr Sanford built on the site was named the Lynton Cottage; Travis, *Illustrated History*, 18–9, 23, 46–7.
7. Advertisements for the sale of the two farms appeared in 1840. See, for example, *Trewman's Exeter Flying Post*, 18 June 1840. It seems that at this time a considerable number of the standing stones were still present for this advertisement refers to the 'far-famed Valley of Rocks' with 'its Druidical circles and other ruins of antiquity'.
8. *Select Committee on Commons Inclosure* (British Parliamentary Papers, 1844, V), 187–204.
9. *Select Committee on Commons Inclosure*, 188.
10. *North Devon Journal*, 26 Jan. 1854.
11. *North Devon Journal*, 26 Jan., 2, 16 Feb., 2 March 1854.
12. Hugh Cunningham, *Leisure in the Industrial Revolution, c.1780–c.1880* (1980), 93.
13. See, for example, a lithograph of the Valley of Rocks by George Rowe, c.1828.
14. *North Devon Journal*, 9 March 1854.
15. *Woolmer's Exeter and Plymouth Gazette*, 24 March 1855; *Trewman's Exeter Flying Post*, 29 March 1855.
16. *North Devon Journal*, 11 Sept. 1856.
17. *North Devon Journal*, 5 April 1860.

John F. Travis

44. Peter Orlando Hutchinson and his Cats in the Late Nineteenth Century

Peter Orlando Hutchinson's career as an antiquary, local historian and amateur archaeologist is well known.[1] From his diaries[2] a new person emerges, a lover of cats,[3] not only does he indulge his own pets, he cat-sits at Uffculme Grammar School for Mr and Mrs Jones while they go away for ten days, and when his house keeper is ill, he has her sister to stay with her cat and its kitten and he can imitate a Tom. His portrait of his mother shows her sitting in a rocking chair in her parlour with a large greyish brown striped cat asleep on her knee.[4] The volumes are not paginated but the entries are in date order.

DRO, Z19/36/16a–e

Tuesday 16th Jan. 1849. To-day my Mother lost her purse with £7 in it. She was in a great fluster and sent for the Sidmouth policeman to search. It was finally discovered under some hay in the cat's bed. Rather suspicious.

Monday Jan 27 [1851] I had breakfast: fed the cat: fed the pigs: set the children to needlework; nursed the baby: carved for the whole lot of them at dinner: sent them out on the green to play: had them all at tea: then, after half an hour's riotous play, was somewhat relieved by the appearance of the nurse-maid, who took them off to bed.

Sat. Mar 26 [1853] To-day the cat was discovered playing with a snake on the terrace. It probably came out of the heath under the tree. The women screamed and ran away. They imagined that it got back to the heath again, but I have not been able to find it. Afterwards I saw the cat playing with a lizard, doubtless from the same place.

Th.July 13 [1854] Walked out to Sidbury, and played chess with the Vicar of Sidbury. Went via Snogbrook and the Caves: Coming home at eleven I picked up some glowworms in the hedges and carried them to Sidmouth. Wanting to speak to Mr Heineken, called on him at this unreasonable hour. Did it in a novel way. As he has been much troubled with the caterwaling of tom cats of late, I resolved to play him a trick, Stealing under his window, I imitate the trilling notes. Soon he stealthily opened the front door, and crept out. Then he shied a couple of coals (the first missiles he could lay hold of in his hurry, as he afterwards told me) in the direction of the sound. But when I could contain my laughter no longer, he discovered who and what the tom cat was. We then went in and chatted till nearly two in the morning.

Wed.July 23 [1856] ... Left for Sidmouth, and got home to Coberg Terrace to tea. My cat 'Louis' knew me after a year's absence. We had tea together and he held out his right paw to have it buttered—an accomplishment I taught him before I left, and which he had not forgotten.

Sat. Dec 26 [1874] ... Went home and dined off herrings, and my white cat with me. We enjoyed our dinner amazingly. Curious that cats are so fond of fish.

Fri. Mar 26 [1880] Good Friday. Hot cross Buns for breakfast and salt fish for dinner. My great black tom cat, who sleeps on my bed every night, and has his every meal with me, for I never think of sitting down to a meal without him, and who is as affectionate as a child, thought the buns very good, and my rooks, that I feed under my window every day, considered them excellent.

Th. 27 [July 1882]—Made a cat's ladder. My black tom cat Robbie or Robert has now got three ladders on three different sides of the Old Chancel, by which he can come in the windows.

Mon. Dec 3 [1883] ... The fishermen say the bay is full of sprats as well as herrings, and great quantities have been brought on shore. Herrings to the dealers to go to London, 18 pence a 100. If this is true it is cheaper than I ever remember. My cat and I had a sprat dinner. Curious that cats are so fond of fish.

Th. Jan.17 [1884] The herring season is nearly over. It has been very good, and selling in Sidmouth by retail at sixpence a dozen. Had two for breakfast. My black tom-cat Robert was mad to share them with me. Curious, how fond cats are of fish, though they dislike water or wetting their feet, yet they all do love fish.

Sat.24 [June 1884] After breakfast, the weather being hot and beautiful, I was sauntering about my grounds with my cat in my arms, whem two gentlemen came in at the upper iron gate ...

Th.Aug.21 [1884] My dear old black Tom cat Robert died.

Tu.Mar 31 [1885] ... Mrs Knowles from Budleigh, with cat and kitten, came over for a few days to see her sister Ann Newton, my servant, who is seriously ill with a chill.

Sun.5 [April 1885] ... Mrs Knowles, cat, and kitten went back to Budleigh about 4.30 in a close fly, rain commencing.

M.27 [April 1885] Mrs. Knowles, who came over with her cat last Saturday week at 9A.M. from Budleigh, left at 8 this morning to return, cat and all.

Th. 25 [June 1891] Dine with Mr & Mrs Sanford at Helens. Towards evening Mrs Hunt, widow of the late Vicar of Tipton St Johns came in. Something was said on the question, as to whether there is authority for believing that the lower animals have a future existence. Where we have pet animals that love us, we would naturally hope that they might have such an existence: and I have more than once lost pet animals whose deaths I have felt more that the deaths of some of my christian friends. And why not? It is not what we lose, but whether we love it and it loved us: And if they have only this one life to live, where most of them are subjected to privation, ill treatment, neglect, or downright cruelty, theirs is a hard fate indeed. This consideration ought to make us humane.

NOTES

1. Sid Vale Association, *The Old Chancel and its designer*, n.d.; Catherine Linehan, *Peter Orlando Hutchinson of Sidmouth 1810–1897* (Tiverton, n.d.).
2. DRO, Z19/36/16a–e.
3. I am very grateful to Michael Dickenson for suggesting this source of matters feline.
4. DRO, Z19/2/8d/95.

Alice Wells

45. Surveying the Estates of Henry Courtenay, Earl of Devon, Marquis of Exeter and Traitor, 1543–4

Henry Courtenay, Earl of Devon and Marquis of Exeter, was tried and found guilty on a charge of treason against his cousin, King Henry VIII and consequently condemned to death on 3 December 1538. Six days later he was beheaded on Tower Hill. On 15 December, in a ceremony at Windsor, he was degraded, or stripped of his titles[1] and later, in 1539, an Act of Attainder against him was passed in Parliament.[2] The attainder resulted in his lands and goods being forfeit to the Crown and his heirs deprived of the right to inherit his estates or titles. In the years following these events a number of official surveys, inventories and accounts were produced detailing the extent and value of the Marquis' property, personal possessions and offices, which was considerable. A number of these documents survive in the Public Record Office in a varying state of preservation, including the one set out below, listing the residential properties which had been in the Marquis' possession at the time of his death and showing their subsequent immediate history.

There are actually two documents, written in different hands, which closely resemble each other but which bear some variations. The document transcribed in full below appears to be the earlier version, and the variations in the second document, of a slightly later date, are given in the notes. The surveys are undated but there are several indications to suggest that they were the results of annual audits undertaken in 1543 and 1544. For example, Sir Richard Pollard, described as the 'late Sir Richard', died in November 1542,[3] Lord John Russell succeeded to the office of Lord Privy Seal in October 1542,[4] the patent granting Sir John St Leger the manor of Iddesleigh was dated 2 June 1543[5] and that giving Walter Erle the custody of Colcombe house and park 23 October, 1543.[6]

It was in March 1539 that Sir Richard Pollard,[7] one of the sons of Sir Lewis Pollard of Kingsnympton, a Judge of the Common Pleas, who was already one of the General Surveyors of Crown Lands, was made chief steward of the forfeited possessions of the Marquis of Exeter, receiving a fee of £30 a year and the right to appoint an understeward.[8] It seems probable that he appointed his brother-in-law, Sir Hugh Paulet, to this post.[9] The surveys were prepared by the auditor Roger Kynsey, who had worked for the Marquis of Exeter in the same capacity, and was described in a list of the Marquis' servants taken after his execution as 'Roger Kempsey, auditor of the lands, of the age of 50 years and married, a man of good honest conditions and can do good service in that office, for his wages £8'.[10] Roger Kensey (the surname is variously given as Kynsey, Kempsey, Kensey) is also recorded as general auditor in the diocese of Exeter, so was an experienced practitioner of his profession in the South West.[11]

The properties mentioned in the document at Okehampton, Chulmleigh, Tiverton, Columbjohn in the parish of Broadclyst, Colcombe in Colyton, Exminster and Hillesden in Buckinghamshire were all part of the traditional inheritance of the Earldom of Devon, held by the Courtenays since medieval times.[12] The property at Wardour in Wiltshire had been leased by the Marquis of Exeter from Sir Anthony Willoughby in 1537[13] and the Cornish mansion at Boconnoc belonged to the Boconnoc estates which the Marquis inherited from his grandfather, Sir Edward Courtenay of Boconnoc, created Earl of Devon by Henry VII in 1485, on his death in 1509.[14] The Marquis had purchased the manor of Iddesleigh from Sir John Dudley in 1531.[15]

The survey reveals that the early medieval castles at Okehampton and Plympton had been allowed to deteriorate, the Tudor Courtenays preferring to use their more modern and comfortable manor houses. They had remained traditional landlords, so that traces of feudal duties and manorial rights survived on their estates, but, within a few years of the Marquis' death, in some instances the King's Commissioners had already begun a process of disparking and leasing the land.

PRO, Rentals & Surveys (Miscellaneous Books. Augmentation Office) E315/384

Devon. The names of all the mansions and houses with the parks that the King's Grace hath by the attainder of the late Lord Marquis, within the county there belonging to the Earldom of Devonshire, within the circuit of Roger Kynsey, auditor, as followeth

First at Okehampton a castle being an honour, wherein was all manner of houses of offices, now rewymowse [remiss] and decayed, of the which divers gentlemen holdith their tenures, being yearly at their fine for the maintenance of the garrets [watch towers] of the said castle.[16]

To the said castle was a park adjoining with a chase to the same park belonging, which is now disparked and was set to farm to Peter Carew by the late Sir Richard Pollard, knight, and Sir Hugh Paulet, commissioners in that behalf, for the sum of £66-13-4, then being keeper Wymond Carew[17] esquier and the next before him one John Chamboane,[18] claiming by their patent of the King's grant the herbage, pannage, windfall and browse[19] with all other profits belonging to the same park, for the which herbage and pannage in all the Marquis's time and ever before was yearly answered £20[20]

Upon the death of the said Marquis and before was Machaunt[21] keeper of the same park and chase by patent, which had no more allowed but a yearly fee of £4-6-8 and the pasture of 24 rother beasts [horned cattle] with such commodities as belonged to the Keepers before that time. At the manor of *Chilmelegh* [Chulmleigh] a park with a fair lodge within, the same which is now disparked, of the which park Anthony Harvey,[22] esquier, was keeper, whose fee was yearly by patent 66/8 with the profit of the herbage, pannage, windfall, timber and underwoods and all other advantages to the same park belonging, which park upon the disparking was set to farm to the said Anthony by the foresaid Sir Richard Pollard and Sir Hugh Paulet for the sum of £10.[23]

At *Tyverton* [Tiverton] there being the head and chief mansion house, moated, walled and embattled round like a castle with all manner of houses of offices and lodgings within the same, well kept and repaired, and fair gardens to the same belonging, the oversight and custody thereof George Pollard[24] hath, having a fee for the custody of the same yearly without patent £4-10-3[25]

To the same mansion house belongeth 2 parks, one called *Aisshely* [Ashley] park whereof my Lord Russell[26] hath the custody with the herbage of the same, the fee yearly by patent £4-0-0.[27]

The other park called *Nueparke* [Newpark] whereof Thomas Appowell[28] is keeper and parker of the same with the pasturing of certain cattle and all other profits to the same of old belonging, the said Thomas having a yearly fee by patent of the late Marquis' grant of 60/8[29]

At *Colump John* [Columbjohn] a fair house with divers lodgings within the same, well kept and repaired, lying now in the same Anthony Harvey, esquier, yielding therefor yearly £15 and the same Anthony to be allowed yearly for and toward the reparations 100/- as appeareth by his lease.[30]

At Colcombe a fair large house with divers lodgings in the same, well kept and repaired, set standing and being within the park, which park standeth, the custody of the place and park had one Walter Langley,[31] now departed, his fee yearly by patent by the grant of the late Lord Marquis, attainted, 60/8, with the pasture of 4 kine or bullocks and of 1 horse or gelding with the pannage, windfall, woods and underwoods.[32]

The same Walter had by virtue of the same patent the office of bailiwick of the hundred and manor of Colyton, his yearly for that 52/-

At Plympton a castle, being an honour, wherein was many lodgings and how utterly decayed, one Thomas Vawterd[33] constable of the said castle and bailiff of the manor and hundred, the yearly fee by patent £4-6-8.[34]

Wilts.
At *Warder* [Wardour] a park with a proper castle within it, well repaired, set to justment [farm] to one Mathie Coltehurst,[35] auditor, dwelling in the same, the King's Majesty having little profit thereby.[36]

Bucks.
At *Hillesdon* [Hillesden] a park with a fair house adjoining to the said park, which park standeth. One Gyfford parker and bailiff there, his yearly fee for both by patent 40/-[37]

The mansion house and the park of *Boconoke* [Boconnoc] in Cornwall, which park is disparked and set to farm to my Lord Russell, having the custody of the same mansion, the yearly fee allowed by patent £6-0-10[38]

[Marginal note. This manor of Boconock is not within my office of the Earldom]

Iddesly [Iddesleigh] park which standeth is not in my office but the manor with the park is changed and put to Mr Sellenger [St Leger][39] for other land of his taken to the King's Majesty.

NOTES

1. Letters & Papers, Foreign and Domestic, in the Reign of Henry VIII xiii. 451 (1056).
2. Statutes of the Realm iii. 717.
3. LPH8 xvii. 600 (1075).
4. LPH8 xvii. 688 (1251:7).
5. LPH8 xviii. 449 (802:37).
6. LPH8 xviii. 237 (449:6).
7. J.L. Vivian, *The Visitations of the County of Devon* (Exeter, 1895), 598; W.B. Pollard, *Records of the Pollards of Kingsnympton* (Typescript, 1962), 44–75.
8. LPH8 xiv. 253 (651:47).
9. Sir Hugh Paulet was married to Sir Richard Pollard's sister Philippa: Colin G. Winn, *The Pouletts of Hinton St. George* (1976), 19–22.
10. PRO, SP1/138 755(1).
11. George Oliver, *Ecclesiastical Antiquities in Devon* ii (1840), 154.
12. Margaret R.Westcott, 'The Estates of the Earls of Devon, 1485–1538' (unpublished MA thesis, University of Exeter, 1958), 294.
13. *Victoria County History of Wiltshire* xiii (1987), 221–2.
14. Westcott, 'Estates of the Earls of Devon', 28–9.
15. PRO, Ancient Deeds E 210/9778.
16. 2nd document at their fine for their homage.
17. J.L. Vivian, *The Visitations of Cornwall* (Exeter, 1887), 68.
18. John Champernowne was made parker in January, 1540: LPHG8 xv. 52 (144:13).
19. Manorial rights of pasturing cattle, pasturing swine in oak and beech woods, and taking fallen and waste wood.

20. 2nd document and now set to the said Peter Carew by the King's Majesty's lease for £42 by the year. Marginal note: This park is distant from Tiverton 20 miles.
21. The list of the Marquis' servants records that several offices were held by John Machaunde, 50 years old and married, in Devonshire, including that of keeper of the park of Okehampton, by patent.
22. Anthony Harvey was the Marquis' Surveyor General and after the attainder was made surveyor of his forfeited possessions on behalf of the King: LPH8 xiv.253 (651:52); Westcott, 'Estates of the Earls of Devon', 98–9.
23. 2nd document At the manor of *Chilmelegh* [Chulmleigh] a park with a little lodge within the same of the building of Anthony Harvey esquier, now disparked and set to farm to the said Anthony Harvey by the King's lease yearly for £10, having an annuity out of the same by the King's grant during his life of £6-13-4 and the said Anthony bound to the maintenance thereof. Marginal note: Distant from Okehampton 12 miles.
24. Probably Sir Richard Pollard's brother: Pollard, Records of the Pollards, 119–23.
25. 2nd document. Marginal note. Reparations of the same this year £11-5-1.
26. G.E.C., *Complete Peerage* ii. 73–5.
27. 2nd document one called *Ayssheley* [Ashley] park, the distance of half a mile from the place. The reparations of paling 26/8.
28. Described in the list of servants as '60 years, married, in Devonshire, keeper of the little park of Tiverton and bailiff of Exminster'. He had served the Marquis' mother, the Countess Katherine, when she resided at Tiverton Castle.
29. 2nd document The other park called *Nuepareke* [Newpark] adjoineth to the place. The reparations of the paling 12/8. Marginal note: These two parks standeth.
30. 2nd document lying now in the same Anthony Harvey esquire, having it in lease with the demesnes for 21 years, yielding therefore yearly £25 and the same Anthony bound to the reparations thereof. Marginal note: Distant from *Excetor* [Exeter] 4 miles.
31. The list records him as 'of the age of 40 years, married, in Devonshire, a tall man and a good archer, keeper of the park and place of Colcombe'.
32. 2nd document the custody of the park and place hath one Walter Erle. LPH8 xviii. 237 (449:6). This park is distant from Tiverton 18 miles. Marginal note: The charge of repairs of the manor house 30/4. The charge of paling is 38/10.
33. He appears in the list of servants as being 50 years of age, holding the constableship of the castle of Plympton and the office of bailiff of Plympton hundred.
34. 2nd document has an extra paragraph At Exminster manor there being a stable and a barn, the reparations upon the stable this year 3/3. Marginal note: Distant from Exeter 3 miles.
35. *Victoria County History of Wiltshire* xiii, 221–2.
36. 2nd document the King's Grace having the same park by lease by the attainder of the late Lord Marquis. Marginal note: It is in the tenure of Sir Anthony Willoughby, knight. Wilts. Five miles from Shaftesbury.
37. 2nd document the park standing and so to be maintained by John Gifford, keeper and bailiff there during his life, his yearly fee for both by patent 40/-. Marginal note: Buck. Distant from London 50 miles and 2 miles from Buckingham.
38. 2nd document set to farm to my Lord Privy Seal for £6. Marginal note: Distant from *Excetor* [Exeter] 60 miles.
39. LPH8 xviii 449 (802:37): Estates in Devon, including Iddesleigh, were exchanged for property in Buckinghamshire; Thomas Westcote, *A View of Devonshire in 1630* (Exeter, 1845), 483–4.

Margaret Westcott

46.   A Devon Muster in June 1639

It was the ambition of Charles I to have a perfect militia and so he required the holding of annual musters. The chain of command went from the privy council to the lord lieutenant (in Devon this was the earl of Bedford from 1623, joined by his son William from 1637) and from them to the deputy lieutenants. Devon's deputy lieutenants responded more effectively to their orders than those of many counties; they reported to their lord lieutenant when musters had been held and sometimes gave detail on the numbers attending and the names of officers present. It is over the next link in the series of orders that material is very slight, of the deputy lieutenants ordering a company to muster. This document provides rare details of those orders. They were sent by Henry Ashford esquire of Burlescombe to his distant cousin John Willoughby esquire of Payhembury. The letter is undated but must belong to 1639, as it refers to both pressed and unpressed men and the first indication of Devonians being pressed for service against Scotland was in September 1638 when Willoughby's muster book marked fourteen pikemen and thirty-seven musketeers as 'prest'.[1] The presence of these pressed men in the annual muster of June 1639 increases the interest of this document as it shows how a company was affected by the Bishops' Wars.

SRO, DD WO 56/6/29

[dorse. 'To my well beloved cousin Sergeant Major Willougby Esq for his Majesty's special service—haste haste post haste']

By virtue of Letters from the Lords of His Majesty's most honourable privy Council to the Lords Lieutenant of this county and from their Lordships to the deputy Lieutenants, it is ordered That all the Regiments of this county both horse and foot be mustered, exercised and trained 26th and 27th days of this instant June at such places as the Colonels of each Regiment shall think fittest to put in execution these orders following That all trained soldiers of your Band be and appear before you completely furnished both in men and Arms at the days aforesaid in Kentismoor as well those which were select and stand still for His Majesty's present service as the rest not impressed. And if the select arms impressed be now be made use of at the muster, after they are to be returned where they were formerly kept, there to be continued till farther order be given for the said Arms and soldiers, the spares and spells weekly now exercised are not to be present at this muster other than such as were care of the trained Bands formerly enrolled. That you give order to the Constables to bring ½lb powder and Match answerable for every musketeer for this service to be used the first or second day at your discretion.

That the Constables of every hundred have warning that all Martial Rates be duly levied and all refusers to pay those rates be warned to appear before the deputy Lieutenants on Thursday in next Sessions week and it is to be understood that all parsonages Impropriate are liable to those rates as other lands are.

That all the soldiers be daily paid as well for the present service as all former arrears, if any be, and that all Constables make perfect their Accounts before the end of the training.

That you keep a watch lying in the field the Wednesday night setting forth your sentinels standing upon your guard and appointing Rounders in Warlike manner whereby your soldiers may be made acquainted with the most necessary discipline and yourself being present and providing in the meantime a tent set up in the most eminent place where your Company is lodged. And if you cannot conveniently provide the same so soon get to have one of cloth which you may safely get from the colour makers.

That you give order that every soldier come provided of a knapsack and victuals to serve him for the time of this service and not allowing any sutler or victualler to sit down near you which may give occasion that your soldiers may disband only to allow one or two to bring beer and set it such a distance as you shall think fitting and those to be such only as you shall think fit to command thither, and that the soldiers pay be then brought and duly paid them on the drums head, That your muster books be made perfect and brought in to the muster master at his house in Exeter at the next Sessions without setting down the defects in the same book, but that there be another list of defects made and sent as aforesaid with a note upon those that have been formerly warned to amend their defects and have not or are otherwise notably refractory that a speedy course may be take for reformation accordingly.

Your loving cousin
[signed] Hen: Ashford

Ashford had become a deputy lieutenant in 1635 after years of service as a captain and then lieutenant colonel of one of the two trained band regiments of east Devon. He took over command of a regiment in 1638 on the death of Francis Courtenay.[2] His correspondent Willoughby had become a captain in 1634 and by the time of these orders was the sergeant-major of the regiment, that is third in seniority.[3] Ashford evidently drew up the same orders for all five companies in his regiment. The rendezvous is inserted in a different ink and another company was ordered to gather at Willand Moor on the same day. In accordance with the orders, the clerk of the company, Edmund Cross, produced a fair copy of the muster book showing that sixty-four pikemen and one hundred and two musketeers were present as well as fifteen gentlemen.[4] The officers of the company, in addition to Willoughby, were a lieutenant, an ensign, two sergeants and two drummers. The book also showed who was responsible for the arms of each soldier; ten brought their own arms or those of their father, sixteen collected arms from the common store and the rest had their arms supplied by one or more named persons. As ordered Cross produced a second document showing any defect in these arms; on the muster day he had found sixteen soldiers with missing or defective arms but he had managed to whittle this down to five by the time he produced his fair copy for the muster master.[5] The muster book shows that the men were drawn from the parishes of Hemyock, Culmstock, Clay Hydon, Churchstanton, Buckerell, Uffculme, Kentisbeare, Awliscombe, Willand, Sampford Peverell and Dunkeswell. For some of them Kentismoor (near Kentisbeare) would have been a convenient rendezvous but others would have had to trudge about ten miles, so it was important that they were paid for the time of travelling as well as training. Rates of payment had been decided at a meeting of deputy lieutenants in 1625. Soldiers were paid 8d a day, while the rates for officers were 3/- for captains and lieutenants, 2/6 for ensigns, 1/6 for sergeants and 1/- for drums.[6] The reference to the payment of martial rates suggests that these were based on landholding. At this time there was no uniform practice over the collection of martial rates, some counties based it on subsidy rating, others on residence in the parish. The parish clergy were liable to pay martial rates on their lands and were also assessed to pay for members of the trained band and for their arms; two pikemen and five musqueteers of Willoughby's company were provided by the clergy.

Ashford had to define carefully who was expected to attend this muster because of the complicated situation created by several presses for the Scottish War. The contingent waiting to be sent to the north was raised in three ways; some were pressed from the trained band, others were substitutes found and paid for by these members of the trained band (termed spells) and the rest were untrained men. This contingent had been training weekly since March 1639 and was supplied with the arms of the trained band.[7] Ashford makes it clear that only the members of this contingent who were enrolled members of the trained band should now attend the muster. The deputy lieutenants clearly did not want the organization of the trained bands to be disturbed if the pressed forces were not going to be required, after all, outside the county. This seemed a probability with the Pacification of Berwick being concluded in the same month as the muster. Even so the deputy lieutenants were determined to accustom their soldiers to wartime procedures such as sending Rounders out to ensure that the sentries remained awake. Their order to the sixty-eight-year-old Captain Willoughby to obtain a tent for a night under canvas suggests that this too was not part of a normal peacetime muster.

NOTES

1. SRO, DD WO 53/1/115.
2. PRO, SP16/150/76; 241/55; 291/14; 402/69.
3. Walter and Charles Trevelyan (eds), *Trevelyan Papers, Part III, 1446–1643* (Camden Society, 1st Series 105, 1872), 186.
4. SRO, DD WO 56/1/7.3.
5. SRO, DD WO 56/6/23.2.
6. PRO, SP16/8/14, duplicate DRO, 1148M/add/18/1.
7. SRO, DD WO 56/6/16.1–16, 49.3.

Mary Wolffe

47. An Eighteenth-Century Tour of Plymouth

The transcript below represents approximately two thirds of a manuscript journal of a tour through Devon and Cornwall located among the extensive records of the Incledon-Webber family of Braunton, now housed in the North Devon Record Office. The document is undated, and there is no indication of authorship. Nevertheless, there are a number of clues in the text which enable it to be dated with reasonable certainty, the foremost of these being the reference to the building of the Chapel at Saltram, for records show that work commenced in August 1776.[1] In addition, there is a reference in the untranscribed portion of the journal to a visit to Tehidy, Illogan, where the observation is made that 'Mr B(assett) comes from his Travel & is of age August twelvemonth'. According to the Bassett family pedigree in Vivian's *Visitations of Cornwall* (1887), Sir Francis Bassett was born on the 9th August 1757, confirming a date of 1777. The journal thus begins on 29 April 1777, a Tuesday, and, as most subsequent entries commence with the day of the week, it is possible to reconstruct the itinerary through to the tour's conclusion on Thursday, 22 May. The Cornish stage of the journey, not transcribed, ended on Thursday, 15 May, when the party crossed the Tamar at Saltash. The transcript continues from this point. The identity of the writer remains a mystery, although it was probably a young woman of a similar social standing to the landed gentry visited. There is no obvious connection between the

Incledon family and Newton Abbot, nor does there appear to be any likely candidate in the Incledon pedigree in Vivian's *Visitations of Devon* (1895). Frustratingly, the surviving correspondence of the Parker family of Saltram, now in the West Devon Record office (P1259), which may have provided a clue, commences in 1778.

NDRO, 3704M/FZ23

April 29 Mr & Mrs Peers left *Newton* [Newton Abbot] at 9 o'clock, at 11 Miss Webber & Mrs R with Mrs Q followed them, got to Okehampton after 2 o'clock (20 mile), dined and reach Lifton by 7 (15m), passed by near Oke, a neat House Lord Courtenay built for Mr T Clack. Mr Harris at Hayne, near Lifton left that place at 8 next morning, went through *Lanceston* [Launceston], breakfasted at 5 Lanes (11 m), from thence to Bodmin. Very fine roads, there by 2 (18 m). Mr & Mrs Peers went soon after Dinner, we walked about the County Hall, part of the old Priory, were highly entertained by the Militia band of Musick pratizing which sounded very harmoniously. A remarkably old Fount we noticed and a good Assembly Room ...

... By Mr Morshead's & in sight of a Romantic Rock to *Coldrinick* [Coldrinnick], Mr Trelawney's, which is surrounded by good land, fine trees, etc. The house very old & out of repair. We found them going out to dinner. Staid till the horses came, were shewn through the Grounds, our Guide's horse getting from him retarded us, & changed our rout which was designed by Tavistock to reach Newton next day. But instead we went to Saltash over the Tamar & to Plymouth Dock. Stopped at the King's Arms. Mrs Q sent to Miss Rodd's, the eldest came directly, we gladly accepted of their invitation to their house in Newmarket Street & went as soon as we had supped. Very disagreeable we found the Inn without a Gent to manage for us.

Fryday after breakfast Mrs Q took us to Dr Remmett's, found the Ladies dressing to go out to Dinner so made them a short visit. Drove to the Assembly Room at the Dock, which is elegantly painted the ceiling & walls. Walked in the Bowling Green, which is finely situated. Drove home to dinner. Mr Smith came before dinner to Confession. Capt Vincent of the *Blenheim* & his sister dined with us. Capt Crawford of the 13 Regiment drank tea after Mrs Q, Miss Rodd & Miss Webber went to take a walk on the Lines, Capt Crawford invited us the next even to come to his Barrack. Mr Smith who is Leiutenant of Marines supped with us at which was much laughing at Joe.

Saterday Mr Smith called to attend us on board the *Occean*, Capt Lescrey,[2] on which Lord Shuldham's flag was hoisted.[3] We met Mr Forsar, the Master who returned with us on board, shewed the Cabbins & 3 Decks. A Mr & Mrs Hole & a Mr & Mrs Vaughan from Bristol came also on board, were offered Wine & Bisket; the *Queen*, another 90 Gun Ship, Capt Robinson, was near us. The *Royal George* ready to be commissioned we saw at a distance with several others, amongst them the *Beinfasance*, which is called by the Common People the *Ben Fesent*.[4] We were landed at the Dock, walked by the Warehouses, saw a 90 Gun Ship on the Stocks, were told they reckon the expence of building £1000 a Gun. A smaller ship, the *Vespers*, which was in a few days to launch. Whilst we stood there the Admiral Spry tender sailed out on a cruise to the westward. Walked through the Rope house in our way home to dinner. Capt Crawford & Smith drank tea with us & attended us to George's Square & to the Coll's Barrack. The Band of Musick were called out & played, till roll calling. The Coll & 9 other officers made their appearance, the former very civil, the rest only walked in at door & out at another. Some other Ladies came in, the Gent came home with us & supped, much laughing, even Capt Crawford Spanish gravity was moved to smile.

Sunday went to St Aubyn Chapple twice, in the even Lady Dalston & her daughter called, we went with them on the Lines. Walked in *Grandy* [Granby] & Frederick Squares. The Concourse of all sort of People very great. Saw a son of the famous Churchills coming home. Called at Lady Dalston's Lodging. Monday after breakfast Mrs Q & I in the Chaise, went to Mutton Cove. Miss Rodds & Miss Webber walked, we went over to *Crimbble* [Cremyll] Passage, went into Mount *Edgecomb* [Edgcumbe], up to Maker Church across to the other side, down the road to the Block House, Green House & Orange Trees 17 & 18 feet high, fine Cypress Trees. Eat some bread & butter at Crimble, over the water & back the same way to Miss Rodd. Afterwards went to Dr Remett's, Cat Street, Plymouth. He walked Miss Webber, A Gibbs & Mrs R went in the Chaise to the Citadel but its raining & little & great Shower seeming to come on we ran as fast as we could back to Dr Remmet's where we drank tea.

Teusday Mrs Q, Miss Rod & Miss Webber in one chaise, Miss Alicia & Mrs R in another, sett out with a basket of cold provision, to *Saltrem* [Saltram], Mr Parker. We saw the House which was in confusion, painters at work in the Hall, which is very elegant. The Musick room has Sir John Chichester, Lord Shelburn, Sir Thomas Ackland by Sir J. Reynolds[5] much faded. A beautiful one of Sir J.R. by Angelica Koffman [Kauffmann]. Many fine ones by her in the Drawing Room ... 4 large glasses we were told cost £1500. Fine tables, the ceiling very elegant. We were told the Carpet coresponds with it. A Tutenage[6] Grate & fender, some fine vases, the room painted Bleu, Damask curtains of that colour, the next room hung with crimson velvet, the form of that the corresponding room odd. Coved at the end & pillars. The Library rather low, a very fine inlaid table in the middle, the ceiling painted, all the chimney pieces extremely fine & elegant. One room has handsome worked chairs, & a fine Tapestry Settee. A Marble frame to a Barometer. The room up stairs not be seen, we viewed the chapple that's building, the Banquetting House[7] then filled with greens, near it a large Eagle. We walked through the plantation by the Cold Bath, through the Wood to the Temple of Jupiter which is a ruinous state, however as it rained were glad to partake of our cold meat. Than we set out walking again. Saw a very natural cave made of petrifactions & stellatates, a Grotto with shells, then back to the house till the chaises we ready. Stopped at the Royal Hospital which is a fine Square of buildings, mett Dr Far about & we sett out to return, stopped at the Royal Hos. Dr Farr took us into the Dispensary & one Ward, 'tis a noble building & neatly kept.

Soon after our return, Lady Dalston, Miss & Mr Smith supped with us. Wenesday we attempted walking in the Dockyard, but rain coming we sheltered in Mr Redstone's house from thence run to the Ammunition House. They refused shewing it till Miss A.Rodd sent to the Head Clerk, Mr Atkinson, than saw the whole. Mr Smith & another officer came to us & walked back to Miss Rodd's, dined & after many messages went to Coll Cruthers' in the Citadel, being invited by his Lady to drink tea, before it went round the Ramparts though cold & damp. The well in the lower rampart has a fine eccho & when the cover is laid down sounds like thunder. Left Miss Rodd's [Thur]sday [ab]out 10 o'clock, chang[ed] horses at Ivy Bridge & dined at Sandgate, reached Newton [Newton Bushel written above] about 7 very thankful for having had no accident of any kind & for escaping Cold though often caught in the rain, especially at Mr Parker's.

NOTES

1. Nigel Neatby, *Saltram*, National Trust Guide (1970), 29.
2. Edward Le Cras is listed as Captain of *The Ocean* in the *Royal Calendar* (1776).
3. Molyneaux, Lord Shuldham returned from a two year tour of duty as Commander in Chief on the east coast of North America early in 1777, and from 1778 to 1783 was Port Admiral at Plymouth.
4. The *Bienfaisant, Ocean* and *Queen* appear in a list of ships in commission in the *Gentleman's Magazine* (July 1777), 351.
5. Sir Joshua Reynolds was a close friend of the Parkers of Saltram and a frequent visitor to the House in the 1770s.
6. Tutenag: a whitish alloy resembling silver.
7. Probably the Orangery, built between 1773 and 1775.

Tim Wormleighton

48. Devon Monastic Bells

There is no little irony in the fact that it was in 1556, towards the end of the reign of Mary Tudor, that the first strenuous efforts were made by the government to discover what had happened to the bells which had come down with the monastic churches nearly two decades earlier. The inquiry was not motivated by any sense of piety on the part of the Lord Treasurer, the marquess of Winchester: it was instituted simply to find out whether all the proceeds of sales, of lead as well as bells, had been properly accounted for.

The Dissolution statutes and the instructions to the commissioners had been insistent that of all the former monastic property, real and movable, special care should be taken to set aside all bells and lead, and to place them in safe custody, prior to their sale.[1] Some, no doubt, disappeared without trace, but on the whole the officers of the newly-established Court of Augmentations followed their instructions to the letter. Bells were more valuable in the form of artefacts while lead was more saleable, especially overseas, after being melted down and cast into blocks. Those few laymen, for example Sir Richard Grenville at Buckland Abbey, who acquired whole monastic churches for conversion to secular uses, no doubt found means, if only as 'custodians', of retaining the lead roofs in situ, but the retention of bells was less easily justified and Sir Thomas Arundell, the Crown's Receiver for the former monastic lands in the South West, lost no time in selling them, not necessarily to the highest bidder, but, like the former monastic landed property sold soon after the Dissolution, at a fixed price.[2]

The task of conducting the Marian inquiry in the four southwestern counties was entrusted to one Robert Grove, about whom nothing else is known. Presumably he was expected to make his inquiries locally for he admits to not having visited Pilton near Barnstaple where there had been a small Cluniac priory. In fact, as his returns make clear, he found most of what he needed to know in the accounts of Sir Thomas Arundell, and he probably completed the whole of his return without leaving London.[3] Comparison with the Receiver's Accounts for 1538-9 and 1539-40[4] indicates that, *as far as he went*, Grove did an efficient job, listing for each religious house, including the friaries in Exeter and Plymouth, the number of bells and the price put upon them. Unlike Arundell he thought it unnecessary to include the actual weight of the bells and who purchased them, but, a more serious omission, he did not pursue the actual payments. In most cases we are left to assume that the cash was in hand. Arundell's accounts are more precise: that for 1538-9 records that the two bells of Polsloe Priory near Exeter were sold to Sir George Carew, lessee of the former priory site, for £6 13s 4d but that by the time the account was engrossed for audit Sir George had paid only £3 6s 8d. Pursuing the settlement of arrears year by year in the Receivers' Accounts is indeed a tedious business and there are gaps in the series.[5] But Arundell seems to have sold most of the former Devon monastic bells fairly quickly and for cash, or at any rate to have obtained payment in full within a year or so.[6] Tudor accountancy ensured that 'arrears', however small, were never forgotten.

For the monastic lead Grove's returns for Devon are missing, though they survive for the three other counties, but in the same file of papers is an account, also compiled in 1556, by John Aylworth, Arundell's successor, of money raised in 1549 from sales of lead in the South West, mostly in Somerset but including that from a handful of religious houses in Devon.[7] Altogether, including £40 from Sir Gawen Carew for the bells of Launceston Priory in Cornwall, Aylworth accounted for the very large sum, in cash, of £1997 15s 5d. He further reported that at Wells in Somerset on 4 August 1549, by virtue of a warrant for £2000 from the Protector Somerset dated 24 July, he handed the proceeds of his endeavours to Sir William Herbert, who 'then was going towardes the West with an army of men for the suppression of the Rebellion that thenne newly was begonne'. In fact, as Aylworth makes clear, he himself had not been actually selling lead, the right to do so having been granted by the Crown before the end of the reign of Henry VIII to Sir Edward Baynton of Wiltshire. But whether or not the lead had been sold by 1549, let alone carted away, it is clear that neither Baynton nor the Crown had received much, if any, of the proceeds until, with the latter's desperate need for cash in the summer of 1549, John Aylworth had been sent hot foot to pick up what he could, apparently with considerable success. So, unlike the proceeds of the sales of the Devon monastic bells, which were swallowed up in paying for Henry VIII's French wars of the mid 1540s, those for lead had been, as it were, on ice, and came in handy ten years later for prosecuting military operations nearer home.

The two references to the Western, or Prayer Book, Rebellion of 1549 are themselves of great value, the collecting of such fortuitous details being one of the few ways now left of advancing our knowledge of this cataclysmic event in westcountry history.[8] The link with the Dissolution adds further irony to the story.

PRO, E117/14, 87, 89–90

A Brief Declaration of the Belles belonging to the late suppressed and dissolved monasteries ... by ... Robert Grove ...

DEVON: viz

Plympton	v Belles	xliij^{li}	xiij^s	iiij^d [5420 lb][9]
Exeter, St Johns [Hospital]	iiij Belles	xxxiiij^{li}	v^s	
Bukfast [Buckfast]	v Belles	xxxiiij^{li}	xv^s	
Torre	v Belles	xliij^{li}	x^s	
Pollesloo [Polsloe]	ij Belles	vj^{li}	xiij^s	iiij^d [1000 lb][10]
Hartelande [Hartland]	iiij Belles	xxix^{li}	x^s	
Donkeswell [Dunkeswell]	iiij Belles	xxxij^{li}	v^s	
Bucklande [Buckland]	iiij Belles	xxxij^{li}	ix^s	
New[n]ham	v Belles	xlvj^{li}	xiij^s	iv^d
Canonligh [Canonsleigh]	iiij Belles	xxxij^{li}		
Fourde [Forde]	v Belles	xxxviij^{li}	x^s	[5130 lb][11]
Tavestok [Tavistock]	vi Belles	l^{li}	x^s	vi^d

[right hand margin, translated from the Latin] Charged in Thomas Arundell's account for 1539–40[12]

Totton [Totnes]	iiij Belles	xv^{li}		
Corneworthe [Cornworthy]	iij Belles	vi^{li}	xiij^s	iv^d
Exon [St Nicholas]	vj Belles	lv^{li}	iii^s	iiii^d
Frythelstoke [Frithelstock]	iiij Belles	xvij^{li}	xvij^s	

[right hand margin, trans.] Charged in Thomas Arundell's account for 1538–9][13]

    Pilton   I have not been their nor cannot say any thinge touchinge belles nor leadde.

    Bar[n]stable Their were v belles wayenge by estimaton vi^{Mil} [lb] and were solde by Sir Thomas Arundell knight to one John Stevens of Witheridge in Devon for the some of lx^{li} or theraboutes, as I can lerne, in [1539–40] and the saide Stevens was killed in the Rebellyon tyme.

[left hand margin, in another hand, in Latin] ... the executors of the said John Stephens

The Grey Friers in *Exetor*	ij Belles	vij^{li} xvij^{s} vi^{d}
The Blake Friers in *Exetor*	ij Belles	vij^{li} xvi^{s} iiij^{d}

[right hand margin: as above for Plympton etc.]

The Grey Friers in Plymouth	ij Belles	Sold with the buyldinges as
The Blake Friers their	ij Belles	I can lerne.[14]

NOTES

1. Joyce Youings, *Dissolution of the Monasteries* (1971), 161.
2. Youings, *Dissolution*, 120–21.
3. See text below.
4. PRO, Special Collections, Ministers Accounts, SC6/Henry VIII/7300 and 7301.
5. They are missing for 1540–43, 1545–46 and 1548–51.
6. There are no arrears for bells in the 1558–9 account: Youings, *Dissolution*, 216–19.
7. PRO, E117/14/100.
8. Joyce Youings, 'The Western Rebellion', *Southern History* I (1979), 99–122, passim.
9. PRO, SC6/Henry VIII/7300. The price was specified as 15 shillings per hundredweight (112 lb). The purchaser, for cash, was one Richard Fortescue. One wonders how the bells were weighed with such apparent exactitude, except by eye.
10. PRO, SC6/Henry VIII/7300.
11. These were purchased by the 'parishioners' (presumably of Thorncombe, then in Devon), also for cash, which works out (cf Plympton) at approximately 15 shillings per hundredweight. At Polsloe Carew agreed to pay rather more, presumably to allow for part payment. The 5 bells of Buckfast Abbey were also bought for the parish church.
12. These were the larger houses dissolved in 1539.
13. The smaller houses, dissolved in 1536. The friars were despatched in 1538.
14. To Giles and Gregory Isham of London in 1546: Joyce Youings (ed.), *Devon Monastic Lands*, DCRS, N.S. 1 (1955), 93–4. There is no mention of any payment for the bells in the sale particulars.

Joyce Youings

A CHECKLIST OF THE WRITINGS OF MARGERY ROWE

1964

[with J.Cochlin] Mayors of Exeter from the 13th century to the present day.—Exeter: Exeter City Library, 1964. ix,30p. DUL 25080

[with J.Cochlin] 'Evidence of the existence of St. John's Hospital, Exeter, in the late twelfth century' *Devon and Cornwall Notes and Queries*, 29:8 (Jan. 1964), 211–4.

1970

[with G.E.Trease] 'Thomas Baskerville: Elizabethan apothecary of Exeter.' *Transactions of the British Society for the History of Pharmacy*, 1:1 (1970), 58p.—DUL 62810.

'Exeter Library Society', *Devon and Cornwall Notes and Queries*, 31:7 (Summer 1970), 222–4.

1971

[with G.E.Trease] 'The 1572 bill of an Exeter apothecary', *Devon and Cornwall Notes and Queries*, 32:1 (Spring 1971), 17–9.

Assizes and quarter sessions in Exeter. Exeter: Exeter City Council, 1971. DUL 25050.

1973

[with Andrew M.Jackson] *Exeter freemen, 1266–1967*.—Exeter: Devon and Cornwall Record Society, 1973. xxxv,462p. (Devon and Cornwall Record Society. Extra series; 1). DUL 62800. ISBN 0-901853-18-6.

1974

'Some seventeenth century annals', *Devon and Cornwall Notes and Queries*, 33:1 (Spring 1974), 20–22.

1975

'Cockington manor wills', *Devon and Cornwall Notes and Queries*, 33:4 (Spring 1975), 109–13.

1976

'The Devon and Cornwall Record Society', *Devon Historian*, 13 (1976), 8–10.

'The Queen's lottery', *Devon and Cornwall Notes and Queries*, 33:7 (Autumn 1976), 240–3.

1977

[editor] *Tudor Exeter: tax assessments 1489–1595, including the military survey 1522*.—Exeter: Devon and Cornwall Record Society, 1977.—xix,106p.—(Devon and Cornwall Record Society. New series; 22)

1983

[with T.J.Falla] 'The population of two Exeter parishes in 1641–2', *Devon and Cornwall Notes and Queries*, 35:3 (Spring 1983), 89–95

1984

'Sampford Spiney registers', *Devon Family Historian*, 32 (1984), 6–7; 37 (1986), 6–7.

1986

'The Exeter plot', In: *The Monmouth Rising: aspects of the 1685 rebellion in the West Country*, edited by Ivan Roots.—Exeter: Devon Books, 1986.—ISBN 0–86114–779–0. Pp 73–5.

1987

[with Geoffrey Paley and John A.H.Wylie] 'The Williams family, gold and silver-smiths of Bristol and their association with the Exeter Assay Office', *Devon and Cornwall Notes and Queries*, 36:1 (Spring 1987), 20–26, 69–70.

'Sources for maritime history in the Devon Record Office' in *Sources for a new maritime history of Devon*, edited by David Starkey.—Exeter: Devon County Council, 1987.—ISBN 0–86114–646–8. Pp10–24.

1988

'The new North Devon Record Office', *Devon Family Historian*, 46 (1988), 4.

1989

[joint editor with John M. Draisey] *The receivers' accounts of the City of Exeter, 1304–1353*.—Exeter: Devon and Cornwall Record Society, 1989.—xxxi,128p,plate : ill.—(Devon and Cornwall Record Society. New series, 32).—ISBN 0–901853–32–1.

'Postscript to 1688', *Devon and Cornwall Notes and Queries*, 36:6 (Autumn 1989), 216–7.

1991

[with Louise Rose] 'The new North Devon Record Office', *Archives*, 19:85 (April 1991), 289–96: ill.

1992

[joint editor with Todd Gray and Audrey Erskine] *Tudor and Stuart Devon: the common estate and government: essays presented to Joyce Youings*—Exeter: University of Exeter, 1992.—xix,230p,plates : ill,maps.—ISBN 0–85989–384–7.

The above listing does not do full justice to Margery Rowe's contribution to historical research in Devon. It does not draw attention to her work as editor of *Devon and Cornwall Notes and Queries* from 1970 to 1994 and of the publications of the Devon and Cornwall Record Society since 1993. Above all it ignores virtually completely the immense value of her work as an archivist in Devon. A public view of some of this work has been provided in recent years by the *Devon Record Office Newsletter* which has appeared since May 1988, but

Margery Rowe has been responsible for a long series of reports, hand-lists and other publications produced by the Record Office and has personally listed many of the collections which have been deposited over the years. Among her more important listings are:

Mallock Family of Cockington, Reynell Family of Forde, Ley Family of Trehill, Champernowne Family of Dartington, Shelley formerly Tuckfield, Exeter Mayor's Court Rolls, abstract of deeds and wills, Exeter City Deeds and relisting.

Ian Maxted

INDEX

Abington (Pennsylvania) 104
Ackland,
  John, 159
  Sir Thomas, 209
Adams,
  A., 144
  John, 51
Adderton, William, 83
Aishford, Henry, 160, 165
Aislabie, Mary, 172
Albemarle, duke of, 165
Alewyn, Mr, 118
Alexander III, pope, 3
Allen (Allyen),
  Mrs, 39
  Revd R.P., 39
  William, 51
Allender, Mr & Mrs, 34
Alnod 4
Alured, Robert, 113
Amados Hill 26
Ameredith, Amias, 159
America (*see* **Abington, Boonsborough, Boston, Exeter, Gwynedd, Kentucky, New York, North Wales, Oley, Pennsylvania, Richmond**)
Anglesey (Wales) 131
Antrim (Ireland) 68
Appledore 14, 17, 49, 52
Appowell, Thomas, 201
Arnold, William, 9
Arscott,
  Edmund, 160, 161, 165
  John, 162, 164, 165
Arundel and Surrey, earl of, 159
Arundell, Sir Thomas, 211–13
Ash 160, 161
Ashford, Henry, 204, 205
Ashley 201
Ashreigney 138–40
Ashridge 4–5
Atherton,
  John, 10
  Thomas, 9, 10
Atkins, Edward, 162, 163
Atkinson, Mr, 209
Atlantic ocean xx, 86
atte More, Walter, 114
atte Porche, Thomas, 114

atte Welle, William, 114
Austin, John, 51
Australia, exhibition of, 20
Aveley (Essex) xxi
Awliscombe 160, 161, 206
Axminster 132
Aylworth, John, 211–12

Babington,
  Gervase, 123, 124
  Mr, 89
Bacini, William, 3–4
Bailey, Charles, 190, 192–6
Baldersby Park (Yorkshire) 172
Balle (Ball),
  Peter, 159, 160
  William, 89
Bampfield,
  Sir Coplestone, 163, 164, 165
  Edmund, 160
  John, 160, 161, 162
  Thomas, 162, 164, 165
Barnbary, J.J., 143
Barnes, Ralph, 57–60, 169
Barnstaple 14, 17, 71, 86–8, 173, 180, 213
  Archdeacon of, 1–2, 72, 139
  Crock Street 86–7
  Cross Street 86–7
  High Steward of, 98
  West Gate of, 86
Barrett, Sir Edward, xxi
Barrow, William, 51
Bartholate, Robert, 51
Bartlett, Mr, 63–5
Bassett,
  Sir Arthur, 70, 71, 159–60, 165
  Sir Francis, 207
Bastard,
  family 155
  Baldwin John Pollexfen, 155, 156, 157
  William, 160, 161, 162, 164, 165
Batcombe (Somerset) 14
Bath 53
  third earl of, 21–25, 179–80
  fifth earl of, 159, 160, 165
  Miss S., 118
  Place 174
Bath and Wells, bishop of, 7

Bayeux, John of, 5–6
Bayly, John, 9
Baynton, Sir Edward, 212
Beare (Beer, Bere),
  John, 77, 81, 160, 161, 162, 164, 165
  Thomas, 165
  William, 186
Bedford 5
  Duke of, 150, 204
Beecher, Lionel, 162, 164
Belechere, Robert, 110–14
Bennet,
  Mr George, 37
  John, 38
  Lucretia, 38
  Robert, 162, 164, 165
Bentham, James, 53
Berepouwe, John, 113, 114
Berkley, John, 160
Bevin (Beyvyn),
  Alice, 4–5
  Peter, 114
  Ralf, 4–5
  Robert, 4–5
Bevis, Peter, 160, 161
Bickleigh 91
Bickley (Bicklie),
  John the elder, 62–5
  John the younger, 62–5
Bickton 163, 164
Bickwell Valley, Sidmouth 32
Bideford 14, 17
Birton, Bishop, 133
Bishopsbourne 58
Blackaller, Joce, 138, 140
Blackmore, John, 63–5, 163, 164
Blackpool 129–30
Black Stone Rock 118
Blagg, Richard, 160
Blandford (Dorset) 132
Blatchford, Mr, 11
Blaytwayt, Georgina Sophia, 141–5
Bluett, Francis, 160
Blundell, John, 163, 164, 165
Blundeville, Thomas, 122, 123, 124
Boconnoc (Cornwall) 200, 202
Bodin, Jean, 123

Bodmin (Cornwall) 173, 208
Bogan, William, 165
Boone,
  family 102–7
  Ann, 105
  Daniel, 102
  George, 102–8
  James, 103, 105
  John, 103
  Joseph, 103
  Mary, 103
  Samuel, 103
  Sarah, 103–5
  Squire, 103–4
  Thomas, 161, 163, 164, 165
Boonesborough (Kentucky), Society of, 102
Boringdon 26
Baron, 175
Borlase, William, 133
Boston (USA) 36
Botour, William, 114
Bouffet, William, 113
Bourchier, William, 21–5
Bovy, William, 81
Boyton (Cornwall) 44
Braddon, William, 163, 164
Bradninch xix, xxii, 102–4, 107
  Hall 142
Bradshaw, John, 161, 163, 164
Braunton 207
Brechemont, Miss Mary, 118
Brend, Robert, 9, 10
Brest 66
Brewer, Bishop William, 5–6
Brialey, Humphrey, 51
Briant, Richard, 51
Bridestow 133
Bridgwater (Somerset) 173
Bridport (Dorset) 132
Brightley 165
Brighton 129–30
Bristol 16, 34–5, 104, 180, 208
  bishop of, 7
  channel 86 (see **Brunswick Square**, **Lewin's Mead**, **Queen Square**)
British Museum 33, 56
Britoun, Thomas, 114
Brixham 66
Broadclyst 200
  Institute 19
Broad Street (London) 73
Brock,
  Betsey, 118
  George, 118
  Moses, 28
  Mr, 28–30
  Mrs W., 187
  William, 118

Brockedon, William, 56, 60
Bronovo,
  Betsey, 116
  Mons., 116–19
Brown (Broun, Browne),
  John, 28–30
  Samuel, 160
  Walter, 113, 114
  William, 9, 11
Brunswick Square (Bristol) 35
Buckerell 206
Buckfast Abbey 212
Buckingham, Duke of, 100
Buckinghamshire (see **Hillesden**)
Buckland Abbey 211, 212
Buckland Farm (Somerset) 174
Buckland Filleigh 160, 161, 163, 164, 165
Buckland Monachorum 91–3
Budleigh Salterton 34, 198
Burghley,
  Lord, 21
  Master, 15
Burlescombe 204
Burnell, Dr Laurence, 72, 74–5
Burrator Reservoir 91
Bury 160, 161
  Mr, 74
  John, 160, 161, 162, 164
Busse,
  John, 113
  Robert, 114
Butterleigh 182
Bylling, John, 140

Cabell, Richard, 160, 165
Cadeleigh 38
Caesarius, Joannes, 123
Calamy, Edmund, 82
Callington (Cornwall) 134
Calmady,
  Josias, 160, 161, 165
  Shilston, 162, 164
Cambridge 56, 58, 119
Campbell, Anne, 98
Canada (see **Newfoundland**, **Placentia**)
Canonsleigh 212
Canonteign 164, 165
Canterbury 137
  archbishop of, 3, 55
Caperun, Richard, 114
Capston Hill 16
Carew,
  Sir Gawen, 211
  Sir George, 211
  Wymond, 201
Carey (Cary)
  family 76–82

Mr George, 21, 25
Henry, 160
John, 161, 162, 164
Robert, 165
Thomas, 165
William, 160
Carter,
  Daniel, 38
  John, 53
  William, 10
Cartwright, William, 55
Castle Hill 97–99
Castor Rock 94–6
Catlin, P.C., 31–4
Cavell, William, 55
Cawdor (Scotland) 98
Cecil, Sir Robert, 178–9
Ceely, Edward, 164
Ceylon 95
Chagford 93–7, 183–90
Challacombe 186
Chamboane, John, 201
Champernowne, Arthur, 160
Champneys, John, 160, 161, 162, 164, 165
Chapel (Chappell),
  Christopher, 50–2
  James, 50–2
  William, 113
Charles I 82
Charles II 72
Charley, Thomas, 51
Cheddlewood 3
Chelsea 131
Cheriton Bishop 41–9
Cheriton Fitzpaine 166, 171
Chichester,
  Lord, 71
  John, 159, 165, 209
Chick, James, 104
Chidley, William, 51
Chilcott, Robert, 11
Cholmeley, Richard, 160
Chudleigh, George, 160, 161
Chulmleigh 200–1
Churchstanton 138, 140–1, 206
Clack, Mr T., 208
Clarendon, earl of, 165
Classh, William, 114
Clatworthy 68–71
Clay Hydon 206
Cleaver, Robert, 123
Clerke, Thomas, 9
Clifford Bridge 96
Clifford, Lady, 178
Clobury, Christopher, 162, 163, 165
Clotworthy,
  Bartholomew, 69
  Hugh, 68–71

INDEX

John, 71
Simon, 68–71
Clyst Honiton 74, 132
  Cockram, Robert, 161
Coffin, Richard, 164, 165
Coleford 3
Coles, Richard, 161
Coleton 165
Coplestone,
  Henry, 160, 161
  John, 62, 163, 164, 165
Cobyn, Geoffrey, 114
Cockington 76–81
Colcombe 200, 201
Coldrinnick (Cornwall) 208
Cole, Alan, 17
Coleridge, Lord, 170
Coles, Thomas, 63, 65
Collacombe manor 44
Colle, Richard, 79
Colleton 165
Colley, John, 51
Collingwood, Admiral Cuthbert, 39
Coltechurst, Mathie, 202
Columbjohn 200, 201
Colyton 200, 201
Combe Martin 14, 15, 16
Cook, Mr John, 40
Coote, Sir Eyre, 38
Cornwall 22, 108, 132–4, 136, 150, 184 (*see* **Bocconoc, Bodmin, Boyton, Callington, Coldrinnick, Gwennap, Heligan, Illogan, Launceston, Probus, St Agnes, St Erme, St Ewe, Saltash, Tehidy, Trematon, Truro, Wendron**)
  archdeacon of, 3, 74
Cornworthy 212
Corvyset, William, 114
Cotgrave, Randal, 123
Cotton,
  Mr, 74
  Bishop William, 181–2
Countess Wear 39
Courte, Thomas, 141
Courten, Sir William, xix–xxii
Courtenay,
  Francis, 205
  Henry, 199–203
  John, 160, 165
  Sir William, 21, 25, 165
Cowick 39
Cowper, William, 123
Cox,
  Dr, 74
  William, 75
Cranbrook Castle 96

Crawford, Capt., 208–9
Crediton 27
Cremyll ferry 134, 209
Crewes,
  Henry, 163, 164
  Robert, 163
Crimes, Ellis, 160
Crispin, Thomas, 8–10
Cristoffels, Miss, 118
Crock Street 86–8
Crockenwell 43, 45, 186
Crocker (Croker),
  James, 186
  Philip, 161
Cromwell, Oliver, 161, 162, 163
Cross, Edmund, 205–6
Cross Street 86
Cruthers, Col., 210
Cruwys family 89
Cruwys Morchard 166–71
Cuic, Edmar of, 3
Cullompton xix–xxii, 88–90, 103–4, 180
Culm, river of, xx
Culme, Richard, 160
Culmstock 75, 206
Cunningham,
  John, 38
  Patrick, 9
  Richard, 9

Dallington, Sir Robert, 123, 124
Dalston, Lady, 209
Daniel, Mrs, 15
Dardanelles, 143
Dartington, 79
Dartmoor 44, 90, 93–7, 108–9, 145, 184
Dartmouth 80, 101
  Lord, 88–9
David, John, 114
Davy, John, 160, 161, 162, 163, 164, 165
Davies, Edward, 160
  James, 51
Dawe,
  Jo Davyesan, 2
  William, 1
de Asschebrutel, Walter, 114
de Berbylaunde, Roger, 113
de Bettburghe, Nicholas, 114
de Bradecrofte, Joel, 114
de Breaute, Fawkes, 5–6
de Cadycote, William, 114
de Carswell, William, 113, 114
de Chuddeleye, Alured, 114
de Cridyton, Alured, 114
de Doune, Robert, 114

de Ellehey, Richard, 113
de Elleueheye, Richard, 114
de Fenton, John, 114
de Fortibus, Isabella, 91
de Fougasses, Thomas, 123
de Fyschacre, Martin, 137
de Gatepathe,
  Henry, 114
  William, 114
de Henton, Roger, 113
de Langacre, Roger, 114
de Langedon, Thomas, 114
de la Spynee, Oliver, 114
de Mayerne, Turquet Louis, 122
de Metton, Gregory, 114
de Montaigne, Michel, 123
Denebaud, Philip, 114
de Nimet, Gilbert, 114
Denis (Dennis),
  John, 11
  Philip, 161, 162, 164
  Sir Robert, 21, 25
  William, 188
de Nyweton, Ralph, 113, 114
de Porte, Ralph, 114
de Radeslo, Walter, 113, 114
de Ralegh, William, 5–6
de Reviers,
  Baldwin, 2, 5–6
  Richard, 2
  Thomas, 2–3
Desbrow, John, 161
de Smalecombe, John, 114
de Spaxton, Richard, 113, 114
de Toryton, Gilbert, 113
de Tyverton, Richard, 114
de Vautorte,
  Juhel, 3
  Reginald, 2–4
de Vernon, William, 5–6
Devon, earl of, 4
Dexter, Robert, 120
de Wyndesore, Henry, 114
Dillon, Robert, 161
Disbrowe, John, 162, 163, 164, 165
Ditsworthy Warren 91
Doble, John, 161
Dod, John, 123, 124
Dodda, treasurer of Plympton 4
Doddridge (Doderidge), Sir John, 133, 160
Donegal, earl of, 165
Dorset 108, 132, 137 (*see* **Blandford, Bridport, Otterford, West Buckland, Weymouth, Whaddon**)
Dorsmouth 26
Doun 140
Dousland 91–2

Downame,
  George, 123
  John, 123
Downing,
  Rebecca, 38
  Thomas, 104
Down St Mary 82
Drake,
  Sir Francis, 23, 122, 135, 160, 161, 162, 163, 165
  John, 160, 161, 162, 164, 165
  Thomas, 160, 161, 162, 164, 165
Drewe, Francis, 165
Drewsteignton, 94, 96
du Pui, Mr, 118
Duck Lane (London) 83
Duck,
  Nicholas, 164, 165
  Richard, 160
Dudley, Sir John, 200
Duke, Richard, 160, 161, 163, 164, 165
Dunkeswell 206, 212
Dunmow, vicar of, 148
Dunprust 3, 4
Duntze, Sir John, 35
Durham 53
Durston (Somerset) 174
Dyer,
  family 27
  Thomas, 27–8, 30
Dyrwyne, John, 114

East Budleigh 33
East Indies xix, 38
Eddystone
  Lighthouse 136
  Reef 23
Edmar, of Cuic 3
Elford, John, 160, 161, 162, 164, 165
Elfordtown 92
Elizabeth I 20–5, 177–8
Ellard, Thomas, 9
Elton, Mr, 19
English Channel 66–7, 117
Erisey, James, 162, 164
Erle (Earle), Walter, 160, 200
Ernst,
  Elizabeth, 14–17
  Thomas Henry, 14
Essex xxi (see **Aveley**)
Europe xx
Evans, Robert, 69, 71
Evelyn, John, 90, 100
Exe
  bridge 38
  river 38

Exeter 7–11, 14, 34–6, 37–40, 43, 44, 46, 62–5, 75, 83, 100, 110–16, 119–28, 132–3, 136, 165, 173, 205, 211
  archdeacon of, 3, 137
  bishop of, 2–6, 7, 44, 137
  Bishop's Palace 132
  Carfax 132
  Castle Street 39
  Cathedral 52–61, 72–6, 132–3
  Cathedral Close 8, 132
  dean of, 7, 9, 72–6, 132, 133
  dean and chapter of, 8, 72–6, 133
  Eastgate 8
  Friends Burial Ground 105
  Meeting House Lane 34
  walls of, 77
  Westgate of, 9, 38
Exeter (Pennsylvania) 105
Exminster 200
Exmoor 108–10, 191
Exwick bridge 38

Fairfax,
  Colonel, 72
  Thomas, 161
Falkland, Viscount 159, 160
Fallapit 159
Falmouth 118
Far, Dr, 209
Farleigh Wallop 55, 57
Farr, Richard, 35
Fartheyn,
  Thomas, 114
  Water 114
Fiennes,
  Celia, 77
  Nathaniel, 163
Filleigh 97–9
Finch, William Wesley, 187
Fingle Bridge 94, 96
Fisshare, Maurice, 113
fitzConan, Richard the Fleming, 4–5
Flour, John, 79
Follett, Thomas, 181–3
Ford (Foard),
  Henry, 165
  Richard, 51
  Mr Robert, 75
Ford Abbey 212
Forsar, Mr, 208
Fortescue,
  family 97–8
  Alexander, 63
  Anne, 98
  Arthur, 161, 162, 164
  Edmund, 159
  Henry Inglett, 38

  Hugh, 98, 160, 161, 163, 164
  John, 160, 161, 162, 164
  Matthew, 97–9
  Robert, 165
  William, 163, 164, 165
Fos, Richard, 114
Foster,
  Mr, 38
Anthony, 119
  John, 119–22
  Robert, 159, 165
Fountain, John, 164
Fowell,
  Edmund, 160, 161, 162, 164, 165
  John, 162, 164, 165
  William, 160, 161, 162, 163, 164
France 39, 50, 56, 66, 122, 143
Francis, Philip, 163, 164
Frelard, Sir John, 140
Fremington 88
Frenchbeer Farm 95
Frithelstock 212
Fry, William, 160, 161, 162, 164, 165
Fryers, Mr, 37
Fulford, Francis, 159
Fyllegh, John, 139

Gainsborough, Thomas, 175
Garlaund, John, 114
Garnett, John, 55, 57
Gatty, Mr, 40
Gautby (Lincolnshire) 172
Geale, Henry, 62–4
George III 40
Gerveis, John, 114
Gibbons, Thomas, 165
Gibbs, A. 209
Gidleigh 95–6
Gifford,
  George, 120
  John, 160, 165
Gilbert (Gilbert),
  Isolda, 79
  Sir John, 21, 25
  William, 79, 81
Gisborne,
  Mr, 89
  Mrs, 89
Glanville, Francis, 161, 164
Gloucester 53
  diocese of, 41
Glyde,
  James, 9
  William, 10
Glyn, John, 163
Godbold, John, 160

INDEX 223

Goodridge, James, 103
Goodrington 77
Gooseford Farm 186
Gorges, Ferdinando, 159
Gosling, John, 167
Gough, Richard, 53, 56
Gowlding, Mr, 63–5
Grant, Mrs, 95
Grantham, Lord, 172–7
Gray,
  Ginger, 143
  Lady Jane, 178
Great Badow, vicar of, 148
Green, Mathew, 100
Greenham, Richard, 123, 124
Grenville,
  Sir John, 165
  Sir Richard, 22–5, 211
Grinslade, John, 38
Grobham, John, 141
Grove, Robert, 211–12
Guerney House (London) 73
Gwenfynnyd (Wales) 131
Gwennap (Cornwall) 75, 150
Gwynedd (Pennsylvania) 104–5

Haccombe 165
Haldon Hill 38, 39
Hales (Halse),
  John, 163, 164, 165
  Mathew, 160
Hall 159
Hall,
  Bishop Joseph, 73
  Dr Robert, 72–6
  Mr Webbe, 15
Hallifax, Mr, 39
Hambley, John, 10
Hamelyn, William, 114
Hampshire 55
Hancock, John, 118
Hannaford, Christopher, 87
Hansons, Mr & Mrs, 95
Harberton 4–5
Harding, Rebecca, 120
Hardwick 26–7
Hardy, Elias, 114
Harleston (Norfolk) 59
Harris,
  Mr, 208
  John, 160
  Richard, 75
Harte,
  Joan, 120
  Michael, 119–28
Hartland 212
Hartnoll, Charles, 51
Harvey, Anthony, 201
Harvy, Miss, 118

Hatch,
  Robert, 161, 163, 164
  Thomas, 160, 161, 162
Hatsell, Henry, 162, 164, 165
Hawton, H., 144
Haydon, John, 141
Hayes Barton 33
Hayne 160, 208
  John, 63–5
Haytor 80, 95
Heavitree 38
Hedd, Edward, 93
Heineken, Mr, 197
Hele,
  Matthew, 161, 165
  Thomas, 159, 165
  Walter, 160
Heligan (Cornwall) 68
Hellwort Sluys (Holland) 116
Hemyock 206
Henley, Henry, 160, 161, 162, 164
Herbert, Sir William, 212
Herries, Mr, 16
Heysom, John, 10
High Bray 108–10
Hill, William Holman, 188, 189
Hillersden 88–90
Hillesden (Buckinghamshire) 200, 202
Hilliard, Mr H., 97–9
Hittisleigh 186
Hocken (Hockin), John, 50, 51
Hole,
  Mr & Mrs, 208
  Nathan 38
Holland 50, 116
  king of, 116
Holne 108–9
Holsworthy 162, 164
Holwell 98
Holy Street 94–5
Holye, Robert, 114
Honiton 17, 132
Hood, Lord, 38
Hooker, John, 62
Hopper, William, 189
Horn, John, junior 114
Howard, Lord, 23
Howlett, Revd John, 148
Hoyle, Richard, 51
Hubbard, Mother, 154
Hubert, Mr, 118
Huckmore, Gregory, 160
Humfryes, Henry 11
Hunkin, Joseph, 162, 163, 164, 165
Hunt, Mrs, 198
Hunter, Dr, 90
Hurford family 104

Hutchinson, Peter Orlando, 197–9
Huxtable, Nicholas, 51

Iddesleigh,
  manor of, 199
  park 202
Ilfracombe 15, 16
Illogan (Cornwall) 207
Incledon family 207
Ipplepen 100–1
Ireland 23, 68–71, 86 (*see* **Antrim**)
Italy 50, 56 (*see* **Naples**)

Jaan, Richard, 80
Jackman, Henry, 11
Jago, Revd John, 145, 148–9, 151
James I 177–83
James II 7–8
James III 7
Jefford, Thomas, 8–9
Jennings, Abraham, 11
Jerwood, James, 108–10
Jewel, John, 123, 124
Joce, John, 51
Johnson, Captain, 118
Jones, Mr & Mrs, 197
Joslin, George Adams, 189
Joyson, R., 143
Jugement, Walter, 114

Katenkamp, Herman, 34, 36
Kauffman, Angelica, 209
Keble, Richard, 161, 162
Kellie (Kelly),
  Mr, 63–5
  John, 160, 161
Kellond, John, 165
Kemeys, John, 188
Kempsey, Roger, 200
Kendall,
  Edward, 54
  John, 52–61
Kenn 77
Kennet-Were, Mr, 18
Kensey (Kempsey, Kensey, Kynsey), Roger, 200–2
Kent,
  earl of, 160
  William, 98
Kentisbeare 82–4, 206
Kentismoor 206
Kerbye,
  Emme, 1–2
  Henry, 1–2
  John, 1
  Sylvester, 2

Kerrich, Thomas, 55–6, 59
King, John, 123
Kingsnympton 200
Kingsteignton 38
Kitley 154–7
Knight (Knyght),
  Mr, 38
  Henry, 114
  Robert, 114
  Roger, 114
  Thomas, 51
Knightstone 163
Knowle xix
Knowles, Mrs, 198

La Primaudaye, Pierre, 123
Ladd, B., 144
Ladman, Charles, 51
Ladram Bay 32, 33
Lake,
  Elizabeth, 140
  John, 140
  Margaret, 140
  Richard, 140
Lambeth 3
Lamerton 44
Lamplough, Thomas, 7, 42
Langdown 186
Langley, Walter, 201
Launceston (Cornwall) 208, 211
Laxton, manor of, xix, xxi
le Barber, Thomas, 113, 114
le Bruere, Pagan, 114
le Ercediakene, John, 114
le Grant, Richard, 113
le Gurdlere,
  Henry, 114
  John, 114
le Hopere, Nicholas, 113
le Keu, William, 114
le Mercer, Roger, 114
le Mey, Richard, 114
le Parchemener, Robert, 114
le Perour, John, 114
le Skynnere, Nicholas, 114
le Smyth, Jordan, 114
le Spycer,
  Adam, 113
  Thomas, 114
le Taverner, Robert, 114
le Whetene, John, 114
le Yunge, John, 114
Lee, John, 38
Lee Abbey 192
Lega-Weekes family 141
Leigh,
  James, 10
  Mr, 39
Lenthall, William, 160, 161, 163
Lescrey, Capt., 208

Lettaford 186
Lewes, John, 51
Lewin's Mead (Bristol) 35
Ley farmhouse 192
Lichfield 54
Lifton 208
Lincoln, Abraham, 105
Lincoln (*see* **Gautby, Stamford**)
Lindsay 165
Lisburne, Lord, 89
Lisle, John, 161, 162, 163
Littleton, Lord, 159
Livermead Sands 77, 78
Liverpool, mayor of, 16
Lloyd, Miss, 95
Lock,
  John, 191–2, 195
  Mary, 193
  William, 191, 195
Logan Stone, 94, 95–6
Logue, William, 143
London xix, xxii, 7–8, 23, 35,
  53, 54, 59, 62, 93, 98, 119–
  20, 168, 177–80, 196, 198
  (*see* **Broad Street, Duck
  Lane, Guerney House, Stratford Place, Wimpole Street**)
Longstone Pillar 96
Loos 143
Lovecock, Henry, 114
Loventor 79
Lowsmore, John, 51
Lucombe, William, 88–90
Lucombe's Nursery 88–90
Lugg, Thomas, 87
Luxton, Barnard, 71
Luton 31
Luttrell,
  Dorothy, 131
  Francis, 131
Lyfing, bishop of Exeter 4
Lygon, Mr, 70–1
Lympstone 160
Lynmouth 16, 190–6
Lynscott, Henry, 75
Lynton 14, 15, 16, 190–6

Machaunde, John, 201, 203
Magdalen Gallows 38
Mager, Thomas, 141
Maker 209
Mallock,
  family 76
  Roger, 160
Mamhead 89
Manchester, earl of, 160, 165
Mannington, Sampson, 9
Mardon, Mr John, 39
Marklay, William, 51
Marlorat, Augustine, 123

Marshall,
  John, 162, 164
  William, 98
Martin (Martyn, Marten),
  Mr & Mrs, 118
  Christopher, 160, 162, 164, 165
  Nicholas, 62, 160, 161
  William, 165
Marystow 68
Mauditt, Joseph, 10
Maughridge, Mary, 103
Maunsell, Andrew, 120
Maynard, John, 160
Meade, Joanna, 104
Meavy 90–3
  river of, 90–2
Mechyne, Philip, 79
Meffen, James, 54
Mey, John, 80
Midlands 154
Mileton Hill 94
Mills,
  Dr, 133
  Thomas, 63–5
Milner, Revd John, 53
Mock, John, 51
Moger, Olive, 137
Mogford, John, 51
Molland, Mr & Mrs, 69
Monck, Thomas, 160
Montague, Edward, 163
Moor 27
More, Joseph, 186
More, William, 78, 80
Moreleigh 137
Moreton, Peter, 101
Moreton Woods 96
Moretonhampstead 116–19
Morrice, Sir William, 134
Morrish (Morrishe),
  Joan, 181–3
  William, 160, 161, 162, 164, 165
Morshead, Mr, 208
Mortain, count of, 2
Moungwell (Mongwill), John, 120, 124
Mount Edgcumbe 134–6, 173, 209
Mowbray, Mr, 100
Mulholland, John, 143
Mulys, John, 81
Munckley,
  Nicholas, 35
  Samuel, 34–6
Murchington 95, 188
Murray, Sir Oswyn, 137
Mutton Cove 209
Myon, John, 11

INDEX

Nairn, county of, 98
Naples (Italy) 174
Napoleon 66, 116
Natt, George, 51
Nelson, Admiral, 39, 67
Newby Hall (Yorkshire) 172–3, 175
Newby Park (Yorkshire) 172
Newdigate, Richard, 163, 164
Newfoundland (Canada) 49–50, 52
Newnham 212
Newpark 201
Newton, Ann 198
Newton Abbot 208, 210
New York 34, 36
Nicholas,
  Baron, 163
  Edward, 159
  Robert, 161, 162, 163, 164
Norfolk 59 (see **Harleston**)
  archbishop of, 55
North Bovey 96
North Molton 1
North Wales (Pennsylvania) 104
Northcott,
  John, 160, 164, 165
  William, 160
Northleigh, Henry, 164, 165
Northtawton 160, 161
Northumberland, earl of, 160, 161
Norton, Gregory, 159, 160, 161, 162
Nosworthy, Thomas, 48
Nottegrei, Thomas, 113–14
Nottinghamshire xix
Nywelond, Alice, 139

Offer, H., 143
Ogwell 159, 160, 161, 162
Okehampton 45, 95, 133, 200, 201, 208
Oldershaw, John, 55, 58
Oley (Pennsylvania) 105
Oliver, William, 87
Omerod, George Waring, 93, 95–6
Orchard, manor of, (Somerset) 81
Orcombe Point 34
Ormonde, earl of, 165
Orum, John, 139
Osborn, Mary, 118
Osborne, Mr Augustine, 75
Otter, river 32, 33
Otterford (Dorset) 139
Otterton 33, 160, 161, 163
Oxford 119, 131

Padbrooke xix–xxii
Page, Robert, 113
Paines, James, 54
Palmere, John, 114
Paker, Henry, 51
Papendrecht (Papie) 117
Parker,
  family of, 26, 172–7, 208
  Archbishop 41
  Lady Catherine 172–3
  George, 26
  Gyfford, 202
  John, 172–7
  Mary, 172
  Theresa, 172–7
Parry, George, 159
Parsons, John, 82
Paul, Samuel, 9
Paulet, Sir Hugh, 200
Payhembury, 204
Payne, Thomas, 74
Peace, Henry, 51
Pearce, Mr, 117
Pearse, James, 165
Peers, Mr & Mrs, 118, 208
Pees, Robert, 114
Pelham, Bishop 40
Pembroke and Montgomery, earl of, 160, 161
Pennsylvania 102–6
Pepys, Samuel, 100
Percy, Hugh, 58
Periman, Thomas, 26–7
Perryman,
  Arthur, 160, 161, 162, 163, 164
  William, 189
Persoun, Walter, 114
Peters, John, 160
Peterson, Dean William, 72, 74, 75
Petre,
  Sir John, xx
  Mary, 100
  William, 100
Petre Hayes 100
Philip II, of Spain 20
Piddledown Heath 94
Pierce,
  family xxi
  Mark, xix–xii
  Samuel, xxi
Piers (Pyers), John, 78, 80
Pilton 213
Pineda, Joannas, 123
Pitts, James, 10
Placentia (Newfoundland) 49
Plente, Walter, 114
Pley,
  Mrs Constance, 100

George, 100, 101
Plym river 91
Plymouth 2, 14, 23, 25, 38, 117, 134–6, 153, 208–10, 211
  breakwater 66
  dock 134, 208
  Hoe 100
  Sound 22, 23
Plympton 77, 160, 161
  castle 5–6
  priory of, 2–6, 212
Plympton St Mary 26, 172
Plymstock 77
Pole (Pool, Poole) Courtenay 165
  John, 160, 161
  William, 159
Pollard,
  George, 201
  Sir Hugh, 69–70, 165
  Sir Lewis, 200
  Sir Richard, 199–201
  Samuel, 37–40
Pollexfen,
  family 155
  Henry, 161, 163, 164
Polsloe Priory 211–12
Polson Bridge 134
Polwhele, Richard, 44–5
Ponsford xix–xxii
Ponsford,
  Ann, 118
  John, 116, 117
  Luke, 118
  Mary, 118
Porter, Richard, 39
Portugal 50
Potel, Henry, 113, 114
Power, William, 51
Pratt, John, 38
Prestbury 96
Prestwood, George, senior 160, 161
Prew, Peter, 11
Prideaux,
  Edmund, 160, 161, 162, 163, 164
  Sir Peter, 165
  Sir Richard, 165
Probus (Cornwall) 131
Prouse (Proues, Prouze, Prouz),
  George, 120, 124
  Humphrey, 160
  John, 139
Providence, 186, 187
Prudomme, James, 114
Puddicombe, Dr, 38
Puddington 138–9
Putt, William, 160, 161, 162, 164, 165

Pylche, Walter, 113
Pyleman, Thomas, 114

Queen's Square (Bristol) 35
Quick, John, 160, 161, 162, 164, 165

Radford 160
  farmhouse 44
Raglan, Lord Herbert of, 162, 163
Raleigh, Sir Walter, 33
Ramsey, Fanny, 95
Redruth 150
Redstone, Mr, 209
Remmett, Dr, 208, 209
Repton, George Stanley, 155
Reymes,
  Bullen, 100–1
  Mary, 100
Reynell,
  Rebecca, 74
  Richard, 159
  Thomas, 159, 160, 161, 162, 164, 165
Reynolds, Joshua, 173, 209
Rice, Mr John, 38
Richards,
  Bridget, 140
  Dorothy, 140
  Emott, 140
  Humphrey, 140
  Joan, 140
  Thomas, 140, 141
  Thomasine, 140
  William, 138, 140, 141, 160
Richmond (Kentucky) 102
Richmond and Lennox, duke of, 159
Ridgeway, Lord, 71
Rigby, Alexander, 161, 162
Ringmoor 90–2
Robert, the hermit 5
Roberts, Lord, 160
Robertson,
  Mr & Mrs, 95
  John, 95
Robinson,
  Captain, 208
  Frederick (Fritz), 172–3
  Philip, 11
  Theresa, 172
  Thomas, 11, 172, 174–6
Rodd, Miss, 208–10
Rodney, Frances Jane, 155, 156, 157
Roe,
  John Colwell, 194, 196
  Revd Thomas, 193

Rogemound, Robert, 114
Rogers, George, 9, 10
Rolle (Rolles),
  Henry, 160, 161, 162, 163
  John, 160, 161, 162, 163, 164, 165
  Robert, 160, 161, 164, 165
  Samuel, 160
  Maurice, 161
Rosewell, Henry, 160, 161, 163, 164
Rougemont Castle 133
Rous (Rouse),
  Anthony, 162, 164
  Francis, 160, 161, 162, 163
Rowe,
  Mr, 36
  John, 162, 164
  Roger, 28
  Thomas, 45, 48
  William, 28–30
Royal Glen, Sidmouth 32
Rushford 94
Russel, Richard, 114
Russell, Lord John, 199, 201, 202

St Agnes (Cornwall) 150
St Albans 53
St Andrew, chapel of, 2–4
St Aubyn, Sir John, 134
St Cherris 186
St Croix, Mr, 38
St Edmond, 37
St Erme (Cornwall) 131
St Ewe (Cornwall) 68
St John, Oliver, 160, 162, 163
St Lawrence 40
St Leger, Sir John, 199, 202
St Martin 120
St Mary Major 54
St Mary Steps 37
St Nicholas Island 135–6
St Nicholas Priory 212
St Petrock 120
St Sidwell,
  Fee of, 8
  parish of, 10, 40
St Vincent, Earl, 66–8
Sainthill, Peter, 51, 160
Salcombe Hill 32, 34
Salcombe Regis 32
Salisbury 54
  earl of, 161
Saltash (Cornwall) 207–8
Saltram 26, 172–7, 207, 209
Sampford Peverell 206
Sandwell 88–9
Sandy Park Bridge 94

Sanford,
  Mr & Mrs, 198
  William, 192
Satchfeeld, Thomas, 182
Saunders
  Mr, 15
  Mrs, 15
  Humphrey, 82
  Richard, 82–5
  Thomas, 82, 161, 163, 164
Savery,
  Christopher, 160
  Robert, 160, 161, 162, 164
  Servington, 162, 163, 165
Savile, Viscount, 159
Scotland 98 (see **Cawdor**)
Scott,
  Sir George Gilbert, 56
  Sir William, 168, 171
Seage, William, 186
Searle, John, 163, 164, 165
Seaton Junction, 32
Sermon, Sergeant Major, 17
Servant, Richard, 51
Seward, Walter, 114
Seymour, Edward, 160, 165
Shapcott, Robert, 160
Shaugh 92
Sheepstor 90
Sheers, Mary, 118
Shelburn, Lord, 209
Sherman, Gideon, 163, 164
Shilston 160, 161
Shobrooke,
  parish of, 27–31
  Richard, 11
Shower, Sir Batholomew, 9
Shuldham, Lord, 208
Shute (Schute),
  Agnes, 140
  Isabel, 140
  Joan, 140
  John, 138–40
Sidbury 197
Sidmouth 31–4, 197–8
  Junction 32
Silverton 160, 181–3
Simcoe, Admiral John Graves, 38
Skilton, Robert, 9
Skinner,
  Mathew, 114
  Robert, 28–30
  William, 114
Skippon, Philip, 161, 162, 163
Sladda 4
Slanning, Nicholas, 159, 160
Sloley, John, 51
Smith (Smyth),
  Mr, 208–9

INDEX

Benjamin, 87
Henry, 123
James, 72, 75
Lieut., 119
Snogbrook 197
Somerset 78, 108, 137, 192, 211 (*see* **Batcombe, Bridgwater, Buckland Farm, Durston, Orchard, Taunton, Wellington, Wells, Westcombe**)
Soper (Supper), Susan, 117, 118
Soth,
  John, junior 114
  Peter, 114
South Carolina 36
Southampton, earl of 165
Southcott,
  Edmund, 159
  George, 160
  Popham, 159
  Thomas, 164, 165
South Kensington museum 17
South Molton 68
South Pool 77
South Zeal 186, 187, 188
Southernhay 38
Southey, Robert, 191
Spain 20–5, 39, 50, 122
Sparke, John, 141
Specott, Peter, 160, 161
Spiceland 104
Spreyton 186
Spry, Admiral, 208
Sqwyer, Walter, 113, 114
Stackhouse, family 131
Staffordshire 88–9
Stamford (Lincoln) 180
Stark, H., 144
Starr, John, 10
Steele,
  Chief Baron, 163
  John, 165
  William, 163
Stephens (Stevens), John, 213
Stobback, Revd John, 37
Stockhay, Sir William 138–9
Stoett, William, 51
Stoke Canon 103
Stokeley 4–5
Stokenham 4–5
Story, John, 102
Stowell, Baron, 168
Strachey, Sir Henry, 14
Strange, Geoffrey, 114
Stratford Place (London) 196
Strode, William, 165
Stucley, Sir Thomas, 165
Studley (Yorkshire) 172, 174
Surinam 116

Sutton 2–6
  Court 14
Sweete (Swete),
  Revd John, 191
  Richard, 162, 164
Sydenham 68
Sydenham,
  Richard, 159
  William, 163

Tamar river 14, 207, 208
Tar, Miss, 118
Tavistock 134, 145–54, 208
  abbey 145, 212
Tavy river 145
Tayler (Taillor),
  Mr, 60
  James, 10
  John, 79
Tehidy (Cornwall) 207
Teign river 94
Teigncombe 95
Teigngrace 38
Tetcott 164, 165
Thirsk (Yorkshire) 172
Thomas Hall 89
Thorn 96
Thorne,
  family, 166–71
  Catherine, 166
  Joan, 166
  John, 51
  Mary, 166
  Sarah, 166–71
  William, 166–71
Thorpe, Baron, 163
Throwleigh, 187
Thurloe, John, 163
Till, Gilbert, 64
Tipton St John 198
Tiverton xx, 14, 15, 104, 200, 201
Tolly, Thomas, 48
Tolman Stone 96
Tomlyn, Phillip, 10
Topcliffe (Yorkshire) 172
Topsham 38, 39
Torbay 66
Torbrian 100
Tor Newton 100
Torre Abbey 181, 212
Torquay 129–31, 181
Torridge 17
Tothill,
  Gilbert, 63
  William, 160
Totnes 56
  archdeacon of, 3, 74
Trafalgar 39

Trelawney,
  Mr, 208
  Bishop Jonathan, 7–8
Trematon, manor of, (Cornwall) 2
Tremayne,
  family 68
  Edward, 160, 165
Tremblett, Daniel, 166–71
Trenethick Barton 44
Trevilian, Hugh, 160, 161, 162
Trigg, John, 10
Trobridge 165
  Roger, 165
Troute,
  Joan, 2
  John, 2
  Richard, 1–2
Trowman, Joseph, 11
Troyte Bullock family 100
Trump, George, 9
Truro (Cornwall) 68
Tucker, William, 56
Tuckfield, John, 162
Tug, John, 11
Tukker, Mr, 119
Twickenham 172
Twigge,
  Amy, 10
  John, 10
Tyrling, John, 160, 161, 163, 164, 165
Tyrrell, Thomas, 164, 165

Uffculme 137, 206
  Grammar School 197
Ufflete,
  Edmund, 139
  Isabel, 139
  Joan, 139
  John, 137–9
Union Inn 117
University College of the South West of England 142
University of Exeter 89, 142
Upottery 139, 141
Upton, Arthur, 160, 161, 162, 164, 165
Ursinus, Zacharias, 123
Ushant, 66, 67

Vagge, William, 79
Valley of Rocks 15, 16, 190–6
  Hotel 194
van der Zonde, Captain, 118
Vaughan, Mr & Mrs, 208
Vawterd, Thomas, 202
Venice 95, 122, 124
Venner, William, 162, 163

Venton, John, 81
Vermigli, Pietro Martire, 123
Vicary, Richard, 161, 163, 164
Vienna 172
Vincent, Capt., 208
Vineyard, The, 142
Vyke, William, 113–14
Vyner,
 family 172
 Henry, 172
 Mary, 172

Waddon, Johan, 160
Waleis, Nicholas, 114
Wales 148 (see **Anglesey, Gwenfynnyd**)
Walkhampton 91, 93
Walpole, Horace, 98
Walronds xx
Walrond,
 family 137
 Henry, 160, 161
 Edward, 165
 Walter, Henry, 161, 163, 164, 165
Walther, Rudolph, 123
Warburton, Peter, 163
Ward,
 Miss, 19
 Mr, 19
Wardour (Wiltshire) 200, 202
Warelwast, Bishop William, 2–5
Warren,
 John, 120,124
 Richard, 10
Warwick, earl of, 22
Watermouth 14, 16
Way,
 Catherine, 166
 Sarah, 166
Weare Gifford 17
Webber,
 Miss, 208–9
 John, 51
 William, 189
Weddell, William, 173
Weekes, Georgina Mary, 141
Wellington (Somerset) 139
Wells (Somerset) 211

Welshe, James, 160
Wendron (Cornwall) 44, 150
Westacott, 138–9
West Buckland (Dorset) 139
Westcombe (Somerset) 14
Westcott Cottage 93
West Indies xix, 35
Westlade, Joseph, 87, 88
Westlake, Hugh, 10
Westminster 21, 23, 24
Westmoreland 102
Weymouth (Dorset) 100
Whaddon (Dorset) 100
Wheal Crebor 150, 151
Wheal Crowndale 149–50, 151
Whichalse, John, 162, 164
Whiddon, Roland, 160, 161, 162, 164
Whiddon Park 94–5
Whipham, Revd W., 95
Whipton 77
Whitehaire, Thomas, 11
Whitehall 178
White Hart Inn 118
Whitelock, Bulstrode, 161, 162, 163
Whiteway Barton 38
Whitfeld, Miss Mary Ann, 118
Wich, Sir Peter, 159
Widdrington, Thomas, 163
Wilcocks, Mr, 35–6
Wilde (Wylde), John, 160, 161, 162, 163
Wilkinson, John, 102
Willand 205, 206
Willeland 4
Willet, Andrew, 122, 123, 124
William of Orange 7–8, 133
Williams,
 Lionel, 9
 Thomas, 51
 T.H., 192
Willis, Browne, 53
Willoughby,
 Sir Anthony, 200
 John, 160, 165, 204–7
Wills, James, 11
Wiltshire 108 (see **Wardour**)
Wimpole Street (London) 98–9
Winchester 55
 Marquess of, 210

Windet, John, 119
Winshed, Mr & Mrs, 118
Wise, Edward, 164, 165
Witheridge 213
Wood (Woode),
 Christopher, 160, 161, 163, 164, 165
 Edward, 63–5
 Thomas, 165
Woolfardisworthy East 137–9
Woollacombe (Woolacombe),
 John, 160, 161, 162, 164, 165
 William, 161, 162, 164
Woollard, J.R., 144
Woolston 95
Worcester, Roger, bishop of, 3
Worsley,
 Frances, 172
 Thomas, 172
Worth, Henry, 160, 161, 163, 164, 165
Wye, John, 160
Wynne,
 Owen, 131
 William, 131–6
Wysdom, Thomas, 114

Yard (Yarde, Yeard),
 Revd Mr, 38
 Edmund, 160
 Walter, 160, 161
Yealmpton 77, 154
Yennadon Down 91
Yeo 96
 George, 160
 John, 51
York 119, 173
Yorkshire 174, 180 (see **Baldersby Park, Newby Hall, Newby Park, Studley, Thirsk, Topcliffe**)
Young,
 Mr, 19
 Private, 142
 John, 160, 161, 162, 164, 165
 Walter, 160, 161, 165

Zanchius, Hieronymus, 123
Zucchi, Antonio, 173